THE AUTOBIOGRAPHY

Jackie Stewart

WINNING IS NOT ENOUGH

headline

First published in 2007
by HEADLINE PUBLISHING GROUP

First published in paperback in 2009
by HEADLINE PUBLISHING GROUP

3

Cataloguing in Publication Data is available from the British Library

ISBN 978 0 7553 1539 0

Typeset in Sabon and Gill Sans by Avon DataSet Ltd,
Bidford on Avon, Warwickshire

Printed and bound in Great Britain
by Clays Ltd, St Ives plc

Headline's policy is to use papers that are natural, renewable and recyclable
products and made from wood grown in sustainable forests. The logging and
manufacturing processes are expected to conform to the environmental
regulations of the country of origin.

HEADLINE PUBLISHING GROUP
An Hachette UK Company
338 Euston Road
London NW1 3BH

www.headline.co.uk
www.hachette.co.uk

For Helen, Paul and Mark.

Contents

It was the autumn of 1971 when I first met Sir Jackie Stewart. We were both attending an annual Sports Awards luncheon, and we were seated at the same table. He was to be named Sportsman of the Year because he had just become the F1 motor racing world champion, while, for my part, I was fortunate enough to be given the award as Sportswoman of the Year for winning the European 3 Day Event Championship.

I regarded him as a very professional competitor from a very professional sport where attention to detail increases your likelihood of success as well as survival. He was always interested in other sports achievers and their preparation, although I suspect that, for him, real horses always had too many variables compared to the horse power he was used to. That attention to detail and broad interest has helped him to achieve success in many fields – in clay pigeon shooting; motor racing; business and education.

There is a subtle difference between winning being everything and winning never being enough and for Jackie it was the latter. When he worked in his father's garage, it was not enough for him simply to serve petrol; he wanted to be known for keeping the cleanest forecourt in the west of Scotland. When he drove racing cars, it was not enough for him just to drive fast; he involved himself in improving every aspect of the design and preparation of the car.

When his friends were killed in accidents, it was not enough for him to become world champion three times; he worked tirelessly to make the sport safer for future generations. When he entered into a business association, it was not enough for him simply to fulfil the terms of his contract and bank his salary; he wanted to over deliver and nurture a relationship to last, in several cases, a remarkable four decades.

As I can personally attest, when he becomes your friend, it is not enough for him to drift in and out of your life; he makes a point of keeping the relationship alive, offering support and outstanding company through good times and bad times. In all these endeavours, in all these diverse activities, over all these years, he has been heroically supported by Helen.

I am delighted Sir Jackie has decided to take the time to sit down and write this book, and provide such an entertaining and inspiring memoir of a truly remarkable British life.

Anne

HRH The Princess Royal

Acknowledgements

I would very much like to recognise, with grateful thanks, Her Royal Highness The Princess Royal for agreeing to write the Foreword to my autobiography. Our friendship is well documented in this book but I am both honoured and thrilled that Her Royal Highness was prepared to contribute her own most kind and generous words.

In writing this book, various people have patiently assisted me in remembering names and events. Now I must try and remember all of them on my own. With apologies to anybody who has been omitted, I acknowledge the important contribution of the following people, who either racked their own memories or prompted mine.

In alphabetical order:
HM King Abdullah of the Hashemite Kingdom of Jordan, Jean Albrecht, Rob Armstrong, Kamal Badawi, Joe Beeston, Bruce Blythe, Penny Breia, Niall Brennan, Comte Frédéric Chandon de Briailles, Elizabeth Corke, Neil Davis, Jacques de la Béraudière, Ron Dennis, Dawn DiMaya, Eric Dymock, Bernie Ecclestone, Edsel Ford, Barry Frank, Graham Gauld, Caroline Goodacre, Bob Goodrich, Will Griffiths, François Guiter, Maurice Hamilton, Margaret Hammond, Livy Harrison, Professor Ian Hay, Patrick Heiniger, Alan Henry, Bette Hill,

Roger Hill, Jackie Ickx, Sir Robin Janvrin, Susan Johnston, Justin Jones, Noel Jones, Shan Jones, Ruth Kinnear, Vice-Admiral Timothy Laurence, Peter Lederer, John Lindsay, David Mason, Karen Moss, Andy Miller, Charles Milner, Nigel Newton, HM Queen Noor, Doug Nye, Don Ohlmeyer, Richard Parry-Jones, Captain Mark Phillips, Neil Ressler, Nigel Roebuck, Stuart Rolt, Deborah Rooney, Dick Scammell, Helen Stewart, Jim Stewart, Mark Stewart, Paul Stewart, David Stubbs, Stuart Sykes, Roy Topp, David Tremayne, Kenneth Tyrrell, Audrey Walker, James Walker, Martin Watson, Sir Frank Williams, Ian Wooldridge, Sarah Wooldridge, Eoin Young.

A special thanks goes to my son Mark and his team at Mark Stewart Productions (Paddy Mark, Shawn Tracey, Hannah Rees, Jemima Jenner-Fust, Matt Prior and Guy Farley) who created the ViBE (Visual Book Enhancement) that accompanied the hardback edition of this book.

Many people contributed their time and energies to the content and production of the ViBE and I would like to acknowledge my thanks to you all:

Jean-Noel Bioul, Comte Frédéric Chandon de Briailles, Sir Sean Connery, David Coulthard, Edsel Ford, Emerson Fittipaldi, Dario Franchitti, Sir Fred Goodwin, Livy Harrison, HH Shaikh Salman bin Hamed Al-Khalifa, Crown Prince of the Kingdom of Bahrain, Patrick Heiniger, Nicholas Jellicoe, John Nicholson, Sir Martin Sorrell, Murray Walker.

Thanks also to Ed Griffiths for his diligent editing of my words and his expert suggestions on how to make my thoughts, feelings and recollections come alive on the page. And to David Wilson for his frontline support and input into my book and to his colleagues, Rhea Halford, Caitlin Raynor, Sarah Kellard and all the team at Headline for ensuring my book looks, feels, reads and is promoted in the way that, when I decided to write it, I hoped it would be.

Finally, thanks to the motor racing enthusiasts, marshals, officials and media who have supported me throughout my driving career. The waving, cheers and words and letters of encouragement have sustained me through moments of success and terrible loss. I owe more than I can express here to you, and to all those who have advised and supported me in my business activities since I retired from the track.

I hope you enjoy my book. It has been almost seventy years in the making and a great adventure.

SIR JACKIE STEWART

Introduction

Titles mean different things to different people.

Some choose not to pay much attention, believing they don't add up to much in the wider scheme of things. In my view, however, the title of a book you have written about your life does mean something because it is invariably placed right beside your name and, in theory, it gives an indication of the kind of life you have lived.

Throughout the preparation of this autobiography, the choice of the title has prompted a lively debate between me, as the writer with a personal preference, and the publishers, as a group with vast experience in the field and an understanding of what might be successful in an inevitably crowded marketplace. The team at Headline, led by David Wilson, have been immensely cooperative and creative and, at one point, they strongly believed the title of this book should be *Driven*. Their view was that this would reflect my career as a racing driver and also my nature as somebody who has always preferred to be busy and active, even now, at the age of sixty-eight, when many have decided to slow down and escape from the rat race. 'A one-word title has more impact on the shelf,' they said.

I appreciated the logic. One of the significant influences on my life was Walter Hayes, an extraordinary man who became a widely respected public affairs expert at the Ford Motor Company on both sides of the Atlantic, and I remembered how often he used to say 'simple is successful'. However, I also felt it should be possible for the title of this book to do more than reflect the nature of a life and to somehow explain the essence and principles of its subject.

One bright early morning, I was walking our two Norfolk terriers, Pimms and Whisky, as I do whenever I am at home – it's one of my favourite times of the day – and a particular phrase flashed across my mind which, I hoped, would at least serve as a useful working title. I bounced it off Helen, my wife for the past forty-five years, when we sat down for breakfast, and her immediate response was positive. '*Winning Is Not Enough*,' she mused. 'Well, it's never been enough for you.'

I suppose it is a fact that, whether in my competitive shooting days, or in eleven years of earning money as a racing driver, or subsequently in a business environment, the mere act of winning has never seemed enough. From my youth, when I benefited so much from the support of my parents and my elder brother Jim, and the counsel of Glynne Jones, then captain of the British shooting team, and Bob MacIntyre, the great Scottish motorcycling hero, I have believed that real, lasting success is defined not only by the accumulation of winning but also by the manner of victory. It's not enough simply to win. It is considerably more profound if success is achieved with integrity and care.

My former teachers at the Dumbarton Academy will readily confirm I am no mathematician, but maybe this concept could be represented by the following equation:

Winning (over a long period of time)
+ Integrity
+ Care
= Success

Simply winning is often regarded as the ultimate, overriding goal. Of course, it is an ingredient of success, but sometimes winning is not such a big deal. The example I often use is of a driver winning the Formula 1 world championship when he is driving the very best car, with the very best engine, and working with the very best team of people – it's still a major achievement, but it's really not that difficult. The greater challenge for that driver is not simply to win the world championship, or perhaps even to become a multiple world champion, but it is how they have achieved that success.

Some may ridicule the idea. 'Integrity and care?' they will jeer. 'They don't count. Look at the scoreboard. It's a dog-eat-dog world out there, and the reality, in sport as in business and everything else, is that nice guys come last. Winning is not everything, it's the only thing' etc., etc.

I categorically disagree.

Soon after Her Majesty the Queen granted me a knighthood in June 2001, I was contacted by the Court of the Lord Lyon, the judicial body that conducts Scottish heraldic business. The Lord Lyon proposed I might like to create my own coat of arms. It was explained to me that such a coat of arms would incorporate a crest and a motto usually written in Latin. After some deliberation, we developed a crest that incorporated various elements representing important aspects of my life, such as a racing helmet and a gun, and for a motto we settled on three simple English words: 'Integrity and Care'. The coat of arms was duly created, and it remains available to be used by my descendants, if they so wish; and, if they do, I hope the motto will serve to remind them that, while winning will always be an essential ingredient of success, so will those two elements.

Over all these years, I have had the opportunity to meet many winners in many fields – in sport, in politics, in business, in public life, in technology, in entertainment – and it is only those who have won with integrity and care, over an extended period of time, who have become universally regarded as 'successful'.

Two individuals who have fulfilled this ideal in the world of golf are Jack Nicklaus and Arnold Palmer. They did not just win many tournaments around the world; they triumphed in such an exemplary manner that they are now recognised and admired far beyond the global golfing community. The statistics are unequivocal – Jack won 113 professional tournaments, including 18 Majors, and Arnold won 92 professional tournaments, including 7 Majors – but they only reflect part of the story of the two men who are widely credited with turning golf into a mass spectator sport.

Jack was born in 1940, but he continues to undertake a breathtaking schedule of travel and commitments all over the world in a purposeful but relaxed manner, treating everyone with respect. In recent years, we have both been associated with the Royal Bank of Scotland and, at various events, I have had the opportunity to admire the way this naturally shy and understated man conducts himself and fulfils his responsibilities.

In May 2006, we were both invited to attend an RBS golf day at Hoylake, in Lancashire, the course where the Open Championship was going to be played two months later. Jack decided not to play that day, so he and I opted to drive around in a buggy, spending time and chatting with each four-ball group, having photographs taken. Approaching one particular tee, we were greeted by a couple, sitting on a bench. Jack immediately recognised the gentleman as John Morgan, a one-time touring pro and a former club professional at the Royal Liverpool golf club, and it soon emerged the ex-pro was suffering from a brain tumour. It was an emotional conversation and, at one point, Jack and I were both struggling to maintain our composure, but Jack took his time, talking to John and his concerned wife, Chris, with real compassion and, as we left, he hugged them both. Even with a frenetic schedule, amidst the endless blur of faces that confronts him almost every day of his life, Jack had been able to pause and demonstrate integrity and care, and I'm sure those few minutes would not only have been appreciated by Mr Morgan, who sadly passed away a few weeks later on 23 June 2006, but I believe they also proved a great comfort to his wife.

Arnold is eleven years older than Jack and personable by nature. I met him several times when I was working in America during the 1970s and 1980s and was always amazed by the way he lit up a room as soon as he arrived. That may be a cliché, but it accurately describes the Arnie factor. The remarkable courtesy and kindness he showed to so many people over so many years made him extraordinarily popular and provided a foundation for his great success in business beyond golf. Like Jack, Arnold also maintains a remarkable pace for a man of his age, travelling frequently, generally at the controls of his own Cessna Citation X jet aircraft, and still playing the game – it has been said he has played more rounds of golf with prime ministers, heads of state and presidents of the United States than anyone else. People have always somehow been drawn to him, and, once again, winning with integrity and care has ensured he is universally acknowledged and revered as a success.

Someone who has applied similar principles to the business environment is Warren Buffett. I have never met the man, but his record in creating the Berkshire Hathaway group of companies speaks for itself, and his remarkable gesture in donating shares worth an estimated $31 billion to the Bill and Melinda Gates Foundation, because he believed in its capacity to spend the money wisely, is evidence of care and integrity.

Winning Is Not Enough: the maxim has worked for me, but I am determined this book should not seem to be somehow preached from any kind of pulpit. I certainly would not claim to have all the answers: very far from it.

At heart, I am a proud Scot of 'average height': one who was fortunate to be the driver in a racing team led by an extraordinary man who brought together a group of dedicated designers and mechanics that won three Formula 1 world championships; one who was lucky to survive in an era when so many of his friends and colleagues were killed; one who has been privileged to meet many stimulating people around the world; one who has taken great pleasure in the progress of his sons, Paul and Mark, and their families; and one who has been endlessly supported by a strong, patient and resilient woman, my wife Helen. That's all I am, and my simple hope is that this autobiography unfolds as an entertaining account of a life spent primarily in motor racing and business, as a narrative that amuses, intrigues, moves and maybe even motivates.

The story begins in Scotland, that small, remarkable country of beauty and courage. It is a place where I have not resided for the past forty-odd years, yet it remains rare air, a place that touches me in a most profound sense.

CHAPTER I

Born Scot

Scotland's greatest export is not our whisky or our shortbread; it's our people. Travel almost anywhere in the world and the chances are you will find expatriate Scots in positions of influence, leading successful companies, creating opportunities and wealth. It's a remarkable phenomenon but, over and over again, Scottish men and women have packed their bags, left their homeland and excelled. Perhaps it's because they are more determined; perhaps it's because they are more ambitious. Some reckon Scots typically feel inferior when they arrive in what may appear to be a more sophisticated and polished society than their own, so they work twice as hard to make an impact. Others think these people are driven by a fear of failure, a dread of having to return home without having been successful.

Maybe the answer lies in a combination of all these elements. Whatever the reason, I have criss-crossed the globe for many years and I have always felt tremendously proud to be a Scot. Wherever you look, Scots are thriving. For many years, London's Metropolitan police force has relied upon a significant Scottish contingent, and the same is true of the British army. Small countries often produce more than their share of achievers, and Scotland is a very good example of this phenomenon.

Consider Scotland's inventory of scientists and inventors in recent centuries: among others, Alexander Fleming discovered penicillin, James Chalmers invented the postage stamp, Robert Thomson invented the pneumatic tyre (later improved by John Boyd Dunlop), Alexander Graham Bell invented the telephone, John Logie Baird invented the television, John McAdam invented tarmac, and James Gregory, a Professor at St Andrews, invented a reflecting telescope three years before an Englishman, Sir Isaac Newton, perfected the instrument and was given the credit.

By nature, Scots are sentimental; we tend to be canny, and we generally prefer to avoid rushing in; we can be stubborn, and determined, and aggressive, and we don't give up; occasionally, we can be dour and pessimistic. Yet, in every one of us, the Scottish roots run very deep . . . so deep that, whatever we are doing, wherever we may be living, those roots are rarely removed from our lives.

English people now and then say Scots often seem to be harbouring a grievance of some kind and that we are quick to take offence. Maybe they're right; maybe we do have a chip on our collective shoulder; maybe it's an important element of the motivation that drives so many of us to travel well and succeed. I clearly remember how I felt when I first headed south as a young man, initially as a competitive shooter in my middle to late teens and later as an amateur racing driver, and I did feel inferior. The top English gun clubs usually had better facilities, and the range of exotic cars parked in the paddock at the English racing circuits, with all the supporting technology, was unlike anything I had ever seen. I used to stand staring at the cars, feeling like an unsophisticated outsider with heather growing out of my ears. And the Englishmen whom I was competing against often seemed to have more money, were smarter in dress and had better equipment than me. Of course, that just made me more determined to work harder, and beat them.

It was Hunter Davies, the writer and sports journalist, who once wrote that, as a Formula 1 driver, I seemed to be 'defiantly Scottish', and that may well be true. Whatever or wherever I was driving, throughout my career, I always asked if the Saltire flag could be displayed somewhere on the bodywork of my car, and I invariably wanted that car to be painted Scottish royal blue – in fact, in 1968, when I was negotiating the possibility of signing to drive for Ferrari, the Italian manufacturers eventually agreed that my Formula 2 car would be painted in the famous Ferrari red on top and Scottish blue below. However, for other reasons, the deal didn't happen.

Thinking back, I have always been defined by my nationality: by the tartan band that Helen used to stick around my racing helmet in the early days when I was driving; by my distinct accent when I was a presenter for the ABC's *Wide World of Sports* in the United States; by the Racing Stewart tartan trousers that I wore in the Stewart Grand Prix days. As a result, almost without exception, I have been described by the media as 'Scottish' rather than 'British'. Either would be OK, but Scottish is just fine.

Being a Scot moves me and touches me in profound and unexpected ways, just as it did moments after the Canadian Grand Prix at Mosport Park in 1971: it was a race I had never won before and, with so many Scots in the crowd waving flags, I was thrilled to cross the line and finally give them a victory to celebrate. At that stage of my career, my post-race routine was to escape from the frenzy of the podium presentation and retreat to a caravan – there were no fancy motor homes in those days – where I would relax and wait for the crowds to disperse before leaving the circuit. On this occasion at Mosport, I happened to be with a good friend, Edsel Ford, and, when the bedlam and excitement seemed to have subsided, we decided to leave and slowly make our way through the mist of what had become an eerily cold, foggy evening. We were slowly driving past some kind of old wooden hut when, out of nowhere, there came the sound of a lone piper, no doubt seeking shelter from the rain and cold. I stopped the car, got out and recognised the tune as 'Amazing Grace'. The melody was coming from inside the hut, and there was nobody else around. As a racing driver, I always took pride in my ability to control and compartmentalise my emotions, but the skirl of those bagpipes so far from home pricked the bubble. Tears started streaming down my cheeks. Edsel was a bit concerned, but these were not sad tears, they were tears of pride.

Being a Scot also moves me whenever I see the unique beauty of our country. I have visited many impressive places around the world, but nothing in my mind compares with the magnificence of the Scottish landscape. It can be rugged, angry and desolate but, in its ever-changing light, it is always majestic. Anybody who has travelled through Glencoe, in good weather or in bad weather, would surely agree. Anyone who has sailed among the Western Isles, or visited the peaks and glens of the Highlands, or relaxed in Speyside or Deeside, or wandered among the rolling pastures of the Borders can only be spellbound by the natural beauty of a landscape that, as home to just five million people, remains wonderfully uncluttered.

Growing up in Dumbarton, an industrial town on the River Clyde not far from Glasgow, I was first exposed to the magnificence of the land when, as the younger son of the local garage owner, I was invited to go deer stalking with a man called Duncan Macbeth, who worked on the estate of Sir Ivor Colquhoun.

Clan Colquhoun was well known in the area – it was said that Sir Ivor's father had liked nothing more than to walk barefoot in the hills – and the family lived in a house called Rossdhu, which has since been turned into the clubhouse at the exceptional and acclaimed Loch Lomond golf club.

Duncan Macbeth lived with his wife Catherine in a wee cottage in Glen Luss, overlooking the loch. I used to make my way there early in the morning, and this tall, thin, distinguished man would take a packed lunch, a flask of coffee and a dram and lead me into the hills above the villages of Luss and Inverbeg. We would walk and walk, for miles and miles, with him striding ahead and me only just managing to keep up.

'Jackie, do you smell the deer?' That was one of the many things he taught me – to look out for and recognise the scent. When Duncan picked up the smell he would raise his hand, and I would crouch down in the heather. 'Come along,' he would whisper, 'we need to be downwind to get close.'

And he would lead me halfway around a hill, clambering across the slopes to get into position, and every once in a while we would pause for a moment to catch our breath and enjoy the view across Ben Dhu. Eventually we would be in position, and I would crouch down again, hanging on his every word.

'Look, Jackie,' he would say. 'The stag has poor antlers – that's the one to cull because that will encourage a good hill of deer. The only way to preserve the herd is to take the poor stock.'

I would look across and watch the stag standing, as poised, strong, dominant and unequivocally majestic as any beast in the animal kingdom.

'Wait,' he would tell me. 'He's surrounded by hinds, and it's awkward. Be patient and wait a while. Always remember: never shoot unless you have a clear shot.'

Duncan's job was to manage and maintain the estate's herd of red deer, which meant keeping the numbers at a manageable level by culling stags in the late summer and autumn, and hinds in January and February, but no later than that because, by

March, they would be pregnant and producing calves. He discharged his responsibilities with unconscious style, integrity and wisdom, and I was privileged to look, listen and learn.

'When we shoot a deer,' he would say, 'it's our job to bring it off the hill.'

The larger estates keep ponies at the bottom of the glen for this purpose, and nowadays, in the age of mobile telephones, even special off-road vehicles are summoned to take the deer away. But, back then, when I was walking the hills with Duncan Macbeth, it was just him, me and the carcass.

We would start by 'gralloching' the stag, which meant cleaning out the guts. This traditional process reduced the weight and enabled us to carry or drag it down the hill. It was tiring work, and it was not unusual for us to shoot three stags in a single day, which meant I was exhausted by the time I got home. But these were great days in my life and, boy, I enjoyed every single minute.

Duncan is dead now, but he was a wonderful man with fantastic values, and it's one of my greatest regrets that, once I had started shooting competitively and then went into driving racing cars, with my life beginning to resemble a rocket-ship ride with not enough time to take stock and really enjoy anything, I simply couldn't find the time to visit him. I somehow lost touch and gradually became detached from what he represented.

Even now, sitting in our home overlooking Lake Geneva, I can still close my eyes, taste the air and once again see the view from the slopes of Ben Dhu, across Loch Lomond, across the islands of Inchfad, Inchcailloch, Inchmurrin and Inchconnachan, to the village of Rowardennan and the majesty of Ben Lomond on the eastern shore.

The emotional pull never goes away and it is important to me to renew a physical connection whenever I can. I recently visited the churchyard behind the lovely Luss church where

Duncan and Catherine Macbeth were laid to rest. The church was rebuilt by Sir James Colquhoun in 1875 in memory of his father and five ghillies, who were lost in a drowning accident nearby, and as I stood there I felt close to Duncan once again, to everything he had taught me and to his way of life.

Those days spent on the hills around Loch Lomond gave me an appreciation both of the countryside and the people who live and work within it, to an extent that, while motor racing has afforded me the opportunity to meet many celebrated and famous people around the world, many of the most impressive people I have met have been these unsung guardians of the land: the gamekeepers, the ghillies and the stalkers. These are the people who pass knowledge and wisdom from father to son, third-, fourth- and fifth-generation specialists who drain the hills so the heather stays young so the grouse can feed, who restore the river banks after they've been damaged by a spate of water, so re-creating pools where the salmon can rest as, by a miracle of nature, they make their way upstream back to the same place where they spawned the previous year. And these are people whose livelihoods have come under threat in recent years because landowners have struggled to sustain the cash flow required to run their estates, which will often include a castle, shooting lodges, houses and cottages. Most continue to employ a factor, as estate managers are called in Scotland, but, whenever costs need to be cut, the easiest option has been to lay off other members of staff.

The plight of the countryside tends to be pushed down the big-city political agenda nowadays, but, amid the animosity of the hunting debate and the marginalisation of rural communities, the fact remains the land will never look after itself. These issues concern me because I am a patron of the National Gamekeepers' Organisation Charitable Trust, and also because my own grandfather, on my father's side of the family, was a head gamekeeper. His name was James Stewart, and he worked on the Eaglesham estate and the neighbouring Polnoon estate, not many miles from Glasgow, both of which were owned by Viscount Weir, whose family ran Weir's of Cathcart, a well-known marine engineering company, which still exists today.

James Stewart lived in a wooden cottage on the Weir estate called Netherholm, which I remember visiting regularly during my childhood. My grandparents kept kennels behind their cottage, and there was a hen run laid out across the road. There was no running water supply, so they had to pump water by hand from the cottage's own well. There was also no electricity, so they used oil lamps for lighting and wood and coal stoves for heating and cooking. However, there was a telephone on a shared line because the head gamekeeper needed to be able to contact the boss or to call the beaters to work. You had to crank the telephone up to reach the operator at the local exchange, who would then connect your call.

Their home was a place of fun, and discipline. Grandfather Stewart was tall and he had a neat moustache and he invariably seemed to be wearing a hat – I think that was to distinguish the head gamekeeper from the under-keepers. He often took me out on the estate, talking about the land and teaching me how to shoot rabbits and pigeon, both of which are regarded as vermin.

'Jackie, always open your gun,' he would say if I ever forgot to make the gun safe. 'And never shoot at a rabbit unless you're absolutely sure there's nobody in the bush behind.'

Both my grandfather and my father always stressed the importance of etiquette and safety in shooting, always carrying your gun in the appropriate fashion, taking precautions, and their words have remained with me ever since.

My grandmother Margaret was known as Maggie; she was a strong character, who made light of the arthritis in her fingers and played the piano with gusto, often accompanied by my father on the fiddle.

For the greater part of my childhood, I was fortunate that both my paternal and maternal grandparents lived within three miles of each other near Eaglesham. My mother's parents, John and Jean Young, farmed at a place called Castlehill, which hit the headlines in May 1941 when the deputy leader of Nazi Germany, Rudolf Hess, suddenly dropped out of the sky in an audacious attempt to broker a peace deal. He was confronted by David McLean, a ploughman and neighbour of my grandparents, with a pitchfork, and taken away to prison. The level of local excitement was unprecedented.

We were frequent lodgers at Castlehill during World War II, when the bombardment of the great shipyards on the River Clyde became so intense that my brother and I were evacuated to safety on the farm, where we were always expected to do our share of milking the cows and other chores. I have vague memories of my grandmother, who died after a stroke, but Grandpa Young was stout and dapper, rarely without his walking stick and happiest sitting in his armchair to the left of the fireplace. They left the farm in the late 1940s and moved to live in a more manageable bungalow in Eaglesham.

In his youth, my father worked for Viscount Weir as a draughtsman at Cathcart, reproducing diagrams of designers' concepts to start the manufacturing process, and all was well until, in 1928, apparently out of the blue, Robert Paul Stewart, my father, only son of a gamekeeper, made a decision that completely changed the course of his life, and ultimately mine. He announced he was going to run a garage near Dumbarton. The business would stand or fall on its location, and my father secured what appeared to be a prime site at a place called Dumbuck, where the busy main road leading from Glasgow to Loch Lomond divided into two, with the A814 heading left beside the Clyde to Helensburgh and the A82 continuing towards the loch. His plan was to sell petrol and oil to passing traffic and, with his own hands, he built the garage and forecourt.

Not long afterwards, he asked Jeanie, the eldest daughter of the Youngs of Castlehill, if she would marry him. She said 'yes', and her parents declared that, as a wedding present to the young couple, they would provide the funds for a bungalow to be constructed alongside the new garage.

My father drew the plans with a sitting room to the left of the front door and a dining room to the right, and two bedrooms, a bathroom and the kitchen at the back. There was a further bedroom on top, which you reached by climbing up a so-called Slingsby ladder that dropped down from the ceiling. A builder from the nearby town of Cardross, James Ritchie, was contracted to build the house.

'So what are we going to call the place?' my mother asked, when it was finished.

My father stood just outside the front door, from where he enjoyed an uninterrupted westerly view towards the River Clyde, just half a mile away, and the local landmark, Dumbarton Rock. 'Well, we can see the rock pretty well from here,' he replied, 'so we may as well just name it "Rockview".' That solid, homely bungalow became a cornerstone in the lives of two generations of Stewarts. My parents both lived there until they died, and my brother and I were both born there, on the dining-room table. It was home to me for the first twenty-three years of my life, and I only moved out when I got married to Helen in 1962.

My parents worked hard, settling into a new environment, and my father's courageous vision of a garage at Dumbuck gradually developed into a successful business. Their first son, Jim, was born in 1931 and, on 11 June 1939, almost as an afterthought, a second boy arrived and was christened John Young Stewart, taking the middle name from his mother's side of the family. Everyone called me Jackie.

So, this typical Scottish family lived contentedly on the outskirts of a typical Scottish town. Dumbarton stood at a spot where the River Clyde narrowed, and it has been an important place in the history of Scotland. The castle had long been of strategic importance, and I remember how they put out nets during the war to make sure no German submarines would make their way up the river.

In those days, the Clyde was widely recognised as the ship-building centre of the world – it used to be said the slipways on our river could accommodate all the shipping tonnage in the entire world – and Dumbarton was an integral part of this crucible of engineering expertise and skilled labour. It was here that Hercules Linton, of the local firm Scott & Linton, designed a beautiful tea clipper called the *Cutty Sark*, and construction was completed by William Denny and Brothers. And it was here, in a factory adjacent to Dennys' shipyard, where Blackburn Aircraft constructed the Sunderland flying boats during World War II.

You knew about these things when you were brought up in Dumbarton. You knew all about the massive red buildings of the Ballantine's whisky distillery that dominated the town, and you knew about Dumbarton FC, the local football club that played its home matches at Boghead Park and whose players were nicknamed 'The Sons' because people who came from the town were known as 'sons of the rock'. You knew all this and you were proud to come from Dumbarton. I remember how fantastic it felt to stand at the front door of our bungalow and watch the great ships pass by, newly built, carefully feeling their way down the Clyde before powering out into the open seas and oceans, and across the globe.

We watched HMS *Vanguard* pass by in November 1944. The largest battleship ever built for the Royal Navy had been laid down by John Brown and Company, of Clydebank, and launched by the then HRH Princess Elizabeth before it made its imperious way down the river, past our front door. Three years later, we stood and stared in amazement at the *Caronia*, a great passenger cruise liner built by John Brown for Cunard following in the tradition of the *Queen Mary* and the *Queen Elizabeth*.

Those days are all gone now. Shipbuilding on the Clyde fell into decline in the 1960s and 1970s, at least in part because the rest of the world started welding and the Scottish companies continued using rivets; and then shipyards elsewhere discovered aluminium to be lighter and more economic, while the companies on the Clyde kept building with steel. We thought we knew best and we paid the price. With many companies closing and communities suffering, William Denny and Brothers struggled against the economic tide before closing its doors in 1963.

The garage continued to grow and, when we became local dealers for Austin, I suspect we started to appear more affluent than we were. There were always fancy cars on the forecourt, and, with my mother and father using the demonstrators around town, the Stewarts started to look quite respectable.

My parents were always resourceful. During the years after the war, T2 tankers started coming up the Clyde, bringing oil supplies from America to places like the depot at Bowling, near our house, so they started a taxi service, taking captains and pursers from their ships to the shipping agents, Denham in Glasgow. I was usually put in the back of the Austin 16 – registration FGG 184, I recall – and taken along for the ride, and our Canadian and American passengers used to give me sweets. In an austere era when almost everything still seemed to be rationed, it's difficult to explain how excited I was to be given treats like Hershey chocolate bars and Wrigley's chewing gum. One particular man always brought my mother a bottle of maple syrup, and we would pour it over pancakes for supper. It's no wonder I developed such a sweet tooth.

A constant stream of interesting people seemed to be passing though our lives and, even as young boy, I always kept my eyes open and learned whatever I could.

There were my father's friends from the bowling club, the Rotary club and the Burns club. There was Jim Fitzgerald, who ran Burroughs Adding Machines, and Russ Kitchen, a Canadian who was in charge of Westclox. There was the local rep for Dunlop, and the local rep for Esso. And all these people intrigued me, and started me wondering what kind of world lay out there, way beyond the garage at Dumbuck.

There was Ronald Teacher, a great man from the famous whisky family, who used to arrive at the garage, where I would fill up his Bentley which, I remember, was light grey with all the parts that were supposed to be chrome painted blue. He lived in a big house in Rhu and owned a yacht, and it was said he knew Briggs Cunningham, who sailed in the America's Cup and later became a well-known racing car driver, owner and constructor in America.

These were the giants of my world and, now and then, we would venture into the gleaming and glamorous metropolis of Glasgow, just fourteen miles away up the Clyde. The city may have passed its heyday at the turn of the century, when it grew wealthy from the boom in shipbuilding, coalmining and steel production and was dubbed the 'Second City of the Empire', but in my childish eyes, even through the war years and into the 1950s, it still represented everything that was opulent, lavish and successful, with big cinemas, large houses and expensive apartments. I used to wonder at the beautiful sandstone Art Gallery and the extravagant magnificence of the City Hall, and my parents would take Jim and me to watch shows such as the *Five Past Eight* at the Alhambra Theatre, 41 Waterloo Street. We enjoyed the pantomimes and, one year, we saw Harry Lauder, the 'Laird of the music hall'.

Music was an important part of our family life. We had an upright Bechstein piano in our sitting room, which my mother played, and a series of well-known visiting singers and musicians used to rehearse in our house before performing concerts for the Dumbarton Choral Society or at venues like the Burgh Hall in town. I recall sitting in a corner and listening to stars like Owen Brannigan, Joan Alexander and the great Robert Wilson, renowned as the 'Voice of Scotland', who sang popular songs like 'Bonnie Strathyre'. And when these great people stopped for a break, I would run in and ask if they would sign my autograph book, which soon became the most cherished possession of my boyhood.

Our lives revolved around the garage but, now and then, we did take day trips down the Clyde – or 'doon the water', as Glaswegians used to say – on famous paddle steamers like the *Waverley* and the *Jeannie Deans*, and we spent summer holidays at Grantown-on-Spey and Aberlour, where my father went fishing with his friend, Jim Walker, the son of Joe Walker, who founded the shortbread company. My brother and I played with the three Walker children, Joe, Jim and Marjorie – and fifty years later, it was Marjorie whom I dealt with when we signed Walkers as a sponsor of Paul Stewart Racing.

In 1952, out of the blue, my mother announced she was taking me on holiday to America. My friends didn't believe me when I told them but, exactly as she had said, we boarded a Boeing C-97 Stratocruiser, complete with bunk beds as an optional extra which you pulled down from the ceiling and clambered into with a stepladder. Our flight stopped in Reykjavik, Iceland and Halifax, Nova Scotia en route to New York.

I remember we stayed on Staten Island, at the family home of a man who had been captain on one of the tankers that brought oil to Dumbarton and had since retired; and every day, we took the ferry across to Manhattan, where my mother bought me my very first pair of long trousers. We also visited Niagara Falls on a journey that felt like a trip to the moon for me back then, but later became a regular feature of my life.

My mother was the forceful member of our family. Jean

Clark Stewart knew what she wanted and, one way or another, she usually got it. There had initially been a fashionably stained pane of glass in the porthole window in the house that overlooked the forecourt, but my mother replaced it with clear glass so she could see what was going on and, if ever a customer was left waiting, she would be on the phone, telling the staff to get out and serve them.

Her greatest passion was driving. She loved it, adored fast cars and could not wait to get behind the wheel of every smart vehicle that came through our dealership – at stages, she drove a 1.5 litre Riley with doors that opened the 'wrong' way, and then the 2.5 litre RMB version. Then, she used a light-blue convertible Austin Atlantic A90 with the long wheelbase and an electric power top that could be retracted and latched down in just twenty-two seconds. It was unheard of in Britain and, as she liked to tell everybody who listened (and the car never lacked admirers), the A90 had a top speed of 92 mph and, in 1949, had broken sixty-three stock car records in the space of seven days at Indianapolis. Next, there was a horrible orange-and-white two-tone Nash/Austin Metropolitan, which looked like something out of a cartoon and, with half-cut wheel arches and soft suspension, appeared to be nodding at everything.

'Mummy, your car is certainly looking friendly today,' Jim and I used to laugh.

'Come on, have you two got nothing better to do?' she would reply.

On one occasion, my brother took her out in his Healey Silverstone, which was a classic British hand-built sporty two-seater, and they drove up to the Bo'ness hill climb, near Linlithgow. Jim eased the car up towards 100 mph on the straight, and our mother cooed with pleasure.

'Gosh, Jim,' she said, smiling broadly, 'it's got loads of punch, hasn't it?'

So did she. People often said 'Jeanie' was the most talented

driver in our family, and I would not disagree. If I was born with any particular racing genes, they were certainly inherited from her.

My father was a gentle man, a gregarious and popular mixer who seemed to know anyone and everyone in the Dumbarton community, which was naturally great for the business. He enjoyed motor sport and had been a competitive motorcyclist in his youth. I knew he had once raced at the Isle of Man, but we never spoke about it much. Robert Paul Stewart was a typical Scot in the sense that he valued his friends, didn't talk much about himself and preferred to avoid any kind of fuss.

He loved the countryside and not only used to go grouse and pheasant shooting with Ronald Teacher but was also so keen on fly fishing that he joined a syndicate which included Jack McPhee, the Provost of Dumbarton, and a Dutchman in the dredging business called Peter Callus. This group leased a stretch of the Spey called Wester Elchies, near Aberlour, for the last two weeks of May each year, at the time when the salmon were freshly running up the river from the North Sea, with sea lice still attached to their silver scales and, together with the ghillies Jimmy Milne and Jock Duncan, steeped in common sense and local wisdom, they fished during this particular fortnight for more than three decades. In fact, it was at this place, where five of us – his friends Russ Kitchen, Andy Thompson, James Walker and my brother and I – gathered in 1972 and, one after the other, scattered my father's ashes at a spot between the ghillies' hut and the water, beside a pool called Delagyle on the magnificent River Spey.

Brought up in a family that ran a garage and Austin dealership, it was perhaps inevitable that I should start to drive at a relatively early age, and I was only nine years old when I first placed a two-gallon can on the driver's seat of a dark-blue Austin 16, clambered into position, made absolutely sure my feet could reach the pedals, which they did, just, at a bit of a

stretch, and excitedly turned the key. The car tentatively started to move around the forecourt, with me somehow managing to see where I was going by peering through the narrow gap between the steering wheel and the dashboard. The long chromium-plated gearshift lever with a big bakelite knob presented a real challenge, but I eventually got the hang of it and, within a few days, I was having a great time, buzzing around the forecourt.

Sadly for me, however, as a nine-year-old boy, feeling good about myself and my place in the world, feeling confident and in control, was quite unusual.

CHAPTER 2

Am I Stupid?

It was a monday morning in the autumn of 1948 in the primary school of the Dumbarton Academy: I was nine years old, just another face in the row of young Scots. Spring-heeled Jake, my father called me because I could never sit still, but at that moment I was stock still in my seat – the moment I had been dreading for weeks was upon me – I was about to be asked to read aloud in class for the first time.

'All right, Jackie, it's your turn,' the teacher said.

'For what, Miss?'

'For reading, of course. Come up here.'

She beckoned me to make my way from the front row; that was where I always sat because that was where the not-so-clever students were supposed to sit – where she could watch us, I suppose. And she kept beckoning me, until I was standing right beside her, facing the entire class of fifty-six boys and girls.

'Now,' she barked, passing me a book, 'read aloud from the start of the chapter.'

I looked down at the page and saw nothing but a jungle of letters. I searched for the first word, something to grab on to, but there was nothing, just a mass of indecipherable, impossible letters. Everyone seemed to regard me as a sparkly character at school, a cheeky wee boy with a twinkle in my eye, but, in that terrible moment, the thin veneer of confidence was stripped away.

As I started to blush, I became aware of my smarter schoolmates starting to snigger. There was coughing as well. I felt trapped in a nightmare and sensed the tears welling in my eyes.

'Come on, Stewart, get on with it.'

I kept staring at the page, now desperately wanting to find words that I recognised, sentences that I could understand. Instead, there was just a mass of letters that meant nothing to me.

'Stop playing the fool,' the teacher said, now getting angry. 'The class is almost over, and you are wasting everybody's time. Hurry up and start reading.'

'I can't,' I mumbled.

'What?' she yelled.

'I said I can't.'

'Stewart, you're a stupid, lazy boy! Get back to your desk.'

I walked back to my place, with most of my classmates laughing out loud. I cannot exaggerate the pain and humiliation that I felt that day. Maybe it's only something that people who suffer from a learning disability such as dyslexia can really understand. Yet this pitiless torture, albeit unwittingly inflicted by a teacher who simply did not understand my problem, was repeated whenever I was told to read in front of the class thereafter. However hard I tried, I couldn't do it. I didn't understand why. Everyone was saying I was dumb, stupid and thick – the teachers said so in the classroom, and other children said so in the playground – and, in the absence of any other explanation, I started to believe they must be right.

I was being made to feel inferior over and over again, day

after day. I began to dread going to school and started to look for any excuse to stay at home. First, I had flu, then I had a stomach bug, and then my leg was sore. My mother realised I had always been small and frail as a boy, but she became increasingly frustrated by my constant ailments. The truth was I didn't want to be made to read out loud again and suffer the embarrassment of being exposed in front of my friends.

That was how I felt when I was nine years old; and, more or less, that was how I felt for the first forty-one years of my life. The fact is that, even when I became a Formula 1 world champion, even when I was mixing with the rich and famous, even when I was closing major deals, I still felt hopelessly inadequate in any matters relating to the three 'r's – reading, writing and arithmetic. Ever since my schooldays, I have had the idea that other people were better than me. You occasionally hear ambitious people say their goal is to be the best in the world. Well, I never had that kind of confidence. I have always believed that, because the other person was better, I would have to work harder, do something in a slightly different way and maybe pay more attention to detail just to keep up. I thought I was stupid, and it took me more than forty years to realise that I am not, and have never been, stupid. I am dyslexic, and there's nothing wrong with that.

The Dumbarton Academy has always been a magnificent, robust, sandstone building, standing high above the town. The school looks majestic, whether viewed from the north, the south, the east or the west. It's the kind of place where any young person would want to be educated. That was my privilege in the late 1940s. In those days, the primary school was situated on the ground floor with the secondary school on the first floor. There was an internal quadrant, and we used to look up and watch the older boys walking along the corridors between their classes.

'It's going to be great when we get up there,' I remember

telling my friend, John Lindsay. John and I both played in the school football team, him in goal and me at outside right, and we did quite well most of the time, even if we always seemed to lose against St Patrick's, the local Catholic school. Anyway, I was in the school side, and that didn't do my self-confidence any harm.

My problems started in the classroom, where I struggled to consume information and learn and be educated. The main exam in those days was the eleven-plus. I sat it twice and I failed it twice. The year before I was meant to go upstairs to the secondary school, my parents were called in to see the head-master.

'Jackie doesn't seem interested,' he told them. 'His teachers say he doesn't pay attention and doesn't try. I'm afraid, without an eleven-plus pass, he'll have to leave the Academy.'

There was no discussion. In those days, nobody recognised learning difficulties, much less wondered how young children who were struggling in the classroom might be helped. They were just branded as stupid. My parents listened, accepted the judgement and made arrangements for me to move to Hartfield, a school just a quarter of a mile down the road.

Most of the boys or girls who failed their eleven-plus in Dumbarton usually ended up on the roll at Hartfield, but, more than disappointed, I was really distressed to be heading in that direction. The whole place felt second rate, from the metal windows to the rough-cast concrete walls. In my mind, every-thing about the Academy had represented class and quality, and everything about Hartfield didn't. I started to feel consigned to the scrap heap.

There was an official ranking structure in the Scottish educational system at the time: if you were bright, you studied Latin and French; if you were half-bright, you learned French; if you were really not so bright, you did woodwork; and if you were downright stupid, you were sent to woodwork and metalwork. To nobody's surprise, I was put in the woodwork and metalwork set. Every aspect of my life seemed to be defined by my apparent lack of intelligence. There were boys and girls whom I liked, and who I wanted to be my friends, but they didn't want to be friends with me because everybody said I was thick.

I recall I used to think Anne Turner was the prettiest girl at our school, and there were many occasions when I was on the brink of approaching her and talking to her, but I always backed away because she seemed so much cleverer than me and, so I reckoned, she would never be interested in what I had to say. So I started to hang out with youngsters who found themselves in a similar position to me, because they were not demanding or threatening and they didn't laugh at me. I began to drift towards the periphery of our Dumbarton community. While clever students were socialising at the Denny Institute, named after the local shipbuilders, my friends and I would usually be found at a billiard hall, up a close off the High Street. It was a rough place, and fights were common: the cues became weapons, and billiard balls were hurled in all directions. Yet, however rough, however unsophisticated, this was starting to feel like my proper station in life. I was fourteen years old, and mere survival seemed to be the limit of my ambition.

Then, one cold November evening, I left the billiard hall, walked down the close, turned right on to the High Street and headed to the bus stop.

'Hey, who do you think you are?'

The voice was aggressive. I didn't know it.

'You're trouble. That's what you are.'

It was a different voice, snarling, nasty, and I didn't recognise that one either. I turned to find a bunch of them, maybe four or five youngsters, bearing down on me, and I saw nothing but a blur of fists and boots. The attack was brutal and brief and, not more than a minute later, I was left lying on the pavement, a few yards away from my bus stop, with a fractured collarbone, three cracked ribs and a broken nose.

In years to come, people would notice the bump in my nose and automatically assume it was caused by an accident suffered in a brave dash for glory at a glamorous Grand Prix. The slightly more mundane reality is that I was beaten up on Dumbarton High Street, and I've never had my nose fixed.

On reflection, that beating didn't hurt me; it saved me. It was a wake-up call because it made me realise, in the bluntest possible way, that that sort of thing was going to happen to me on a regular basis if I kept putting myself in the wrong place with the wrong people at the wrong time. The message was clear: change your lifestyle, or else. I clearly remember sitting at home, with my mother dabbing disinfectant on my wounds, and reaching a decision that I would get my life on track. I was not going to slide away and give up. I would find something I could do. I would succeed and earn the respect of all the people who were laughing at me.

'All right,' I told myself, 'you may not be the brightest boy in the school, but you know as much about cars as any of your friends, and there aren't many who have such a deep knowledge of the countryside. You may have to work a bit harder. You may have to do things in a slightly different way. You may even have to pay extra attention to detail, but you can do it.'

In my youth, I was fortunate to have friends who pushed me in the right direction, and it was people like John Lindsay, Willie McGilchrist and his sister Ann and the Woodbridge brothers, George and Henry, who did as much as anybody to keep me away from the world of the billiard hall, and the slippery slide that it grew to represent. The group of us used to watch movies in the village hall next to the Co-op in Milton, down the road from our garage. They were called 'Magic Lantern' nights, and I enjoyed them. But much as I enjoyed being part of that social group, I still didn't have the confidence to join the Cubs or the Scouts because I imagined they might do something that was beyond me and I was still terrified of being exposed as inferior.

I had already started to work part-time at my father's garage, doing something I found I was good at, when my life changed on New Year's Day 1953, when I went along to take part in a local clay pigeon shooting competition and, out of the blue, I won. It may be true that some of the other competitors were the worse for wear because they had celebrated Hogmanay the previous night, but that didn't matter to me. Against every expectation, it was me who was called up to stand in front of everybody else . . . this time, not to read aloud and be mocked, but to receive a trophy and be applauded. It was as if somebody had blown away the clouds of gloom. I still had to get through six more months at school, but that period flew by because, even though I struggled in the classroom, I had proved I was able to succeed at something.

Shooting gave me a precious confidence boost but, as the years passed, working at our garage, then as a racing driver, then as a colour and expert television commentator for the ABC's *Wide World of Sports* in the USA, then under contract to major international companies such as the Ford Motor Company, Rolex, Elf, Goodyear and Moët & Chandon . . . through all this, whenever I was asked to deal with anything related to spelling or reading, I still harboured this sense of being inadequate. Deep down, away from the public gaze, I still felt vulnerable. What would people say, I used to wonder, if they discovered that, in reality, Jackie Stewart was not too clever? There were a few close calls.

In 1967, I was invited to record a television commercial for British Railways, the first I ever did, and I was to make the recording while standing in front of a railway engine at Waverley Station in Edinburgh. I was scared I would not be able to remember my lines, so I learned them so well that I can still repeat them word for word today, forty years later.

'Hello, I'm Jackie Stewart,' I said to the camera. 'The most powerful engine I've ever driven produced 750 horsepower. This beauty produces 7,500 horsepower. It's fast, very fast, it's alive with power. It can take you from Edinburgh to London in under five hours. Even I can't do that.'

Even the wonderful exhilaration of winning a Grand Prix was always tinged with an element of fear because it meant I would have to stand on a podium, in full public view, while the British national anthem was played . . . and the fact was that, as hard as I tried, I couldn't remember the words. It was impossible for me to learn them. It is the same with the Lord's Prayer. So once again I devised a way of working around the problem. I did that, by learning to sing or pray just a millisecond behind everyone else, effectively repeating the words as soon as I heard them. I became so adept that nobody ever seemed to notice.

It has always seemed a paradox. On the one hand, I can't recite the alphabet beyond the letter 'p', but on the other hand I know every single gear change and braking distance required to negotiate the 187 corners around the 14.7 mile circuit at the old Nurburgring in Germany, and all that complex information remains banked in my brain to this day. Does this mean I am stupid or clever? I have never really understood. It appers as though it may be a trait particular to a dyslexic like me – although, oddly, somehow I did manage to learn the scripts for the commercials I appeared in. It took a long time and a lot of effort, but I did it. Perhaps it had something to do with the pressure of being in front of a camera. Or the fact that I would be getting paid!

The years passed and, in 1980, in a strange reversal of roles, I found myself cast as the concerned parent being called to see the headmaster. This time, the school was Aiglon, the boarding school in Villars, Switzerland, and the boy who was struggling with his academic work was our twelve-year-old son, Mark. My wife Helen and I had thought there could be a problem when the teachers at two of his previous schools had expressed concern, but he seemed such a creative boy that we were never overly worried. Even at that age, he used to take the home video camera into the garden and shoot his own films.

'Do you think Mark may have learning difficulties?' the Aiglon headmaster asked.

I looked at Helen, and Helen looked back at me. The fact was we were not aware of learning difficulties, so I gave the only honest answer: 'I don't know.'

'Maybe you should have him tested.'

'OK,' I replied, uncertainly.

We were referred to Lord Renwick, who was then chairman of the British Dyslexia Association; he directed us to Professor Colin Stevenson, of Southampton University, an expert in the field, and we met him in London. I was about to experience the most startling moment of realisation in my life. The professor took Mark away for a series of tests, which cannot have lasted more than twenty minutes. He then returned to where Helen and I were sitting and said: 'Your son is dyslexic.'

'What?' I replied. To be honest, I didn't know what he was talking about.

'Your son is dyslexic. He has a learning disability, which explains his difficulties at school.'

'How could he have got that?'

'Well, it can be hereditary.'

A pause followed, and the professor seemed to be thinking exactly what I was thinking.

He asked, 'Are you in a rush?'

'No,' I replied.

'Well, if you have time, I could test you.'

Twenty minutes later, after forty-one years of feeling stupid and inferior, I was diagnosed as dyslexic. It felt as if somebody was reaching out an arm and saving me from drowning. A professional was standing before me saying I was not stupid, and my sense of feeling inadequate was suddenly erased.

I was pleased for Mark. Now we knew the problem, we could get around it. It was important that we all adopted a positive approach, as so often people allow themselves to be defeated by situations not so much because the situations are impossible as because they *believe* the situations are impossible. It has been said that, 'There are no problems, there are only solutions,' and that sentiment is extremely important to me.

Whether I was confronted by a mechanical fault in my racing car, or a sticking point in negotiations, or my son with dyslexia, I always believed every problem could be solved. It is sometimes called the power of positive thinking, and I have certainly applied the principle to whatever I have done in my life.

Helen and I decided we wanted to keep Mark at the same boarding school as Paul, his older brother, who was fourteen and we now suspected had himself suffered from a mild form of dyslexia. So we discussed the issue with the teachers at Aiglon, who had initially indicated they could not cater for Mark's needs. Eventually, it was agreed I would fund the appointment of a specially trained teacher to assist dyslexic students. The search was on, and we eventually found an exceptional teacher in England called Jenny James and persuaded her to relocate to Switzerland and take up the challenge at Aiglon.

I attached a single proviso to my financial commitment of around £45,000, specifically that, if it emerged that other Aiglon students needed Jenny's specialist assistance, then their parents would be asked to contribute towards her salary. Less than twelve months later, Miss James was offering invaluable guidance to more than twenty dyslexic students, and Aiglon was being praised for its pioneering decision to appoint a specialist teacher. The Learning Disabilities Unit at Aiglon thrives to this day.

It seemed entirely natural that, as soon as the pace of my life allowed, I should become involved in the wider campaign to raise awareness of dyslexia. In 1988, at the invitation of two fine Scottish ladies, Julia Trotter and Maive Mowbray, I agreed to become president of the Scottish Dyslexia Trust, which later became known as Dyslexia Scotland. The organisation has become a particular passion for me. Julia and Maive provided me with the bare facts and, to be honest, I was startled: 10 per cent of the UK population were dyslexic; between 15 and 20 per cent of the UK population suffered from some kind of learning disability; 70 per cent of sufferers were boys, and their inability to develop basic literacy skills meant they struggled to find employment, and often drifted into a twilight world of drugs, alcohol abuse and crime. It was a fact that more than 70 per cent of all prison inmates in the United Kingdom suffered from some kind of learning disability. The scale of the problem was enormous. Dyslexia was costing the country billions of pounds in wasted potential and needlessly derailing millions of lives, and yet it seemed to me that the educational establishment in the United Kingdom was somehow in denial of the real issues: attention appeared to be focused on soothing the effects of learning disabilities rather than on addressing the core of the problem.

Yes, there were plenty of high-profile people attending fund-raising dinners, and money was being allocated to help a few, but the recognition and management of the condition remained largely in the hands of the private sector. Well-off parents of children with learning difficulties raised monies to assist families who did not know where to turn for help. The education authorities were inadequate and, in schools up and down the country, dyslexic children were still suffering exactly the same kind of humiliation and mishandling that turned my school years into such an ordeal.

Eventually, midway through a speech at a Dyslexic Institute dinner in the Dorchester hotel, London, something snapped. The event was going to raise more than £300,000 to help families who lacked the knowledge, resources and funds to have their children helped, and I was relating my personal experiences of the condition when, suddenly, I sensed the content of what I was saying was somehow inadequate. I put aside my notes, and spoke straight: 'Ladies and gentlemen, in all honesty, we're on the wrong track here. It's all very well us gathering tonight and giving money, probably because either one of our children is dyslexic or maybe we know somebody who is dyslexic. That's fine. But are we doing enough? Is shaking our heads and writing cheques doing enough? Or should we rather be getting involved and working to change the way dyslexic people are treated?'

There followed what public speakers call a 'pregnant pause'. For a moment, I wondered if I had gone too far. In hindsight, maybe this was just an example of classic dyslexic thinking: looking at a familiar problem from a new and different perspective. In essence, I believed it was time to stop saying, 'Poor thing, he's dyslexic, let's give him and his family some money,' and to start saying, 'At least 10 per cent of our population are not realising their potential, so let's do something concrete and insist our government helps these people.'

I increased my commitment to the cause and soon realised the most effective approach to the problem would be to improve the rate of early detection; this meant training teachers to recognise the symptoms. It seemed ridiculous that only a fraction of the 450,000 teachers in the UK were aware of learning disabilities and I'm afraid it remains the same today.

When he was elected in 1997, British Prime Minister Tony Blair had declared one of the major priorities of his New

Labour government would be 'Education, Education, Education' and that impressed me at the time but, from where I was standing, not much was happening for ordinary dyslexic people. Yes, special learning units were introduced at most of the private schools, largely because parents were in a position to insist to the board of governors that such facilities be created, yet that kind of assistance and understanding still seemed depressingly rare in state schools across the country. A two-tiered situation was developing where wealthy children with learning difficulties were called dyslexic and being helped to overcome the problem, while less affluent kids with exactly the same difficulties were called stupid and were still being dismissed. It wasn't good enough, and something needed to be done, not just because the government was obliged to fulfil its promise of better education but also because the situation flew in the face of its often declared emphasis on social inclusion.

I raised the issue during a speech at the Gleneagles hotel to a group called Scotland International, which brings together a group of influential Scots from home and abroad who meet annually to discuss what can be done to improve our country.

Professor Duncan Rice, vice-chancellor and principal of the University of Aberdeen, was among the audience and he telephoned me soon afterwards to ask if we could meet and have lunch the next time I was in Scotland. A date was set, we met and, together with Duncan's vice-principal for learning and teaching, Cathy Macaslan, we began to develop a plan whereby we would approach the then First Minister of the Scottish Parliament, Jack McConnell, and the Scottish Minister for Education, Peter Peacock, and seek government funding for a Chair of Inclusive Studies to be created at the University's teacher training college. Duncan and Cathy agreed that, if we could train teachers to recognise the symptoms of dyslexia and assist the affected children accordingly, we would start to make a real difference.

A meeting was duly arranged, and it unfolded as one of my most fruitful interactions with government, maybe because the First Minister had trained as a teacher himself, and so he and his Minister for Education seemed to understand the logic of what we were saying.

'This professorship would be the first of its kind,' I explained, 'not just in Scotland, not just in Great Britain, not just in Europe . . . a world first. It is needed. The only issue is funding.'

'Are you contributing?' the First Minister asked.

'No,' I replied. 'With respect, this is not something that should be borne by the private sector.'

It has always seemed to me that taxpayers should be entitled to expect three things from government: first, that the National Health Service will assist their recovery from either ill health or an accident; second, that the police are equipped and able to enforce law and order in their community; and, third, that every child is offered a complete education, whether or not they have learning difficulties, within the state system. In my view, using private money to drive projects to address learning difficulties is wrong. It is government's responsibility, and doing their job for them solves nothing in the long term.

Jack McConnell was listening, and Duncan proceeded to explain how not one of seven teacher training colleges in Scotland had any capacity to prepare future generations of teachers to learn not only how to recognise basic learning disabilities, but also how to help dyslexic learners progress through the curriculum.

'What's the cost for the pilot project?' he asked.

'One and a half million pounds,' I replied.

'When do you need an answer?'

'Within four weeks,' I said, which may have been asking a bit much but, having already experienced the continuous procrastination of politicians in Westminster on other issues, I was eager that we should execute the closed loop philosophy, and get the job done without any unnecessary delay.

Four weeks to the day after our meeting, I received the official response, approving an allocation of £1.4 million to create a Chair of Inclusive Studies at the University of Aberdeen. The initiative was duly launched in September 2006, and it is now thriving under the leadership of Professor Martyn Rouse and an American professor named Lani Florrian, both of whom were recruited from Cambridge University. The project reinforces Scotland's reputation for breaking new ground in education, and it has been enthusiastically endorsed by the First Minister, Alex Salmond. The fact is that every teacher qualifying at a teacher training college in Scotland will be trained to identify children with learning disabilities. These early recognition skills are crucial and, so far as I am aware, this development is a world first for Scotland.

Working in tandem with the British Dyslexia Association, I am now proposing similar courses are launched at teacher training colleges in England, Wales and Northern Ireland. However, it remains considerably easier to get things done at the Scottish parliament than at Westminster. I have dealt with first Lord Adonis and more recently Ed Balls, the Secretary of State for Children, Schools and Families, and, while both men have shown interest and understanding of the problems associated with dyslexia, it almost feels as if 'the system' is there to make sure reasons are created to delay progress.

In my experience, the approach and the mood is over-whelmingly negative. Just imagine how much could be done if all this energy could be directed away from decision procrastination and into making things happen in a better way.

Westminster seems to me to be a wasteland of open loops. Projects and initiatives are proposed, but too few people seem to have the skill, the energy or the will to get the job done and actually close the loop.

So, while we continue to make progress with all seven teacher training colleges in Scotland, we have struggled to get any real traction at Westminster, a situation that is not helped by the reality that the British Government is run by a merry-go-round of ministers. Just when Andrew Adonis had got his feet under the table at the Department of Education, and developed the understanding and relationships to take the situation forward, he was moved to the Department of Transport, where he had to start learning all over again.

No single person is to blame. It is a fault of our system of government that our major departments are run by generalists, politicians who usually only stay in a job for a few years before being moved on. At risk of repeating myself, I strongly believe ministers need to be left in one job to gain experience, and then knowledge and then wisdom.

Even so, we are playing with the cards we are dealt and, before long, we hope that every teacher training college in England, Wales and Northern Ireland will catch up with their Scottish counterparts and introduce the modules to ensure every qualified teacher is able to assist dyslexic pupils.

Our position is straightforward: unless every teacher in the UK is trained to make early recognition of children with learning difficulties, we will effectively deny the rights of a minimum six million people to realise their potential, at immense cost to the country. There is not a manufacturing company in the world that could afford to abandon close to 15 per cent of its production capacity, and the same principle applies to every country whether it is small, like Scotland, or enormous, like China or India.

It was my misfortune to be educated in an era when dyslexic students were humiliated. There was a particular teacher at the Dumbarton Academy who regularly used to punish me for what she believed was pure laziness. She knew no better. She wasn't aware of learning disabilities or dyslexia. I wish she had been in a position to understand what was wrong because it is that kind of ignorance that has denied so many children a proper education. The era of ignorance should have passed, but it hasn't. It angers me and frankly amazes me to hear how, even today, in twenty-first-century Britain, some teachers are still shouting at terrified, humiliated children because they struggle to read out loud. As president of Dyslexia Scotland, the least I can do is work to ensure that, in this country, the teachers of the future are properly trained to understand and assist their pupils with learning difficulties.

These children are not a national liability; on the contrary, they should be regarded as a national asset. Winston Churchill was dyslexic, which helped him become one of the greatest orators in history because, like many dyslexic people, he had an ability to 'colour in the pictures' and express himself vividly. Charles Schwab is dyslexic, which meant this great American entrepreneur was able to see the potential of selling stocks and shares on the mass market because, in common with many dyslexic people, he could look at issues differently and pursue his own solution. Such tendencies are recognised in many dyslexic people, and they were evident in my own career as a racing driver. When I needed to communicate with engineers or designers and make them understand how the car was performing, I found myself able to express myself more vividly than my colleagues. It's true that dyslexic people can sometimes over-explain issues – maybe because we need to be totally sure we have made ourselves clear before we can move on to the next issue – but an overflow of information has rarely been a problem for an engineer who needs to understand how a car is behaving, or for an executive who needs to understand every aspect of a proposal.

'Dyslexia can be good for you!' This was the message I wanted to convey when, in November 2006, with David

Swinfen, chairman of Dyslexia Scotland, and Mary Evans, another leading official in the organisation, I was invited to visit a special unit for ten-year-olds with learning difficulties at the Kaimhill primary school in Aberdeen. I had written a letter to encourage the children and been touched by the letters they sent back.

James Riach, aged nine, wrote: 'I am new here. I miss my friends but Shane is my friend. I think it is good to get on with your life. I want to follow you. I want to get a medal from the Queen. I was told I had dyslexia when I was eight. When I was told I had dyslexia, I was upset. When you knew about it, did it still hurt? Did you feel weird at school? I did but now I come here it is better. We do a lot of work . . . Mrs Mackay read out your letter to the whole class. I am glad you know you aren't stupid now.'

The visit to Kaimhill started with me joining the children in playing the innovative games designed to help them improve their reading and spelling skills. I then addressed a school assembly and, mindful of my own experiences, I warned the other children in the school that they should not tease their friends with dyslexia.

'Watch out,' I told them. 'Dyslexic kids are often very successful later in life and, you never know, one day you might just find yourself working for one of them.'

At one stage, earlier in the classroom, Eileen Jessamine, the specialist teacher, had asked me to recite the alphabet.

'OK,' I responded, 'but here comes a failure!'

She countered firmly: 'We don't have failures here, Sir Jackie. We only have successes.'

I looked across the classroom at her. There she stood: upbeat, seeing solutions not problems, trained and informed, the model of a modern teacher for children with learning difficulties. At least none of the children in her class were going to grow up believing they were stupid, dumb and thick.

That was progress, but there were just twelve children in Eileen's class, and there are an estimated 1,250 dyslexic primary-school children in the Aberdeen area. So, a start has been made . . . that's all, and that's just in one city, let alone the rest of Scotland, let alone the rest of the UK, let alone the rest of the world.

That's the reality.

There is still so much to be done.

CHAPTER 3

Trigger for Success

FIRST PRIZE ON NEW YEAR'S DAY 1953 at the Gartocharn and Kilmarnock gun club was a surprisingly large trophy and a £5 note. Clay pigeon shooting was suddenly offering me, an apparent failure in the classroom, the chance to be successful, to be good at something and to earn people's respect. A new world was opening up before me, and I was soon travelling all around Scotland, meeting new people, performing well, gaining confidence and sometimes winning.

My entire approach to life was changing. I clearly remember starting to feel nervous on the night before a competition. This was something new, something different from the paralysing sense of fear that I had always felt before an academic exam. Fear was a negative emotion, because I categorically knew that, whatever I did, however long I studied for the exam, however hard I worked, there was no way I would finish anywhere near the top of the class; so I was fearful of the challenge and I went to those ridiculous lengths to avoid going to school. Nerves were something quite different. Preparing for a shooting event, I became nervous because I knew I could do quite well, but there was no guarantee, and I became apprehensive because I realised that one error was usually the difference between winning and losing. So, I gradually began to work out for myself, the burden lay with me to prepare as meticulously as possible. The essential difference was that, at school, I had been disheartened by facing what seemed impossible, but, in my shooting, I was being stimulated by dealing with challenge.

This process was the introduction to a key principle of my life – to be better prepared than any of my rivals in whatever I was doing – and, as a teenager, I learned to develop a ritual of preparation that helped me stay single-mindedly focused on what I was doing. Whenever I approached the shooting stand, I developed the habit of making my way through a series of procedures and little idiosyncrasies before I called for the target to be released. I used to adjust my shooting jacket, so there was no risk of creases on the shoulder where the stock of the gun snuggles in. I tugged the peak of my cap to create total comfort. I added a few cartridges to the pockets of my jacket, and over the years learned when was the right time for me to swallow so that my breathing was not interrupted when I was ready to call for the clay to be released. I did all of those things before I shot each of the twenty-five targets in every round. My preparation became mechanically timed to eliminate all unnecessary disruptions that might interfere with my concentration and total commitment. As I matured, I developed and refined such routines and skills to a level where they helped me significantly, both when I became a racing driver and in business. My overriding goal in everything I have tried to do has always been to remove the unnecessary hazards and reduce the downside risks through good preparation, good structuring and good planning; and it all started when I was clay pigeon shooting.

Risk management has always been important to me. If you eliminate potential problems in advance, or at least minimise them, then whatever you are doing is bound to go better and more smoothly. Never more so than when I was filming a commercial for Goodyear tyres on Bridport pier in the early 1980s. The plan was that I would drive at speed along the pier – towards the sea – and at the last minute I would slam on the brakes and the car would come to a halt, inches from the end, with the sea looming. There was a marker positioned out of camera shot which was to be my indicator as to when to brake. I arrived and I didn't fancy the set-up one little bit. The weather was rough with waves periodically soaking the pier, making the surface very slick. The director of the shoot assured me that all was safe. 'We've planned it all thoroughly,' he said. And with that a stunt driver took off on my route to demonstrate the manoeuvre. Sure enough, he braked in time and remained high and dry.

'I'd like to see that once again,' I said.

So off the stunt man went and, again, he stopped at the designated spot.

'That's all very well, but what if it goes wrong. What happens then?'

'It isn't going to go wrong, Jackie,' responded the director, with more than a hint of exasperation in his voice.

'Yes, but what if it does and I end up in the sea, strapped into that Ford Granada? How do I get out?'

'That's not going to happen. Look, we'll demonstrate it again.'

At that he indicated for the stunt man to do one last demonstration. Off he went . . . just as a huge wave came crashing over the pier. The car skidded and spun, coming to rest literally inches from the edge.

'This is what we are going to do,' I said to the shell-shocked director. 'There will be a frogman in a boat next to the pier, just out of camera shot.'

'Fine.'

'And,' I continued, 'a frogman in the back of the car. With a hammer. If I'm going under I want someone there, inside the vehicle, to get me out.'

All was arranged and off I sped, speaking my lines to the on-board camera. I was all but done, just about to hit the brakes, when a loud 'Shhhhh' could be heard emanating from my blanket-covered passenger crouched in the back seat. He'd tried his hardest – but he could no longer hold his breath. He'd had to exhale, and the noise was loud enough to be clearly picked up by the microphone. Another take – and a deeper breath – was required. You can't eliminate every possibility it would seem.

My father had always encouraged me to shoot, setting up a small clay pigeon hand trap in the field behind our bungalow and letting me use his 12 bore shotgun. It was heavy and had a recoil that thudded into my shoulder with such force that I was bruised black and blue by the end of a competition, or even after a practice session. I suppose a 20 bore gun would have suited me better at that age, but the 12 bore was what we had, and it was fine.

As soon as we could afford it, my father let me buy an A1 base model Browning Over Under, manufactured by the Fabrique Nationale in Belgium. It cost £119, which was a fortune for me in those days, and I cherished it. I used to spend hours tinkering with the settings and making wedges of sellotape and paper which I used to adjust the height of the comb on the wooden stock and make it just right for me; I needed to make certain I could rest my cheek comfortably on the comb, so that my eye could easily line up with the bead at the end of the barrel. That gun repaid me with many years of consistent and reliable performance.

In the early days, I competed in eight- and ten-bird competitions, before progressing to twenty-five birds, and to fifty- and a hundred-bird events. Gun clubs like Fasnacloich and Taynuilt, Stirling, Kelso and Dundee became increasingly familiar to me. Personalities like 'Bulls-eye' McClellan, whom I met at Fasnacloich, Tom Brockie, Abe Bruce, Bill Louden and Ralph Haliburton all made me feel welcome, and they started saying I had reasonable hand–eye coordination, and a few more trophies found their way to our home.

Most of the competitions followed the Down the Line (DTL) format in those days. It was the simplest form of the sport, with the clay birds being released from one trap, and shooters moving down a line of five stations, one after the other, thereby varying the angle of the shot. You would start at full left, move to mid-left, to straight, to mid-right, to full right, and then you would walk from the fifth stand back to the first.

This format suited me well, and I continued to improve. So, when I left school, without any qualifications, as soon as was legally possible, at the age of fifteen years and one month, in July 1954, I was very far from downcast or depressed. I literally threw away my school uniform on the Friday evening, and the following Monday morning, enthusiastically slipped into a routine of working at the Dumbuck garage from Monday to Friday and entering a shooting competition at the weekend.

Shooting was everything to me. It felt like the only thing I could do well and the only way I could make something of my life. In fact, I am sure I put more time, effort and commitment into my shooting during this period, until I turned twenty-three, than I ever applied to motor racing.

It didn't matter I was so much younger than most of my competitors because I was doing OK; and it didn't matter that I usually had to travel far away, and was always asking for lifts here and there, because the shooting community was filled with gamekeepers and rural folk, so I felt at home and at ease among them. Young Jackie Stewart from Dumbuck near Dumbarton may not have been the type to turn up wearing his plus-fours in the tweed of his home estate – the tradition in those days was for shooters to wear their laird's tweed – but I felt quite comfortable in the company of those other shooters, even in my normal jacket and trousers.

I started to be recognised by a beige American skip cap that I wore. It had a particularly long peak and a small green visor that flipped down, protecting my sensitive eyes from the sun. That meant I didn't have to squint, which had been distracting me. Even back then, I was focused about being well prepared.

Competition followed competition. Sometimes the top four shooters received prizes, sometimes it was the top six, and prizes ranged from jugs to cups to plates, and before long a bunch of this stuff was being displayed on the sideboard in our living room. I used to enjoy gazing at the clutter, which gradually spread to any available space around the home, and it was important to me because it was clear proof of success.

My boundaries grew, and I started to compete at events in the north of England. The trips south, across the border, were big adventures for a wide-eyed sixteen-year-old Scot: I would either catch a lift with somebody who was driving straight to the gun club or my father would drive me into Glasgow, and I would take a train down the old west-coast line to somewhere like Carlisle, where I would be met by a friend. In fact, I quite literally would not have got anywhere without the kindness of people like Gordon and Hugh Cameron, two brothers who worked on Robert Crawford's farm next door to our garage and who, as keen shooters, drove me all over Scotland in their Vauxhall Velox, and Louis Barrett, who had a small car repair workshop in Dumbarton, and Andy Thompson, who never minded taking me along in his Ford Zephyr, with a Raymond Mays conversion that raised the performance to a frightening level; it was so quick and exciting that I almost looked forward to the drive as much as I did to the shooting competition.

My first major event was also my first major disappointment. Some of my friends said they thought I could win the British Colts Championship because I would be competing in my own age group at a time when I was holding my own in adult events. So I travelled south to the Harrogate gun club in Yorkshire with real hope but only finished second to Paul Wilkinson, a fine shot who became a friend.

Good loser? Far from it, I'm afraid. I have never enjoyed losing, at all, and I remember feeling intensely disappointed on the drive back to Dumbarton. What upset me was that I was going to be too old to enter the Colts event the next year. My chance had gone and subsequent wins in the English and Welsh Colts events never compensated for missing out on the British title. Even so, I continued to make progress, and was named in the Scottish senior clay pigeon shooting team at the age of sixteen and selected to represent Great Britain at nineteen. I managed to win my first major event, the Grand Prix of Great Britain, at the North Wales gun club soon after my twentieth birthday.

Through these formative years, a pivotal five-year window of my life, when I was transformed into a competitive young sportsman who felt comfortable in adult company, I benefited immeasurably from the counsel of two great men: Glynne Jones, the captain of the British shooting team, and Bob MacIntyre, a Scottish motorcycling champion.

Glynne Jones lived in the village of Rhosesmor, near Mold in North Wales, where he and his brother, David, ran Jones Balers, one of the finest baling companies in the country, so successfully that it was eventually sold to New Holland, the American multinational. Glynne was always known in the local community as 'Jones the Baler', effectively distinguishing him from another Mr Jones, who lived not far away and worked in a small clay pigeon factory; he was called 'Jones the Pigeon'.

The Jones family home became my base down south, and I spent many happy weekends with him, his wife, Hazel, daughters Vivian and Sylvia, and sons Noel and Allan. They welcomed me, assisted me, supported me and fed me with a kind of generosity that is hard to explain. Allan became one of my best friends and not only was he the best man at my wedding, but his girlfriend Shan was our bridesmaid. I often used to say their house was like my second home, and it was also the case that Hazel Jones was like a second mother to me. In my eyes, she was a shining example of motherhood, bringing up her children with such love and care, keeping a beautiful house. Ever modest, calm and wise, she took me in.

Glynne Jones taught me so much. In all the time we spent together, over meals at his home, travelling to and from competitions, I watched and listened, and learned how to be competitive, about the importance of leading a balanced life and, above all, about maintaining a consistent level of performance.

One of the greatest feats in clay pigeon shooting is to score '100–straight', which is hitting a maximum 100 out of 100 targets. This achievement proved beyond me for some years until, finally, I shot '100–straight' during the Scottish Championships at Sherriffmuir in the Lead Hills, not far from Gleneagles. Every career seems to have its tipping points and, from that day, aside from being able to stitch the prized '100' patch on my representative blazer, alongside the '25', '50' and '75', and being allowed to wear a silver lapel badge in the shape of a clay pigeon with '100–straight' engraved on it, my form took off. Everything suddenly seemed so easy, and I shot 100–straight in eight of the next nine times out. I just turned up at the club, raised my gun . . . 'bang' . . . and there was another trophy to be squeezed on to the sideboard in the living room at home.

Like many young sportsmen before me, many since and many to come, early success made me complacent, cocky and overconfident, and it was predictably followed by a severe loss of form. It is at this stage where the top competitors typically regroup and recover, while the one-hit wonders fade away. I recall feeling terrified. One day, I was feeling super-confident;

the next day, I was super-desperate. Everything that had seemed so easy now felt so difficult; everything that had seemed so natural and simple that I had almost competed without thinking, now seemed so complex and difficult to understand. Suddenly challenged to work out what was wrong and what needed to be put it right, I felt completely lost.

'Take it easy, Jackie,' Glynne Jones told me, in his steady, gentle voice. 'Stay calm and concentrate on the basic elements of what you want to do.'

'OK, but it's not working for me,' I told him, getting agitated again.

'Stay calm,' he repeated. 'You don't have to make any dramatic changes to what you were doing. It worked for you then, and it will work again. Just keep it simple and stay focused.'

With firm guidance and empathy, I was led out of what had seemed a very deep hole and, within a few months, I had recovered my confidence and form. I later applied his words to my motor racing career and my business life and with a bit of luck, over the years, have managed to even out the ups and downs and maintain a reasonably consistent level of performance.

The phenomenon of high-flyers suddenly making a mistake and struggling to recover has always interested and intrigued me. The trend is perhaps most visible in the corporate world, but there have been many examples in the political arena, in the armed services and even in religion. You sometimes see leaders who appear on top of the world. All their decisions turn out right and all their initiatives prove successful. As a result, everyone follows them and, perceptibly, they start to walk with a kind of corporate strut. They are rarely seen without an entourage of support people, nodding and agreeing with every word they say, and they live by the dictum: 'If the boss eats bananas, everyone eats bananas.' Then, out of the blue, something goes wrong and, in many cases, the boss suddenly seems incapable of successfully dealing with the situation. Like me at that difficult stage of my shooting career, one day they could do no wrong, the next day they could do no right.

Part of the explanation may lie in the fact that many leaders operate in a comfort zone, where mediocrity is concealed by the size, prominence or wealth of the organisation. Sometimes the mere fact of being president, chairman or CEO of a major international company, or being a cabinet minister, or a general or even an archbishop can be enough for you to be recognised as a giant in your field, almost irrespective of how well or how ineffectively you are doing the job. Such people can become over-protected by the infrastructure they inherit. They become self-important and distracted by their title, the acreage of their office, the private elevator, the prominence of their parking space and the sycophancy of their advisers. The endless courtesies and privileges are often highly intoxicating, not just for them but also for their spouses and even for their secretaries, yet they serve only to distract the leader from the key elements of what he or she is supposed to be doing. Power and influence can be destructive and dangerous commodities, and it is therefore not surprising that, when problems arise, many of these people prove unable to deal with them.

Of course, there are similar excesses in the world of sport, but, by nature, sports people are different. They tend to be more resilient because they learn to cope with adversity from an early age and, when they reach the higher levels, they soon discover there is no comfort zone where they can hide and exist. It is a transparent and relentlessly analysed world, where every performance is assessed and judged, where nobody can argue with the scoreboard, where, in reality, nothing less than victory and winning really counts. It may be satisfactory for a company to be ranked in the top ten, or the top thirty or even the top hundred, but for most sporting champions even second place is regarded as just another form of losing. If anybody offered me a million pounds today to tell them how many times I finished second in a Grand Prix, I wouldn't know the answer because it doesn't matter. On the other hand, I remember each of my wins. And when people lose form and fail to recover in sport, it is often painful because the failure is so public, but the consequence is rarely worse than criticism in the media and the sad end of a career. The consequences are often far more serious when a big name stumbles in the corporate world because that mistake or error of judgement can seriously affect the fortunes of an entire company, and send a share price tumbling, and put people's jobs at risks and jeopardise tens of thousands of livelihoods.

Maybe, confronted by such crises, it would be helpful for the bosses to bear in mind the advice that Glynne Jones offered me all those years ago: stay calm, make sure you are not intoxicated by the first flush of success and apparent achievement or by the publicity and new-found prominence and don't be distracted by the temptations that accompany the good times . . . stay firmly focused on the basic elements of the challenge, keep your head down and get on with it.

I remained close to Glynne for many years, right up until the brisk winter's day in January 1985 when, out pheasant shooting with friends, Glynne suffered a heart attack while going for a high bird, keeled over backwards and passed away. Characteristically, even in that terrible moment, he somehow remembered to open his gun and make it safe. His funeral was held in a classically solid Welsh church, and I was privileged to be asked to deliver a eulogy in which I tried to express everything this wonderful man had meant to me. He had offered me excellent counsel at a decisive period of my life, I explained, and for that I would forever be in his debt.

The same was true of Bob MacIntyre, one of Scotland's most famous motorcyclists, who had made his mark in 1957 when he set a one-hour speed record at Monza, Italy, and also won both the Junior and Senior TT races on the Isle of the Man. That was when, pushing his Gilera 500cc to the absolute limit, as was his style, he became the first ever rider to complete a lap of the 38-mile TT circuit at an average speed of more than 100 mph. Almost everybody seemed to have heard of him and, when we first met at a shooting competition and fell into a casual conversation about sport, I remember sitting there and thinking to myself how incredible it was that this famous man was actually talking to me. I idolised Bobby from the start. He was the epitome of the canny Scot, a down-to-earth character, unaffected by success, who never forgot where he came from. I loved listening to his stories, about how he began his career riding for a small independent team before moving to MV Augusta and then Honda, and none was better than the tale of how he rode for a man called Joe Potts, a car and motorcycle dealer on the south side of Glasgow. That was typical of Bob – never mind the glamour and glitz; if it was good enough for his home town, it was going to be good enough for him.

Motorcycling was widely regarded as a blue-collar sport during the 1940s and 1950s, in an era when motor racing was dominated by the sons of rich fathers, or more mature drivers. They had the cash to buy the fancy cars around at the time, like the Ferraris and Maseratis, the HWMs and Fraser Nashs, the Jaguars and Aston Martins. In those days, the reality was absolutely clear: if you couldn't afford to buy one, you rarely got a chance to race one. The motorcyclists appeared to be more grounded, and the sport produced solid champions, like Alistair King and Bobby in Scotland, and Geoff Duke and John Surtees in England. A rare exception in later years was Mike Hailwood – 'Micycle the Bicycle', as I used to call him – who came from a wealthy family and became a multiple motor-cycling world champion before making a successful transition to motor racing. Mike was a great competitor and a wonderfully modest and charming personality in a sport gilded by many good men.

'So, Jackie, do you want to come testing with me at Glencoe tomorrow?'

I could hardly believe what I was hearing. Bob MacIntyre had become a familiar customer at our garage on the A82, ever since he had ordered a brand new maroon Mark II Jaguar, with chrome wire wheels, a 3.8 litre engine and all the trimmings, but now he was asking me to go out testing bikes with him.

'Sure,' I replied, for once somewhat lost for words.

'Good. That's settled then.'

The next morning, we loaded an impressive-looking racing bike into the back of his Bedford van, together with all his kit, and drove up there, just the two of us, to Glencoe, one of the most beautiful glens in the world, and one of the most extraordinary parts of our country. We stopped at a long, straight stretch of road, which, Bobby said, had an ideal gradient for putting a racing bike through its paces. Much more than just a rider, he was also an excellent engineer, who helped design the bikes he raced.

'Come on, jump up here,' he said, and he would shift forward in the racing saddle, making room for me to perch at the back, and he would hand me his spare pair of racing goggles and tell me to grab hold of him around the waist. Then, with a blast of power and speed, we would take off.

On that first run, I thought I was going to come off the bike, and I was holding on for dear life but, as the fear subsided, the excitement and exhilaration remained. We used to reach hideous speeds at Glencoe, but these were special days for me, plucked from my wildest boyhood dreams.

Bobby was everything I ever wanted to be, the perfect role model: he was a winner, he was respected, he was incredibly modest about what he had achieved and yet he remained confident of his own abilities, and he was a proud Scot who never forgot the people and places that made him.

'And Jackie,' he would say, 'never forget the importance of staying fit. Don't ever think that just because you only have to stand still and point a gun, or sit in a car or on a bike and drive or ride, that you don't have to be as fit as an athlete or a footballer. Always make sure you keep in good condition.'

I listened and began visiting him two or three nights every week, so we could train together in a gym he had created at his home. He and his wife Joyce lived in the Glasgow suburb of Bearsden, and he had built a maze of weights and bars, held together with rubber bands, in the spare room. It did the job, and I gradually learned how to develop and stick to a proper fitness regime. Today, more than half a century later, I am still sticking to a proper fitness regime.

As time passed, more and more observers began to suggest Bob could transfer his talent from motorcycling to motor racing. I was desperate for him to follow the path blazed by John Surtees, and was probably even more excited than he was when an invitation arrived from a man called Ken Tyrrell, asking him to travel down to the Goodwood circuit, in Sussex, and test drive a Formula Junior car.

'This is your chance,' I said.

'It may be,' he replied, smiling. 'Do you want to come along with me?'

On the long drive south, I remember Bob asking if I had heard of this Ken Tyrrell, and I said I thought he was someone important in motor racing. He said that Tyrrell had helped Surtees make the move from two to four wheels and that maybe he would be able to do the same for him.

As it turned out, I stood quietly among the small group of people as Bob drove the car and, so far as I was concerned, he performed brilliantly and should have been signed up there and then. Unfortunately others said he was struggling to get the car sliding through corners, because in those days it seemed motor-cycles seldom drifted in the way cars did when they reached the limit of adhesion, and he never got the break into motor racing that he craved. In retrospect, maybe they had a point.

One miserable, wet afternoon in March 1962, Bob MacIntyre was riding in a national motorcycle event at the Oulton Park circuit, in Cheshire. As one of the big names in the field, he was expected to do well but, out of the blue, he went off the track at Druids Corner and crashed into some trees. I was at home when the telephone rang that night. It was Joyce MacIntyre, calling to tell me Bobby had suffered serious head injuries in an accident and was being treated at the Chester Royal Infirmary.

'Is he going to be OK, Joyce?' I asked.

'We don't know,' she said. 'We just don't know.'

My head was spinning. I had previously been vaguely aware of my grandparents dying, but nobody this close had ever been in this kind of situation before, and my instant reaction was to take an E-type demonstrator Jaguar from the garage and drive down to Chester as quickly as possible.

Amid a flurry of telephone calls, it was arranged that I would drive down with Margaret King, the wife of Alistair King, who had been riding in the same race. A tight-knit community was pulling together, but we scarcely spoke as we sped through the night. He'll be OK, I told myself, he'll be OK. There may be a few broken bones, I thought, but he's the fittest man I know and he'll be all right.

We arrived at the Chester Royal Infirmary just after six in the morning and walked in to find a group of motorcycling people standing in a group, with expressions that instantly confirmed all my worst fears.

'Bobby's died,' somebody said.

The shock hit me in the pit of my stomach. It was almost as if somebody had walked up and punched me, winding me. How

I hated those words, how I hated the news. Bobby was just thirty-four years old, in his prime, and now he was gone. I felt crushed and deflated, dazed and stunned. I turned on my heel and, leaving Margaret with her husband Alistair, Joyce MacIntyre and other friends, I walked to the E-type in the car park and drove straight home to Dumbuck, through an appropriately wet, grey and desolate morning. It was the saddest and loneliest drive of my life.

The death of Bob MacIntyre was a great blow to motor-cycling as a sport, to Scotland as a country, and to me as a young man. In a very real sense, however, he remains with me, and I have lost count of the number of times when, in trouble, I have paused to ponder what Bobby would have done.

In their own ways, in their own worlds, in the windows of my life that they so substantially and meaningfully filled, Glynne Jones and Bob MacIntyre shared much in common. Through them both, I learned leadership is not about dominating; it is about stimulating people, creating an environment where they can grow, thrive and succeed. I learned how the place and community in which you were bred provides the bedrock for the rest of your life, and that you should never lose touch. Watching Glynne, I learned how to prepare properly for a shoot. Watching Bob, I learned how to get ready for a race. Watching them go about their business, I learned how to address people. Watching how they dressed, I began to learn what to wear. Watching their manners and habits, I learned how to behave. Perhaps above all, I learned how to learn . . . to be nothing less than a voracious consumer of information, relentlessly seeking out wisdom which had never been available to me in formal education and which I could take and deploy in my efforts to become successful in my own wee way.

My chosen field, at this stage of my life, was clay pigeon shooting, and I continued to make progress. As soon as I had passed my driving test, a few weeks after my seventeenth birthday, my parents allowed me to take my newly acquired Austin A30 and head south on my own, and I celebrated this new-found independence by winning the West of England single-barrel championships at the Blandford gun club in Dorset. The first prize was a magnificent solid silver biscuit barrel with carved ivory handles, and it remains on display at home today.

In fact, it turned out to be a busy day in Blandford, because the single-barrel event was over by lunchtime and one of the chief organisers said that, since I had travelled so far, they wondered whether I might like to enter the double-rise competition, scheduled to take place that afternoon. In 'double-rise', forty pairs of birds were propelled from the trap and, evidently in form, I managed to hit eighty out of eighty targets.

'Gosh, Stewart, that's never been done before,' said an English gentleman, in tweed.

My first shooting trip abroad proved less successful, but equally memorable. I was pleased to be selected in the Great Britain team for the European Championships at the Bois de Boulogne, Paris, and even more delighted to hear that Glynne Jones was captain and his son Allan had been included as well. Allan and I behaved like excited schoolboys, hiring a Vespa scooter and hurtling through the streets to see as many of the sights as possible, but there was a competition to be won.

The event was contested over the challenging Olympic trench format, where a battery of fifteen traps below ground level shot clay pigeons with 'brains', which meant they flew at varying angles, heights and speeds. Two targets could be released on the same trajectory, with one travelling at 130 mph and the other at 70 mph. The task was to assess the speed and angle in a millisecond, adjust accordingly and somehow break the 4.5 inch disc.

It was exciting, but I finished some way down the field, and returned home not with another trophy for the living room, but with a wealth of experience that would prove invaluable.

'Never drink the tap water in France,' Glynne Jones had warned Allan and me, as we prepared to dash off on another Vespa adventure. 'If you feel thirsty, get a bottle of Coca Cola and make certain it's a snap top that has not been tampered with, so you can be sure it hasn't been opened.'

Allan had asked: 'OK, anything else, Dad?'

'Actually there is,' Glynne said. 'Watch out for the food. Don't eat the salad, because that will have been washed in water, and that could make you sick as well. The safest choices are probably steak and chips or chicken and chips, but keep your eyes open and take care. An upset tummy and a sore head won't help your shooting.'

I lapped up the advice and, while the standards of hygiene in France have improved immeasurably since Glynne's era, I have always taken exceptional care of what I eat and drink when I am travelling abroad; as a result, I have only fallen very ill abroad on one occasion, before the Mexican Grand Prix in 1966.

Many other trips followed the adventure in Paris, and the merry-go-round of European clay pigeon shooting took me all over Germany, Denmark, Switzerland, Belgium, Spain, Sweden, Italy and Norway. The events followed a standard pattern, with the exception of one grotesque occasion when, after the European Championships in Barcelona, a promoter appeared and invited Allan and me to take part in a live pigeon-shooting contest. This was a dubious practice where specially reared pigeons were released from traps in a designated area. It was totally unpredictable where the pigeon would choose to fly, and the shooter only scored if he killed the bird before it reached the small-mesh perimeter fence.

The 'sport', if it could be called that, was reportedly associated with some serious gambling and it seemed to be enjoyed by some well-heeled members of the European and

Middle Eastern aristocracy, but this was the first and the last time for me. I didn't enjoy it, and was pleased when live pigeon-shooting contests were banned throughout Europe. In Monaco, where it was very big at one stage, I remember it was stopped at the personal insistence of Princess Grace.

Allan Jones and I lived life to the full on these trips, and he was always great company. On one occasion, we drove to Geneva in an Austin A35 to join the British team at another European Championship, and started by taking what was called the air ferry, when you put your car on a plane at Southend airport, flew across the Channel and drove it off at Calais. That was no problem, but the drive on the wrong side of the road through France proved such a hassle that, when we eventually arrived in Switzerland, we spent half a day trying to sell the car, so we could afford to fly back to England. This proved impossible, and we had no option but to grin and bear the drive home.

Looking back now, I can see that the five years spent competing at the highest level of clay pigeon shooting proved an ideal preparation for my career as a motor racing driver. In so many ways, big and small, I gathered a quantity and quality of experience and knowledge that simply could never have been made available to me at any college or educational institution. The University of Shooting served me well. It taught me how to deal with the pressure of club, national and international competition and how to compete overseas. It taught me how to mix with people from different walks of life. It taught me how to conduct myself when I won and when I lost. It taught me important lessons like how to take the positives out of a defeat and move on and it made me aware of more personal, but no less valuable, lessons such as that I invariably performed best when I was hungry; so I didn't eat before any shooting competition and, in the years that followed, I never ate before a Grand Prix.

I can say with certainty that the University of Shooting proved so beneficial to me because the records show how quickly I was able to settle as a Formula 1 racing driver . . . pole position in first Formula 1 race, sixth in first Grand Prix, victory in fifth race (the non-championship Daily Express International Trophy at Silverstone), victory at the Italian Grand Prix in my eighth Grand Prix, third in the drivers' world championship in that first season. There is no doubt that none of this would have been possible if I had not first been an international shooter.

Today's Grand Prix drivers are reared in the karting structures, which are highly competitive, but they invariably race against people of their own age, and this remains the case as they progress through the formative classes of the sport. That path was not available to me in the early 1960s but, even if it had been, I believe it would have provided me with a much narrower experience in almost every respect compared to my shooting career, where I was always competing against the best. Just imagine how well Lewis Hamilton would be doing if he'd been a successful clay pigeon shooter! When I turned up at Fasnacloich as a fouteen-year-old, I was shooting against Bullseye McClellan, who was known as the best shot in Scotland. When I travelled down to England, I competed with Percy Stanbury, Joe Wheater, Teddy Fear, Bill Heald and Alan Posket, who at that time were the very best shots in Britain. And when I started travelling abroad, I was competing against the likes of Liano Rossini, the world and Olympic champion from Italy, Maurice Tabat from Lebanon, and Francis Eisenlauer from the USA. All of these people were much older and more mature than me and I can see now that I was incredibly fortunate to serve my sporting apprenticeship in their company, where I was able to develop my natural ability and mental skills at the very highest level of a highly demanding sport. In addition, I benefited greatly from the experience of having had to adapt to the entire culture of international shooting, from being a youngster in the primitive gun clubs of Scotland to being an entrant at the most sophisticated clubs in the world, growing with the pressure and the worldliness of the environment; and this meant that, when the time came, I was more able and better prepared to step into another global arena, and embrace the completely different culture of top-line motor racing.

In quiet moments, I had always imagined the crowning achievement of my shooting career would be a place in the British team to compete at the 1960 summer Olympic Games in Rome. There seemed no greater honour for me than to wear the blazer with the five interlocking rings on the pocket. I didn't mention it to my family or friends but, as the days lengthened in the spring of 1960, my goal came within reach. There were two places to be won in the British Olympic trap team, and, with just one competition left in a complex series of qualifying events, I was lying a strong second behind Joe Wheater, a wonderful shot from Yorkshire. Everything was going to be confirmed at the final designated event, at the North Wales gun club.

'It's a foregone conclusion, Jackie,' one official told me. 'You can pack your bags for Rome.'

Nothing is ever a foregone conclusion in shooting, or in anything else. I knew that much. I doubted whether any sport required such intense concentration and focus because, in shooting, there was rarely a second chance. Miss a target at the start of the day, and the reality was that you would never get it back. Even if you were perfect for the rest of the competition, you could only finish with 99 out of 100. Other sports are more forgiving: a golfer can hook his drive into the rough, but recover with an accurate iron shot and a long putt; a racing driver can make a mistake on a corner but recover time on the other fifteen corners of that lap; a striker can miss an open goal, but score with a sensational volley moments later.

I was feeling nervous when I arrived at the club, even though, as Allan Jones had noted, the fates seemed somehow to have taken control of events – the decisive competition was to be held on Saturday 11 June 1960, the day of my twenty-first birthday. 'It's meant to be,' he laughed. 'It's meant to be.'

There would be 100 targets, split into four rounds of 25, and my guess was that any score around 92, well within my capabilities, would secure my place in the Olympic team. Stay calm, I told myself, prepare, concentrate. Get the first couple of rounds out of the way. You can do this, you know you can.

I scored 24 in the first round, and then a decent 23 in the second round. Glynne Jones was standing among the crowd, watching this drama being played out at the shooting ground he had created. Somehow he caught my eye and gave me a thumbs-up and a smile. All was well. I was two rounds from Rome.

What happened next? I don't know. Perhaps it was nerves, maybe it was pressure: whatever the reason, in the third round, I so seriously lost my sense of timing that I hit just 18 targets. It was a catastrophe. I did manage to recover and score 23 in the last round but, when I stepped back from my stand to await the official announcement, the result seemed too close to call. I glanced across at Glynne Jones, but he was staring at his feet. Did he know something? I was guessing.

A silver-haired, blazered official stepped forward, cleared his throat and announced: 'Ladies and gentlemen, we have the final selection ranking . . . in first place, Joseph Wheater.'

That was expected, and Joe deserved his place. The official continued: 'Ladies and gentlemen, the contest for second place could not have been closer, and in fact the gap between second and third position was one single target, but the second place in the Olympic team goes to . . .'

He paused for dramatic effect. I held my breath.

'. . . Brett Huthart.'

My heart sank, and the Olympic dream instantly dissolved. I walked across to congratulate Brett, which was an easy thing for me to do because we got on well. He had many times gone out of his way to meet me at the train station in Carlisle and drive me to wherever we were shooting that weekend.

That was that. I was named as the official first reserve for the Olympic team, but that was no compensation for me at the end of a bitterly disappointing twenty-first birthday. I later heard Joe Wheater finished just out of the medals in the Olympic trap final and couldn't help thinking it could so easily have been me who was competing so fiercely.

I continued to shoot competitively until the autumn of 1962, when I decided to stop, not because I was no longer enjoying it, but because I realised I couldn't pursue the sport and fulfil all my responsibilities as a newly married man.

So, I retired after a successful but relatively short shooting career, in which I won the British Grand Prix of Shooting on two occasions, as well as the English, the Irish, the Scottish and the Welsh championships, finished sixth at the world championships and twice won the Coupe de Nations, a major event in Europe.

I was satisfied, and it was enough, and if anybody had asked me what I was going to do next, I would have replied that I was going to concentrate my efforts on working full-time and making a career in the service area of my father's garage.

Yet by then a man called Barry Filer had walked into our garage and asked me if I wanted to drive his grey Porsche Super 90 in a sprint at Heathfield in Ayrshire, Scotland . . . and that invitation triggered a remarkable sequence of events that put me not under the bonnet of the car, but behind the wheel.

CHAPTER 4

Catching the Bug

THERE WAS USUALLY A BUZZ AROUND THE DUMBUCK GARAGE whenever Barry Filer drove on to the forecourt but, on this particular day, with everybody still talking about the events of the previous weekend, there seemed even more interest in what this quiet, likeable and well-off young man was going to say.

Barry's family ran a successful business that produced packaging for the whisky industry, and this provided him with the means to indulge his passion for fast cars. However, in an arrangement that was not unusual in the early 1960s, the terms of his family trust prevented him from going racing himself. So he had arranged for his two cars to be maintained and prepared at our garage, where we took great care to keep them in pristine condition. I can still see them now, parked on the forecourt, always attracting attention – a dark metallic blue AC Bristol with red upholstery and Borrani wheels, and a battleship-grey Porsche Super 90. He would often take his cars on the road himself and, every now and then, he would invite a driver to enter one of his cars in a local event.

Jimmy McInnes was one of the trusted few. He was so

tall, dark and handsome that the rest of us thought he was a bit of a lad, especially when he used to arrive at the track in powder-blue racing overalls with a white helmet dangling from his wrist. As the mechanic, it was my job to prepare the car and have it warmed up on the start line, all ready for the amiable Jimmy to jump in and drive to glory. However, the previous Saturday, he had been driving one of Barry's cars in a club event at a disused airfield and he had managed to hit one of the five-gallon oil drums, which were being used to mark out a chicane. The aluminium bodywork of the AC Bristol was damaged, and, when Barry arrived at Dumbuck this particular morning, we all wondered how he would react to the incident.

'Morning, Jackie,' he said, as ever dressed conservatively in a jacket and tie.

'Hello, Barry,' I replied.

He walked over towards me, apparently in a good mood. He had always said he liked the way I worked, endlessly polishing the bodywork, wheels and every crevice of the car, as well as checking the engine, transmission and technical system.

'Jackie, there's a sprint at Heathfield next weekend, isn't there?'

'I think so.'

'Well, how would you like to take the Porsche Super 90 up there?'

I was surprised, not just because it appeared Jimmy McInnes was paying a heavy price for the small incident, but also because, at that time, in 1961, I was either shooting competitively for Scotland and Great Britain or working at the garage; I certainly wasn't attending races or pressing for a drive. Perhaps Barry was rewarding me for preparing his cars so well or perhaps he just thought I'd like to have a go myself. However, the idea that I would be a racing driver seemed a far-fetched dream.

'Well, would you?' he repeated.

'Yes, that would be wonderful,' I said. 'Thank you very much.'

'Good, let's do that. You'll keep the car on the island for me, won't you, Jackie?'

'I'll do my best.'

'Keeping the car on the island' was a popular expression in those days, and it meant keeping the car on the road and, hopefully, avoiding the five-gallon oil drums.

The prospect of driving a Porsche at Heathfield was exciting, but I knew the issue was not going to be quite that simple because my mother had made it absolutely clear she did not want me to be a racing driver. There was no discussion. Jeanie Stewart had spoken, and that was that.

'There's been one racing driver in this family,' she declared, 'and that's more than enough.'

The 'one driver' had been my elder brother Jim, and it was his career that created my appetite for motor racing, which made me so excited by the prospect of driving Barry's car. My brother was always known as 'Jim' to me, my parents and at the garage, but in the wider international motor racing community he was 'Jimmy' Stewart, one of the best and smoothest sports car drivers in the world during the early 1950s. I had always looked up to Jim as 'the clever one'. Eight years older than me, he passed all his exams and was such a talented boy soprano that some smart people arranged for him to record a classical song called 'Who Is Sylvia?'. It was a '78' record and it sold quite a few copies.

Jim was the rising star, and I was content to be wee Jackie, the ten-year-old boy in short trousers following his big brother around. He first went racing when he was eighteen and, from the start, he took me along to hill climbs, sprints and the races. Many would have left their wee brother at home, but Jim always looked after me and, through the five years that followed, I was given a front-row opportunity to see, feel and taste British motor sport at what was, as those years passed, the highest level. I caught the bug, and I've still got the bug today.

My brother started by competing in the two local hill climbs that every year formed part of the British hill climb championship: the first was held at Bo'ness, near Grangemouth, and the second was always staged two weeks later at a place called Rest-and-Be-Thankful, the name reflecting what most people wanted to do when they reached the top of this stretch of road that wound its way up through Glen Croe before leading on to Inveraray. Imagine a classically beautiful Scottish landscape, dramatic and spectacular, with a strip of tarmac making its way up from the bottom of the glen, up between the wild, green and rocky peaks. That is Rest-and-Be-Thankful: it's a special place for me, the cradle of my life in motor racing, and I feel a great sense of nostalgia whenever I go back.

We had some great days there. On the big day of the hill climb, my parents and I would arrive early and sit on a grass bank at a particular spot just below the hairpin bend where we knew we would be able to keep sight of up to eighty cars as they screamed their way up the hill, one after the other, in different classes, over the 'hump and the bump', through Bridge corner and on through the Cobbler corner, around the hairpin and through to the finish line. My mother would have prepared a picnic, and we would spend the entire day there, cheering Jim in between slurps of lemonade and a generous consignment of 'jelly pieces', my favourite food – slices of thick white bread bought from the City Bakeries in the Dumbarton High Street, with a black crust at the top and a lighter crust at the bottom, filled with my mother's homemade raspberry jam . . . not strawberry jam, mind . . . it had to be raspberry jam, and they taste as good today as they did then. We would sit on the grass bank, together, among a crowd of several thousand, with the public address announcer shouting out the names of the drivers and their cars, and all their split times, and his voice would echo through the glen, and I used to sit there wide-eyed, enjoying a spectacle as thrilling and exhilarating as any young boy could ever imagine. I watched everything, hardly daring to blink.

There would be Jim driving his super-quick Healey Silverstone, and Raymond Mays wearing his amazing cloth helmet with a buckle and driving a wonderful black ERA with twin wheels bolted together at the back, and Ken Wharton with his yellow overalls and helmet in a dark green ERA, and Spike Rhiando in the Rhiando Special, and Basil Davenport in a GN Spider, and Hartley and Sheila Whyte from the famous Whyte and Mackay whisky family in a Jaguar XK120, and Dennis Poore in his dark-green monster Alfa Romeo, Freddie Mort in a metallic light-blue Jaguar XK120, and Jimmy Gibbin from the family that were the Rover distributors in Glasgow. And John Melvin would appear in a Fraser Nash replica, in British racing green. That was my favourite. What a sports car! It cost £3,500 in those days, but a decent one would be worth not less than £250,000 today.

Sydney Allard would be there as well, driving a Steyr Allard, which was all polished alloy with no paint at all, and we would give him a special round of applause because, on his way up to the hill climb, he usually parked his transporter by the side of our garage during the days between the hill climbs at Bo'ness and Rest-and-Be-Thankful, and we would help prepare his cars.

And at the end of the climb, when all these drivers and enthusiasts would be standing around and mingling, and looking at each other's cars, and discussing who had gone well, I was the eager ten-year-old darting this way and that, clutching a brown leather autograph book and asking the drivers to give me their signature.

Jim soon moved to race at circuits like Turnberry, on a track beside the golf club, and Winfield in the Borders, and we would mix with drivers like the great Stirling Moss, Lance

Macklin, John Heath, George Abecassis, Gillie Tyrer, Reg Parnell, Don Parker, Alex McGlashan, Pat Prosser, Ninian Sanderson, Ron Flockhart and two French drivers, Louis Rosier and Philippe Etancelin. This was the Scottish motor racing scene at the time, which congregated at various hill climbs and circuit races throughout the season. In the winter, another great assembly of drivers and navigators could be found at the RSAC (Royal Scottish Automobile Club) clubhouse in Blytheswood Square, Glasgow. It seems astonishing now, but back then this was where the Monte Carlo Rally started. It was a wonderful spectacle and Jim and I would follow the rally closely on the radio, having given all the cars a rousing send-off. The drivers I met at such events were just names in my autograph book in those days, but many of them I have since got to know well.

My brother was soon winning races on a regular basis, and I was tremendously proud when he was offered a contract to drive for Ecurie Ecosse, the famous Scottish motor racing team. He signed on the dotted line without hesitation, and followed in the footsteps of well-known drivers like Bill Dobson and Sir James Scott Douglas, Ian Stewart and later Desmond Titterington. These drivers came from wealthy families – as we used to say, they were 'posh' – and in an era when the driver was expected to buy his own car, my father needed to take £1,800 plus £200 car tax from the proceeds of the garage to buy a competitive C-type Jaguar for Jim to drive.

Ecurie Ecosse was a phenomenon. Owned and run by a polished, sophisticated man called David Murray, with the support of his ever-elegant wife, Jenny, who assisted as a timekeeper, it was a business with a wonderful spirit and ethos. Jim took his place alongside stalwarts like Wilkie Wilkinson, who was in charge of preparing the team, Stan Sproat, the chief mechanic, Sandy Arthur, who was also the 'truckie' responsible for moving the equipment from the team's base in Merchiston

Mews, Edinburgh to circuits at Silverstone, Snetterton, Goodwood, Oulton Park and others, and Wendy Jones, who was David Murray's secretary and was always at the centre of everything.

Jim became part of all this and he kept winning, travelling to compete in distant and previously unimagined places like Buenos Aires, and later he was taken on by Jaguar as a factory driver, and then by Aston Martin as a works team driver. It seemed the Stewarts of Dumbuck were becoming famous because my brother was succeeding at the highest level of international sports car racing. He was competing with the best drivers in the world, men like Stirling Moss, Duncan Hamilton, Tony Rolt and Mike Hawthorn, heroes like Juan Manuel Fangio and the famous Italian *piloti* of the time: Alberto Ascari, Luigi Villoresi, Piero Taruffi and Giuseppe Farina . . . and I was right there, at Jim's side, in amongst them.

In these years, even at the British Grand Prix, the paddock area was open to the public, which meant people like me could wander around at ease, getting close to the drivers and their cars. Today, this zone is a high-security fortress, accessible only with paddock or pit passes that are as valuable as platinum or high-carat gold. Of course the sport has changed out of all recognition, although the size of the crowd is typically no larger, but it is a pity that the modern drivers seem to have become so remote from the enthusiasts. In 1953, I was walking up to drivers and asking them for their autograph, standing and watching mechanics prepare the car, seeing, feeling, smelling and hearing the power and glory of this extraordinary spectacle and, through this first-hand experience, I became hooked. Nowadays, a fourteen-year-old boy can only experience a Grand Prix through television coverage, through the media or through his binoculars.

I was incredibly privileged, and the images have stayed with me . . . of Fangio and Ascari sauntering into the paddock with their jackets draped over their shoulders, of Tony Gaze, the tall, handsome Australian who had been a fighter pilot in the Battle of Britain, and of Harry Schell, who always seemed to have a cigarette in the corner of his mouth and spoke with an American accent but whose nationality was a mystery.

The Italians were always so impressive, so stylish and charismatic. Manufacturers like Ferrari, Lancia, Abarth, Maserati, Alfa Romeo and Osca were producing amazing cars, Colletti made the best gearboxes, Magneti Marelli were renowned for their excellent electrics, and Weber produced the best carburettors in the world; all this activity provided unequivocal confirmation that, in the 1950s, Italy was universally recognised as the capital of motor sport. Britain seemed a poor relation in comparison, a country apparently on the margins of the sport, home to successful sports car manufacturers but unable to muster a serious contender in Formula 1.

Everything would soon change.

Why? Because, through the late 1940s and 1950s, an extraordinarily talented generation of Britons were also 'catching the bug' – men like Tony Vandervell, John Cooper, Colin Chapman and Eric Broadley, who would become extraordinary racing car constructors. Sir Alfred Owen, Raymond Mays and Peter Berthon produced 1.5 litre supercharged cars for BRM (British Racing Motors) that were exciting to look at, and particularly to listen to, and which would eventually deliver the success so long promised. Other faces in the crowd were men like Ken Tyrrell, Frank Williams, Ron Dennis and others who were destined to become giants of the paddock. Through their efforts and achievements, by the mid-1960s, the recognised capital of motor sport would have moved from Italy, not to France or Germany, but to Great Britain.

And where did these men 'catch the bug'? They caught it at precisely the same place as I did, at the British Grand Prix at

Silverstone, where they went along and were exposed to the sport at the highest level and all its possibilities. There is no question that, if there had not been a British Grand Prix, the motor sports industry would not have moved to Britain, creating jobs and prosperity for more than 50,000 people and their families. These are the facts. This is our history and our heritage, and yet today there are some people who question whether Britain needs to host a Grand Prix every year. In recent years, I have spent a great deal of time arguing that we do, because it is the race that spawns, feeds and inspires the industry and its personalities. If this country wants to remain as the capital of the motor sports industry, it simply needs to retain the Grand Prix.

I attended my first British Grand Prix in 1953, and there can have been few among the 80,000 people who gathered at Silverstone as excited and proud as me because my brother was the youngest driver on the grid, driving a Cooper Bristol in the colours of Ecurie Ecosse.

My father and I drove down from Dumbarton, and we stayed in a vicarage that had been taken over by the Ecurie Ecosse team. I don't recall the name of the village, but it cannot have been far from the circuit because, amazingly, Harry Schell drove his Formula 1 Maserati back there after each practice session. It was a wonderful sight, this character happily driving his single-seater on the public road, hair flowing in the wind.

Jim drove exceptionally well that day and was lying in fifth place, the leading British driver, when he went off the circuit at Copse Corner (precisely the same spot where I was destined to crash my car in the Daily Express International Trophy race seventeen years later) and was forced to retire.

There were other great trips with Jim and Ecurie Ecosse – racing at Aintree, near Liverpool, where we stayed at the Adelphi hotel, and at Goodwood, where we checked in at the Ship hotel in Chichester – but my brother announced his retirement in 1955, when he was still just twenty-four years old and in his prime. He had damaged his elbow in an accident at Le Mans the previous year and been involved in other shunts at the Nurburgring and Silverstone, but he has always said the major factor in his decision was the negative impact his racing had on our mother's health. She was a fantastic motoring enthusiast, but the pressure of seeing her elder son take part in such a dangerous sport caused her tremendous concern, to such an extent that she sought medical assistance. The anxiety, quite literally, brought her out in a rash.

Jim was a remarkably smooth and stylish driver – so smooth in fact that, later in life, his Ford Focus was still on its first set of brake pads after 56,000 miles – but, for him, life after motor racing was not always such an easy ride. He worked in motor vehicle sales in Scotland, England and America, married and had two children, Jane and Iain, but was then separated from his wife, Elizabeth. Eventually, he settled in the village of Rhu on the banks of the Clyde.

I was incredibly proud of my brother when I was following him around the motor racing circuits of Britain in the early 1950s, but perhaps not half as proud as I was when he showed incredible courage to confront and defeat the alcoholism that for too long dominated his life.

When many would have quietly slipped away, Jim squared up to the problem in 1999, pulled back from the brink and did not touch another drop until he passed away on Thursday 3 January 2008. As a result of his determination, he got his life back and I got my big brother back. I hope and believe those nine years of sobriety were a period of peace and contentment for him, rekindling his friendships, playing golf, driving his own car again, travelling and living in comfort.

Jim died from complications following heart surgery. He had not been well for some time, suffering from diabetes and circulation problems in his legs that meant he was unable to play golf or walk without pain. I remember he decided not to come with us to the 2007 British Grand Prix at Silverstone, because he knew he would have to be on his feet for a fair amount of time. He didn't want anyone to make any fuss, but his health was deteriorating.

He developed a heart problem and, with the help of my good friend and fellow Scot, Ian Hay, who is a professor at the Mayo Clinic in Rochester, Minnesota, we were able to have him seen by a leading heart specialist in Glasgow. It was decided Jim would require an operation, so he checked into a very comfortable private hospital on the banks of the River Clyde.

Helen and I had booked accommodation on the maiden voyage of the *Queen Victoria*, over Christmas and New Year, but I asked the doctor whether he felt it would be appropriate for us to cancel our trip. He said the operation was routine, and there was no need to change our plans. So we set off, and kept in touch with Jim by telephone. All seemed well.

A week or so passed, and still the operation had not taken place. I called the doctor and he explained the private hospital was running a skeleton staff over the holiday period and they were running behind schedule. Thankfully, Ian Hay happened to be visiting his family in Scotland at the time, and he was able to arrange for Jim to be transferred immediately to the Royal Infirmary in Glasgow where the operation could be done without delay.

I was growing agitated, and began spending a lot of my time aboard the ship on the telephone either to Jim or to his doctors. The operation did take place, and the surgeon called immediately afterwards to let us know everything had gone well. It was New Year's Eve and we were visiting the Madeira isles. Barely forty-five minutes later, the doctor phoned again to tell me Jim's condition had suddenly worsened – his heart had stopped and he had had to be resuscitated. The prognosis was not good. His heart stopped again the following morning and again later that afternoon. The doctors took him back into the operating theatre, but still could not detect the problem.

On the morning of 1 January, we decided we needed to get to Glasgow as quickly as possible but, of course, the commercial flights were fully booked over the holiday period and even flying privately was not an option, so we resigned ourselves to having to travel via London. That was clearly going to take additional time, and time was something we did not have.

The British Airways staff in Madeira could not have been more helpful, and they managed to find us two seats on their next flight to London but, just as we walked into the airport at Madeira, Helen happened to look up at the departures board and saw there was a Thomson Holidays flight heading straight to Glasgow and leaving in less than an hour. We rushed over to the desk, and tried our luck. The flight seemed full but, after a while, they said they had managed to make room for us.

God really was on our side. The Thomson Holidays staff were fantastic, so kind and obliging, and I will always be grateful to the company for enabling Helen and me to reach my brother's bedside in Glasgow.

Our friends John and Nan Lindsay were already there, right on the ball as usual. Jim's children, Jane and Iain, whom I had telephoned, arrived from their homes in Germany later in the afternoon and Ian Hay and his wife Eileen were also with us, offering support, fantastic back-up and sound counsel. By the evening of 2 January, we had all gathered, and sadly prepared ourselves for the worst.

Jim was being looked after in the intensive care unit, and he never came out of the coma before quietly passing away. In a way, I think my brother made up his mind to move on. It was almost as if he felt he could no longer sustain a decent quality of life, and he was content his time had come.

I know there are some members of the medical profession

who will say this is all philosophical nonsense, and maintain Jim's death was the unavoidable result of a major physical problem but I believe that, for many of us, there does come a moment when you are prepared to lie back and just let go. My brother had tackled life, and conquered his demons. He had won his greatest battle over alcoholism, and he had been reunited with a quality of life, and everything he could have wanted. That was enough.

Jim was cremated at Cardross the following Tuesday, with only the immediate family and very close friends in attendance. Emma Galloway sang a wonderful solo in the hymn 'The Day Thou Gavest, Lord, Is Ended', using the refrain of 'St Clement', and we left to the majestic, fantastically emotional swirl of 'Highland Cathedral'. As I walked away, head bowed, I happened to notice a card attached to one of the floral tributes; it read: 'To a real Scottish sporting hero, from all his friends at Ecurie Ecosse'.

Jim was nothing more and nothing less. He was my hero, my older brother who blazed a trail that I was so proud to follow. The age gap between us meant Jim and I had never been side by side on the same circuit until, in 2006, we were invited to take part in an event arranged to mark the 50th anniversary of the first Ecurie Ecosse victory in the 24 Hour of Le Mans, and we drove together at the Knockhill track, near Dunfermline.

It was an emotional occasion with Jim driving a Cooper Bristol, the very car he drove in the 1953 British Grand Prix at Silverstone, and me driving one of the original Ecurie Ecosse cars, a Jaguar XK120, now owned by a fine Scotsman called Hugh McCaig. I followed Jim in the parade of historic cars and, at the end of the first lap, accelerated the XK120 and pulled alongside him. He turned and seemed surprised to see me. It's taken me this long, I thought to myself, to catch up but, after all these years, we were still together.

What did I owe Jim? I owed him almost everything because,

when I was a youngster struggling at school, the world seemed an extremely dark place. I somehow found my way into competitive shooting, but that road would only take me so far. I found my real salvation in motor racing, and I found it because, in my time of need and confusion, it was my brother who carried the torch and selflessly showed me the way. Through my formative years, when my life might so easily have gone wrong, it was as if Jim was beckoning me to join him on a magic carpet ride, carrying me out of the wilderness at school into the exciting and glamorous world of motor racing.

To me, he was a wonderful brother. To others, he was something else. Obituaries appeared in all the major newspapers, with glowing tributes in the *Daily Telegraph*, *The Times* and the *Scotsman*. Eric Dymock and Graham Gauld, the two great doyens of Scottish motor sport journalism, both men who Jim and I had known so well over the years, captured the general tone. Graham wrote: 'If you wanted to introduce a typical British driver of the 1950s to a modern day enthusiast, you could not choose a better person than Jimmy Stewart. He was a gentleman through and through, and was constantly smiling and great company even though he faced and overcame many sad moments in his life.'

We decided to organise a memorial service at Glasgow Cathedral, not too soon after the funeral and not too long, giving Jim's many friends an opportunity to gather, reminisce and celebrate his life. The date was fixed for 3 March, and we were fortunate to have the help of Victoria Thorburn and Gael Pollitt, from the Royal Bank of Scotland, who gave up their own time to assist with the planning.

More than 600 people made their way through the torrential rain to attend the service, arriving at the cathedral and walking past, parked outside like guards of honour, the two cars with which Jim was most often associated – the Cooper Bristol from the 1953 British Grand Prix, which was made available by

Barry Wood, and the Jaguar C Type raced by Ecurie Ecosse in the early 1950s, made available by Dick Skipworth.

Helen and I, together with our two sons Paul and Mark, had undertaken the difficult task of clearing out Jim's belongings in his flat in Rhu; and, in the process, we had come across an old gramophone recording of my brother, as a thirteen-year-old boy soprano, singing 'Who is Sylvia'.

Our son Mark took the vinyl record to London and, together with his team at Mark Stewart Productions, started work on cleaning and clarifying the recording. Nick Mason, the drummer from Pink Floyd and a family friend, also got involved and, using sophisticated modern technology, they produced a fantastic result. Early in the Memorial Service at the cathedral, we were able to play the recording and literally hear my brother singing.

Music had always been important to Jim, so it needed to be an important part of the service, and we arranged for the pipe band of the Royal Highland Fusiliers to play outside the cathedral as the congregation arrived and for the Glasgow Cathedral Choir, the BBC Scottish Symphony Orchestra and the National Youth Choir of Scotland to take part during the service.

I wanted everything to be right. As ever paying attention to detail, we had gone up to Glasgow beforehand and attended a service at the cathedral just to check the acoustics. They were not great, so we arranged for our good friend Roger Lindsay, from London, an expert in the field, to install a quality sound system, enabling everybody to hear every word and note.

Dr Laurence Whitley conducted the service with great dignity and, in between the beautiful music, one after the other, a series of speakers all named Stewart proceeded to reflect on various aspects of Jim's life. Ian Stewart, no relation, one of Jim's teammates in his years at Ecurie Ecosse, spoke about the early motor racing days; Iain Stewart, Jim's son, and Mark

Stewart, our son, both delivered readings and Ken Stewart, no relation, spoke movingly about the period Jim spent at the Priory Hospital, when he recovered from alcoholism. It was important to recognise what Jim had achieved.

We had received many touching letters, including a note from David Grierson, Director of Clinical Services at the Priory Hospital in Glasgow, who wrote: 'I remember Jimmy as a true gentleman who was always immaculately turned out with a warm and jovial personality which was endearing to all staff and patients alike. In particular, he was popular with the young addiction patients, entertaining them with his stories and inspiring them to work hard in the programme to succeed in the same way he had with his sobriety.'

Jim would have appreciated those words. He had the courage to talk publicly about the pain and suffering he endured through his addiction and how, with help at the Priory, he had emerged as a new man, giving a strong message of hope to many in similar circumstances.

I took on a fair chunk of speaking in the service as well, retracing Jim's life through all its various phases and I thought I had managed to get the job done pretty well until the moment when I returned to the pulpit after Karen Cargill, one of Scotland's finest mezzo-sopranos, sang 'Ave Maria'. As I reached the lectern, I said, 'No wonder Jim loved music,' and I think that is when it hit me. He was gone. I just stood there and wept, and took a few moments to pull myself together. I was not embarrassed or annoyed at all, but it had been the music that triggered the overflow of all my emotions.

As with Jim's funeral, the service ended on an uplifting note with 'The Day Thou Gavest, Lord, Is Ended', again using the refrain of 'St Clement', this time played on the guitar by Eric Clapton and our son Paul; and then the congregation moved away to the reception, held at the opposite end of the nave. I remember looking around and starting to realise just how many people were present – there were so many familiar faces from Scottish motor sport, and old friends who I not seen for fifty years or more, and people who worked with us at the garage in Dumbarton.

It was a great attendance and, I hope, a fitting tribute. If I close my eyes and think of him now, I see Jim standing and smiling as he received a trophy after a race at Goodwood in 1954. That was him . . . my big brother, so happy, so talented, representing everything I wanted to be.

After Jim had retired from racing in 1955, I channelled my teenage enthusiasm for cars into my work at the garage, where my chief responsibilities were initially serving petrol and fixing punctures. I have always felt that if something is worth doing, then it's worth taking the time and trouble to make sure it is done properly, and I have tried to apply this principle to every area of my life, from shooting to motor racing, from business to running a Formula 1 team and even the preparation of this book. This approach has been very important to me, and it started nowhere else but the forecourt of the Dumbuck garage. Perhaps I was just a youngster serving petrol at a garage near Dumbarton, but if that was what I was going to do, then I told myself I had to do it as well as I possibly could and, so far as I was concerned, that meant I had to keep the cleanest and smartest forecourt in the west of Scotland.

One day, Alan Whicker, the BBC television presenter, turned up unannounced at our garage, accompanied by his film crew. He was making a documentary on Scotland and investigating the origins of the lyrics in the traditional song which refers to a 'high road' and a 'low road' on the way to the 'bonnie, bonnie banks of Loch Lomond'. This very well-known personality, whom I instantly recognised, walked up to Jim and me and, having established that we were true Scots, asked if we would be interviewed on the crossroads outside our garage because it could have been said that both these roads led to Loch Lomond.

I was dressed in my white overalls and, all of fifteen years of age at the time and full of conviction, despite having no knowledge of the subject at all, I categorically told the camera: 'Yes, indeed, the A82 is the high road, and the A814 is the low road.'

The interview was later broadcast – my first public appearance – but it was not particularly distinguished because, as I later discovered, the 'high road' is spiritual and the 'low road' is the path taken by those still living. Many years later, we got to know Alan Whicker quite well, because we used the same tailor in London, and Helen and I have admired him as one of the great British broadcasters. Of course, whenever we meet, he rarely fails to remind me of my unequivocal certainty on the road to Loch Lomond.

Not every day was so exciting at the garage.

'There you go, Jackie. There's a customer wanting five gallons of Extra and a pint of XL' – that was the voice of Willie McColl, who was in charge of the forecourt, calling me to action. Our big sellers were Esso petrol, which came as normal fuel or high-octane Extra, and Castrol oil, either the Castrolite, the XL or the XXL. Willie McColl always seemed to be wearing a cap, inside and out, and he lived with his sister Murn in the nearby village of Dumbuck, now part of Milton. He had two wooden legs, but that didn't stop him walking to the garage every morning, unlocking the padlocks on the pumps and opening for business at six o'clock.

'Hey, Pintel, get to the vulcaniser and sort out that tyre' – that was Willie Derris, the head mechanic, using his nickname for me (the origins of which I never knew), calling me to the next job. I would not have minded if it had been a puncture on a private car, but far too often the tyre that needed fixing was one of the giants from the articulated petrol tankers that brought fuel from the depot at Bowling. That was hard work: deflating the tyre; removing a spring ring, a wheel rim and a gater; using a heavy hammer to get the tyre off the rim, so you could get to the inner tube; reinflating the tube and submerging it in a tank of water, which was often iced over in winter, and finding one or more holes; vulcanising patches on the holes; then using the hammers and levers to put everything back together again. And all the time, everyone would be telling me to hurry up because the tanker drivers needed to get back on the road and be on their way.

Willie Derris was responsible for the workshop, organising other members of staff, like Alex Mauchlin, Marshall Duff, Hugh Birch and Willie White.

They were good people and I enjoyed my work, especially when John Lindsay was doing the same shift. He and I used to ride a moped which was an amazing present from the famous racing driver Ninian Sanderson, and we used to take it out on a circuit we created around the garage, running from the forecourt, through the car park, up around the back, past our bungalow and back to the front, and the two of us were always competing to see who could set the fastest time. And, whenever John happened to be quicker, I would run over to the garage and fetch a new sparking plug from the box beside the till. Willie McColl would ask me what I was doing, and he would say cars ran for thousands of miles with the same plugs, but I didn't pay any attention . . . in my mind, it was the new sparking plugs that would give me the crucial edge to go faster than John.

'Hey, wee Taruffi, get back to work' – that was the voice of my father. He called me after Piero Taruffi, the Ferrari driver, because I had said I liked the flamboyant Italian.

My wages were exactly £1/12s/6d per week, of which I gave my mother a pound, not because anybody said I should, but because I wanted to pay my way in the house like any other working man. Anyway, I told myself, work hard and do the job properly, and you'll make more than a pound every week in tips, which I did, to my great delight.

One of our regular customers was a multi-millionaire called

Mr Pickford – at least, we thought he was a multi-millionaire because he owned a Rolls Royce, and employed a chauffeur – and one day, after I had filled his car with petrol, he wound down his window and pressed a sixpence into my palm. That was fine by me, but he seemed to sense some disappointment in my eyes because he looked straight at me and said, 'That might not seem a lot to you, but it cost me a pound to give you that.' It seemed a peculiar thing to say at the time, but I have never forgotten these words and, in years to come, when I was exposed to high rates of income tax myself, I understood exactly how Mr Pickford felt.

My future seemed tied to the garage and, even though I dreaded the idea of more education, it was clear I needed to secure my City and Guilds certificate as a motor mechanic before I could start my full apprenticeship, so I enrolled at Stow College in Glasgow. There was no other way and, working around my difficulties and attending night classes three evenings a week, I managed to manoeuvre my way through the examinations.

I was starting to recognise the sense in the strategy that 'you get praise for the things you're good at, and you hide everything else', and I was becoming increasingly adept at concealing my severe problems with literacy and numeracy, and focusing people's attention on what I could do well.

The garage was thriving, and, in 1955, we were ready to expand and start selling Jaguars as well as Austins. It was a major decision to become a Jaguar dealership because it meant we would have to build a large showroom and maintain a fully stocked workshop, and all of that cost money. But my father wanted to develop the business from the status quo where it was supporting four of us under one roof quite comfortably to a position where, as Jim and I grew older and got married, it would be able to feed three families instead of one. With the help of Ken Williamson, his friend at the Clydesdale Bank, the arrangements were concluded.

Jim was given responsibility for completing the new showroom, and he was getting things in order when, at the age of sixteen, I decided I would have my say in the planning.

'We need a proper lubrication bay as well,' I said.

Jim sighed, because he wanted as much space as possible to display the cars.

'Yes,' I said. 'Cars get serviced every 1,500 miles these days, and we need to look after them.'

My father agreed and then gave me the job of looking after the new lubrication bay. That place became my pride and joy: it had a blue floor and white tiles on the wall, and the ramp was painted red with white edges, and I made sure every part and surface was always clean, gleaming and immaculate.

'It looks like a space ship,' John Lindsay used to joke.

'Hey, don't be rude,' I would reply. 'That happens to be my "lubratorium".'

Everyone used to smile at my enthusiasm, but I didn't mind. I even arranged special lighting, so everything would look good, and we created a system where the oils, greases and sprays were dispensed from guns on long pipes that rolled in and out. In those days a Jaguar had as many as twenty nipples needing lubrication, and the heads of our grease guns were made to fit over the nipples and ensure nothing was wasted.

The Dumbuck lubrication bay became famous in the Dumbarton area, and customers began leaving more and more tips, until, in 1956, I counted my savings and realised I could afford to buy myself a car. Still six weeks before my seventeenth birthday, when I would be able to take a test and get a driving licence, it was agreed that I would pay my father the sum of £375 and become the very proud owner of my Austin A30. Spruce green, yellow and red jeweller's enamel lions rampant on each side, fashionable seat covers made from Hunting Stewart tartan, numberplate ASN 500, an instrument panel that was regularly wax-polished, every accessible surface

Simonised to permanently shine: it was an object of beauty, and – although I could never have guessed it at the time – it turned out to be the only car I have ever bought. Every other vehicle I have driven was either a demonstrator belonging to the garage or, from 1964 onwards, was supplied to me by the motor company with which I was associated at the time.

After the A30, there was an A35 and then a high-spirited Austin Healey demonstrator, which I regularly took down to North Wales for the weekend, to attend a shooting competition and, when there was some spare time, Allan Jones and I would take the Healey to the Oulton Park circuit, near Chester. In those days, anyone could turn up, pay £5 and take their car on the track for an hour, but we generally nipped in without paying and usually earned a bollocking from Rex Foster, a great character who was the track manager at the time.

Allan bought his own Healey soon afterwards and, one memorable afternoon, when the track was covered in snow, we had a tremendous time hurling our Healeys around the circuit, getting such a thrill from sliding our cars into the corners and correcting them with what I later recognised as opposite lock.

In 1960, my father asked me to take charge of the workshop, and I shifted my enthusiasm for cleanliness to a different area of the garage. I soon launched a routine where, every month, some friends would come round and help me move all the cars outside to the forecourt; then we would scrape and scrub the oil and everything else off the workshop floor and finally we would give the whole place a new coat of red paint. We also created a mezzanine level above the spares department, making space for a sales office, a secretary's office and a service office, which is where I was sitting on the infamous morning when one of our most distinguished regular customers, Captain Featherstone-Haugh, arrived wearing his full dress uniform, complete with a burnished Sam Browne leather belt and cross strap, and all his medals and decorations.

'Jackie,' my secretary, Anne Rennie, announced, 'it's the man from the AA to see you.'

George Burns, a wealthy landowner in Argyllshire, was another notable customer: his legs were so long that the front driver's seat of his dark-green 3.8 litre Jaguar had to be moved so far back that it touched the rear seat.

And there was Leslie Milne, a fruit merchant from Glasgow with a Jaguar Mark 9, who had an extraordinary habit of throwing his electric cigarette lighter out of the window as if it was a match, instead of putting it back in its slot in the dashboard, and we ended up having to order a huge stock of these things so we were always able to supply him with a new one.

There was also a well-known businessman who wore double-breasted suits and lived in Kelvin Court, which was a very posh and exclusive apartment block on the Great Western Road in Glasgow, and he used to bring his Jaguar in for a service and, if he ever had any kind of complaint, about a rattle or something not working correctly, he would unfailingly begin by declaring: 'I have passed many other garages to come to you today . . .'

And each time one of these characters pulled on to the forecourt, one of us would run into the workshop and grab one of those long rubber hoses that we kept as spares for the petrol pumps, and blow it like a trumpet, giving out this great 'woo-ooo-ooo' sound that reverberated through the garage; and all of us would burst out laughing, and the important customer would be confused but completely oblivious to our messing around.

It was into this happy, relaxed environment that Barry Filer walked on the Monday after Jimmy McInnes had slightly damaged the AC Bristol, and invited me to drive the grey Porsche Super 90 at Heathfield.

'Your mother won't let you drive,' somebody said.

They were right, so I didn't ask her. Instead, I came up

with the bright idea of entering the Sprint under the name of A. N. Other. The organisers didn't mind, and so, in my first ever competitive outing, I finished runner-up to a talented man called Charlie Harrison, from the north-east of England, driving a TVR. Most importantly, I had kept the car 'on the island' and, as other opportunities came my way, Mr A. N. Other began to develop a bit of a reputation in the world of Scottish club motor racing. Everything was going so well that the young Mr Other started to think he might have a future in this game.

'You should see how you go on a proper circuit,' one of his friends suggested.

'OK,' he replied. 'That sounds like fun.'

'Well, the nearest circuit is Oulton Park in Cheshire, isn't it?'

'That's right, so let's go there.'

It was arranged that he and a group of friends would travel down to the north-west of England and spend a day driving cars, just to see what sort of times the promising Mr Other could produce. Barry Filer heard about the plans and decided to join the convoy south, which included Jimmy Stewart, the famous retired sports car driver, and his girlfriend at the time, Dorothy Paul, a young motor journalist called Eric Dymock, local amateur golfer and farmer Jimmy Pirie and a salesman from the Rolls Royce dealer in Glasgow called Gordon Hunter, known as 'Gogs'.

The party left Dumbarton soon after noon and, reaching Cheshire that evening, checked in at the Rising Sun Inn, in the quaint village of Tarporley. The next day, on a track strewn with autumn leaves, the youngster took the garage demonstrator E-type Jaguar and posted a lap time faster than those set by well-known drivers Graham Hill and Roy Salvadori the previous month, driving a similar car on the same circuit.

Barry Filer was smiling broadly as the twenty-one-year-old mechanic climbed out of the car.

'Well driven, Jackie,' he said. 'That was fantastic.'

A. N. Other won his first race at Charterhall on 22 April 1961, in Filer's Marcos, an amazingly light and fast car designed by Frank Costin, made out of laminated plywood and powered by a Ford 1,100 cc engine. At the end of the year, he won again, in Filer's extremely glamorous Aston Martin DB4 GT, a car notable for its two fuel tanks.

Into 1962, the comprehensive records kept by Graham Gauld, then editor of *Motor World* magazine and the recognised chronicler of Scottish motor sport, show that A. N. Other managed to win quite regularly in GT class events at his local circuit, Charterhall, and continued to make progress.

It's hard to overstate the role played by Barry Filer in my early motor racing career. He offered me not only the opportunity to drive some remarkable cars, but also encouragement and support. I remember once when I had to pay an insurance premium of £50 to enter a race, and I had decided to withdraw because it was more than I could afford at the time. Barry stepped forward and paid the premium. There were so many happy days when, after a day's racing at Charterhall, we used to put the Marcos on the trailer, and Barry and the rest of us would stop at the Carfraemill Hotel and join the other participants for a boisterous dinner – there were people like John Milne, brothers Graham and Gerry Birrell, brothers Nigel and Ronnie Morrison, Eric Liddell, Eric Dymock, Graham Gauld, Jock Russell and another good pal, Tim Morrison, who later became godfather to our son Paul; and it would be late when everyone made their separate ways home.

Such kindness can never be completely repaid and, in 2006, I was delighted to sit next to Barry and his wife Margaret at a lively Scottish Motor Racing Club dinner in Edinburgh. He seemed not to have changed at all and was still the quiet, unassuming man who had walked into our garage almost fifty years before. In simple terms, he gave me the chance to drive fast cars and changed the direction of my life.

In fact, in 1962, everything was changing for me. Shortly after two o'clock in the afternoon on Tuesday 28 August 1962, I exchanged marriage vows with Miss Helen McGregor, from Helensburgh, and sealed what has been beyond any doubt at all the most important partnership of my life. Helen did not marry a Formula 1 world champion or even a promising racing driver. She wed a twenty-three-year-old mechanic with an uncertain future, and, forty-five mildly busy years later, we're still together.

It all began with a blind date at Dino's Radio Café in Helensburgh. Jim Macpherson, a fine golfer from Cardross and a friend of mine, called to say that he and his girlfriend, Irene Fraser, were going out that evening, and he asked if I would come along and make up the four with a girl called Patricia Singleton. I had nothing else on, so I turned up at the café and sat down at a table with Jim and Irene, and her friend, Helen McGregor. Patricia was at another table and, even though the Pat Boone hit 'Love Letters in the Sand' was playing on the juke box, I sensed I had not made an immediate impression. This was confirmed when Patricia declined Helen's invitation to swap places and, for a moment, I sat at the table, feeling jilted and a little embarrassed by the apparent rejection.

'Well, will you come with us, Helen?' Jim asked.

Helen took one look at me and, out of pity rather than with any great enthusiasm, said she would.

The juke box had shifted on to 'Diana' by Paul Anka and, as we started talking, Helen told me her parents owned a bakery in the town. We got along quite well, the evening picked up and, later on, I took her for a drive up to nearby Glen Fruin because I thought she would enjoy the view. I was eighteen, she was sixteen.

Dino's Radio Café is still open for business today, on Front Street, Helensburgh, overlooking the River Clyde, and whenever I'm in town, I always make a point of calling by and asking for a 'single nugget' – that's a double scoop of vanilla ice cream and a special wafer filled with a kind of chewy cream and coated in chocolate.

I very soon became very keen on Helen from Helensburgh and was a frequent visitor to the family bakery in James Street, where I soon discovered her father, Evan, and her mother, Grace, made the finest cherry and sultana cake in Scotland: a Madeira cake with a layer of marzipan on top, coated in icing sugar. Helen used to make sure my piece was taken out of the oven a fraction early, so it was still soft and moist on the inside, exactly the way I liked it.

So the years rolled by and our relationship survived a few ups and downs, until, in the autumn of 1961, on a bright and breezy evening, Helen and I found ourselves together, sitting in my car in Kidson Park. People were starting to gather at the Helensburgh yacht club across the road, as I cleared my throat.

'Erm, Helen,' I mumbled.

'Yes?'

'You know, you'll be twenty-one soon,' I said. 'If we get engaged, nobody will be able to say anything.'

'OK,' she replied.

That was all arranged, then. Perhaps not the most romantic of proposals, I accept, but we were happy and we promptly told our respective families. We may have seemed young to be getting married by today's standards, but, in Scotland at the time, your early twenties was when you were encouraged to start thinking about settling down. And it certainly turned out to be right for the two of us.

We were married at St Bride's Church, Helensburgh, in brilliant sunshine, with Allan Jones as my best man and his girlfriend Shan Gorst as the bridesmaid. The new Mr and Mrs Stewart were then photographed in a garage demonstrator red open-top E-type Jaguar with black upholstery, registration FSN 1, the very same car in which I would later win quite a few races. Cocktails and lunch were laid on at the Lomond Castle hotel on the water with a perfect view of Ben Lomond beyond.

Planning the honeymoon had been more problematic, because the week clashed with the German Grand Prix of clay pigeon shooting at Darmstadt, and I was eager to compete. I explained the situation to Helen, and, after a brief discussion, it was agreed we would spend our honeymoon in the heart of Germany.

We had a wonderful time, with plenty of sight-seeing interspersed around the shooting, where I came second, winning the Silver Cartridge. We were blissfully happy, our lives seemingly perfect. Until we arrived home that was. A photograph of our wedding had been published in the Dumbarton *Lennox Herald*, the local newspaper, while we were away in Germany, and the caption referred to me not as a shooter but as a young racing driver. My mother had read it and realised that, without her permission, against her will, for the past nine months, I had been driving Barry Filer's cars behind the mask of A. N. Other.

'She's not pleased,' my brother Jim told me.

'Well, I suppose we had better go and talk to her,' I said.

'You go,' he replied. 'It's got nothing to do with me.'

I persuaded Jim to come along, and we walked across from the garage to our home and found our mother sitting in the front room, looking out of the window towards the River Clyde.

'Mother, I have to tell you something,' I started, 'and you're not going to like it.'

She looked at me, briefly and unsmiling, and then turned back to the window.

I continued: 'Mother, I'm going to go motor racing. I have been to a few events already, and people think I might be quite good at it, and there is money to be made.'

She said nothing, and continued to gaze into the distance.

'Mother, please,' I continued. 'I think I can make a name for myself.'

'Well,' she said, still looking out the window, 'do you think it might rain today?'

That was all, and I went back to work in the garage.

In her mind, the situation was clear: I had lied to her, so she saw no reason why she should take any notice of my motor racing . . . not that day, not the next day . . . in fact, never. During my entire career, through three world championships and twenty-seven Grand Prix victories, my mother – my mother who adored cars and loved driving fast – never once acknowledged me as a racing driver. In all those years, the subject was never mentioned in her company, not once.

I had lied to her, so why should she?

CHAPTER 5

Decisions, Decisions

THE PERIOD FROM FEBRUARY 1963, when I signed my first driver's contract with Ecurie Ecosse, until January 1965, when I competed in my first world championship Grand Prix, unfolded as a frenetic blur of opportunities and changing circumstances. Time and time again, as a young man in his mid-twenties trying to make his way in the sport, I had to make a series of potentially crucial decisions. Should I sign for this team or that team? Should I race in this car or that car? Should I be associated with this entrant or that entrant (the people who actually entered and ran the cars in the races)? Should I attend this event or that event? There were so many options.

Through twenty-three races during 1963 and fifty-three races in 1964, I started to gain experience driving a car as quickly as possible; and I also learned a lot about making decisions. The popular perception of a racing driver is of an individual who needs super-quick reactions and lightning reflexes to do his job, and in many cases to stay alive; and it is often assumed that such people apply the same speed of thought to every other area of their lives, and are able to make instant assessments of every situation and decide what to do. Not true. That was never the way I drove, and never the way I thought. If I learned anything during these years, it was the paramount importance of always allowing sufficient time to consider all the options and consequences before making an important decision. When I took my time and studied all the implications, I invariably got it right. When I rushed and took things for granted, I invariably made a mistake. That's not complicated. It's just common sense, but it's amazing how many people, in sport, business, politics and every walk of life, fail to give themselves enough time to make an informed decision and therefore make mistakes. In my career, I soon realised that I would generally make better decisions if I acted with care and caution, and maybe even a kind of Scottish canniness, rather than try to fit some caricature image of a glamorous racing driver, charging through life, foot down on every accelerator, making colourful and inspired, but not always accurate, decisions.

So when, in February 1963, David Murray phoned and asked if I would like to drive for Ecurie Ecosse, the famous Scottish racing team with the metallic blue cars, my instinctive response was to pause and consider. Of course, I knew the team well from the days in the early and mid-1950s when my brother Jim was driving for them. I had great respect for David Murray, Wilkie Wilkinson and the rest of the staff, and we had celebrated their success when drivers Ninian Sanderson and Ron Flockhart combined to win the 24 Hour of Le Mans in 1956; then, as if to prove that had been no fluke, they returned the following year with two D-type Jaguars and triumphed again, with Flockhart and Ivor Bueb winning the classic event and Sanderson and his new partner John Lawrence following as runners-up.

The move seemed to make sense for me, and a contract was agreed whereby I would be paid £500 for the season plus 50 per cent of all prize money and bonuses, and my expenses. Initially, I was to drive the Tojeiro Buick and, if everything went well, in due course I would get a chance to drive the faster Cooper Monaco, a potent motor car with a rear-mounted 2.5 litre Coventry Climax engine. With one signature, I was transformed from a mechanic driving cars owned by a customer of his family garage into a young racing driver with a genuine chance of making his way in the sport.

'Who's the new boy?' people would ask.

'It's Jimmy Stewart's young brother,' came the reply.

Jim was always going to be a tough act for me to follow, but I managed to make my mark during 1963: one week, I won in the 'Toj', when I could see nothing out of the back window; another time, I won in the Cooper Monaco at Charterhall, completing a lap at an average speed of 92 mph, faster than the previous record held by Jim Clark.

Success meant the telephone started to ring more often in our first home, a lovely rented apartment in a block called Strathclyde Court, Helensburgh, which was probably more than we could properly afford. It was often Helen who had to take the calls and let the entrants know where I was and whether or not I might be available to drive. This meant she was centrally involved in my career from the very beginning. We were newly-weds, who had decided to wait before having children, so she was able to attend most of the races, and this proved excellent preparation for all the excitement and turmoil that lay ahead.

'Your racing helmet looks very plain,' Helen mentioned one day in 1963.

'You think so?'

'Well, I mean, it's just white, isn't it?'

She had a point and, after some discussion, she went out and bought half a yard of Royal Stewart tartan silk, which she literally stuck around the helmet, and then sealed with nail polish. It looked smart, even though half a yard turned out to be not quite enough to reach all the way around, so the tartan band didn't quite join at the back.

'Shall we get a bit more to fix that?'

'Oh no, we'd have to buy another half yard, and that would be too expensive,' she said.

We needed to watch our expenses in those days – Helen used to have a little black book where she wrote everything down, to make sure we would be able to make ends meet – and my salary of £22 per week from the garage plus a bit of money from the motor racing usually left us with just a pound to spend on ourselves each week, but that was enough to take us to see a movie at the cinema in Helensburgh, or maybe in Dumbarton.

Slowly, almost race by race, our financial position began to improve. I remember winning one particular club race at Charterhall, and we both decided we would take the prize money and splash out by buying a brand-new washing machine, which meant Helen no longer had to put our clothes in a bag and wash them at the local launderette.

Eventually the bungalow two doors down from my parents' house was put on the market for £3,500, and we seized the chance to climb on to the property ladder and buy our own home, not least because it was so much more convenient for me to walk past Rockview and across the forecourt whenever I had to open the garage at six o'clock in the morning. We called the house 'Clayton', a name that reflected my two main sports, *clay* pigeon shooting and motor racing, where we always wanted to reach speeds of 100 mph or, in the popular phrase, to do a *ton*; in fact, every home we have ever lived in – in Dumbuck, Helensburgh, on the banks of Lake Geneva in Switzerland, and in Buckinghamshire – has had the same name.

This was progress and, towards the end of 1963, a motoring magazine made reference to me as 'the most successful club driver in national events anywhere in the United Kingdom'. That surprised me. I had been doing quite well in national club racing around Scotland and at events down south but, in all honesty, I was not able to recognise whether it had been such a good year.

An individual who seemed to think I did have genuine potential was Robin Mackay, then the circuit manager at Goodwood; he had just happened to be watching when I managed to set a new sports car lap record at the Sussex track, driving the Ecurie Ecosse Cooper Monaco, which was starting to look quite dated alongside models like the Lotus 19 driven by John Coundley. Mackay apparently related what he had seen to a friend of his, Ken Tyrrell, who was preparing a team for what was going to be the first ever season of the new Formula 3 racing. Ken just happened to be looking for a new young driver and I was duly asked to travel down to Goodwood in early March 1964 for a test drive. Almost exactly three years after I had accompanied Bobby MacIntyre on exactly the same journey of hope, I was being asked to make the trip myself.

Another big decision loomed and, once again, I hesitated.

I was being asked to drive a single-seater car, and I wasn't sure that was what I wanted. My ambition at the time was to make a modest living driving touring cars and GT cars for teams like Ecurie Ecosse and perhaps one day for entrants like John Coombs, Rob Walker or Tommy Sopwith, who ran Equipe Endeavour. This was the world I knew well, and the prospect of climbing into a single-seater and going open-wheel racing was something I didn't properly understand. Should I go to Goodwood, or should I decline? In need of guidance, I telephoned David Murray, and he encouraged me to grab the opportunity and see what happened. Next, I called Jim Clark, who had driven in almost every category of racing car. I'd got to know Jim pretty well over the course of the previous year when our paths had crossed at various races in Scotland. I asked him what he thought I should do. He would, I felt sure, understand the nature of my dilemma.

'Well, Jackie,' Jimmy replied. 'If you want to be a top driver, you are going to have to drive single-seaters one day; and if you are going to drive single-seaters, at this stage in your career, the best man to drive for is Ken Tyrrell.'

That was good enough for me and, on the appointed day, I arrived at Goodwood to find the same transporter that had been there on my previous visit with Bobby. The mechanics were the same as well: both Alan Stait and Neil Davis had been working with Ken Tyrrell in 1961, they were still with him in 1964 and they would still be there when I retired in 1973.

I looked around the group of people gathered in the pit lane, and felt in awe of the company I was keeping.

John Cooper was there: he had left school at the age of fifteen, like me, trained as an apprentice toolmaker in the Royal Air Force and later become co-founder, with his father Charles, of the Cooper Car Company. They effectively revolutionised motor sport from grass-roots to the highest level with the introduction of a rear-engined chassis design, and their cars won no fewer than sixteen Grands Prix in a nine-year period, which culminated in back-to-back world championships for Jack Brabham in 1959 and 1960. Cooper was now supplying cars to race in the new Formula 3 series as a works entry under the name of Tyrrell Racing, and that was why this great man, this giant of the sport, had come to Goodwood on this particular day, to watch a young Scottish racer test drive the new F3 car. Wearing his familiar 'Tammy' with a chequered band, John Cooper said he was going to walk over and stand on the first corner after the pits because he reckoned he would see more from there.

Bruce McLaren was also there: the New Zealander had been a Cooper Formula 1 driver since 1959, and became the youngest man to win a Grand Prix when he won the 1959

United States race at the age of twenty-two years and eighty days, setting a record only broken when Fernando Alonso won the Hungarian Grand Prix in 2003, at the age of twenty-two years and twenty-six days. Bruce had travelled to Goodwood that day in 1964 because he was going to set up and drive the F3 car and maybe set a benchmark for me.

Ken Tyrrell took charge. 'Jackie, thanks for coming down,' he said, confidently. 'We've got the new car this morning, and Bruce is going to take it round the circuit for a couple of laps, then we'll give you a go and see how you get on, OK?'

'Fine,' I said quietly, working hard to take everything in.

Exactly what happened next has been embellished, enhanced and exaggerated over the years. The myth is that the F1 star and the unknown rookie soon became embroiled in an aggressive head-to-head rivalry, taking turns to drive the F3 Cooper, the one going faster than the other, on and on through the day, with the established driver becoming increasingly angry and exasperated as the young Scot finished with the quickest lap, and the glory. It's a good story, but it simply didn't happen. There was no element of competition, and certainly no tension, between Bruce and me. It's true we took turns to drive the new car, but I was not aware of the lap times and I didn't know whether I was driving faster or slower than him, until the end of the day. My goal was simply to make a good impression on everyone.

Bruce was the one of the kindest, gentlest, most mild-mannered men I have ever known, and my main memories of this pivotal day at Goodwood are of him being so generous, supportive and constructive, and the car being so tremendous to drive. It was underpowered, in comparison to the sports cars I had known, but it was so precise and agile, so different. I felt like a pilot who, accustomed to flying cargo aircraft, had suddenly been given the opportunity to take the controls of an acrobatic aircraft.

After a few laps, I returned to the pits and noticed John Cooper rushing back from his vantage point on the first corner. He shouted at Ken Tyrrell, within my earshot, 'You've gotta sign him, you've gotta sign him.' As the day progressed I became more accustomed to the car and its behaviour and by the end of the day's testing, I had set the fastest lap. Faster than Bruce McLaren. I was amazed. In his typically understated way, Ken was clearly impressed by what he had seen.

'Jackie, what are your plans?' he asked, as everything was being packed away.

'I'm driving back to Scotland,' I replied.

'Well, why don't you come and stay at our house tonight, and set off tomorrow?'

My first impression of Ken Tyrrell was of an authoritative man who was absolutely practical and clear about what he wanted to achieve. There were no airs and graces about him at all; I liked that.

Over dinner, prepared by his wife, Norah, he came straight to the point. 'Jackie, you have clearly got potential and we would like you to drive our Formula 3 car this season,' he said. 'My proposal is that we pay you £10,000 up front and, in return, you will pay us 10 per cent of your total earnings over the next five years from all sources.'

Ten thousand? That was a hideous amount of money in those days, and part of me wanted to shake hands on the deal there and then and rush to the nearest telephone so I could call Helen and tell her the good news. Calm down, I told myself, maybe there is a bit more to this than meets the eye. Slow down, take your time and consider all the options.

'OK,' I said, after a while. 'Is there an alternative?'

'Sure,' Ken stated, matter-of-factly. 'We could give you £5 up front, just because that is legal tender for any contract, and you will receive 50 per cent of all the prize money and bonuses you earn from my team.'

Facing another major decision, I asked Ken if I could think it over and give him a call when I arrived back home. I didn't have a manager or an agent, and I wanted to talk to Helen and get everything straight in my head.

Tyrrell Racing seemed the best team for me because they were effectively the 'Works' Cooper outfit, which meant they offered much better prospects than any enthusiastic amateur entrant, and Jim Clark had said this was the best option. It was more difficult to decide whether to take such a lot of money up front or take the risk of only earning 50 per cent of the prize and bonus money. I thought there must be more money in this business than I had imagined. Someone was offering to pay me £10,000 in advance and take a risk of getting his money back from 10 per cent of my total earnings in motor sport over the next five years. It was very tempting. I asked Helen if she happened to know the balance of our current account that day. Less than £50, she replied.

After running through everything in my mind, I decided to back myself and my earnings potential. I walked over to the service department office at Dumbuck garage, where I dialled Ken Tyrrell's number.

'Hello, Mr Tyrrell? It's Jackie Stewart speaking.'

'Yes, Jackie.'

'I've decided to take the five pounds.'

'That's fine. I would like you to start driving for us at Snetterton on Saturday.'

'I'll be there.'

Amazing.

So began the single most influential professional relationship of my motor racing career, perhaps of my life. It would be true to say that, over the course of the next nine years, Ken Tyrrell – avuncular, unsophisticated and utterly loyal – made me whatever I became.

The following weekend, it was pouring with rain when I

arrived at the Snetterton circuit in Norfolk, and it was hard to blame the spectators who had given up and gone home by the time the Formula 3 race was scheduled to start. However, I was determined to make a good impression and, fortunately, everything went well.

Somebody later explained to me how, once the race had started in a cloud of spray, everybody in the main stand had settled back and waited for the cars to reappear after the first lap. He said that I had sped past, but that it was then a while before any other car appeared. He said people were starting to think there must have been a big accident. In fact, the records show I managed to lead by eleven seconds after the first lap, by twenty-two seconds by the end of the second lap, and by forty-eight seconds after three laps. It was just one of those days when everything went my way.

The race would not have been allowed to start today – there were loads of puddles on the track and cars were aquaplaning at almost every corner – but I was not complaining because my winnings for the day amounted to £186, which was my 50 per cent share of the prize money and bonuses, and the comforting, and until then spectacularly rare, imaginary bulge in my wallet made me feel that, just maybe, I had made the correct decision in turning down the £10,000 that had been dangled before me earlier in the week.

Decisions, decisions . . . it wasn't easy, and I certainly was not coasting through this pivotal period of my life with any kind of smug certainty that I was getting everything right. I was every bit as hesitant and unsure as any youngster just starting out, but I was trying to get into good habits of taking my time and never being rushed into anything.

In March 1964, when I was just newly installed as a Tyrrell F3 driver, my career quite literally took off. All aboard the rocket ship . . . the phone at home hardly stopped ringing with offers to drive, and every weekend seemed to bring a new car, a new entrant and a new challenge. Before long I was feeling as comfortable and assured in driving an F3 car, an Élan, an E-type Jaguar, a Formula 2 Works Lotus or a Ferrari as I was in either of the two stalwarts, the Cooper Monaco and the Tojeiro Ford.

These were wonderful days of variety and opportunity, meeting so many great characters and seeing so many places. In fact, they were as stimulating, frenetic and downright enjoyable as any in my entire career.

Certain occasions remain vivid memories: the day when I drove a Lotus Élan for entrant Graham Warner and managed to hold off the Lotus Works entries to win the race; the day when I drove a 3.8 litre Jaguar saloon for Charles Bridges, a great racing enthusiast from the north of England, and helped the Red Rose Motors team to victory in a relay race at Oulton Park; the exhilarating day at Crystal Palace when I competed in four races – driving a Cooper for Tyrrell Racing in a Formula 3 race, an E-type Jaguar for John Coombs in a GT race, a Jaguar XK 120 for Eric Brown and a Lotus Cortina for Charles Bridges – and won them all.

'Who's the new boy?' more people were starting to ask.

'You remember Jimmy Stewart?'

'Sure.'

'It's his younger brother.'

'Really?'

John Coombs was to become an important person in my life, as an entrant who started to believe in my ability, who trusted me to drive his cars efficiently and who has remained a close friend ever since.

Always dressed immaculately and instantly recognisable with his wavy, almost blond, hair, he owned a large Jaguar dealership on the Guildford bypass and was very well connected. It was said that 'Mr Coombs', as I knew him, only ever recruited big-name drivers for his cars, so I was particularly flattered when, at the suggestion of Lofty England, then Jaguar competition director, and later the chairman of Jaguar, he asked me – maybe a little reluctantly – to test drive his lightweight E-type Jaguar. All went well, thankfully and, in the years that followed, we enjoyed considerable success together in various categories of racing, and shared many, many happy days. He married relatively late in life, to Ellie, and they have moved to live in Monaco.

Colonel R. J. 'Ronnie' Hoare was another influential man at the time. By far the poshest man in motor racing, a gentleman through and through, he owned Maranello Concessionaires, a company created in July 1960 to bring Ferraris into the United Kingdom, and it was in June 1964 when he asked me to join his team as a reserve driver at the 24 Hour of Le Mans race. Maranello Concessionaires, named after the home town of Ferrari, entered two cars, with Tony Maggs and Innes Ireland driving a Ferrari GTO, and Graham Hill and Jo Bonnier driving a Ferrari P2. My job, as the reserve, was to qualify both cars, practise in both cars, so that, if anything happened to any of the drivers, I would be ready to slot in and take his place.

It turned out to be a memorable week, not least because Colonel Hoare only ever took his team to the very best hotels, and we all stayed in a smart place with a three-star Michelin restaurant. Our caravan at the circuit was also fantastically well equipped and ahead of its time but, even so, the noise of the racing cars and the incessant music being blasted through the loudspeakers made it almost impossible for any of us to get even a few hours' sleep at any stage during the twenty-four-hour race.

I never drove for Tommy Sopwith or Rob Walker but, with Mr Coombs and Colonel Hoare, they made up an extraordinary quartet of deeply committed, serious 'gentleman entrants' widely admired as doyens of taste, style and dignity. These were the men who set exceptionally high standards in

British motor sport, who unfailingly ensured their cars were pristine, and their mechanics were neatly dressed. They were responsible for creating the stage of quality and class upon which people like me could perform.

The Formula 3 season continued, and, with the Tyrrell Cooper running so well, I particularly looked forward to competing in what would be my first ever event outside the United Kingdom, the 1964 Formula 3 Grand Prix of Monaco.

Getting to the Principality proved an adventure in itself because, still trying to save money, Helen and I had decided that instead of flying, we would drive from Helensburgh down to Dover, take a Channel ferry and then drive down through France. We had arranged to stay with Bruce and Patty McLaren at their flat in Surbiton, outside London, to save on the cost of a hotel, and, the following morning, I placed my plastic briefcase, with money, passports and ferry tickets on the roof of the car while we were packing and saying goodbye . . . and I left it there, as we drove away and continued our journey south. I only realised what had happened when we reached Dover, so I immediately phoned Bruce who told me the good news was that he had found my briefcase in the road outside his flat but the bad news was that he was on his way to catch a flight to Nice, because he was going to drive for Cooper in the Monaco Grand Prix.

This was a crisis. Our intended schedule was very tight, because wherever possible I had wanted to save on hotel costs, and this meant there was not enough time to drive back to London, fetch the briefcase, catch a later ferry and still get to Monaco on time. So our only option was to drive back to Surbiton, retrieve the briefcase and fly, but we then discovered all the flights to Nice were fully booked.

In the end, we managed to buy one-way air tickets to Geneva, from where we somehow organised another flight to Nice, and it was with considerable relief that Helen and I eventually checked into the Westminster hotel, in a small village called Roquebrune.

'What room would you like, Mr Stewart?' the receptionist asked. 'We have a room with a view of the Mediterranean and we also have a room with a view of the rock?'

Relishing this first taste of what seemed a kind of jet-set lifestyle, many worlds from our lives in Dumbuck, I finally cast aside my Scottish prudence and decided to splash out on the sea view. This was the life, I thought.

The view from the room was great and, choosing to ignore the railway line just below our window, I enthusiastically suggested we go for a quick swim in the sea. I had bought a pair of swimming trunks in anticipation, but even that outing didn't work out well because I somehow managed to sit on some wet tar on the pebbled beach and completely ruined the trunks.

Our first motor racing weekend abroad was starting to feel like some kind of Abbott and Costello film, with everything that could go wrong going wrong, and the next morning, reverting to my initial instincts, I told Helen we would walk from our hotel to the scrutineering, where the cars are given a technical inspection prior to practice, because it would be stupid to waste any more money on a taxi fare.

Despite all the mishaps, this first visit to Monaco proved wonderfully exciting. I walked a complete lap of the circuit, taking in all the sites that would become so familiar to me, the Hotel de Paris, the Casino square, the tunnel that was so poorly lit and the harbour. In those days, cast-iron lamp posts stood right beside the track and there were no barriers in front of the buildings.

Ken told me to take it easy in the F3 race, and his advice had a sobering effect on an eager, young driver. I made a strong start and managed to pull away from the rest of the field and go on to win the race. The fairytale ending meant that, like Cinderella, we went to the ball . . . specifically the traditional black-tie gala banquet at the Hotel de Paris held on the Sunday night after the F1 Grand Prix, where I met the F1 winner, Graham Hill. There, as the F3 race winner, I was seated on the left of Princess Grace and, right across the table, Helen was placed on the left of Prince Rainier.

It did cross my mind that, flush with 50 per cent of the prize money from what was regarded as the most prestigious race of the Formula 3 season, we should just take a flight back home, but, after all the dramas, I didn't want to waste any more cash, so we scouted around the paddock and eventually found someone who needed their car and trailer driven back to London. That was the ideal solution for me, because it meant we would be able to get home all expenses paid, effectively for free.

Our future trips to Monaco, I am pleased to say, would prove to be more relaxing.

The race itself was remarkable for an incident that occurred soon after the finish. My delight at winning instantly turned to wonder when I looked up and realised that a thick-set, relaxed and instantly recognisable man from Argentina was walking directly towards me. It was Juan Manuel Fangio, the greatest racing driver of all time, and he had clearly made his way down from a balcony, from where he had been watching my race.

Escorted by his friends Bernard Cahier, a well-respected French journalist, and Fima Ruchman, from Venezuela, the great man smiled and shook me firmly by the hand. He spoke in Spanish, in quite a high-pitched, almost squeaky voice, his eyes darting between me and Fima, who translated his words.

'Well driven, young man,' he said, 'that was very impressive.'

You take compliments from whom they come and, without wanting to exaggerate the significance of this incident in the context of my career, I believe that this moment – when, having won my first race abroad, and as a twenty-five-year-old driver standing in the pit lane and being congratulated by the great Fangio, a man whom I had idolised for as long as I could remember, whose autograph I had collected at Silverstone eleven years before – ranks as one of the most cherished experiences of my life. It was truly extraordinary and, in the years that followed, I was privileged to spend more time with the 'Maestro' of our sport, the man who won five world championships with four different constructors (Alfa Romeo in 1951, Mercedes-Benz in 1954 and 1955, Ferrari in 1956 and Maserati in 1957), always displaying extraordinary judgement in ensuring he changed teams at precisely the correct moment.

I have so many wonderful memories surrounding this man. I remember feeling so proud when Fangio presented me with the trophy after I won the Gold Cup at Oulton Park. I recall another evening, before the 1966 Grand Prix in Monaco, when four of us – Fangio, Fima Ruchman, Helen and I – went for dinner at a place called Le Pirate, across the border in Italy. Fangio drove us to and from the restaurant in his Mercedes-Benz, with Helen and me sitting in the back seat. I felt completely star-struck. For me, to be driven by Fangio was almost too much to take in. I also remember an occasion following my retirement when I stayed with him in his apartment in Rome before driving together to an event in Bologna, where he presented me with an award. That time, he drove up the A1 autostrada, and I drove back.

This man was not just an enormously skilled and talented racing driver, he also carried himself with a dignity that has never been surpassed before or since. In so doing, he became the finest ambassador our sport has ever known. His statistical record is amazing – twenty-five Formula 1 wins in just fifty-one starts is an incredible batting average – but it was his serenity, dignity and modesty that set him apart. He was in so many ways, on and off the track, the ultimate world champion, embodying the very best qualities of motor racing.

People have always debated who is the greatest racing driver of all time. In my view, all any driver can be is the best of his era, and Fangio was certainly that, but his manner outside the cockpit took him to a different level. Some may say he competed in a less-demanding age, when there were fewer cars on the grid and fewer races on the calendar, but I do not accept passing time can in any way detract from his achievement. For example, he was no athlete by modern standards of physical conditioning, and yet it is a fact he was able to produce incredible performances in searing temperatures and sapping humidity. On many occasions, when other drivers were retiring or collapsing through heat exhaustion, Fangio remained on the track, winning with apparently effortless ease.

I make no secret of my admiration and praise for this man. Fangio was so special. On 17 July 1995, I was playing in a charity golf day at the RAC country club at Epsom, when somebody approached me on the ninth green.

'Jackie, can I have word with you?' he asked.

I walked over to him, and he said: 'I'm sorry, but I have some very bad news.'

My heart sank. When someone says that, you immediately think something has happened to a member of your family.

'I'm afraid there has been a death.'

My heart sank further.

'It's Fangio. Your office wanted you to know. The funeral is in Argentina tomorrow at three o'clock.'

I absolutely felt compelled to attend and pay my last respects and, having arranged that the correct suit, a white shirt and a black tie be brought to the golf club, I rushed to Heathrow and caught a British Airways flight to Buenos Aires, via Rio de Janeiro. Stirling Moss, who had been Fangio's team-mate at Mercedes, was on the same plane, and everything seemed on course until the pilot came over the intercom and announced that, since there was dense fog in Rio, the plane would have to be diverted to São Paulo. He added the plane would have to wait there until the weather cleared, go back to Rio and only then make its way to Buenos Aires. So we were sitting on the runway in São Paulo, wondering how on earth we were going to get to the funeral, when I looked out of the window and spotted an Aerolineas Argentinas plane. That must be going to Buenos Aires, I told Stirling. It was, and, travelling with hand luggage, we managed to get the necessary clearance from some fairly high-powered people, all of whom understood exactly why we needed to get to Argentina in such a hurry, and were able to make the tarmac transfer from one aircraft to the other, without passing through immigration and customs.

A friend of mine, Constantio Vigil, had arranged for us to be cleared by police and immigration as soon as the door of the plane opened after landing in the federal capital, and be rushed in a private plane to the town of Balcarce, where Fangio was to be buried. We landed there, at a grassed airfield, to be met by his brother Toto, who immediately took us to the Fangio Museum, where the great man was lying in state, and where Stirling and I paid our respects at the open coffin.

The funeral was held in the packed church of this small town, which resembled something out of a western film and, at the end of the service, six of us – the Argentine F1 drivers Froilan Gonzalez and Carlos Reutemann, the president of Mercedes Benz, Fangio's brother, Stirling and I – carried the coffin down the aisle and out into the glaring sunlight, into the dusty town square. Into complete silence. There were not less than 15,000 people standing there, and there was not a single sound. Then, one individual started to clap, not fast, just a slow and rhythmical clap; and somebody else joined in, and the crescendo of slow rhythmical applause soon became deafening, reverberating through the square. It was the most remarkable demonstration of grief I have ever experienced – thousands of people in this modest, proud village, united in respect, all clapping, slow and heartfelt, in perfect time. I was struggling to control my emotions, and tears welled in my eyes as the great racing driver was carried on his last journey with the most amazing dignity.

There was one final twist to this extraordinary day.

At the church I had noticed an immaculate man in a camelhair coat who looked and spoke exactly like Fangio, and whom I recognised as the illegitimate son whom the family steadfastly refused to recognise. Fangio had never married and had no other children, and his son, in his fifties, unwelcome as he may have been, was attending his funeral. I saw him again an hour later, standing alone, keeping his distance, after we had laid the coffin to rest in the family tomb, a ceremony from which he had obviously been excluded. I waited until the rest of the family had moved on, then walked up to him, introduced myself and said I would like to take him into the small tomb. It just happened. I simply felt this man should have a chance to say goodbye to his father, and he was very emotional when he thanked me. We have never seen each other again.

I flew back to London that evening and quietly reflected that Juan Manuel Fangio was my greatest hero. To have carried him to his last resting place was without doubt one of the truly important things I have done in my life.

His words of encouragement after that memorable race in Monaco gave me the impetus to continue my rocket-ship ride through 1964, and I managed to win eleven of the thirteen Formula 3 races held that season.

I drove whenever, whatever, wherever possible: a first racing trip to the United States to co-drive a Lotus Cortina with Mike Beckwith at the Marlboro twelve-hour race, in Arlington, Virginia; driving a Lotus Élan for Graham Warner and the Chequered Flag team; driving Formula 2 cars for a great character called Ron Harris and Team Lotus, and many more. It was, however, my performances in Formula 3 that prompted speculation about whether I would join a Formula 1 team for the 1965 season and, if so, which one.

'Young Jackie Stewart has driven twenty-six different cars, and won twenty-three races from fifty-three starts this year,' reported the *Daily Mail*. 'He is all set for Formula 1, but it is now a question of whether he will join Cooper, Lotus or BRM.'

The article was entirely accurate.

In my own mind, I felt an emotional pull towards Cooper, and I was aware of the crucial role John Cooper had played in securing my opportunity to join the Tyrrell Racing team.

Colin Chapman, of Lotus, had registered his interest, inviting me to try out Jim Clark's Formula 1 car after the official practice session on the Saturday lunchtime before the British Grand Prix at Brands Hatch. I hesitated, but he made arrangements for the marshals to remain in position, just so I could get a chance to drive the car. In the event, I actually missed a gear change and spun at Druids Corner, but it was a magnificent machine, more precise and agile than the F3 Cooper.

I had also had an opportunity to consider BRM when the team's three principals – Louis Stanley, team manager Tony Rudd and senior adviser Raymond Mays – had approached me after I won the Formula 3 support race, held before the French Grand Prix in Rouen, and inquired whether I would be interested in driving for them in 1965.

Another big decision loomed. In those days, the future of a young racing driver was very often determined by his first F1 team. He may have been the most talented and gifted driver of his generation, but if he was not supported by the right mechanics, and the right designer, and the right team director, and the right infrastructure, then his chances of success were significantly reduced. I had worked my way through the Formula 3 season, and proven myself in what amounted to a scaled-down Formula 1 car, but I was keenly aware that my fate depended on whether I could select the right team to join.

Take your time, I told myself, as usual, consider all the

options. The simple reality of me getting a F1 drive meant some other driver would have to lose a drive, but such considerations never crossed my mind. If a team owner felt I could deliver, that was all there was to it.

My analysis began with the realisation that the Cooper team appeared to have lost their way and were no longer front-runners in Formula 1, and this left me with a straight choice between Lotus and BRM.

I studied the cars: the Lotus unquestionably seemed to be the fastest car on the grid but it appeared to be more fragile than the more robust BRM. Did I want the speed of the Lotus, or did I need the reliability of the BRM?

I also looked at the teams. Lotus was the glamorous domain of Colin Chapman, an enormously charismatic and dynamic man who was perhaps the most brilliant creator of revolutionary technology in the history of Formula 1. Jim Clark, my friend and fellow Scot, was the apple of Colin's eye and the undisputed No. 1, to a degree that, for whatever reason, none of the team's No. 2 drivers – talented men like Peter Arundel, Trevor Taylor and Mike Spence – had ever come close to challenging him. I started to wonder whether it would be too hard to develop and grow as a No. 2 in a team where the No. 1 was so admired and so dominant.

In contrast, BRM was solid, dependable and maybe a little less charismatic. The team was based in Bourne in Lincolnshire, which was hardly recognised as a destination for the jet set. However, the mechanics and the engineers were rock solid and utterly dedicated, and team manager, Tony Rudd, was well rounded, in more ways than one. Graham Hill was the No. 1 driver and, in all our previous meetings, he had never been less than generous, helpful and supportive.

I started to conclude that, as a young and inexperienced single-seater racing driver making this important step up to the highest level of the sport, I needed stability and reliability rather than raw speed and glamour and required the comfort of both a racing car and an administrative organisation that was emphatically solid and robust.

So, after long consideration, I decided to join BRM. It was the last and most significant choice of a frenzied and at times bewildering period of my life when any wrong turn might have cost me dearly and propelled me in the wrong direction.

Touch wood, I thought at the end of 1964, I have got most of the major decisions right. Time would tell.

CHAPTER 6

Ideal Education

JIM CLARK WAS THE FINEST RACING DRIVER OF MY ERA. He was also one of my closest friends and even now, almost forty years after his death, just the mention of his name triggers so many memories and emotions. We were so similar in so many ways – the same height, the same build, the same measured approach to our racing and the same pride in being Scottish. Yet in other ways, we were so different – Jimmy was quiet, I was rarely at a loss for words; he was an introvert, people used to say I was an extrovert. Nonetheless, we always seemed to get along and, during my club racing career and through my first three seasons in Formula 1, this humble, unaffected genius became my benchmark and role model. Just his presence at an event somehow seemed to make me more relaxed and, as a result, more successful. I did not fully appreciate it at the time, but I now look back and see that Jim Clark, together with my BRM teammate Graham Hill, offered me an ideal education in racing at the highest level.

It was July 1958 when we first met, on the evening after the hill climb at Rest-and-Be-Thankful. The much-heralded young

Scottish driver had competed in the event and stopped for petrol at Dumbuck on his way home. Jim Clark stepped out of his car on to our forecourt wearing, I recall, a blue round-neck sweater and grey flannels. The pundits were talking about him as a star of the future, and I had read all about him in the various motor sport magazines on sale at the time – the comics, as I called them. I knew his family were farmers in the hills around Duns and Chirnside in the Border region of Scotland, I knew he had started his racing career in cars provided by Ian Scott Watson and I knew he was a member of the Border Reivers racing team run by a great enthusiast called Jock McBain. And here he was, visiting our garage. I continued to follow his career with great interest, once standing in the crowd at Oulton Park and watching him dominate a Formula Junior race, right through to 1961, when he signed with Colin Chapman and Lotus and became a Formula 1 driver.

Jimmy and I were formally introduced by Graham Gauld, the editor of *Motor World* magazine, at Charterhall in 1962; by then, he was recognised as one of the top racing drivers in the world, and I was competing as A. N. Other, and yet he greeted me and seemed so mild and modest. Jim was a brilliant driver, however his great popularity throughout the sport owed as much to his endearing shyness and total humility.

There was more contact the following year when I started to race for Ecurie Ecosse and, as we became friends, I believe Jimmy Clark was somehow looking out for me: 'Don't force it,' he told me once, 'don't try and drive too quickly. Just keep it smooth.' That was *his* style, of course. You never saw arms and elbows when he was driving. There was minimal hand movement because he was so precise and accurate. I used to watch him intently, studying his preparation and his mannerisms, and it seemed to me entirely logical that this was the correct way to drive.

As the pace of my life increased during 1964, Jimmy became

a kind of anchor for me, always encouraging me, always supporting me and, when I started getting drives for prestigious teams like Chequered Flag and Team Lotus, I suspected it was because he had put in a good word for me.

I used to visit him at his farm, getting to know his parents and four elder sisters, and I enjoyed listening to him talk about racing and his experiences. We became close and, in the frenetic world of motor racing, perhaps we helped each other: for me, it was a friendship forged by my utter respect for him as a driver and as a person; for him, maybe I was a fellow Scotsman in the same business whom he felt he could talk to and, now and then, confide in.

However, Jim was not always too forthcoming. One afternoon at Silverstone, when we were preparing to race in a couple of Lotus Élans, I wandered over to where he was sitting and asked where he braked for Stowe corner. He mumbled and looked away. Bloody hell, I thought, nobody knows this circuit better than him, and he doesn't want to tell me. Maybe he thought there were some things I should be left to work out for myself; perhaps I was becoming fast enough for him to feel he shouldn't be giving me tips.

'Morning, Jackie, will you drive Jimmy's car in South Africa?'

It was November 1964 and, out of the blue, Colin Chapman was asking me to drive for his works Lotus team in the Rand Grand Prix, a non-championship Formula 1 race, in Johannesburg. He explained how Jim had suffered a freak injury – he had travelled to Cortina in the Italian Alps to attend the launch of the new Ford Cortina and slipped a disc in his back while throwing snowballs – and this meant Lotus urgently needed a driver for both the F1 race and a touring car race at Kyalami. Colin wanted to know if I was available.

'That would be very nice,' I replied, 'but you know I've signed to drive for BRM next season.'

'Yes,' he said, 'but what if I cleared it with them?'

'Well, if you do that, fine.'

I had enormous respect for Chapman as a great innovator in the history of our sport. He had an amazing ability to produce cars that were frighteningly quick and, as the years passed, strangely, he seemed to play a pivotal role at key stages of my racing career. This was one such moment and, with his amazing charm, he persuaded BRM to let me drive, and I was boarding the flight to Johannesburg.

It was my first ever Formula 1 race, and I put the car on pole position. I don't know how. Coming out of club racing and the formative classes, I was shocked to find myself on the front row of a F1 grid. Only Jacques Villeneuve has achieved the same feat in recent times, and that was after he switched from IndyCar racing, where he had already been the CART World Series champion. Maybe it was the combination of a fantastically quick car and a bright-eyed, bushy-tailed young driver who was thrown in at the deep end, against big names like Graham Hill, Mike Spence and Frank Gardner, feeling as if he had nothing to lose and an awful lot to gain.

The brand new Lotus had been designed specifically for Jim Clark and its adhesion and grip was incredible, but this was the first time the car had ever been raced competitively and, on the start line, just as I released the clutch, a tubular metal drive shaft snapped, and a rubber doughnut that was part of it flew 100 feet in the air. I was stranded and the rest of the field roared past in a blur of noise, power and dust. This particular event was run in two heats, and I managed to redeem the situation in the second part of the race when, with my drive shaft repaired, I made my way from the back of the grid, recorded the fastest lap of the day and won. Graham Hill was the overall winner and he took home a spectacular diamond and gold trophy, but my first taste of Formula 1 racing could hardly have been more exciting.

The 1965 season was scheduled to start at the South African Grand Prix on New Year's Day, in the coastal city of East London. I was nervous ahead of my first F1 championship race having qualified the previous day in eleventh place and, just as the New Year's Eve party was getting underway at our hotel, the King's Arms, I decided to escape the bedlam by going to watch a movie at a local drive-in, together with an emerging Austrian driver called Jochen Rindt.

There was a great spirit among the drivers in those days and, on the morning of the race, I recall spending some time sitting and chatting with Graham Hill and Jo Bonnier in their hotel rooms.

That afternoon, I focused my mind on getting the basics right and performed reasonably well, picking up my first championship point in a race won by Jimmy Clark at his most immaculate, driving the same Lotus that I had driven in the Rand Grand Prix.

'Finished sixth Jackie,' read the telegram I sent home to Helen.

Everything was going well . . . although maybe not quite as well as Ken Tyrrell had anticipated: he had laid a bet with John Cooper that I would out-qualify Bruce McLaren in South Africa and he lost. The setback must have upset him, because years later he was still telling me how I let him down.

The fast start to my Formula 1 career continued: second place in the non-championship Race of Champions at Brands Hatch, pole position for the non-championship Sunday Mirror Trophy race at Goodwood and, on Saturday 15 May, I was leading the field in the non-championship Daily Express International Trophy at Silverstone. There were no world championship points at stake, but this was a major motor sporting occasion. More than 80,000 people packed into Silverstone, and the British crowd were becoming increasingly noisy and excited as the new, young British driver moved into the lead.

Keep it smooth, I tell myself, repeating Jimmy's words in my head . . . only a few laps to go . . . keep concentrating . . . in my rear view mirror, I see the reigning world champion, John Surtees, in his Ferrari . . . ahead of me, I see his team-mate Lorenzo Bandini in the other Ferrari . . . I am concerned . . . I have to lap Bandini, but maybe he will give me a hard time, and let Surtees get closer . . . don't get outfumbled by the Ferraris . . . stay calm . . . I head for Becketts corner . . . ease on the brakes . . . OK, there's a gap . . . go for it, nice and smooth . . . that's it . . . I slip past Bandini . . . open road ahead . . . Surtees won't catch me now.

Victory in what was just my fifth Formula 1 race seemed to confirm my potential, and, ahead of the next date on the calendar, the Monaco Grand Prix on 30 May, the *Daily Sketch* newspaper invited me to start writing a weekly column. Everything was happening so fast, and my excitement coursed through the words I babbled to my contact person at the *Sketch*, motor sport writer Michael Kemp.

'This place is special,' I dictated. 'One moment, I am driving at 130 mph in bright sunlight along the streets of Monte Carlo. In a flash, I drive into a wall of darkness. It is a pitch-dark tunnel. Instead of slowing down, I have to pile on speed until I return to the dazzling daylight at 140 mph. This is the most hair-raising part of the circuit, before I swoop down to the harbour. This burst from light to dark to light will happen 100 times; it's cruel on the eyes and hard on the nerves. Driving must be more precise here than anywhere else because there is no room for error. There are sharp stone kerbs on each side of the road and, if you hit them, there could be a burst tyre, a broken wheel, or a bent or broken piece of suspension, and that could spell disaster.'

The BRM P261 was flying. Graham Hill, and then I, broke the lap record during practice on the Saturday, but my inexperience showed in the race when, leading through lap twenty-nine,

I failed to notice an oil spill on the tarmac and spun the car. It was a mistake any over-eager youngster might have made, but I was very annoyed, even though I did go on to finish in third place. On reflection, that is not bad for my first Monaco Grand Prix, but I knew I could, and should, have done better.

In years to come, my capacity to consume information and take appropriate action, usually within the space of a few milliseconds, would improve to such a degree that I would avoid such errors. With experience, I would be able to spot a black streak on the track and instantly register an engine had blown or a car had dropped oil and I would be able to straddle the spill or avoid it without losing speed.

However, if carelessness was one product of my youth, another was naivety. A fortnight after Monaco, I noticed some of the experienced drivers seemed apprehensive about starting the Belgian Grand Prix at Spa-Francorchamps in driving rain. What's the problem, I thought. I was so keen and eager that I didn't know any better than to throw myself into one of the most notoriously dangerous circuits in extremely difficult conditions. Courage is one thing but, in years to come, I would learn to respect the thin line between what people call 'bravery' and what is actually downright stupidity.

It was an extraordinary race. Only two drivers completed all thirty-two laps, the two Scots. Jimmy Clark won, and I came second. At stages, I had started to sense my compatriot was almost pacing me around Spa, past the barbed-wire fences and the telegraph poles, past full-grown trees at the edge of the track and farm buildings constructed a few feet from the edge of the tarmac. Jimmy seemed to be backing off when possible, ensuring we took no stupid risks, making certain we both stayed safe.

Actually, standing on the podium afterwards, he turned to me and asked: 'Are you OK? I was getting worried about you out there.'

'No problem, Jimmy,' I replied. 'I'm fine.'

Back home in Glasgow, the *Herald* was preparing a headline acclaiming the one-two finish of the 'Scottish speed twins', but I was already focused on my next challenge. At the end of every race, win or lose, my first instinct has always been to get away as soon as possible and move on.

The next adventure was Le Mans, where Graham Hill and I had been invited to co-drive something called the Rover BRM Gas Turbine. This was a good-looking car, with an engine revving at 64,000 revs per minute, compared to the 11,000 rpm of the BRM Formula 1 car. It generated speeds of 150 mph on the Mulsanne Straight, but there was no engine braking, so the only way to decelerate was to use the brakes.

'It feels more like flying,' I remember telling Graham.

We finished tenth in the 1965 race, and I returned the following year and qualified a Ford GT 40 Mk II for Alan Mann Racing, but injury prevented me from taking part in the actual race.

Historically, the 24 Hour of Le Mans is one of the three great events in motor sport, ranking alongside the Indianapolis 500 and the Monaco Grand Prix, but I have to say the race never particularly appealed to me. It was certainly a test of machines, pushing cars through the equivalent of a year's motoring in one single day, yet for a driver it seemed less challenging, driving to finish more than anything else. Aficionados of the race will disagree, but it seemed to me that, to win a Formula 1 Grand Prix, the driver has to drive pretty much on the limit, at 9/10. To win Le Mans, it was necessary to drive at 6/10 or 7/10 for twenty-four hours. That was the difference. One was a blue riband 100-metre sprint; the other was a slog.

The 1965 Formula 1 season continued through June and July, with Jim Clark sweeping all before him and me following not far behind. After my second place in Belgium, I again took second place behind him in the French Grand Prix at Clermont-Ferrand, and yet again at the Dutch Grand Prix in Zandvoort on 18 July. Such results were far beyond my expectations, and I felt tremendously proud each time I stood on the podium alongside my fellow Scot.

It was an ideal education, seeing Jim perfect the art of doing just enough, going just fast enough, pushing the car just hard enough to win. There was no wasted effort.

Sandwiched between the French and the Dutch races was my first British Grand Prix, which turned out to be a disappointing event for me. I qualified well enough, on the front row, although in reality I was in fourth position. Unusally, the grid was set up in a 4–3–4 formation. Throughout the whole race I was uninspiring. That is the best word for my performance that day. I hadn't set the car up as I should have, I didn't drive as well as I should have and I certainly didn't deliver as I should have, finishing fifth.

In practice for the Grand Prix of Germany at the Nurburgring, which followed the race in Holland, I came within a few hundredths of a second of being the first man ever to complete the 14.7 mile circuit at an average speed in excess of 100 mph. Almost as if to put me back in my place, Jim jumped into his Lotus and claimed the milestone for himself, which meant hardly anybody seemed to notice when I posted a lap at 100.07 mph a few minutes later.

Jimmy always seemed to be one step ahead of me, and I remember how we laughed about the rivalry the next week, over dinner at an Italian restaurant called Trattoria, around the corner from the flat where we used to stay whenever we were in London. The Balfour Place apartment belonged to Sir John Whitmore, who became a great friend to both Jimmy and me, and he put it at our disposal.

John was a very talented racing driver and a great character, who once famously forgot to lower the wheels when landing his private plane in Geneva and caused the airport to be closed for the rest of the day. He has since built a highly successful business, becoming one of Britain's experts in leadership and organisational change. His flat became known as the 'Scottish Embassy', and we enjoyed many happy times there, with Jim and his girlfriend Sally Stokes taking the main bedroom, and Helen and I using the smaller one.

It's odd how life turns in circles because Trattoria has since closed and the building is now home to a private dining club called George's, where I am a member and frequent visitor.

The 1965 Italian Grand Prix was held on 12 September at Monza, but this was not the Monza of today, punctuated by a series of chicanes to reduce speed. This was the high-speed circuit through the wooded royal park where the lead could change four or five times during a lap, where you could pass or be passed before or after Curva Grande or before Curva di Lesmos, or at Ascari, or at the Parabolica and perhaps eight cars would be slipstreaming, taking advantage of the drag produced by the air pockets, racing nose to tail and wheel to wheel.

It was uniquely exciting to watch and exhilarating to drive in and, year after year, hordes of knowledgeable, fanatical, feverish Italians would get to their feet and roar with delight as the drama unfolded before their eyes.

BRM senior management and drivers typically stayed at the Villa d'Este during the week of the Italian Grand Prix. It was one of the finest hotels in the world, on the banks of Lake Como, and I checked in with the team: Louis Stanley and his wife, Jean, whom everyone called Mrs Stanley and who was, in fact, the sister of Sir Alfred Owen, the owner of BRM, Tony Rudd and Graham and Bette Hill. Helen stayed at home as she was just about to have a baby and was not able to travel.

The race was remarkable for the fact that the lead at the

start/finish line changed no fewer than forty-three times during the seventy-six laps. Jim Clark, Graham Hill and I were driving in a cluster of cars, each of us taking the lead at various stages, then losing it, and surging again. Jim was for once forced to retire with a mechanical problem so, with thirteen laps left, Graham and I found ourselves out in the lead, ahead of the rest of the field. Tony Rudd immediately started to signal from the pit wall that we should ease off and consolidate our control of the race, and, as drivers, neither of us had any reason to do otherwise. However, to Tony's frustration, the more we 'eased off', the faster our laps became.

I was intrigued by the experience and, thinking about it, realised that when someone tells you to slow down, you change up a gear a little earlier, you use fewer revs and you don't brake as aggressively into a corner . . . and, as a result, you actually go faster because you are not unduly upsetting the car. Riders will understand the concept because it also explains why similarly, if you loosen the reins, a horse tends to run more freely and quickly. It was a useful lesson, and the theory applies in other walks of life: sometimes the best way to raise your level of performance is to back off rather than to push even harder.

The two BRMs continued to hurtle around Monza. Graham led with two laps remaining, when he went wide at the Parabolica, got into the loose stuff, losing speed and leaving a gap. I slipped inside, drove through and easily seized the lead. Thrilled beyond words, I was able to complete the race and secure my maiden Formula 1 victory.

Tens of thousands of Italian fans, *tifosi*, flooded the track at the end. The typically Italian tidal wave of adulation, passion and enthusiasm for motor sport was overwhelming.

'*Il Grande Jackie, il Grande Jackie*,' they chanted.

Monza was special for me in 1965 and it has been special for me ever since.

Only when I escaped from the mayhem and returned to the hotel did I have an opportunity to phone Helen and tell her what had happened, and then to call my father at Rockview. I remember hearing the pleasure in his voice, the simple pride that his 'stupid' younger son had won a world championship F1 Grand Prix.

After such a 'bang', my debut season ended with a whimper. Mechanical failures meant I failed to finish the USA or the Mexico Grands Prix, which cost me a chance of finishing second in the world championship. My total of 34 points left me third behind Jimmy, the world champion on 54, and Graham on 47. Even so, I was happy. The BRM had proved every bit as robust and reliable as I could have hoped, and one victory and five podium finishes in ten races represented a very satisfying promising debut season.

Early in 1966, I flew around the world with Jim, Graham and Dick Attwood to compete in the Tasman Cup, a series of eight races, four in New Zealand and four in Australia. Jimmy later reflected on these two months as among the happiest trips of his career, and everyone enjoyed the mix of tough, competitive motor racing with flying, surfing, trap shooting, water-skiing and plenty of laughter along the way.

Chris Amon was not competing that year, but he was one of New Zealand's finest drivers and an extremely likeable man and he invited us all to visit his family's beach house after the New Zealand Grand Prix at Pukekohe, and before the second race at Levin. It was arranged that Jimmy, Dick and I would drive down in the red 3.8 litre Jaguar with cream upholstery provided for us to use during our stay. However, for whatever reason, Jimmy was not ready to leave on time. 'Don't wait for me,' he told us. 'They have given me an E-type Jaguar, so you go ahead and I'll catch you up.'

To a fellow racing driver, this casual remark amounted to a clear challenge. So Dick and I set off, determined Jim would not catch us and we were soon speeding through the countryside, regularly glancing back to check for any sign of Jim. Approaching a town called Bulls, I moved wide to overtake a school bus labouring up a steep hill and, a few minutes later, stopped at a set of traffic lights in the main street. Suddenly, a police patrol car appeared from nowhere and screeched to a halt across the front of our car, blocking our way.

The policeman was agitated. 'Do you have any idea what speed you have been doing?' he asked.

'No,' I replied.

'Well, I've been trying to catch you for the past twenty miles, and I must have been going at over a hundred miles per hour.'

'I see.'

'Do you know the speed limit in New Zealand is fifty miles per hour?'

'No, I'm sorry. I didn't.'

'Well, it is, and I'm charging you with dangerous and reckless driving.'

As he spoke, the school bus stopped nearby, and some of the children came over to look at the Jaguar. The policeman's mood was not improved when the boys recognised us as racing drivers and asked to borrow his pen because they wanted to get our autographs. The officer eventually told me to follow him to the Bulls police station and, once my attempts to charm my way out of the problem failed, the reality started to dawn on me that reckless and dangerous driving was a serious charge, and I could lose my road licence; and if I lost that, I would lose my competition licence as well.

When I had been warned to expect a summons and allowed to leave, we joined our group at the barbeque with the Amons, where I told everyone what had happened, but not before I made it clear that Jimmy hadn't passed us on the road!

'You need to get yourself a decent lawyer,' I was advised, firmly.

'Who?'

'Well, the man you want is Trevor de Cleene. He got P. J. Proby off a charge of indecent exposure.'

P. J. Proby was an American pop star known for wearing skin-tight trousers that used to split during his live performances. When this happened during a concert in New Zealand, he was charged with indecent exposure and, apparently, only Mr de Cleene's expertise resolved the situation.

I called him on a Sunday evening and, having been told he was out fishing, spent two hours waiting beside his white Mercedes for his boat to return to shore. I eventually met him, explained what had happened and asked if he would take the case. He said he would, so long as I paid his fee of £1,100 up front and in cash. It was a lot of money, but my career was under threat, so I didn't have much choice.

The following Saturday, I was served with a summons by an embarrassed Scotsman who had emigrated to New Zealand; he handed me the papers when I was still sitting in my car after finishing second to Jimmy in the Gold Leaf International race in Levin, which ensured that the case was splashed over the newspapers, but Trevor did his homework and got the charges dismissed on a technicality.

The story didn't end there. Many years later, back in New Zealand to present a Sportsman of the Year award, I was surprised to read in a newspaper that the government minister with responsibility for taxation was none other than Trevor de Cleene. Interviewed live on television, I was asked to relate an anecdote about my experiences in New Zealand, and I couldn't resist telling the tale of my adventure in 1966.

'So Mr de Cleene took my money and insisted I paid in cash,' I concluded, with the studio audience in stitches, 'but don't worry, I'm sure the minister would have declared the income in full.'

Early the next morning, the telephone rang in my hotel

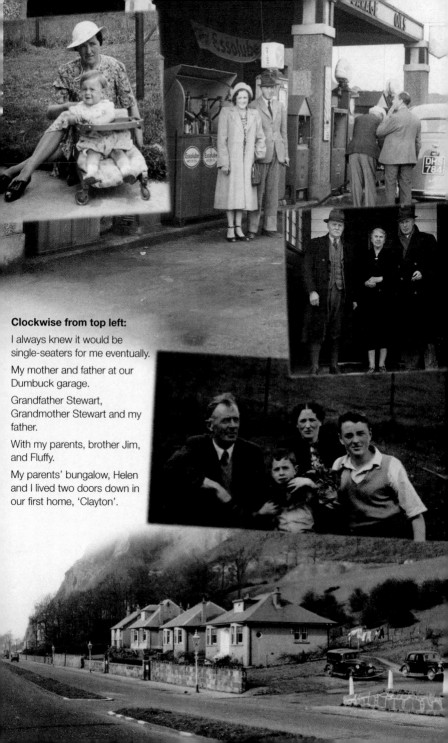

Clockwise from top left:

I always knew it would be single-seaters for me eventually.

My mother and father at our Dumbuck garage.

Grandfather Stewart, Grandmother Stewart and my father.

With my parents, brother Jim, and Fluffy.

My parents' bungalow, Helen and I lived two doors down in our first home, 'Clayton'.

Left: A day that changed my life: New Year's Day 1953 with my first shooting trophy.

Above: Christmas 1957, sporting my Scottish Shooting Team jacket.

Above: 1957 Scottish Shooting Team. I'm front row, centre. 'Bulls-eye' McClellan is front row, far right. Tom Brockie and Abe Bruce are standing ninth and fourth from the right.

Left: The most important partnership of my life. Allan Jones is best man and Shan Gorst (who later married Allan) is bridesmaid.

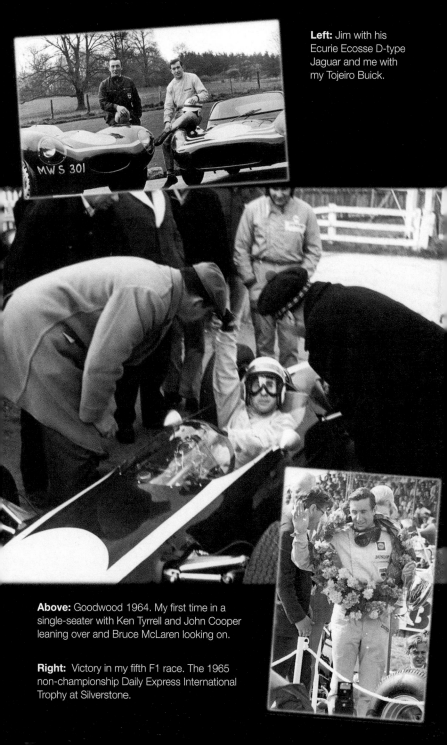

Left: Jim with his Ecurie Ecosse D-type Jaguar and me with my Tojeiro Buick.

MWS 301

Above: Goodwood 1964. My first time in a single-seater with Ken Tyrrell and John Cooper leaning over and Bruce McLaren looking on.

Right: Victory in my fifth F1 race. The 1965 non-championship Daily Express International Trophy at Silverstone.

Top left: Monaco Grand Prix 1965. Challenging for the lead until I hit the kerb and span. I ended up third.

Top right: Monza 1965. Passing Graham Hill...

Left: ...to win the race. My first championship victory.

Below: Le Mans 1965. I co-drove the Rover BRM Gas Turbine with Graham Hill. It felt more like flying.

Top left: Making a pit stop in my Lola in the 1966 Indy 500.

Top right: At the Indianapolis Motor Speedway in 1967, with US driver Ronnie Buckman and Italian driver Lorenzo Bandini. Lorenzo was killed at Monte Carlo a week or so later.

Right: Brands Hatch 1967 for the BOAC six-hour. Helmet on and about to take over from team-mate Chris Amon in the beautiful Ferrari 330P4.

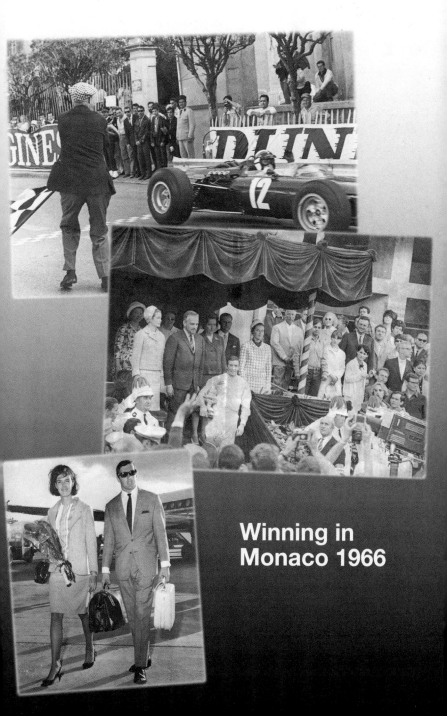

Winning in Monaco 1966

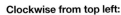

Clockwise from top left:

Scottish Motor Show, 1965. Is Jimmy Clark concentrating fully on the cars?

Corks flying at the Dumbuck garage opening, 1966. The Provost of Dumbarton joins the celebrations with Graham and Jimmy.

Grand Prix Drivers' Association in session, 1966.

Continuing clockwise from left:

The Doghouse Ball. Tony Brooks, Dick Atwood, Denny Hulme, me, Graham Hill, Jack Brabham, Jim Clark, Innes Ireland, Colin Chapman.

Jimmy interrupting my 'celebratory' photo shoot, the night before the 1967 Tasman Series New Zealand GP. I'd have looked very foolish if I hadn't won the following day.

room. It was the man himself on the line. 'Jackie,' Trevor declared, laughing. 'You've made me a hero!'

He was a talented man and a terrific character and, when he succumbed to cancer in April 2001, I called his wife, Raewyn, the following day to express my sincere condolences.

I actually managed to win the 1966 Tasman Series, but my abiding memories are of the parties where the touring group drank the bottles of local sparkling wine we were given on the podiums because we couldn't take them home, and where we held Maori war canoe races, where we sat on the floor, bare-footed, in lines and rowed in time together, pushing ourselves backwards by digging our heels into the carpet. Jimmy and I laughed and laughed. If people weren't referring to me as Jimmy Stewart and to him as Jackie Clark, they were calling us the Speed Twins, or the Poison Dwarfs, or Batman and Robin.

For someone so commanding and clear-minded when driving, Jim was frustratingly uncertain in other areas of his life. He was one of the world's great procrastinators, and I lost count of the times we missed dinner or a film because everywhere had closed by the time he made up his mind where he wanted to go.

I tell the story of the time we were driving to a race in Sebring, Florida, when we arrived at a single-track level crossing. The railway stretched away straight as a die for miles to the left and right, and there was no other traffic. Jim was driving, so he stopped and looked left and right. There was nothing. He glanced at me warily and said, 'Well, what do you think?'

I thought I must have missed something. So I looked left and right and saw again that there was nothing within miles of us. He was still sitting there, in a quandary.

'I think it's safe to go, Jim.'

'OK,' he said, and we continued on our way.

The general expectation ahead of the 1966 Formula 1

season was that the BRM would be competitive, with Lotus, Ferrari and the new Brabham Repco team also strongly in contention, and our optimism seemed to be borne out when I managed to win the opening race of the year in Monaco, which was, and still is, regarded as the most prestigious race of the season.

Next day, Jimmy, Graham and I caught a flight to America to drive in the Indianapolis 500. We had all been there the week before Monaco to qualify our cars and now we were returning for the race itself.

The contrast between the prestige and luxury of Monte Carlo and the flat, open plains of Indiana could hardly have been greater. Leaving La Grande Corniche, we arrived at the Indianapolis International Airport, which in fact only handled domestic flights. Having checked out of the Hotel de Paris, we experienced the raw charm of the Speedway motel. Having negotiated the Monaco circuit, where there are sixteen corners and you have to make at least 2,800 gear shifts during the race, we were confronted by the Indy race track, where you turn left, left, left and left again and you don't have to change gear at all after leaving the pits. All the two events shared in common was their eminent status in motor sport.

For me, in 1966, the Indianapolis 500 represented an exciting driving challenge and the biggest payday of the year because I had been guaranteed a minimum fee of $25,000 to drive a Lola for John Mecom Jr, the larger-than-life owner of the New Orleans Saints American football team and son of a Texas oil billionaire, who owned various hotels, newspapers and a fleet of seventeen private aircraft, including a Caravelle. That really impressed me: the Caravelle was the most glamorous and renowned commercial passenger aircraft of the day, and the Mecoms not only had one of their own but they had also kitted it out with every imaginable luxury.

My car was called a Bowes SealFast special, which pleased me because Bowes SealFast was the product we always used to fix the punctures back at the garage in Dumbuck. It was hard to believe that, in two years, I had moved from the service area to the starting grid at the Indianapolis 500.

Jim Clark, as ever, kept me in line, prodding me in the right direction. He had established his reputation at Indianapolis the previous year when he became the first non-American to win the race since 1916, and his genial, humble and relaxed manner seemed to go down well with the crowds.

'Listen, Jackie,' he told me, 'get as close to the concrete walls at entry and exit of the corners as you can. If you can't see the shadow of your tyre on the wall, you're not close enough and therefore not fast enough.' That was the trick back then.

One or two notable British drivers have dismissed the Indianapolis 500 over the years, claiming it's not real racing because you just keep turning left and that's it, but these tend to be people who have never competed in the race, never sat in an IndyCar and had to maintain intense concentration through 200 laps of the circuit at speeds of up to 180 mph in the 1960s, and as much as 250 mph nowadays.

Our preparations for the 1966 Indianapolis 500 ran smoothly, at least until I was persuaded by a personable agent called Chuck Barnes to make a public appearance at an Elks club function. He arranged for me to be picked up at the Speedway motel and taken to the venue in a police car, a Ford Galaxie, as I recall.

The police officer introduced himself as Joe Harris and, no sooner had we reached the freeway on our way to the venue, than he said he thought there was something suspicious about the car in front of us.

'You think so?'

'I do,' he said.

He made a call on his police radio, read out the numberplate of the car and, sure enough, was told the vehicle was listed as stolen.

'Right,' he said, turning on his siren and flashing blue light, 'we're after him.'

In an instant, sitting there in my Savile Row suit, I found myself hurled into a scene straight out of a police TV show, chasing this car down the freeway and up and off the ramp at full speed before turning into a quiet suburb of streets lined with bungalows called Edinburg, Indiana. The car screeched to a halt. The driver and passenger doors swung open, two men leaped out and started running in opposite directions. 'Hey, Jackie,' Joe yelled, 'I'll take this one, you chase that one!'

Me?

Was he serious?

There was no time for discussion, so I did as the policeman told me and chased my man through a couple of gardens, over a few fences, ducking under lines of washing being hung out to dry – it was a Monday. Joe was firing warning shots in the air, raising the stakes, when I turned into an alley and found myself standing face to face with the man I was chasing. Assuming I was armed as well, he put his hands on his head.

'OK, just stand there,' I said and, embarrassingly, for some reason, I then made my hand into the shape of a pistol, with my thumb up and forefinger pointing. 'Don't move,' I barked.

What now, I thought. A few nervous seconds passed like minutes. I had absolutely no idea what to do and, just as my 'prisoner' was starting to sense my confusion and make a move, Joe appeared on the scene, holding his man in an arm lock with one arm and pressing a gun in his back with the other.

'Good work,' he said, grinning. 'Let's get them back to the police station.'

The situation seemed almost surreal, and even more so when we pulled into the station precinct and heard the sound of a policeman practising on his bagpipes.

I eventually arrived at the function an hour late, but at least I had a decent story to tell. My 'arrest' was widely reported in the newspapers, in America and back home. A delegation of policemen came to see me in the pit lane a few days later and said that, in appreciation of my efforts, they wanted to make me an honorary sheriff of Indiana, and they presented me with my own badge and baton.

Several years later when I was the unsuspecting subject of the *This Is Your Life* TV show, the main and last surprise guest called on stage by host Eamonn Andrews was . . . Officer Joe Harris.

Meanwhile back at the raceway, the British drivers were causing a stir. It would probably be fair to say that, as always, we stood out from the American IndyCar drivers. In fact, over the years it was clear to those in and around the US circuits that we were totally different. Another occasion I remember was when, flying in from Europe, I drove directly to the circuit from the airport, and I was wearing a bespoke pin-striped Kilgour French Stanbury suit, a collar and tie and, in my lapel, one of the red carnations that TWA used to give their first-class passengers when they left the aircraft. So, dressed like this, I strolled into the area known as Gasoline Alley, and amazed Americans wearing jeans, boots and cowboy hats were gazing at me, as if to say, 'Huh? What's that?'

The culture shock worked both ways. During that '66 race Graham Hill was so appalled to discover there were no doors on the cubicles in the gents' loos at Gasoline Alley that he told Tony Hulman, then president and owner of the Indianapolis Motor Speedway, that he would never return unless some kind of privacy was introduced. New doors were installed by the next morning, and we laughed when we heard one local tell another: 'Jeez, what's going on? Have you been in the stalls this morning? They've got doors!'

Always held on Memorial Day at the end of May, the race

attracted around 400,000 spectators in 1966, of which approximately 150,000 were seated in the various grandstands around the circuit. In my view, the Indianapolis 500 was, and indeed remains, the most impressive spectacle in world sport. The pre-race ritual began with marching bands, followed by a rendition of 'Star Spangled Banner' and then 'Back Home Again in Indiana'; and the crowd would join in the chorus:

> Back home again in Indiana,
> and it seems that I can see,
> the gleaming candlelight, still burning bright,
> through the sycamores for me.

Thousands of balloons would be released from an infield tent when the singing reached the line:

> the new-mown hay sends all its fragrance,
> through the fields I used to roam.
> When I dream about the moonlight on the Wabash,
> how I long for my Indiana home.

It really was something, and I would defy anybody to stand in the midst of this amazing atmosphere and tension, with all the crowds, singing and colour, and not have goose pimples.

Then Tony Hulman, Jr, whose family have presided over the race for so long, stepped forward and took a piece of paper from his pocket and read, 'Gentlemen, start your engines.' As always, the words were broadcast around the raceway, booming through the stands as if uttered by some greater being. I was always amused by the fact that, year after year, Tony was never content just to say the words. Taking the piece of paper and reading them was all part of his performance.

A pace car then set off, leading the field of thirty-three cars around the circuit until they were perfectly aligned in eleven rows of three; then, when they were ready, with the crowd going wild, the starter stood on his gantry suspended 20 feet above the cars and waved a green flag.

In 1966, my concern was to survive the usual crush at the first and second corners, so I focused intently on keeping out of trouble. When I reached the back straight, I glanced in my rear-view mirrors and saw no one there. Wow, Jackie, I thought to myself, you're driving so well, you've blown them away. In fact, there were a few cars ahead of me, and there had been a mass pile-up behind me, even before the first corner, which meant the race had to be stopped and resumed an hour and a half later.

This time, the Lola was still running fantastically well, and, with eight laps remaining, I had managed to establish a lead of nearly two laps – a distance of five miles – over Graham and Jimmy. It appeared certain that, barring a major setback, I would match Jimmy's achievement of the previous year and win the race.

On lap 192, that major setback occurred. In one of the most frustrating moments of my racing career, I felt the engine tighten as I approached Turn 1. The oil pressure began to fall away, and I had no option but to turn off the engine, knock it into neutral and coast to the exit of Turn 4, where the car came to a halt.

I climbed out of the car, took off my helmet and started pushing the car back towards the pits, because that seemed the right thing to do. It was hard work and, when I stopped for a rest every fifty metres or so, the crowd in the adjacent stand would start cheering, I would wave, and what should have been an intensely disappointing moment for me turned out to be something quite enjoyable.

There was no reason for me to feel bad, even when Graham and Jimmy roared past to finish first and second respectively, and I was actually quite content to be ranked sixth, based on laps completed, in my first Indianapolis 500, and named as the Rookie of the Year. That title carried an intriguing range of prizes, including a yellow leather jacket and free butcher meat for the year, which was of limited use to me living on the banks of the River Clyde.

As my career turned out, I only competed in one other Indianapolis 500. That was in 1967 and, once again, I had to retire when the oil scavenge pump failed while lying in second place. In 1968, I was booked to drive but withdrew with a broken wrist and then watched in horror as Mike Spence died during practice in the car I would have been in.

Thereafter, I decided to concentrate all my efforts on Formula 1, and only returned to the Brickyard raceway in the 1970s and 1980s, in my commentating role for US television.

After the Indy interlude in 1966, Jimmy, Graham and I flew back to Europe in time for the Belgian Formula 1 Grand Prix at Spa-Francorchamps, held the day after my twenty-seventh – and nearly my last – birthday.

It is strange how catastrophic incidents are often preceded by events that don't feel quite right and proper but which, at the time, we are prepared to rationalise and accept.

That weekend at Spa, the organisers unexpectedly announced there would be no warm-up lap before the race, prompting the wry joke among the drivers that they didn't want us to drive around the notorious circuit too slowly because we would see all the hazards and drop-offs and refuse to race. So we grumbled because it was unusual, but that was all, and we pulled on our helmets and settled into the small single-seater cars, which resembled high-powered tubes on wheels.

I had secured a place on the first row of the grid but, in dry and overcast conditions, I completely cocked up the start and had slipped back to ninth by the third corner. Then, at the entrance to the sweeping downhill right-hander at Bonneville, without any warning, we ran into heavy rain.

This part of the Ardennes forest was known for sudden changes in climate, where it could be mild and dry in one place but raining heavily less than a mile away – I used to call it T-shirt and overcoat weather – and, with no warm-up lap, the downpour caught all of the drivers completely by surprise.

My terrible start left me so far off the pace that I had a grandstand view as seven of the world's top drivers accelerated into a flooded part of the track, lost control of their cars and became involved in a multiple collision fortunately not resulting in any serious injury. It was all I could do to get on the brakes, reduce my speed and carefully weave my way through the debris, finding a path between the detached wheels and twisted bodywork.

In similar conditions at a F1 Grand Prix today, yellow flags would be waved to indicate the hazards ahead, enabling the drivers to proceed with care. There was no warning system in 1966.

I was lying third when I reached the Masta Straight, with only John Surtees and Jochen Rindt ahead of me. It had been an eventful start, but I had survived and seemed well set. It was still raining heavily, but, easing on the accelerator, I headed towards the Masta Kink, a right-left-right swerve in the middle of the straight. I drove into a river of water on the track at 170 mph, immediately lost control of the BRM, and aquaplaned off the tarmac. My car had effectively become a missile and it proceeded to flatten both a woodcutter's hut and a telegraph pole before careering over an eight-foot drop and finishing on the lower patio of a farmhouse. The chassis of the car was severely bent around me.

What had prevented me from smashing into a tree and being instantly killed? Good fortune, that's all. I was slipping in and out of consciousness but I was still alive, and lucky to be so.

'Jackie? Are you down there? Jackie?'

The voice was familiar and it belonged to Graham Hill. I

later learned that my team-mate had hit the same river of water and spun off the track on the same trajectory, but, in my wake, there was nothing else to hit and his car came to a stop, pointing in the right direction for him to rejoin the race. Preparing to do just that, Graham glanced to his right and saw me looking, as he put it, 'very second-hand'. When he could have continued, he jumped out of his car and came to help me. He was joined a few minutes later by an American driver called Bob Bondurant, who had rolled his car at the same spot, and been fortunate to escape without injury. It was now more than twenty minutes after my accident and no sign of any race marshals. Graham and Bob had decided they needed to get me out of the car as quickly as possible. The fuel tanks, full at the start of the race, had ruptured, and the corrosive liquid had flowed into the driver's area of the BRM, a part of the car that resembled a bath tub. Any spark from the electrics might easily have caused an explosion and killed all three of us.

'He's trapped by the steering wheel,' Graham said. 'We need a spanner.'

What followed is hard to believe. Still with no emergency crews in sight, Bob wondered how on earth he would get hold of a spanner. He looked around and decided he had no option but to run across the track to a place where some spectators had parked their cars and ask if any of them happened to have a tool box.

He was in luck. Somebody produced some spanners, one of which fitted the nuts required to remove the steering wheel, and the two of them were finally able to pull me out of the car. From that day forward, until the steering wheel quick-release mechanism became standard as a safety feature . . . I always took the precaution of keeping a spanner taped to the inside of my cockpit.

They then carried me to a barn beside the farmhouse, and laid me on the back of a hay truck. By now, I could feel my skin being burned by the high octane aviation fuel, which was soaking through my overalls, thermal underwear and normal underwear.

'Graham, get my clothes off,' I pleaded, still sliding in and out of consciousness.

He obliged and then set off to find an ambulance because, at least half an hour after the accident, with the Grand Prix continuing a few metres away, still no emergency crew had come to help.

At this precise moment, three nuns arrived at the barn – I have no idea why they were there, or where they had come from or where they were going – but they were there.

I have included this story in many speeches over the years . . . and I always say the nuns' first response was surprise at the sight of this naked man lying on the back of a hay truck. Second, they were mightily impressed by what they saw because the only naked men they had seen before were American (or whatever the nationality of my audience). Third, they tried to get me dressed again.

Just then, Graham arrived back on the scene.

'No, no, sister,' he said. 'Don't put his clothes back on.'

The nuns must have been appalled as they watched this tall English man, with long hair slicked back with Brylcreem, a trim moustache and a twinkle in his eye, insist on once again undressing this defenceless man. As I tell my audience, you can imagine what was going through their minds . . .

It's a good story, it always goes down well and it's all true.

I was eventually taken to the so-called medical centre at Spa, where I was left lying on a canvas stretcher on a filthy floor strewn with cigarette ends. More minutes passed, until it was decided I should be put in a converted Cadillac ambulance and, with a police escort, transferred to the hospital in Liège. Helen had first realised something was wrong when I didn't come round on the next lap, and she later told me she had eventually been informed of the accident by race control. She had immediately made her way to the medical facility where, apparently, there was a general concern that I might have suffered serious back injuries. It had been decided that Helen, Jim Clark and Louis Stanley would travel with me in the back of the ambulance. I was lying in considerable discomfort and, at one point in the journey, I started to moan and groan.

'For goodness' sake, Jackie,' Jimmy snapped. 'Pull yourself together. Helen is here.'

'Oh, OK,' I replied, instantly. 'I'm all right now.'

Then I would drift off again, which was probably just as well because, while all this was going on, the police escort somehow managed to lose the ambulance, which then also got lost.

It occurred to me during one of my moments of consciousness in the ambulance that I ought to thank Louis Stanley for his help and, not quite on the ball, I decided it would sound overly formal to call him Mr Stanley. So I addressed this most distinguished man as 'Lewis'. He tolerated this on three or four occasions, but then leaned over and said quietly in my ear: 'Stewart, if you insist upon calling me by my first name, it is Louis, not Lewis.'

Louis certainly looked after me well, arranging for a Medicare jet to be flown in from Zurich so it could take me straight to London where I was admitted to St Thomas' Hospital. Once I'd been fully examined it turned out I had broken my collarbone and ribs, but mercifully not my back. There was also some internal bleeding, but I had escaped a serious shunt without a mark on my body. In fact, in twelve years, I never lost a single drop of blood in a racing car.

I was amazingly lucky . . . lucky to have survived, and lucky that, on 12 June 1966, a true gentleman such as Graham Hill had stopped and, with the help of Bob Bondurant, with no regard for their own safety, pulled me out of a car that was flooded with fuel and might have exploded.

There were three sides to Graham, and I admired each of them as much as the other two.

First, he was a serious, almost dour competitor. Perhaps it was his background in the Royal Navy and as a mechanic first with Smiths Instruments and later with Lotus that made him so meticulous. He used to keep a small black book, in which he recorded every race and lap time, every mechanical detail of the cars he drove – spring ratings, valve settings on the dampers, every roll stiffness. Nothing was omitted.

Second, he was a remarkably dignified man. It cannot have been easy for him, world champion in 1962 and runner-up in 1963, 1964 and 1965, to see me arrive as his BRM team-mate and settle so quickly and yet he was a man of such quality that he only ever appeared supportive and encouraging.

Third, he had a wonderfully dry, urbane sense of humour which became a regular feature of the prestigious and well-attended BBC Sports Personality of the Year function. He and I used to appear together, reflecting on the past F1 season, and, year after year, it was our repartee and Graham's perfect timing that stole the show.

For the 1969 show, he was confined to a motorised wheelchair and he started by asking me, in his deadpan voice: 'So, Jackie, did you have any funny moments during the year?'

'Er . . .'

'Any that you can talk about?'

'Not very many I can talk about.'

'No, neither did I, now you come to mention it. Anyway, I'd like to congratulate you for a fabulous season. I would like to wish you a lot of luck for next season – not quite as much as for myself.'

Two years later, before the same audience of sporting stars, he started the conversation by asking: 'Leaving aside your undisputed skill – dammit – what single factor contributed towards your success?'

We were close friends who shared an interest in golf, and I later enjoyed introducing him to shooting on a grouse moor in Scotland. Helen and I saw a lot of Graham and Bette over the years and watched their children, Brigitte, Samantha and Damon, grow up. It was with every bit as much pride as Graham would have felt that I saw Damon pursue his driving career and become F1 world champion in 1996.

Graham had left BRM at the end of 1966 and joined Lotus, with whom he won a second world championship in 1968. He subsequently drove for Brabham, Shadow, Lola and his own team, Embassy Hill, before finally retiring in 1975, after a career that spanned two generations of our sport. At his first Grand Prix, in Argentina in 1958, he shared the grid with Juan Manuel Fangio, Stirling Moss, Luigi Musso and Mike Hawthorn. In his last F1 race, in Monaco an incredible seventeen years later, he lined up against Emerson Fittipaldi and Niki Lauda. And, of course, he remains the only man ever to win the so-called Triple Crown of Motor Sport, with victories at Le Mans, the Indianapolis 500 and the Monaco Grand Prix.

I was staying at Hambleden on 29 November 1975, preparing for a day's shooting. I'd gone to bed reasonably early and was just dozing off at around 11.30 when there was a knock on my door. It was Lady Hambleden, informing me that Helen had just telephoned to tell me Graham had been killed in an air crash. He had been flying his own Piper Aztec from the Paul Ricard circuit in France and come down in fog over north London. Five members of his racing team, including the young driver Tony Brise, and four mechanics, also died.

I was in shock when I heard the news. 'This isn't fair,' I thought. 'We are both retired. We should have passed this stage in our lives.' I just couldn't understand how Graham could have gone so suddenly when he was no longer racing.

I wanted to be able to do something, to escape into my racing driver mode in order to cope. When there had been death on the track there was always something to do. I could be of practical assistance. But not here. All I could do was lie in my room and think of Graham's family. There was no sleep that night.

The following week I escorted Graham's widow Bette to all six funerals. It was a horribly sad and depressing time.

I was racing again just five weeks after the accident at Spa, in the British Grand Prix at Brands Hatch, but the rest of the 1966 season unfolded as a disappointment with only a fourth place in Holland and fifth in Germany to show for my efforts, and I finished seventh behind world champion Jack Brabham.

Away from F1, I did manage to win the Grand Prix of Japan for IndyCars at Mount Fuji, which was a major achievement on my first visit to the Far East. This event was a big breakthrough in the increasing global reach of motor racing. It was a major logistical exercise just getting all the cars to Japan, but it was well worth it. The Japanese fans were incredibly enthusiastic about racing – they used to show the Indianapolis 500 in cinemas – and they came out in their thousands to cheer on the drivers.

The 1967 season started well for me with victory in the non-championship New Zealand Grand Prix, edging out Jim Clark by four seconds in an exciting finish, and then a more comfortable win in the Australian Grand Prix at Warwick Farm; yet, even so, we were struggling to produce a car to be competitive in the F1 world championship season.

As the season gathered pace, the BRM H16 engine started to seem so cumbersome in comparison to its competitors, using too much fuel, too much oil and too much water. Its chronic unreliability was such that I was forced to retire in no fewer than nine of eleven F1 championship races.

Fortunately, I was able to maintain the momentum of my driving career by enjoying a much more successful Formula 2 series, in the Matra MS7–Ford, being run by Ken Tyrrell. In those days, all the leading drivers competed in these races, and victories at the Kanonloppet at Karlskoga in Sweden, the Mediterranean Grand Prix at Enna in Sicily and the Grand Prix of Albi in France sustained my reputation and my self-confidence.

One of the highlights of my year was partnering Chris Amon at the BOAC Brands Hatch six-hour race, and finishing second in the 4 litre Ferrari 330P4, maybe the most beautifully designed racing machine of all time. I had initially been approached by Porsche to drive for them in the race, but when I enquired what I might be getting paid they were somewhat bemused.

'The German drivers in the race drive for the honour,' I was told.

My reply was simple. 'But I'm just a wee Scotsman. I drive for money.'

I ended up in the Ferrari and was behind the wheel for almost five of the six hours because Chris had fallen ill. Our second place confirmed the world championship for the Italians, depriving the Germans who had had a chance of snatching the title if they had won.

Jim Clark continued to thrive in the Lotus 49, winning four F1 races in 1967 but still finishing second behind the new world champion, Denny Hulme of New Zealand. However, Jimmy won the last two races of the season, in the US and Mexico, and seemed to be driving as smoothly and brilliantly as ever. When he triumphed in the first race of 1968 in South Africa, he had won three F1 Grand Prix races in succession.

Then, it was Saturday 7 April 1968. Major races were being run at Hockenheim (Formula 2) and at Brands Hatch (BOAC 1000km sportscar), but I had chosen to take the weekend off and conduct a safety inspection of the circuit at Jarama, near Madrid, on behalf of the GPDA (Grand Prix Drivers' Association). Late in the afternoon, as I was walking round with my notebook and camera, I suddenly saw one of the

Spanish officials driving around the circuit towards me. He stopped and said, in broken English, that he had heard a news report from Hockenheim saying Jim Clark had been involved in a big accident.

'What does that mean?' I asked.

'No know if he live or die,' he replied, understandably stumbling over his words

'Well, you'd better find out for me,' I said.

The official rushed away, and I was left out on the empty circuit, alone. Not Jimmy. Not Jimmy. I felt numbed by the shock but, somehow, in an instant, I managed to rein in my emotions and continue with the inspection. Jimmy was in Germany, so there was nothing I could do to help him. Whatever needed to be done to find out exactly what had happened, the official was much better equipped to do and would understand the Spanish radio better than I could. I was not uncaring. Nobody cared more. My response was typical of the racing driver's mind. Even in the face of the most devastating news and the most intense emotions, our nature is to be precise and clinical.

No more than ten minutes later, the same official returned.

'Clark dead,' he said.

And he said it exactly like that. Someone who spoke English as a first language may have couched the news in gentler words, but there was no mistaking the meaning.

'Who says?' I snapped.

'Radio.'

'You are 100 per cent sure?'

'No.'

I suppose I wasn't ready to accept the news, so I told myself there might have been a mistake. It wasn't confirmed. I was then driven round to the control tower, where I asked if somebody could give me a lift back to the airport in Madrid.

On the way, I suddenly felt a need to speak to Helen, so we

stopped at a small restaurant beside the main road, and I persuaded the owner to let me make a phone call to Scotland. Helen was at home in Helensburgh, packing suitcases because it was this weekend, of all weekends, that we had fixed as the date we would go non-resident and move to Switzerland.

'Hello,' she said, answering the phone.

'Hello, it's me . . . ' I said.

And then there was silence . . . complete silence on the line . . . an awful, empty silence of final confirmation. She didn't have to say anything to me and I didn't have to say anything to her. Jimmy Clark, the man we wanted to be godfather to our second son, Mark, was gone.

'They've just announced it on television,' Helen said, and we both broke down in tears.

The death of Jimmy Clark stunned the world of motor sport. A friend of mine was at Brands Hatch that day and he described the stunned silence that spread across the circuit. This shy and humble man was mourned across Scotland, but the enormous impact of his loss was felt across Britain and Europe, across Australasia, where he had become so familiar during the Tasman Series, and throughout America, where ABC television broadcast a substantial tribute in his honour.

It later transpired Jim had been lying eighth in the European Formula 2 championship race at Hockenheim, trying to make progress with an engine that didn't seem to be giving full power. On lap five, on a wet track, entering a broad, fast right-hander at 160 mph, it was reported that his car seemed to twitch from left to right before travelling almost straight ahead, veering off the left of the track and smashing into a densely wooded area. The force of impact completely destroyed the chassis of the Lotus, and the medics insisted Jim died instantly.

Was it mechanical failure or driver error? Even in wet conditions, it seems inconceivable that Jim could have gone off the track at that particular place without there being a problem.

The spot is today marked by a small, rough stone cross, engraved with his name and the date he died.

Jim Clark's funeral was to be held in Chirnside on 10 April. It was arranged that I would fly from Geneva to Edinburgh, and back, in a private jet with a friend of Jim's and mine called General Lassiter, an ex-brigadier general in the US Air Force who had also moved to live in Switzerland and started Executive Jet Aviation Inc.

The motor racing world seemed to converge on this quiet corner of Scotland – Dan Gurney flew in from California – and the service was remarkable for the dignified courage and stoicism of Jim's parents and his sisters. Welcoming all the mourners in their farmhouse afterwards, they seemed to feel that what had happened was somehow meant to be, and that we should not be sad.

Helen and I were deeply affected by Jimmy's loss and, in many ways, we still miss him today. I remember the days and weeks following his death as among the saddest of my life, so sad that – for the only time during my racing career – I seriously considered whether I should leave the sport.

In low moments, I wondered what my friend would have advised if he were there and I decided he would have smiled in that wonderfully modest way and told me to 'get out there, do what you do best and keep it smooth'. So I did, but after all these years, recalling these events as vividly as if they had happened last week, two facts seem abundantly clear: first, my life was hugely enriched by being a friend of Jimmy Clark; second, my life has been so much poorer because he left, at the age of thirty-two, much too soon.

CHAPTER 7

'Oh No, Not Again'

IMAGINE AN ELEVEN-YEAR WINDOW OF TIME WHEN YOU LOSE FIFTY-SEVEN – repeat fifty-seven – friends and colleagues, often watching them die in horrific circumstances doing exactly what you do, weekend after weekend. Helen and I didn't have to imagine. We lived through it. To be a racing driver between 1963 and 1973 was to accept the probability of death – not the possibility, the probability, because the statistics suggested, during that period, that if a F1 driver was to race for five years or more, he would be more likely to lose his life on the track than to survive and retire.

What the cold statistics don't record is the hush that used to descend over the pit lane when an ambulance appeared . . . the sense of foreboding that spread through this small community when a plume of black smoke rose on the other side of the circuit . . . the unimaginably brutal way people died . . . how it felt to be a driver continuing a race, speeding by and catching a glimpse of a crumpled car or the body of a friend . . . the agony of a devastated wife . . . the fear in the eyes of other wives as they wondered if it might be their turn next.

It would be easy for me to reflect on this element of my career and to say it was tough, but it is in the past, and we have all moved on. It would be easy, but it would not be true.

Hardly a day goes by when I don't think of those who died during that period, particularly my closest friends Jimmy Clark, Jochen Rindt and François Cevert. The sense of loss remains acute. It is always there, lingering just below the surface of my frenetic daily schedule, and every now and then this reservoir overflows, and the grief and the hurt pour over an emotional wall. I still break down in floods of tears. This is odd because, back then, when I was immersed in the aftermath of so many accidents and attending so many funerals, I used to feel pain but I hardly ever cried. I somehow taught myself to compartmentalise my emotions, effectively to lock them in a box and put them away, and that enabled me to do whatever needed to be done, whether it was to make arrangements with undertakers or to make sure the widow was being looked after; and then I would be able to climb back into my car and go racing again.

How do I explain that? Well, I always believed there was a little pouch somewhere inside my chest, and this pouch contained a rich and precious potion that effectively diluted the grief and pain and helped me carry on; but it has emptied as the years have passed, and there is now no potion left, and I find myself feeling more emotional and vulnerable than I ever did when I was racing. A psychologist would probably have a field day with me, analysing the repressed emotions and maybe even detecting a subconscious sense of guilt that, for some reason, I have been allowed to survive and live a full life and enjoy many of the wonderful opportunities so many of my friends were denied.

I don't know. I don't pretend to understand everything. I suppose I have tried to deal with what I saw and what I felt in the best way I could and, by and large, I have managed to get along.

We were so much more than just an itinerant group of professional sportsmen. We were a small, tight-knit group of friends . . . genuine friends who travelled together, always stayed in the same hotels, partied, holidayed together and had wives who became close as well. But every now and then, because we were racing in exposed cars on amazingly dangerous circuits, one of us would have a shunt and be killed. This was the reality of our lives and as drivers we accepted the risk partly because we were paid reasonably well, partly because that was just what we did and mainly because we were stimulated by driving fast and living fast in such an exciting, colourful, intoxicating and glamorous environment.

An analogy has sometimes been drawn between the F1 drivers of the 1960s and 1970s and the squadrons of fighter pilots in the Battle of Britain during World War II, and – accepting the obvious differences between heroes defending their country and those being paid to pursue their sport – there were parallels in the camaraderie that bonded us together and the way we accepted danger as part of the job. Just as they jumped into the cockpits of their Spitfires or Hurricanes on the runway and wished each other well, aware that one or more of them might not come back, so we climbed into the cockpits of our racing cars on the starting grid, conscious that one or more of us may not cross the finish line.

'See you later,' drivers would typically say to each other.

'Let's hope so,' came the reply.

Nobody ever said 'yes', because nobody wanted to tempt fate.

I've heard it said that fighter pilots revered their colleagues killed in combat or an accident, but tended to disown those who lost their lives because of over-confidence. Our thinking was similar. We used to admire the bravery of a driver who pulled a friend from a burning car but despised the misguided 'courage' of anyone who threw their car around the circuit in a way that endangered not only themselves but everyone else as well. The pilots, I'm sure, were able to block out any apprehension when they pulled forward the canopy of their cockpit and prepared to go; in the same way, we managed to pull down our visors and become so consumed by the challenge of driving fast that there was no time to contemplate the danger.

I was first exposed to death at the track on the night Bob MacIntyre died in Chester, and, as I started racing, the harrowing experiences became more vivid and more frequent.

One night I remember watching a Movietone news bulletin in a cinema, and seeing footage of a big crash at the Indianapolis 500. I was staggered by the sheer scale and violence of the accident. Gearboxes were sent flying, engines became detached and were propelled hundreds of metres down the track, and the cars literally disintegrated. I was starting to understand how, in terms of impact and devastation, a high-speed motor racing accident more closely resembles an air crash than any incident on an ordinary road.

Next, on 11 September 1966, there was a major incident at the Grand Prix Ile de France at Montlhery, near Paris. A driver and two marshals were killed, but the race continued, and, as I drove out of the pits in a Ferrari 250 LM, I happened to look to my left and see two dead bodies, shattered beyond recognition, lying just a few metres away from me. This kind of scene was more suited to a medieval battlefield, but my response was to block out all my emotions and stand on the accelerator pedal. Later, when I returned to the pits, I discovered the stopwatches showing I had posted the fastest lap ever recorded in a GT car at the Montlhery circuit during that stint in the car.

Then, during the Monaco Grand Prix of 1967, I remember standing in the pit lane after my car had retired with a mechanical failure, looking towards the chicane, and being shocked to see an inferno of leaping flames and billowing black smoke. Somebody said Lorenzo Bandini had gone off the track. Soon afterwards, there was confirmation Lorenzo had died. And had become another statistic. Helen and I knew him well.

I kept a diary during these years, as I have done ever since. In 1968, the slim booklet was a complimentary gift from a garage in Glasgow and, although the ink is fading, it is still possible to read the entries from the middle of that year as the accumulation of horror and grief reached unprecedented proportions.

7 April: Jimmy crashed.

10 April: Jimmy's funeral.

7 May: Indy practice. Mike crashed.
(Mike Spence had been my F1 team-mate at BRM the previous year and, when a broken wrist meant I was unable to compete in the Indianapolis 500, he was signed to replace me and drive the exciting new Granatelli STP Lotus 56 turbine. I attended the practice session at the race track when Mike had an accident at Turn 1. His front right wheel came off, bounced and hit him on the head. The impact sent him into a deep coma. I went to the hospital that evening, hoping he might somehow recover, but he didn't. Mike died that same night. Distressed, upset and far from home, I was left to come to terms with the loss of a friend and the fact that it should have been me driving that car.)

8 June: Ludovico crashed.
(Ludovico Scarfiotti was an impeccably mannered gentleman, a nephew of Fiat chief Gianni Agnelli and a hugely popular home winner of the Italian Grand Prix in 1966. He had been my team-mate with Maranello

Concessionaires on that grim weekend at Montlhery, and even now I can picture him at the wheel of a Ferrari, wearing a blazer and bow tie, with no helmet. He had been practising before the relatively minor Rossfeld hill climb in Bavaria, Germany, when a reported technical failure sent his car off the road, crashing into some trees, and he was killed.)

7 July: French GP. Jo crashed.
(Jo Schlesser was an effervescent Frenchman and a good pal of Guy Ligier, the former international rugby player who became a successful driver and team owner. Honda had developed an experimental air-cooled F1 car, which the team entered for the French Grand Prix at Rouen-les-Essarts, and, as the crowd's favourite, Jo was hired to be the driver.

On the third lap, going downhill very fast, the Honda left the track at the Six Frères corner, spinning and smashing violently into a bank. The full load of fuel ignited, and the magnesium-bodied car exploded. Jo never stood a chance.

The burning fuel ran across the track, feeding a horrific wall of fire. The race continued and, each time we passed the scene of the accident, the rest of us literally had to drive blind through the flames, smoke and debris. It had been raining heavily, and the spray dramatically reduced visibility. I had rarely felt frightened in a car, but I did that day at Rouen. And Jo was dead.)

Four established drivers had been killed on the same weekend of four successive months, but the season had to carry on, and it did. There is a photograph, taken in July 1968, which shows a dozen F1 drivers sitting on three benches. Everybody looks happy and relaxed, smiling and joking with each other. It's amazing. I look at the photo now and, recalling what we were all living through, I wonder how we coped.

I am always wary of drawing parallels between generations

– and, of course, the sport has changed beyond recognition – but I don't believe today's F1 racing drivers have any understanding at all of what we experienced. They simply have no conception of how it felt to travel around the world, as they do, to race week after week, as they do, and to lose people you care for on a regular basis . . . and I hope to God they never find out. We just got on with the job. That's all we could do, and each of us dealt with the losses in our own way.

For me, the grief quickly turned to anger. I wanted answers.

Why were so many of my friends being killed?

Why did our community have to cope with so much carnage?

Why were people so regularly walking down the pit lane, saying: 'Oh no, not again,' and shaking their heads?

Why was I, who had always felt composed and had always been superstitious about not being superstitious, suddenly finding myself unable even to glance at a cemetery, whether I was driving past one in a car or flying over one in a plane?

Why did I look in my rear view mirror every time I left home to race at Spa or the Nurburgring and see our house fill the frame and wonder whether I would survive to see it again?

Why did we all attend a dinner at the end of the year and bow our heads in memory of those who had died but do nothing to prevent more drivers being killed the next year?

Why was the chief medical officer at one circuit a gynaecologist with minimal experience of neurology, burns or internal medicine, who apparently got the job because he was an enthusiast?

I decided my first response should be to do everything within my control to minimise the downside risks I faced as a racing driver. I owed that much to Helen and the boys.

First, I found a highly qualified doctor in Switzerland, and arranged for him to be present at each of my races. I paid him well to look after me. Dr Marty held degrees in seven areas of medicine but he was principally an anaesthetist and, according to all my research, if I did have a serious accident, it was expert anaesthetics that would keep me alive. If required, he would be able to jump-start me and keep me going until I reached the nearest specialist hospital best equipped to deal with whatever life-threatening injuries I might have suffered.

'Have you heard? Stewart's got himself a personal doctor!'

Nobody had taken such a precaution before and some people scoffed. I didn't mind what they said, but I was annoyed when officials at certain tracks denied Dr Marty access to the medical centre, claiming he was not required, saying he needed a licence and suggesting his presence was an insult to their doctors. I told them he was not there to perform operations, but his role was to supervise any treatment that it might become necessary to give me. Most of them, but not all, grudgingly allowed him to stay. Their antagonism was ridiculous because I was certainly aware that several drivers had died unnecessarily because they had not received adequate medical support.

The second element of my initiative was to compile and maintain a comprehensive list of leading specialists in each country that I raced. So, if I was competing in Argentina, I would make sure we had the name and contact numbers of the leading orthopaedic surgeon, the leading neurologist and the leading burns man in Buenos Aires and I would telephone each of them in advance and make them aware of my situation. Again, some people ridiculed my idea. Again, I didn't mind because I knew that, if I had a big accident, any one of these doctors could turn out to be the person who saved my life.

The greater challenge was to prevent 'the worst' happening in the first place, and the only group capable of leading an effective campaign for improved safety measures at the circuits was the Grand Prix Drivers' Association (GPDA). Membership was by invitation only and was restricted to F1 drivers who were current and established; for example, we would not invite somebody who had competed in only a handful of races.

Some progress had been made, and the GPDA had started to send drivers to undertake track inspections at the circuits, as I was doing at Jarama, near Madrid, on the day of Jim Clark's accident; and we would politely request the removal of unnecessary hazards at key points.

'Does that telegraph pole have to be there, right beside the track at the exit of the corner?'

'Could those trees be removed, please?'

The response of the governing body and the track owners was sometimes constructive but often obstructive. In 1968, for example, the authorities at Brands Hatch were asked to install a crash barrier in front of trees right beside the track. 'It's not necessary,' they replied. 'They're only small trees.'

Jo Bonnier served as president of the GPDA and was followed by Graham Hill. In 1968, I was elected to the position and began to lead the campaign.

'What happens if a car goes off the track here?' I would ask.

'It's OK, Stewart,' irritated officials would reply, 'we have grass banks to stop the cars.'

'They're no good, they're just launch pads.'

Some officials were more cooperative, and an innovative Dutchman called John Hugenholtz, track manager at Zandvoort, developed a kind of chain-link fencing, which was installed in three rows, and offered a deformable structure that 'collected' the car at high speed and effectively reduced the impact. A racing car hitting one of these fences resembled a tennis ball hitting a net and, for some time, they seemed to work well.

However, in due course, it emerged that if a car turned over during an accident, this chain-link fencing had a tendency to wrap itself around the car and finish up looking like a rolled-up carpet, trapping the driver in the cockpit – this happened to

Jack Brabham at Zandvoort, and he was fortunate to escape unharmed.

The next product was the Armco barrier, which was corrugated steel bolted to metal uprights, which could be used as single strips, or as two or three on top of each other. These were typically installed in front of trees, buildings or drop-offs and they were positioned in such a way that, in the event of impact, cars would be more likely to take a relatively safe glancing blow rather than a head-on collision.

I became an enthusiastic advocate of these barriers, to a point where people used to say that, if anyone wanted to know where Jackie Stewart lived, they only had to follow the Armco barriers. We began to ask every track owner to have these potentially life-saving barriers installed around their circuits. We didn't stop there. The GPDA also started to demand that every F1 driver should be compelled to wear flameproof overalls, thermal underwear, officially certified helmets, six-point safety belts or harnesses, and high-quality thermal socks and gloves to provide effective protection against burns.

Through 1968 and into 1969, we resembled dogs with a bone. In every interview, at every opportunity, we raised the issue of safety, alternating dire warnings with new demands. At one stage, the team owners said they agreed with everything we were saying but asked if we couldn't give the circuits more time to make the changes. No, we said, because that could be one year too long for some driver, and his widow and his family. We were adamant, and insistent.

As time passed, unhelpfully but maybe unavoidably, what was always a GPDA campaign became increasingly personalised and identified with me. As president, I was more often the spokesman in the media, but the situation was not helped when the GPDA would take a decision and, under pressure from some team owners, some of my colleagues would back off and say, 'Well, it was Jackie who told us to do that.'

People were getting irritated. I kept talking about unnecessary hazards. People were getting annoyed. I kept talking about barriers. People were getting angry. I kept talking.

Eventually, the guns were turned on me. Letters began to appear in motor magazines.

'There is little in motor racing today for which I can thank Stewart,' wrote T. C. W Peacock. 'I have enjoyed the motor racing scene less since he arrived rattling his money box and waving his petitions . . . It is unthinkable for any professional to accept the challenge and then try to change the rules to make it all safe and cosy. This is plain cheating. Perhaps this insecure driver, diarist and emotional motorist should concern himself with the less dangerous but equally lucrative world of entertainment.'

G. W. Binks put pen to paper in similar vein: 'I feel your magazine underrates the problem that motor racing has with Stewart. Really we have had enough of this timidity of his. I suggest he retires to Switzerland and leaves motor racing to the men. I hope your excellent magazine will see fit to defend the sport from Stewart's attempt to eradicate all risk, except that of his being run over on the way to his bank.'

Many leading journalists joined the attack. Denis Jenkinson was the doyen of the era, and I respected his writing enormously. He had excelled in the sport himself, riding in the sidecar for world champion Eric Oliver and navigating for Stirling Moss in the famous Mille Miglia. It was heroic stuff, and he believed the essence of motor sport was the courage and passion of the driver. In his view, our campaign was too clinical; he saw it as the head overruling the heart.

I took issue with an article he wrote in *Motor Sport* magazine and sent a response, which was published in the following edition: 'I have tried terribly hard, devoting considerable time and effort to make motor racing as a whole for as many people as possible – officials, spectators, drivers and even journalists –

safer than it has been in the past. The sport will never be totally safe, and I perhaps know that better than Mr Jenkinson could ever know, but it is imperative that people act in a positive and constructive way to bring race track safety, medical and fire-fighting facilities up to modern standards.

'It is very easy to sit on the fence and criticise. All Mr Jenkinson seems to do is lament the past and the drivers who served their time in it. Few of them, however, are alive to read his writings. There is nothing more tragically sad than mourning a man who has died in circumstances that could easily have been avoided. Therefore, it always angers me when people oppose measures to make our sport safer.'

We evidently disagreed but, in later years, Denis and I spent more time together and even drove some cars together. He was a genuine eccentric, who was always stimulating company, and I remember one occasion, long after he retired, when I heard him say, 'Stewart's all right.' That was just about as good as it got from 'Jenks' and it was one of the more important compliments I have received in my life.

In the late 1960s, even some of the drivers reckoned we were pushing too hard. At one stage in the pit lane, I looked up to see Innes Ireland flapping his elbows and making chicken noises at me. Innes was the first Scot ever to win a F1 Grand Prix, when he triumphed at Watkins Glen in 1960. He was a broad, brave character who enjoyed his shooting and fishing and, at one stage, was captain and owner of his own trawler. I liked and admired him but, on this issue, we differed.

Still, I kept talking about safety. It was not much fun being portrayed as a loud-mouthed troublemaker set on ruining the spirit of a great sport, and there was worse abuse than that. My response was to talk about safety in a TV interview before a Grand Prix, get in my car, drive as strongly and as quickly as anybody else, if possible win the Grand Prix and then get out of the car and go to the press conference and start talking about safety all over again. Of course, my life would have been much easier, less tiring and less stressful if we had stopped talking, but the issue would then have petered out, and little would have been changed. Our friends were being killed! We had to keep talking, and keep working at the situation.

On the afternoon of 2 June 1970, I happened to be in Paris, attending a book launch with a great friend of mine called Michel Finquel, who used to make my racing overalls. He had called his office and received a message from my secretary to say Bruce McLaren had died while testing his M8D CanAm McLaren car at Goodwood.

'Bruce is dead,' he said.

'Oh no, not again,' I replied.

It transpired a piece of the rear bodywork had flown off at 130 mph, and the New Zealander's car veered off and crashed heavily into an obstacle, built to protect a marshal's post no longer in use. It did not have to be there. The car could have and should have glanced off a proper Armco barrier, or merely spun across the grass. A human body simply does not survive immediate deceleration from 130 mph to zero. There was no fire, but Bruce died instantly, and his wife Pat became a widow. I remember talking to Jochen Rindt soon afterwards, and I'll never forget his words. 'Nobody is immune,' he said sadly.

The Dutch Grand Prix was held just over a fortnight later, on 21 June 1970, and our small, happy band of drivers, together with their wives or girlfriends, and the teams, gathered at the Circuit Zandvoort, just outside the resort town of the same name on the northern coast of the Netherlands.

Race day brought a familiar scene with the drivers and mechanics busy in the pit lane, and the various wives sitting in a row on the pit counters, holding stopwatches and assisting their respective teams by doing lap charts and taking lap times. As Helen told me later, there was herself, Lyn Oliver, Sally Courage, Bette Hill, Nina Rindt, Marianne Bonnier and others, and the race started without incident, and all seemed well as each car passed the start/finish line, completed a lap, passed by again, on and on . . . until the twenty-third lap, when there was no Piers Courage.

Just then, every head seemed to turn and notice a cloud of pitch-black smoke rising from the far end of the track, and, in an instant, that horribly familiar chill of dread descended upon the pits.

'Who is missing?' Nina asked.

'It's No. 4,' somebody replied.

That was Piers' car.

At first, apparently someone told Frank Williams his driver was unhurt in the accident, so the team owner waited for the ambulance to return, but ten minutes passed and it was clear that he was becoming concerned. He had told Sally he would bring Piers straight to her, but now he could not be sure.

More confusion followed, with people speaking Dutch, until Frank was eventually informed by Eric Corschmidt, the head of the governing body in Holland, that Piers was dead. Frank has told me that he asked him to repeat it three times before he was prepared to accept the news. It was a most terrible day for Frank but, characteristically, he took it upon himself to telephone Piers' parents back in England and inform them what had happened to their son. Sally was quietly led away by Louis Stanley, with Nina in support. Everybody rallied round, and Helen was later asked to go back to the Palace hotel, where we were all staying, to pack Piers' and Sally's belongings. She remembers pausing for a moment in their room and noticing the imprint of his head still on the pillow.

Out on the circuit, with the race continuing, the moment when we, as his fellow drivers and his friends, realised what had happened was no less poignant and no easier to bear.

Heir to the Courage Breweries empire, Piers was an Old Etonian who was determined to make something of his life through his own efforts rather than his inheritance, and he used to wear a pale-blue helmet with a single black stripe, broken diagonally, running from front to back. That day he was driving a De Tomaso and, for some reason, on a very fast part of the circuit, towards the end of the lap, he veered off the track and hurtled into a grass-covered sand bank. The car dug in, rolled and was quickly engulfed by flames.

The first time I drove past the fire, I glanced quickly to my left but could not make out any markings on the car with all the flames, fumes and smoke. The next time I passed, the blaze was still raging but, amid the debris and burning rubble, I spotted Piers' helmet lying in the middle of the track; and in that moment, I knew the worst because, if Piers had been OK, he would have taken that with him.

The race ran its course, Jochen won and I finished second, but nobody was celebrating on the podium. Our thoughts were with Sally, the Courage family, Frank and his team, and what needed to be done.

'Jackie,' somebody asked, 'how do we get Piers back to England?'

I thought we would have to find space on a cargo plane because, in those days, few passenger airlines were prepared to carry coffins, and the coffin would have to be lined in lead or zinc, but I didn't know any undertakers in Holland, so I telephoned my most reliable source of sensitive information – a man called Andre Dimonte, who was head concierge at the Carlton Towers Hotel in London – and asked if he could find out the name and contact number of the best international undertaker in Amsterdam. He called me back within minutes, and I was able to make a start on the enormous volume of arrangements that had to be made.

First Bruce, now Piers. We had passed the stage where our campaign for safety could be waged with track inspections and press conferences. It was time, I felt, for us to raise the stakes.

Our next GPDA meeting was held on 24 June 1970, immediately after we had all attended a beautiful memorial service for Bruce at St Paul's Cathedral. Louis Stanley served as GPDA secretary, and we arranged to meet in the palatial surroundings of his usual suite at the Dorchester hotel, in London.

Emotions were running high.

'Gentlemen, we have reached a crucial moment,' I began. 'Bruce and Piers are dead, and I think it is fair to say both might well have survived if the governing bodies and circuit owners had listened to what we have been saying for the past three years.

'People say they agree, but nothing gets done. When Piers' car burst into flames, there was not even enough of the appropriate fire-fighting equipment to extinguish the car. This is ridiculous. How long are we going to let the organisers be so careless and disrespectful with our lives? We must do more.

'I think we have reached a point where we need to be strong. We must say we will not race at any circuit that fails to implement the safety measures we have requested. And this is not a Jackie Stewart issue, it's a GPDA thing, so let's have a debate and decide together.'

An animated discussion followed, and it soon became clear that a significant number of the eleven F1 drivers in the room had major reservations about my approach.

'We're paid to drive,' someone said. 'We can't say where and when we will race.'

'Look,' I replied. 'Two weeks ago, I did a track inspection at the Nurburgring. It's the greatest circuit in the world, no question. I know that, but currently it's also stupidly dangerous. There are 14.7 miles of track, and there's hardly a barrier to be seen on either side. That means they're short of 29.4 miles of guard rail. There are just trees and who knows what. So I told the owners what needed to be done. I was fair and logical. I went right around the circuit, saying this needs to be put right here and that needs to be sorted out there, and they just said no. They refused. I'm sorry, but I just can't accept that.'

'Boycott the Nurburgring? You're out of your mind.'

'If doing that saves one life, yes we should.'

'Jackie, you just can't do that.'

'Why not? There are huge fir trees two feet in diameter right next to the track. There are places when you come to a corner and you see small Christmas trees ahead of you. It's only when you actually walk the track that you realise those aren't small Christmas trees – there is a huge drop-off and what you are seeing is just the tops of trees that are at least 100 feet tall. It's crazy. It's that dangerous, so why should we race there?'

'Look, even if you're right, we're drivers and it's not our job to make these decisions.'

'So who will make them?'

'The governing body.'

'The governing body has done nothing!'

'People will say we're scared.'

That particular remark provoked Jochen Rindt.

'I am not scared of anything,' said the Austrian. 'But if my car has a technical failure, and goes off the track at 150 mph, I would certainly prefer not to smash into a tree.'

The GPDA was divided. It seemed the vote could go either way, and I was starting to consider whether I ought to resign as president if it went against me. Then, Jack Brabham spoke. The Australian was a hard man on the track, as tough to pass as anyone, three times world champion and widely respected. 'I have listened,' he said, paused, and then added: 'and I agree with Jackie.'

The vote was held soon afterwards, and we decided by seven to two with two abstentions that we would send Jochen, as a German speaker, to inform the authorities at the Nurburgring that we would not race at their circuit unless they implemented the eighteen safety measures we had identified.

The reality was that, with only thirty-nine days until the scheduled date of the German Grand Prix, there was not enough time to make the changes, and this was confirmed not long afterwards with the formal announcement that the race would be switched to the lesser, but safer, circuit at Hockenheim.

Media reaction to the news was predictably hostile, particularly towards me, and I received a series of death threats from Germany. Of course I recognised the serious impact of our decision on the economy of the Eifel region, and I understood the anger of 375,000 spectators who would have watched the race at the Nurburgring.

The irony was that, while I was being cast as the enemy of the place, I actually revered 'The Ring', and I took enormous pride in being elected as a '*Ringmeister*' after I won there in 1968. I affectionately christened the circuit as the 'Green Hell', a name that seems to have stuck over the years and is featured in the museum they have there, and I have always joked that if anybody says they enjoyed driving around the Nurburgring, they're either lying or they weren't going fast enough. However, notwithstanding all the history and prestige, the fact remained that, at that time, the track was simply too dangerous, and we could not compromise on safety.

During the weekend at Hockenheim, I started to grow weary of the glowering antagonism and hostility and, when my gear-box forced me to retire from the race after the twenty-second lap, Helen and I decided we might as well drive to Frankfurt airport and catch the next flight out of there. Nowadays F1 drivers are not allowed to leave a circuit until the Grand Prix has ended, but back then we could leave as soon as were out of the race.

So it was still quite early when we arrived in London, and we decided to go and see a movie. We watched *Midnight*

Cowboy at the Odeon Marble Arch, and when we stepped out of the cinema – I remember it so clearly, as if it was yesterday – Helen and I suddenly had absolutely no idea where we were. We looked around, and neither of us knew what country or what city we were in. Was that Marble Arch or the Arc de Triomphe? Was it Paris or London? We categorically did not know. It was a surreal moment. Perhaps we were simply physically and emotionally exhausted.

This strange flash of confusion was followed by a sublime sense of peace. On this idyllic, balmy English summer's evening, we strolled into Hyde Park, past the animated orators at Speaker's Corner and into the wide open spaces. It almost felt as though we had escaped into another world, a million miles away from all the anger and controversy of the past few days and weeks, as we wandered anonymously through the happy crowds. It really was an extraordinary experience in both of our lives.

Maybe the criticism was getting to me. Even if I seemed to be generally upbeat and chirpy, I certainly wasn't bullet-proof, and it hurt when people said I was somehow working against the sport. I wished they could understand that it was possible for me to campaign for safety and still to love my motor racing.

Perhaps they would have been surprised to know that, even while we were sitting in that GPDA meeting at the Dorchester hotel, the racing bug was still biting. As we were discussing what to do about the Nurburgring, I was called away to take a telephone call from America. It was Jim Hall, inviting me to drive the 'Chapparal' in a sports car event at Watkins Glen, and, even in the middle of all that, I found myself getting as excited about the prospect of being behind the wheel of such a special car as I had at any stage of my life. I instantly accepted his offer because the Chapparal was known as the most advanced racing car of its time. It was called 'the vacuum cleaner' because it was designed with a small additional secondary engine which removed the turbulent air from beneath the car and effectively sucked it to the ground.

Jochen Rindt was dominating the 1970 season with Lotus, and, as we arrived at Monza for the Italian Grand Prix in the first week of September, I was teasing my serious and sometimes dour Austrian friend about how he would cope with the media onslaught when, as everyone expected, he became world champion.

'You'll have to do a bit more smiling for the cameras, you know,' I told him.

Helen and I had become extremely close to Jochen and Nina Rindt, and we were so pleased when they bought a piece of land from Jo Bonnier and started to build their own house close to us, in a village overlooking Lake Geneva in Switzerland. At the time we left for the Italian Grand Prix, they were renting a place which belonged to the former heavyweight world champion, the Swedish boxer Ingemar Johansson.

Jochen and I had grown up together in F1 racing, and he was one of the most sincere men I ever knew, who said what he thought and, as a result, upset as many people as he befriended. If he didn't agree with the way someone led their life, he ignored them and refused even to acknowledge their presence.

I also admired him tremendously as a driver and, even though he had waited six seasons to win his first F1 Grand Prix, he seemed to relax and mature after that victory at Watkins Glen in 1969 and he proceeded to win five Grands Prix during the 1970 season. It looked as though he was no longer forcing or overdriving the car, as he recognised that 'loosening the reins' invariably generates speed.

We trusted each other completely on the track, developing a kind of mutual understanding that I had not known since the Jimmy Clark days. Jochen and I never put each other in trouble, even if we were in opposing teams, for example by going into a corner heavy-handed, daring to see who would chicken out.

In practice on the Saturday afternoon at Monza, amid all the crowds and excitement, Jochen seemed to be driving the Lotus 72 as smoothly and efficiently as he had all season . . . until, approaching the braking area before the Parabolica, his car swerved sharply to the left and crashed into a barrier. Subsequent reports suggested one of his front brake shafts had failed. Denny Hulme was driving immediately behind him, and the New Zealander's first instinct was that Jochen was OK, so he completed the lap and, instead of stopping in his own McLaren area, he drove on to the Lotus pit, where he told Colin Chapman and the rest of the team what had happened. Bernie Ecclestone was Jochen's business partner at the time so as soon as he heard about the shunt he ran out to the Parabolica to see for himself what had happened.

I heard the news from Peter Gethin, the other McLaren driver, who had stopped at the Tyrrell pit, and I immediately went to find Nina sitting on the pit counter. I told her I would find out what was happening and come back to her. So I ran along to the control tower and asked the officials. The clerk of the course didn't want to talk to me. That was odd. I was the reigning world champion, and he was ignoring me.

'Come on, what's the story?' I persisted.

'Well, we think he's out of the car,' he said.

'OK, so where is he?'

'He's in the field hospital.'

The behaviour of the officials unsettled me, and I sprinted through the crowds and arrived at the medical compound, which was fenced in. There was a guard on the gate, who recognised me and let me in.

I looked around . . . and saw Jochen. He was lying on the back of an open Volkswagen pick-up truck, and there was nobody attending to him, which shocked me. His head seemed to be propped up, but his eyes were closed. I looked more closely and saw he had a serious open wound at his left ankle and foot. It wasn't bleeding.

In that moment, I knew Jochen had gone.

As a Catholic priest approached him and seemed to start administering the last rites, I hurried back to the pits and found that Nina and Helen had left. Someone told me Colin Chapman had gone with them, but in all the confusion nobody could say where. I ran back to the medical compound and found that Jochen had been moved. They said he had been taken in an ambulance, and Nina, Helen and Colin were with him.

There was nothing more I could do. So I returned to the pits and told Ken Tyrrell where I had been and what I had seen. I said I was convinced Jochen was dead.

The track was closed while repairs were made to the barriers that Jochen's car had struck, so I sat quietly in the pit, trying to gather my emotions. Maybe another twenty-five minutes passed before Ken walked over, said the track was open and solemnly suggested I should put my helmet on and complete the practice session. Jochen had literally just been killed on the track, but our team was preparing to get me back into my car so I could go out again.

That was our reality and recalling these events makes me so grateful that safety procedures and the entire racing environment have improved so dramatically over the years. What we have in F1 motor racing today is heaven. What we had in the late 1960s and the early 1970s was hell.

As I prepared to drive again, my head was full of sadness, confusion and thoughts of Jochen and Nina, and I felt the tears welling. It was too much, and I started to cry. I don't think anybody saw because I was wearing my racing helmet and my tinted visor was down. Perhaps Roger Hill and Roy Topp, my two mechanics who, as usual, were busy strapping me into the car, might have detected something unusual in my breathing pattern or in the way my chest was heaving. I don't know.

As I accelerated out of the pit lane, I could taste the salt of my own tears.

My first lap was an out lap and relatively slow, and, reaching the Parabolica, I took a long look to my left at the scene of Jochen's accident. The second lap was a little faster and, by now completely focused on the car, my third lap turned out to be the fastest lap I had ever recorded at Monza.

At least one journalist wrote later that I had driven with a kind of death wish and that, after Jochen's death, I didn't care any more. That was wrong. For those six or seven minutes, I was able to remove the emotions and exert clinical control over my mind, exactly as Jochen would have done if it had been me who had crashed. The truth is that I drove no differently from normal. It was just an exceptionally good lap.

Roger Hill was holding the signal board with my lap time when I drove down the pit road, and I recognised it was fast but, as I brought the car to a halt, the awful reality of the day overwhelmed me again. I stopped and stood up, and the tears started all over again. John Lindsay was with me that week in Monza, and my best friend passed me a bottle of Coca-Cola. I took two swigs and almost unconsciously hurled the bottle with all my force against the concrete wall. It smashed into smithereens. Nobody said a word. That was completely out of character for me, and it never happened again.

Jochen had been taken to hospital in Milan, where he was pronounced dead on arrival. In Italy, few if any drivers were declared dead at a track because, if a fatality occurs, there had to be an inquiry before the event could proceed. That could take weeks, and organisers didn't want that to happen. Once again, plunged into another tragedy, our small community rallied round. Helen stayed with Nina all the time at the hospital and brought her back to the hotel. Nina flew to

Geneva that evening, and arrived to find her great friend Sally Courage had already flown in from London and was there at the house, offering her support and helping with Natasha, the Rindts' two-year-old daughter. Sally had heard the news and immediately driven to the airport and caught a flight. A racing widow of only three months herself, she knew better than anyone what Nina was facing.

The Grand Prix took place the following day, and I finished second to Clay Regazzoni driving a Ferrari, but the result didn't seem to matter. Jochen's team-mate at Lotus, an Englishman called John Miles, was so affected by what had happened that he never drove another F1 Grand Prix.

Helen and I then flew straight back to Geneva that evening, and spent time with Nina and her parents.

More than 30,000 people attended Jochen's funeral in Graz the following week, as Austria mourned the loss of a sporting hero and I contemplated the death of another great friend. The unanimous view of the drivers in mourning was that Jochen deserved to be crowned world champion, albeit posthumously.

However, three races remained, and, when Jacky Ickx won the following Grand Prix in Canada, it became clear that if he won the last two races of the season, in the USA and Mexico, he would finish with 46 points, one ahead of the 45 points that Jochen had secured before his accident.

So we moved on to Watkins Glen, where Jacky was leading the race at one stage, with me in pursuit, when his car suffered a mechanical failure and forced him to withdraw (as did I later on), leaving Emerson Fittipaldi to win the race for Lotus. The result confirmed Jochen Rindt as the 1970 F1 world champion.

As I prepared to leave, I happened to notice a small banner in the main stand. It was not being waved. It was being held perfectly still and, in silver letters on black, it read: 'JOCHEN LIVES'.

The annual FIA awards dinner was held, as usual, in lavish

surroundings on the Place de la Concorde in Paris, and I was pleased to be given the emotional task of presenting the F1 world championship trophy to Nina, who accepted on behalf of her late husband.

Even now, almost forty years on, I find it difficult to accept what happened. I understand part of it: how it happens in a split second . . . how you can be driving with no problem . . . you are the master of your car . . . in complete control of everything around you . . . you feel you can do almost anything . . . you can put the car on the same mark in the road every lap . . . then something breaks, and you know it's a mechanical problem . . . all your senses go into defensive mode . . . in that moment, you cease to be the driver and you become a passenger . . . you are just along for the ride . . . you try to regain control . . . you never give up.

If you are an experienced driver, you know what to do: millisecond fast, you work out what you're going to hit, you take your hands off the steering wheel and, in that last split second before impact, you cross your arms across your chest, and you hope. In that moment, your life hangs in the balance, and you are at the mercy of the fates. You might smash into a tree beside the track and be killed instantly like Jimmy, or you might hit a grassed sandbank and burst into flames like Piers, or you might crash into a barrier and die like Jochen.

Or you might be amazingly lucky like me on one occasion at Watkins Glen when I spun at 140 mph and the car veered on to the grass and towards two bridge parapets, and passed clean between them without touching either. The car hardly decelerated, so I steered it back on to the track and rejoined the fray . . . and the strange thing is I didn't tell anybody what had happened. I didn't need to. Life just moved on.

Jochen had gone off the track at Monza in a spot where there was 40 feet of grass and one small barrier. He could easily have steered back on the tarmac and continued the practice. He could easily have hit the barrier in a way that might have damaged the Lotus but left him unharmed. In fact, his car crashed into the base of an upright in just the wrong way, and that was that.

Not long ago, I was browsing through Heinz Prueller's biography of Jochen, and I came across the account of a conversation between the two just before he died.

'I want to retire when I become world champion,' Jochen said.

'But, if you won the title, wouldn't you want to continue and try to beat Jimmy Clark's record of winning the most Grands Prix?'

'No,' Jochen replied, 'look where Jimmy is now.'

Helen and I kept losing people close to us, among others Jo Siffert at Brands Hatch in 1971, Jo Bonnier at Le Mans in 1972 and François Cevert at Watkins Glen in 1973.

Spurred on, perhaps, by those dreadful events, the GPDA continued to pursue the safety campaign and we sparked more controversy during 1973 when we took a decision that we would not race at Spa-Francorchamps unless safety measures were implemented. Spa and the Nurburgring were regarded as the two most prestigious circuits in the world, and our blunt refusal to race there was regarded throughout the sport as a kind of sacrilege. The race was moved to Zolder, and we had to take action again when the tarmac started to break up during practice. Immediately after the end of practice on the Saturday afternoon, we informed the track owners we would not race unless the surface was repaired. The work was done overnight.

It was my job as GPDA president to act as a spokesman, both in discussions with the owners and the governing body and in dealing with the media, with the result that, yet again, our collective decisions became personalised, and the responsibility for 'causing all the trouble' was pinned squarely on me.

'I wish Stewart would just shut up and drive,' somebody said.

'He's always got a problem with something,' another added.

In these circumstances, the eventual result of the 1973 Belgian Grand Prix at Zolder – a Tyrrell one-two, with me winning and François Cevert coming second – was perhaps not the most popular outcome.

The F1 drivers had established extraordinary power and influence within the sport, but 1973 proved to be a high-water mark, and the governing body of the sport and other parties gradually started to erode this position to a point where, as the years passed, the GPDA was left with few teeth.

The torch of the safety campaign was eventually passed to a remarkable man called Professor Sid Watkins, the teaching professor of neurosurgery at the Royal London Hospital. Appointed Chief Medical Officer of the FIA in 1978, he proved to be magnificently strong and resolute, a pillar of integrity. I recall one occasion when Prof. Watkins, as everyone called him, said there should be a helicopter on hand at every F1 race, so a seriously injured person could be taken to hospital as quickly as possible. The authorities agreed.

Sid wasn't finished. 'That's fine,' he added, 'and if someone is injured and the helicopter takes them to hospital, the practice session or the race obviously has to be stopped.'

'Why?'

'Well, there would then not be a helicopter available if someone else was injured.'

'What about the TV coverage?'

'Well, in that case, you will need to have two helicopters at every circuit.'

The chances of two drivers being seriously injured, and needing to be taken to hospital by helicopter at the same time, were quite small, but Sid made his point calmly and got his way.

Prof. Watkins almost single-handedly improved human and

technical resources at the tracks to a point where today's F1 medical centres are better equipped than most major hospitals to deal with the kinds of injury typically suffered in single-seater racing cars. He proved able to remain removed from the politics and to focus on the key measures that were necessary and he has made a historic contribution to the sport. He has become a great friend of mine and has grown close to many, many people involved in the sport, the drivers and the teams, and their respective families. If the child of a mechanic happened to contract measles, the parents would take him to Prof. Watkins, who would cheerfully prescribe the medicine.

The combined effect of the GPDA campaign in the late 1960s and early 1970s and Prof. Watkins' efforts over twenty-six years until his retirement in 2004 prompted nothing less than a revolution in F1 Grand Prix racing, absolutely transforming the sport in terms of its safety procedures and saving lives, and the benefits of these advances and improved regulations have rippled through every form of motor sport worldwide.

At the time of going to press, nobody has lost their life in F1 racing since the weekend of the 1994 San Marino Grand Prix, when Roland Ratzenberger and Ayrton Senna were killed at Imola, in Italy. This is a remarkable record, and a wonderful example of good risk management. It pleases nobody more than me. However, it is no cause for complacency. F1 racing remains an inherently dangerous sport. It can hardly be otherwise when cars are racing a few centimetres apart at speeds in excess of 200 mph, or 320 kph. As much as ever, it remains the responsibility of the drivers and the governing body constantly to review the safety procedures and never, ever to believe safety has ceased to be a priority.

I stress: it is the responsibility of the drivers as well as the officials. Technologists and scientists can assist, but it will always be the men behind the wheel who are most intimate with the risks. For this reason, I believe motor racing would benefit if the GPDA was awakened and its authority restored to the level of years gone by. The moment is ripe for one or more of the current generation of drivers to pick up the torch and carry it forward and seek to make the sport even safer.

Nobody should ever forget that any F1 racing driver is always just a mechanical failure or a tiny error away from paying the ultimate price. Just like fifty-seven of my friends and colleagues.

CHAPTER 8

Family Tyrrell

To be competitive, I would have to find a new team. This blunt reality became increasingly clear as the BRM H16 struggled through the 1967 F1 season. It was not something I wanted to accept, partly because it wasn't in my nature to jump ship – I have always preferred to stick to situations and try to make them work – and partly because I knew Tony Rudd and his team were working hard to make us something more than midfield runners. There was talk of a new V12 engine, but as the year rolled on, each spark of optimism seemed to be squashed by the dead weight of poor results. The engine was a 16-cylinder H configuration, something never seen in modern F1 racing; it was unnecessarily large, used more fuel, carried more oil and needed more water – all of which added weight and diminished the vehicle's agility. I wondered what to do and eventually faced a choice between signing for the most prestigious and glamorous motor racing team in the world and joining a private entrant from Surrey with no F1 experience. It turned out to be the most important decision of my career as a racing driver, and the best.

One afternoon, after another mechanical failure in the BRM, I was talking to Keith Ballisat, formerly a driver for Tyrrell in Formula Junior racing who had become competitions manager for Shell, the company that supplied fuel and lubricants to several F1 teams, notably BRM and a well-known Italian organisation.

'How are things going?' Keith asked.

'Not well,' I replied.

'I've been talking to the people at Ferrari.'

'And what did they have to say?'

'They're interested.'

'Really?'

'Yes. Do you think you could visit Maranello and have a look around?'

'I could do that,' I replied, 'but we'd have to keep it quiet.'

'OK, I'll let them know.'

A trip was arranged, and Keith and I were met at the airport in Milan by a senior Ferrari executive called Franco Gozzi, who drove us to the team headquarters in the type of high-performance sports car that was always going to attract the attention of a racing driver like me.

We arrived at Maranello to find Enzo Ferrari himself standing at the gates. The legendary 'Commendatore' cut a familiar figure – snow-white hair swept back, pitch-black sunglasses, shirt and braces, no jacket – and he seemed to have gone to some trouble to make sure he was there to welcome me in person. I couldn't work out whether he had been waiting, or whether he was just there by chance or whether, in this age before mobile phones, he had installed some kind of early-warning system – whatever the explanation, I was pretty impressed.

We shook hands, and he led me past the front of the factory, past all the manicured flower beds and the flaming-red banners with the black horse logo and straight through to his private office. The room seemed dark, even in the middle of the day, and most of the extremely soft lighting was provided by lit candles. On the walls, there were several photographs of his late son Dino, who had died of muscular dystrophy in 1956 and who was clearly still profoundly mourned.

Enzo Ferrari spoke to me in Italian, with Franco Gozzi translating phrase by phrase, and he proceeded to outline his plans for the following season, finishing by expressing the hope that I would agree to drive for Scuderia Ferrari in 1968.

'Anyway,' he said, 'why would you want to drive for those garagists?'

He smiled, delighting in his description of the British racing teams who bought engines and other parts from third parties and preferred to concentrate on chassis design. Then he suggested it was time for me to take a guided tour of the factory where Ferrari proudly produced all their own engines and gearboxes; in fact, they effectively manufactured the total car.

It was impossible not to be impressed by the scale of Maranello, and yet I was still wary. There were so many stories about the Machiavellian politics within the team and so many people had told me how Ferrari liked to dominate and manipulate his drivers, treating them like pawns on a chess board, seldom allowing them to gain confidence and authority. I was a keen student of the history of motor racing and I had read how Ferrari had behaved towards drivers like Luigi Musso and Eugenio Castellotti. In fact, while Enzo Ferrari was in charge, it was only a handful of strong-minded, tough and self-centred characters who managed to win the F1 drivers' world championship for Ferrari. Only men like Juan Manuel Fangio, John Surtees, Niki Lauda and Jody Scheckter got the job done. Phil Hill did win the F1 world championship for Ferrari in 1961, and he is the nicest, most mild-mannered man you could ever wish to meet, but he is the exception to the rule.

However, having said all this, the fact remains that, in 1967, and in all the years before and since, the combined effect of the outstanding facilities, the aura of the brand and the charisma of so many of the officials and staff has been to ensure that there has hardly been a racing driver in the world who, at one stage or another, did not want to drive for Ferrari.

Moreover, it was the case that the 'Old Man', as people affectionately knew Enzo Ferrari, had appeared very straightforward with me throughout my visit.

I was warming to the idea of Wee Jackie Stewart driving for Ferrari. I had to pinch myself. It simply didn't get much bigger for a youngster from Dumbarton. I agreed to visit Maranello again en route to drive for Ken Tyrrell in the F2 Mediterranean Grand Prix at Enna in Sicily just a few weeks later. So I duly returned on Wednesday 16 August 1967, ready and willing to discuss terms and do the deal.

Enzo Ferrari came straight to the point and asked me how much money I wanted. Without blinking, I looked him straight in the eye and asked for £20,000 per year, 50 per cent of all prize money, 50 per cent of all bonuses, plus a Ferrari road car for my personal use. Without blinking, he accepted the terms.

Next, I said I wanted to continue driving for Ken Tyrrell in the F2 championship. The Commendatore was not keen on the idea but, after a long discussion, he agreed Ferrari would provide the F2 cars and equipment to Tyrrell; and, after more debate, he even accepted my request that the F2 car be painted Ferrari red on the upper half of the chassis and Scottish blue on the lower half.

He asked, 'Is OK?'

'It looks fine to me,' I replied.

We shook hands on the deal, subject to the contract being worked out and signed, right there in his office and we left to have lunch together. At that moment, in heart and mind, I was a Ferrari driver. Within four days, I was anything but.

I travelled from Maranello down to Sicily and was talking to Jacky Ickx on the Saturday afternoon after practice. Jacky was my F2 team-mate at Tyrrell and, in many people's eyes, the sport's new rising star. A twenty-two-year-old Belgian, he was talented, cheerful and charismatic, and I liked him very much, but nothing prepared me for what he was going to tell me.

'So, Jackie, are you going to drive for Ferrari next year?'

I was taken aback and said I didn't think anybody knew about my private discussions and that I was trying to keep everything quiet. 'Anyway,' I added, 'who told you?'

'The people at Ferrari told me,' he replied.

Typical, I thought, struggling to believe that they could have already started playing one driver off against another.

Jacky continued: 'They told me you had been to look around, but there were problems because they said you were demanding too much. They said you wanted Maranello itself.'

'I see.'

'Well,' he continued, 'they have offered me the drive for next year on condition I give them an answer by Sunday evening.'

'OK.'

'I don't know what to do. What do you think?'

I told him: 'Jacky, you should accept the offer.'

Snap! That was that. Any chance of me driving for Ferrari completely evaporated in that moment. How could they have offered the drive to Jacky when Enzo Ferrari had shaken hands with me? I had been well warned by many people but, even so, I was amazed. Was this how Ferrari operated? For me, driving a F1 car was hard enough without having to worry about what was happening behind my back. I needed to have total confidence in the people working with me.

I won the race at Enna on the Sunday afternoon and, on the Monday morning, having found a public telephone at the airport in Rome, I called first Keith Ballisat and then Franco Gozzi to tell them, as far as I was concerned, the deal was off.

'You can't do that,' Franco protested. 'You shook hands on the deal with Mr Ferrari.'

'So did Mr Ferrari shake hands with me,' I replied, 'and now you have offered the drive to someone else.'

'What do you mean?'

'Jacky Ickx has been told he could have the drive.'

'No one has authority to do that.'

'Well, the offer has been made and Jacky has even been given a deadline of Sunday night. The deal's off.'

There was a postscript to this saga. Eleven years later, as part of a promotion for Elf, I worked on a television series where I was going to drive each of the 1978 F1 cars, analysing their strengths and weaknesses. Each team made their car available, except one. Our request to Ferrari received a pointed reply from Enzo, saying, 'If my car wasn't good enough for Stewart in 1967, why should it be good enough for Stewart now?'

The series really needed to include the Ferrari, so I phoned Gianni Agnelli, the president of Fiat, who by then had bought a controlling interest in Ferrari, and asked him if he could have a quiet word with the Commendatore, and try to make him change his mind. I knew Gianni quite well, and he called me back not long afterwards to say he was very sorry, but the 'Old Man' was simply not going to budge on this one.

At any rate, looking ahead to the 1968 season, the question remained: if not BRM, if not Ferrari, then who?

I had been driving a Matra for Ken Tyrrell in the 1967 F2 series, and my success partly compensated for the disappointments in F1 and effectively sustained my reputation as a driver. Ken and I got along so well, I had taken him into my confidence and told him all about my discussions with Ferrari, and, completely out of the blue, this utterly straight-forward and uncomplicated man came up with his own proposal.

'Why not drive for me?' he said.

'Ken,' I replied, 'you don't have a Formula 1 team.'

'What if I did have?'

'Well,' I smiled, 'I suppose that if you did have a car, I would obviously love to drive for you.'

This was a man of absolute integrity, whose genuine love of motor sport shone through in everything he said and did, and he started to explain how, to begin with, he wanted to put one of the new Ford Cosworth DFV engines into a modified F2 Matra chassis, and then to enter the car in the 1968 F1 season with me as his driver.

'What do you think?' he asked.

'Well, I . . .'

'That DFV is fantastic,' Ken continued. 'I went to see it at Zandvoort and, I'm telling you, it was infinitely superior to everything in the field. Everything else was rubbish.'

Walter Hayes, vice-president of public relations in Europe for the Ford Motor Company, had secured a budget of $300,000 and commissioned Cosworth, the company run by Keith Duckworth and Mike Costin, to produce an engine for Lotus. I knew exactly why Ken had been so impressed, because I had also been at the Dutch Grand Prix at Zandvoort and seen the DFV power Jim Clark to a spectacular victory in its first race. In fact, driving the BRM H16, I was lapped by the new Ford Cosworth engine.

Lotus had secured exclusive use of the DFV engine for 1967, but thereafter, in what was an extraordinary and probably unique opportunity for private entrants, literally anybody was able to go out and buy one of these top-quality, highly competitive F1 Grand Prix engines for a price of just £7,500. Today, the annual F1 engine bill for a major manufacturer's F1 programme would be something like £125 million.

'Jackie, I'm sure we can be competitive,' Ken said.

'I think you may be right,' I replied.

Some people might have accused me of letting my heart rule my head. The facts were that I was planning to leave BRM, a large and well-funded organisation, and, having said no to Ferrari, was now on the brink of signing for a new and untried F1 team led by a man who had never made a F1 car. Why? I could explain in two words: Ken Tyrrell. He was unique, the outstanding team director of his generation. Simply put, I would have been prepared to trust him with my life, let alone my motor racing career.

Ken was brought up near the village of Ockham in Surrey, and, as he used to boast with a broad grin, his early years were not notably successful, a bit like mine. He failed his eleven-plus, failed his entrance exam to technical school and was initially turned down by the Royal Air Force. Eventually, he was accepted as an RAF flight engineer and he worked there before demobbing and going into business with his brother Bert as timber merchants. He used to play for his village football team, and his passion for motor sport was ignited when the club organised a coach trip to watch the British Grand Prix at Silverstone. Bitten by the bug, he pursued a brief career as a racing driver. However, tall and broad, naturally authoritative, he soon found his true vocation as a team owner, and the Tyrrell Racing Organisation began entering cars in 1960.

Operating from the same woodyard as the family timber business, the team first established itself in Formula Junior racing and then moved on to F3 in 1964 and to F2 in 1965. In the process, Ken earned a reputation for spotting young talent, providing single-seater debuts to drivers like John Surtees, me and then Jacky Ickx. All the while, his overriding ambition remained to reach the highest level of the sport, to compete in F1.

He achieved this dream largely because he developed an outstanding association with Matra, the French aerospace and telecommunications company, who brought with them the backing of Elf, the French petroleum giant. This turned out to be the motor racing marriage made in heaven: the style, sophistication and high technology of Matra and Elf being brought together with Ken's sober professionalism and thorough practicality.

The matchmaker was Jabby Crombac, one of the most experienced motor racing journalists of the time, founder of the French magazine *Sport Auto* and a man whom I met and got to know well during my first year with Ken in 1964. He was also a good pal to Jim Clark, and at one point found a flat for him in Paris. Jabby was involved in many areas of the sport, as a race promoter and organiser, as a writer and a steward, and it was he who engineered the introduction of Jean-Luc Lagardère, the well-respected CEO of Matra, to Ken Tyrrell. Somehow, the chemistry worked.

'Ken, I think we have something exceptional,' Jean-Luc would say, and he would expansively enthuse about the latest concept being developed by his brilliant engineers, scientists and physicists at the Matra headquarters, at Vélizy near Paris.

'It sounds nice,' the down-to-earth Englishman would reply, 'but I don't think it can work.'

'Why not?'

'Because I just don't think it will be reliable. It's too complicated. There's no point having something fast and furious, if it breaks down the whole time. We must remember: if we don't finish the race, we'll never win the race.'

Lagardère typically listened well. Like me, he admired Ken as a very practical man and he completely trusted him to bring success. The Matra chief also understood that motor racing would project a positive global image of his company, so he supplied Tyrrell with its F2 cars and, by end of 1967, was ready to talk about and embrace the challenge of F1.

Jean-Luc was one of the outstanding executives in France, indeed in Europe, and he remains in my mind's eye as the very model of a successful businessman: charming with perfect manners and taste, confident with genuine humility, calm with an exceptional sense of purpose and drive, a wonderful sense of humour and a perfectly cut suit. The combined effect was to make him a most impressive and intoxicating person. Helen and I became very friendly with him and his first wife, Corinne, and then his second wife, Betty, both of whom came from Brazil, and we kept in touch over the years, spending time with him at his home on the island of Mustique in the Caribbean, his lovely stud farm near Deauville in Normandy and his home in Paris. He became one of the leading men in French horse-racing.

The third member of the triumvirate at the heart of this emerging F1 team, alongside Ken and Jean-Luc, was a genius in his own right: François Guiter, the communications director of Elf.

François, a man of generous proportions who loved to scuba dive, however unlikely that is for a man of his vast size, was widely admired as the marketing guru responsible for the revival of motor sport in France.

It began in April 1967, when various French-owned companies were brought together into one giant corporation with a simple, small and effective brand name. 'Elf' had arrived. 'Elf' didn't stand for anything, but it was soon known around the world, becoming smoothly integrated into almost every language. François Guiter believed motor racing represented an ideal marketing vehicle for Elf to project a dynamic worldwide image as a successful global company. Through his enthusiasm and energy, the then state-owned company launched a two-tiered programme to develop French motor sport: they supported the Matra Tyrrell F1 team and also launched 'Volant Elf', a project to nurture young talent at driving schools at Magny-Cours and Paul Ricard, and then to reward the best students with full-budget grants to compete in the Formula

Renault class the following season. Both Ken and I later became judges in the Pilot Elf competition.

The results speak for themselves. Johnny Servoz-Gavin, Jean-Pierre Beltoise, Jean-Pierre Jarier, Jacques Laffite, Jean-Pierre Jabouille, Henri Pescarolo, François Cevert and others reached the highest level of the sport in the late 1960s and early 1970s, and the conveyor belt continued to produce the likes of Didier Pironi, René Arnoux, Patrick Depailler, Patrick Tambay, Alain Prost, Olivier Grouillard, Paul Belmondo, Eric Bernard, Erik Comas, Olivier Panis and others. François Guiter, I am sure, would have felt great pride when no fewer than seven French drivers took their place on the starting grid of the British Grand Prix in 1980. However, when budgets were cut at Elf and other French companies withdrew financial support, the production line ground to a halt, and François will have been as disappointed as anybody to see not a single French driver on the F1 circuit at the start of the 2007 season.

The combination of Tyrrell, Matra, Elf and the Ford DFV engine – of Ken, Jean-Luc Lagardère, François Guiter and Walter Hayes – seemed almost providential, and I duly shook hands on an agreement with Ken, underwritten by Ford, who agreed to subsidise my retainer of £20,000.

I wasn't joining just a team. I found a close group of specialists and mechanics who worked well together and enjoyed each other's company and realised I was joining a family. Ken liked it that way. His wife, Norah, was a wonderful lady from Edinburgh who was always around, offering help and support wherever required, typically making snacks for the mechanics; his eldest son, Kenneth, later helped with the timekeeping before becoming a pilot for British Airways; and, as time went by, his younger son, Bob, assisted with the marketing.

To judge from the way he treated his mechanics, they might as well have been blood relations as well. Long before most people even contemplated such benefits, Ken was offering his staff generous pension plans, private medical insurance and other forms of support and they repaid him with extraordinary loyalty. Many of those who joined him never left. The saying 'once a Tyrrell mechanic, always a Tyrrell mechanic' rang true. Roger Hill was a New Zealander who first came to the United Kingdom by sea, joined Ken and became, in my opinion, one of the greatest mechanics the sport has ever known. Neil Davis was magnificently practical and frank, so rigorous that he turned attention to detail into an art form. Alan Stait was another long-term Tyrrell engineer, who always proved absolutely scrupulous and unflappable. Amazingly Alan and Neil were both part of the Tyrrell team working at Goodwood in 1962, when I arrived to watch Bob MacIntyre's test. Both were present two years later when I tested the F3 car with Bruce McLaren and both were still working for Ken at Watkins Glen in 1973, when I retired as a driver. There was also Max Rutherford, who arrived from New Zealand, worked on my car for three seasons and later returned home to buy and run a ladies' underwear company; Roland Law, who worked with John Coombs before joining the team in 1970; and Roy Topp, who also joined in 1970 and later moved across to work for Paul Stewart Racing. These men were the best in their profession and, through all the years we worked together, it is true to say I always felt they were much better at their jobs than I was at mine.

We were a small group. When the Tyrrell team travelled to a F1 Grand Prix in 1968, we numbered no more than ten people: Ken, Norah, two drivers and six mechanics. That compares with the complement of around forty that Stewart Grand Prix typically took to F1 races in 1997, and the army of ninety highly qualified and extremely busy individuals who travel with major F1 teams like McLaren or Williams today. Ferrari take even more.

Back at the woodyard, Alan Stait ran the workshop, proving as skilful with machines and lathes as anyone I have known. Keith Boshier, a devoted and somewhat eccentric expert, made magic in a separate wooden hut, creating the seats and composite carbon fibre components.

I feel an enormous sense of debt to all these men. Each of them played a central role in my motor racing career, and therefore in my life; and, as the years fly by, I greatly appreciate the fact we have all managed to stay friends and keep in touch with each other on a regular basis. It is probably true to say the best families function as teams, and the most effective teams work as families. The difference is that while we typically can't select all the members of our family, it is possible to choose who we would like to have in our team. Ken chose brilliantly in the mid to late 1960s and through the 1970s, and achieved the same kind of harmony and the same level of exceptional performance that I have often witnessed at musical concerts, both classical and modern.

When you watch a genius like Phil Collins or Eric Clapton perform, they are usually supported by a substantial band, and you can be sure that each and every member of that band is the best: the best bass guitar player, the best keyboard player, etc. The same goes for the stage and sound crews. With the best around them, artists like Phil or Eric are able to breeze through their set without a backward glance, without a moment of doubt or concern.

In the same vein, I never worried about Roger or Neil. I never doubted Max or Roland or Roy. I never questioned Ken's ability. They nurtured each other, challenged each other, kept their standards high and performed with great consistency. Quietly and modestly, through so much testing and so many practice sessions, through six years of F1 racing, they combined to make me look good.

The new Matra MS10 wasn't quite ready so it was MS9

which took its place on the starting grid of the first F1 Grand Prix of 1968, in South Africa and, moments before the start, I took off my watch and handed it to Ken.

'Look after this, will you?'

'No problem,' he said.

I never wore my watch during a race because there had been accidents where they had done incredible damage, 'degloving' drivers and ripping the skin off their hands, and this went on to become a ritual between us. The last thing I did before climbing into the cockpit before every race was pass my watch to Ken, and the first thing he did after a race was give my Rolex back to me. In all the years we worked together, I never passed it to anybody else.

By the time the watch was back on my wrist at Kyalami, Lotus had posted an impressive one-two victory, and I had had to retire with engine trouble after forty-three laps, but Ken and I were pleased because the Matra had been instantly competitive.

I could hardly wait for the next F1 Grand Prix, to see how the Matra MS10 would perform once it was ready – would it be instantly competitive? In many ways, this was a makeshift car in its first season. We believed we had something special but, with each race, we learned a little more.

The momentum of my season was literally fractured when I broke a small bone in my right wrist while driving for John Coombs in a F2 race at Jarama, near Madrid.

'How long will I be out?' I asked the doctor.

'About twenty weeks,' he replied.

'You're joking.'

'No,' he said firmly, 'there's very little blood circulation to the scaphoid, so it takes longer to heal the bone.'

That was no good, I thought, we need to find another opinion. First, I contacted the orthopaedic surgeon who had treated me after my accident at Spa in 1966, and flew him over to Geneva to get his prognosis, but he said the same thing. Next, I visited the doctor of the Indiana college basketball team in Bloomington because I reckoned he would have experience of similar hand injuries. I even travelled to New Orleans to see a doctor who had looked after Muhammad Ali. But everybody gave me the same story: 'no driving for five months'. Still not satisfied, I arranged to see Dr Argand, a leading orthopaedic surgeon in Geneva and at last found a member of the medical profession who was prepared to look at the problem creatively and think out of the box. He studied my options and devised a plastic mould that fitted over my wrist and forearm and supported my hand in a fixed position that enabled me to hold the steering wheel and use the gear shift. We even arranged for one of the Tyrrell steering wheels to be sent over to Switzerland, to make absolutely sure the mould fitted properly.

The brace served its purpose, but it was a nuisance to take on and off. Wherever I was racing, I needed to find a doctor on the Thursday night to help me take the normal plaster off my hand, wrist and arm, cover the area with Vaseline and then put on the special brace, which laced up like a shoe. Then, after the race on the Sunday evening, I would have to go back to the doctor so he could remove the mould and put a new plaster on. I wasn't complaining because, with Dr Argand's brace, I was able to start racing again within four weeks. It's a small world: the doctor's son, young Luc Argand, has grown up to be a lawyer who represents Bernie Ecclestone; and in 2007, Luc served as president of the Geneva International Motor Show.

I returned to the action at the end of May, but by then the 1968 season had been overtaken by a series of tragic deaths: my great friend Jim Clark in April and Mike Spence at the Indianapolis 500, and then Ludovico Scarfiotti in June.

Still the season continued, and the early optimism within the Tyrrell team was borne out at Zandvoort, when I managed to win the Dutch Grand Prix, finishing more than a minute and a half ahead of Jean-Pierre Beltoise in the V12-engined Matra, with both Lotuses, driven by Graham Hill and Jackie Oliver, well down the field.

We were indisputably competitive, and, at the French Grand Prix in Rouen two weeks later on 7 July, in blinding rain, I secured another podium finish, coming in third behind Jacky Ickx, whose win helped him settle into his new life with Ferrari. Even so, the entire day was overshadowed by the death of Jo Schlesser, the final tragedy in that awful four-month period which had started back in April.

The brace was still doing its job, although in practice I wasn't able to do much with my right hand, and that meant I had to do a lot of the driving with just my left hand. This required a level of additional effort that proved tiring over ninety laps at Rouen and almost intolerable in the British Grand Prix on the notoriously bumpy circuit at Brands Hatch. There were stages of the race when I felt it would be sensible to stop, but I managed to keep going and finish sixth. Coming to a halt back in the pit, I was unable to move and needed to be lifted out of the car. Helen and I left the track soon afterwards and, as soon as I got home, I went straight to my bed and slept for eighteen hours. Driving mainly one-handed, I learned, was tiring work.

On Sunday 4 August 1968 – the first weekend of 'the fifth month' in the sequence – a noticeably apprehensive group of F1 drivers prepared for the German Grand Prix at the Nurburgring, which was then recognised by most people within the sport as the most demanding and dangerous circuit in the world, with no fewer than 187 corners on each lap of the 14.7 mile (23 kilometre) circuit. And it was raining, hard.

I had been given a lift to the Ring on the Thursday afternoon by Graham Hill, flying his own Piper Aztec with me, Jo Siffert, Jo Bonnier and Graham's wife Bette as passengers, and we had seen the first few drops of rain splatter on the tarmac just as we were unpacking our luggage from the plane.

'It's going to be the Green Hell this weekend,' I noted.

Graham understood exactly what I meant.

The rain continued to fall through Friday and Saturday, prompting the organisers to declare there would be an additional practice session on the Sunday morning before the race. However, when Sunday dawned, it was still raining heavily, and the fog had come down as well. The weather made it almost impossible to drive, and I didn't see any point in trying to practise. Ken said the car was ready and he told me to prepare to go out.

'I don't think so, Ken,' I replied.

'Well, I think it would be sensible,' he said.

'Ken, you can't see a thing out there.'

'Jackie . . .'

'The rain is ridiculous. Jackie Oliver has just gone off at Adenau and he was lucky to walk away. We could really damage the car, so it's not worth the risk.'

People were starting to notice our increasingly animated conversation. Ken wasn't backing down.

'Jackie,' he said, firmly, 'you have to go out!'

I looked straight at him, realised I wasn't getting anywhere, stood up and walked to the pit, shaking my head. I was angry and also surprised Ken had pushed me so hard. Looking back, I realise he was absolutely right. He wanted me to get out there and drive around the circuit at a pace where I would be able to see the potential hazards, and make a mental note of where the falling rain had either gathered into standing water on the tarmac or where it had created little rivers streaming across the track. He knew it was dangerous, but he told me to go out because he wanted me to be as safe as possible during the race. So I went out, and looked, and learned.

One of the idiosyncratic traits of people with dyslexia can be a photographic memory and, throughout my racing career, I was able to look at a circuit and bank its features in my mind. It might seem impossible for a human being to make their way through the 187 corners of the Nurburgring and remember precisely where you have to brake, to change gear, to accelerate and to take care, especially when so much of the track is bordered by fir trees and so much of the scenery is similar. This would be a major task in perfect dry conditions, but it was even more of a challenge for all the drivers on that incredibly wet and foggy Sunday in 1968.

Yet, almost forty years later, I can still recall: 'out of the pits, accelerate up through the gears down to the south turn, brake, down into third gear in entry, accelerate up to fifth gear behind the pits, brake not too heavily, back into third gear into the left hander, over the bridge, turn left and again up through the gears down through the winding section that is narrow, blind and fast . . .'

The start of the 1968 German Grand Prix was delayed by fifty minutes; as he came to collect my watch, Ken leaned down and told me: 'Today, you are certainly underpaid.'

He wasn't wrong. The rain was still falling heavily, the fog was dense and there were no high-intensity rear lights back then to help pick out the cars you might be following. No doubt at all, he wasn't wrong. I was starting on the third row of the grid, having been sixth fastest in qualifying, almost a minute slower than polesitter Jacky Ickx. Problems with the car had prevented me from getting out earlier in the session, when the track was considerably drier and faster.

The race itself remains vividly etched in my memory.

The starter's flag drops, and Jacky Ickx gets too much wheel spin, forcing me to swerve into the pit lane gutter to get past him, so I am third going into the first corner, behind Graham Hill and Chris Amon. I had known the spray would be bad. In fact, it is unbelievable. Visibility is so pathetically poor I can't see any braking distance markers. I can't even see Chris's car in front of me. I am simply driving into this great wall of spray. If I can just get past these two guys, I'll get through the spray and everything will get much easier, but they are somewhere ahead of me. I hate to think what's going on behind me.

I'm concentrating, working hard, peering through the mist, trying to follow the tyre tracks of the car in front and, approaching Adenauer, I can see I'm getting close to Chris. I pull out to pass him, but the spray is dense, and I'm driving blind. I accelerate and get past and I feel so relieved, not just because I am into second place but because I know I am a little safer. It's like flying an aircraft in bad weather, without radar. These conditions would be hellish on any circuit but they are nothing less than terrifying at the Nurburgring, with its undulations and many fast bends and slow, tight corners. Little streams on the track are almost impossible to see in the shadows of the trees, but you know they are there soon enough as the car aquaplanes on water that feels two inches deep.

So you fight to keep control and with luck you stay on the circuit but, all the time, at the back of your mind you know anything can happen to the car in front of you and, as you plough on, you realise it could suddenly appear, spinning wildly. At least I might have a half chance to react if that happens, I think. The driver in front will have slammed on the brakes if he has lost control, the wheels will lock, and locked wheels mean no spray. It is small consolation.

It's still the first lap, but I need to pass Graham, maybe at the start of the straight. Then a gap appears at the end of Solitaire Corner and I go for it and get past and I feel another burst of euphoria because, as I accelerate into the home straight, there is no more spray – just the thick fog, restricting visibility to approximately forty metres. This is ridiculous. We're travelling at speeds of up to 170 mph.

I complete lap one; there are thirteen laps to go.

It is now a question of driving as fast as possible, to open up a lead. I focus on what is ahead of me, trying to stay on the road. At the end of the second lap, I look out for the signal board at the back of the pits and see my lead has reached thirty-four seconds.

The Dunlops are performing well. The tyres have exceptionally wide grooves to minimise the effect of the deep water. If they're giving me an advantage, then I must make the most of it.

It's a relief to be out in front, and I keep concentrating because I know catastrophe can be looming on any section of the circuit. Two corners after the Karussell on lap ten, I hit a deep river of water and I know I have lost control as the Matra starts to ride over the water. I look ahead and see the car is hurtling towards a track marshal, who dives one way, jumps back the other way and then seems to freeze. I feel sure my car is going to hit him, but then, by some miracle, it bites and finds a little bit of grip, just enough for me to regain control and coax it back on line. It was one of those moments but I get out of trouble, complete the lap and finish the race.

The ordeal is over.

At the end of this momentous race, I drove straight back to the pits, took off my helmet, looked up to find Ken and immediately asked him: 'Is everyone OK?'

'Everybody is fine,' came the reply.

Thank God.

The race statistics showed my final margin of victory was four minutes and three seconds, with Graham Hill in second place and Jochen Rindt third, and many observers have since suggested that, given the conditions, this was perhaps the outstanding performance of my racing career. In my view, it was just as much a triumph for Ken and his mechanics and their reliable engineering. It was also a great win for Dunlop, and their outstanding tyres; and it was a triumph for Dr Argand, and his brace – strangely, the wet conditions had made the steering lighter and eased the stress on my injured wrist; and it was a triumph for the twenty men who had bravely lined up on the grid and survived to drive another day.

The 1968 F1 season was moving towards an exciting conclusion, through the Italian Grand Prix at Monza, the Canadian Grand Prix at Mont Tremblant, near St Jovite, and the US Grand Prix at Watkins Glen, where I won my third race of the season.

'Jim would have been proud of a drive like that,' somebody told me after the podium ceremony at Watkins Glen and, amid all the usual crowds and happy chaos, those words registered with me not only because I still sorely missed Jimmy but also because I thought I knew what the person had meant.

I had held the lead for a long while at Watkins Glen and, for the first time in my F1 Grand Prix career, I had sensed I was able to dictate the pace of the race. When I went slower, the entire field went slower; when I went faster, the whole field went faster. It had been an extraordinary moment of realisation. Jimmy had been able to exert the same kind of control, and, driving a competitive car, supported by an outstanding team, I felt in a position to pick up his mantle and move on.

The contest for the 1968 F1 drivers' world championship came down to the last race of the season, the Gran Premio de Mexico in Mexico City on 3 November, with three of us – Graham Hill in the Lotus, Denny Hulme in the McLaren and myself in the Matra-Ford – still in with a chance of claiming the title.

Denny's hopes faded when he retired on the tenth lap after his suspension failed, and my chances wilted when the Matra's fuel pump developed problems towards the end of the race. It struggled to move fuel from the tank on one side of the car to the tank on the other side of the car, causing fuel starvation and making the engine cut out on almost every right-hand corner.

Graham seized the opportunity, surged ahead and won the race. He secured his second world title, finishing with a total of 48 points, ahead of me on 36, with Denny third on 33.

Lotus won the F1 constructor's championship, and nobody begrudged Colin Chapman and his team the success at the end of a 'peaks and valleys' year which had begun with the deaths of two of their drivers, Jimmy Clark and Mike Spence.

'Don't worry,' Ken told me. 'We've had a great year.'

He was right. It had been a remarkable achievement for this brand-new team to emerge from the woodyard in Surrey, settle into F1 and prove so competitive in their first season.

On a personal level, I don't believe I was ready to be world champion in 1968. Winning the title is about far more than standing on a podium and waving at the crowd, and, with hindsight, I don't think I was equipped to cope with the pressures and the demands not just of the racing but also of having to fulfil my associations with Ford, Elf and Dunlop. Receiving a couple of 'Driver of the Year' awards proved more than sufficient to sustain my confidence, and persuade me my time would come.

Johnny Servoz-Gavin was retained as my team-mate for 1969, and nobody doubted the talent of this good-looking, well-heeled but highly strung French driver. He tried to control his emotions and nerves and, as I saw one day when I peered into the darkness of the Tyrrell transporter, he was one of the first F1 drivers to practise yoga as a means of relaxing before a Grand Prix. It should be added that my team-mate showed far fewer signs of anxiety away from the track, where he moved with the social 'fast set'. I remember him spending so much time on one particular yacht, it became known as the 'Johnny Boat'.

We began the new season in Johannesburg, where our painstakingly thorough programme of testing Dunlop tyres reaped the reward of victory in the South African Grand Prix, and this form was sustained by wins in the non-championship Race of Champions at Brands Hatch and an F2 race at the Nurburgring.

The Spanish Grand Prix, run at the Montjuic circuit on the hill above the city of Barcelona, then provided me with an object lesson in the impact of so-called 'good luck' in F1 racing.

Everybody was talking about the Ferraris and the Lotuses during qualifying, and Jochen Rindt set a new lap record and secured pole position. The new Matra MS80 Ford-V8 was looking solid but unspectacular, and I found myself well back in sixth position as the race settled into its rhythm.

Sixth became fifth place when Graham Hill crashed into a guard rail near the Stadium jump on lap six; his new high 'biplane' front and rear wings collapsed instantly, removing almost all of the down force and therefore the car's grip.

Fifth became fourth place when the same problems resulted in Jochen losing control of his car at the same spot on lap eleven; he suffered head injuries that looked serious at the time, and caused us all concern, but he made a full recovery.

I moved up to second place when two other drivers retired, which meant there was only Chris Amon, in the Ferrari, ahead of me. Then, during the fifty-seventh lap, he ran out of oil.

I had moved from sixth place to first place without passing a single car. I'd been fortunate, and it provided a neat reminder that, no matter what happens, you should never give up.

Now leading the race and under no pressure, I backed off and crossed the finish line. As usual in Spain, the chequered flag was being extravagantly waved by a wonderful character called

Peppe Villapalermo, who was invariably dressed in a distinctive dark-blue and well-cut blazer and red trousers.

'*Hola*, Jackie,' Peppe said afterwards on the podium, giving me a hug. 'That was a well-judged race.'

'Thanks,' I replied. 'It was just good luck.'

I was learning. I understood good luck but, as time went by, I didn't really believe in bad luck. In motor racing, as in other areas of life, you often hear people complaining about their bad luck, claiming nothing is going their way. More often than not, a closer inspection suggests their problems are the result of human error, whether it is bad planning, bad structuring, bad preparation or bad judgement. A racing driver curses his 'ill fortune' when his car suffers a mechanical failure, but luck often has little to do with it. The failure will usually have been caused by poor concept engineering, or a flaw in manufacturing, casting or machining, or maybe the incorrect assembly of a particular component. Similarly, a businessman may arrive late for a meeting and apologise to his colleagues by saying he had been 'unlucky' with the traffic. In fact, a more accurate explanation would be that he had not planned to leave sufficient time for the journey. I am not saying there is never any such thing as bad luck. Of course there is, in sport and in every realm of life. However, in motor racing, there very often seems to be a practical explanation. It was perhaps the meticulous design and careful preparation of the Matra-Fords by Ken and his mechanics, and the Matra people at their headquarters just outside Paris, that meant we suffered so little 'bad luck' in 1969.

That said, I did have to retire from the Monaco Grand Prix that year and, at first glance, many people might have said I had suffered a bit of bad luck because the drive shaft failed. Not so. An investigation subsequently revealed the problem was directly caused by a bad batch of universal couplings that had slipped through the outside supplier's inspection.

The car ran well a month later at Zandvoort, where I won the Dutch Grand Prix for the second year in succession, and again eight days later at the famous circuit in Clermont-Ferrand, where I was able to win the French Grand Prix.

Immediately after the race, I brought the car to a halt on the start/finish line, and an army of photographers started to gather around. As I stood up in the cockpit, somebody handed me a double magnum of Moët & Chandon champagne. I was quite surprised, but I thought the least I could do was open it.

Nobody told me the bottle had been left lying in the sun and so, as I released the cork, the champagne foamed out. I thought it would be a shame to waste any, so I pressed my thumb over the top, but this only increased the pressure and produced a powerful jet of champagne. Everyone was enjoying the spectacle, and so, thinking I might as well have some fun, I started spinning around, spraying the champagne in all directions . . . and so a F1 tradition was born. This was the first time champagne had been used to celebrate victory in a F1 Grand Prix, even though it was the American racing driver Dan Gurney who initiated the practice at the 24 Hour of Le Mans. Jubilant champagne showers on the podium became one of the signature features of F1 racing, and it wasn't long before they translated into another lucrative commercial opportunity, with Moët eventually being replaced as the official supplier.

That afternoon at Clermont-Ferrand, the champagne had rarely tasted better because we had secured four wins in the first five races of the F1 world championship season. Johnny Servoz-Gavin had retired, and had been replaced as my team-mate by Jean-Pierre Beltoise, a promising French driver who had driven for the Matra F1 team the previous year. However, any hint of complacency was erased during a practice session before the British Grand Prix at Silverstone. I was driving behind Piers Courage, when he clipped and dislodged one of the small rectangular kerbstones cemented to the track at Woodcote

Corner. This rectangular piece of stone flew into the air and hit my rear right tyre at 150 mph. The tyre exploded, and my car flew out of control, slamming through three rows of chain-link fencing and finally coming to a stop against a grass bank fronted by railway sleepers. I was fortunately not injured and sensed considerable relief among the spectators in the main grandstand nearby as I stepped out of the car. They realised, as I did, that such a high-speed accident more often than not results in a serious injury or death.

It was clearly going to be impossible to repair my Matra before the start of the race, so Ken decided I should use the spare car. The actual race was notable for a fantastic duel between me and Jochen Rindt, in which the lead changed more than thirty times, but he then developed a mechanical problem, and I was able to move clear and win my first British Grand Prix.

The day was made even more special for me because my father had travelled down from Scotland, bringing some of the staff from Dumbuck garage with him. It must have been a pleasure for him to watch his son win, and it was an even greater thrill for me to see the pride and joy across his face.

Second place to Jacky Ickx in the German Grand Prix meant we arrived at Monza in the first week of September, knowing that victory in the Italian Grand Prix would secure the world championship. Nothing was taken for granted, and Ken and his mechanics worked as meticulously as ever.

The race was one of the most remarkable F1 Grand Prix of all time and, to the delight of the wildly excited crowd, it culminated in the amazing spectacle of four racing cars hurtling towards the finish line almost in a row. Incredibly, after 240 miles of racing, less than a fifth of a second covered the first four cars. In truth, any of us might have claimed the victory but, to my great delight and relief, it was me whose car found something extra to win the race by a hair's breadth from Jochen Rindt, with Jean-Pierre Beltoise third and Bruce McLaren fourth.

What separated the cars in such a blanket finish? Some might say it was luck. Once again, I would take issue with that. In my view, it was no accident that the Matra-Ford crossed the line first. The fact is we had spent a substantial part of the practice and qualifying sessions on the Saturday painstakingly taking time to ensure I had gear ratios that enabled me to accelerate out of the Parabolica, the last corner before the home straight, and then only have to change from third to fourth gear before crossing the line. That exhaustive process involved calculating exactly how much fuel the car would be carrying and the likely weight of the car on that final lap – all to get the gear ratios exactly right. It may have seemed an enormous amount of work to secure a tiny advantage but, from the Parabolica to the finish line, each of the other drivers had to change gears from third to fourth and then to fifth. Every time you change a gear, you risk making a mistake, which could cost you a fraction of a second – and, at that speed, that could equate to as much as 40 or 50 metres. In such a tight finish, that apparently insignificant attention to detail gave me those few extra inches, and that proved the difference between winning and losing because I won the race by a distance of just 12 inches.

Ken had every reason to be delighted when I pulled into the pits. 'You've done it,' he said, beaming, his arms in the air.

'Are you sure?'

'Yes, there's no doubt. You're the world champion.'

'Ken, listen to me. Are you absolutely sure?'

'Yes.'

Following the tradition at Monza, tens of thousands of spectators were soon flooding across the track at the end, but they seemed especially excited on this occasion. I stepped down from the podium straight after the prize-giving and immediately went to find Helen. As I reached her, a heaving crowd surged towards us.

What followed seems scarcely believable. The police and

crowd control officials seemed unable to contain the mass of people, and it seemed obvious to me we needed to get away. So, still holding the trophy and with the winner's wreath around my shoulders, I took Helen by the arm and we scrambled into a washroom on the ground floor of the administration block. Within minutes, a large group of spectators had invaded that building as well, so we had to get moving again, climbing out of the washroom window, sprinting hand-in-hand for 20 yards and then taking refuge in the giant Dunlop transporter.

The crowds were happy and boisterous, and we never felt in any danger because people only wanted to congratulate me, but it was becoming hard to see how we would ever get away.

I looked out of the window of the transporter to see what was happening – that was a mistake because someone spotted me, and the crowd rushed towards us again. We had just left the transporter when the pressure of the crowd tipped the huge vehicle over, leaving it leaning against the vehicle parked beside it.

A friend of ours called Phillip Martyn, a great sports enthusiast and at that time the backgammon world champion, had seen what was happening, and he eventually moved his 6.9 litre Mercedes-Benz into a position where we could jump in.

'How are you?' he smiled.

'We're fine,' I said. 'You wouldn't mind taking us to the Villa d'Este hotel, would you?'

'We are on the way.'

We celebrated that night with the rest of the team, and the telegrams of congratulations started arriving the next day, an early form of text messaging, bare words without punctuation. WONDERFUL MUM AND DAD . . . WONDERFUL SIMPLY WONDERFUL JENNY AND DAVID MURRAY . . . DELIGHTED TO SEE YOU HAVE LEARNED THE ART OF SLIP STREAMING JOHN COOMBS

Strangely, the full impact of becoming F1 world champion

did not truly sink in until the next morning, when, as I was walking down the marble staircase at the Villa d'Este, I happened to overhear the concierge speaking on the telephone. I had asked him to try and change my flight, and he seemed to be having trouble getting two seats on an earlier plane out of Milan.

He said, 'This is important. It's for Jackie Stewart. He is the new world champion, you know.'

I stood still for a moment on those stairs. The words sounded good; no question, they sounded very good.

The season petered out, and we lost our edge in the last three races of the year, but my final margin of victory – Stewart 63 points, Ickx 37 points – and Matra-Ford's triumph over Brabham Ford in the constructors' world championship suggested to most observers the alliance between Ken Tyrrell, Matra, Elf and Ford, supported by Dunlop, would continue to dominate the F1 landscape.

It didn't work out that way.

Our success was rightly celebrated in Paris, but it prompted the notion within Matra that, in 1970, we should dispense with the Ford engine and race in a car completely made in France. Ken disagreed, and so did I. We were adamant the Ford Cosworth engine was the dominant force in the sport and believed it would be madness to seek another option. On the other hand, Jean-Luc Lagardère saw production of a high-quality engine by his own engineers as an entirely natural progression.

I agreed to try out the new Matra V12 engine, at a secret early-morning test in Albi in the south of France, and it produced a silky smooth power curve that sounded magnificent. But it was larger and more complicated and it just didn't have the grunt of the Ford Cosworth.

There was absolutely no animosity between the parties but, with considerable sadness, Ken and Jean-Luc decided their respective companies should go their separate ways.

All of a sudden, as reigning world champions, we became a F1 team in search of a chassis. We made tentative enquiries at Lotus and at Brabham but, unsurprisingly, nobody was interested in supplying a car to their main rivals. In the end, with no options, we opened discussions with Max Mosley, Alan Rees, Robin Herd and Graham Coaker, the founders of March Engineering, and they agreed to supply us with the March 701 chassis. I was hopeful the new car would prove competitive but, in reality, the 1970 season turned out to be every bit as frustrating and disappointing as 1969 had been enjoyable and successful.

We started quite well, when I took pole position and finished third in South Africa. I then secured a slightly fortunate victory in the Spanish Grand Prix at Jarama, when first Jack Brabham suffered a mechanical failure while leading and then Jacky Ickx led until he was involved in a fiery collision with Jackie Oliver which destroyed both cars – once again, the race continued, and the rest of us were forced to drive through the fire and smoke.

However, all I had to show from the rest of the season was a couple of second-place finishes, in Holland and Italy.

There were times when the March seemed fast enough, but we could not maintain the pace and reliability of the previous year, and I struggled to be competitive in a year overshadowed by the deaths of Piers Courage, Bruce McLaren and Jochen Rindt.

For us, all was not lost because, even while we were battling through the 1970 season, in the main hut of his woodyard, deep in the heart of Surrey, Ken Tyrrell was planning our revival.

CHAPTER 9

Rocket Ship

As THE YEARS PASSED AND MY MOTOR RACING CAREER PROGRESSED, the rocket ship of my life seemed to be travelling faster and faster. The pace became such that, in any given time, it was difficult for me to recall the important places I had visited, meetings I had held and people I had met only a year before. My schedule became a frantic blur, with scarcely a spare hour, let alone a spare day or weekend in my diary, but when I think about it now, the challenge of organising this schedule and effectively managing my time was a useful preparation for my life after racing. It was crazy and challenging, but it was also stimulating and exciting, and somehow we packed everything in. For at least four decades to come, not much was going to change.

Now as then, if I thought I was going to enjoy something, whether it was a race in a particularly impressive car or a test session where I thought we might be able to improve our performance, or a corporate function where I knew there would be interesting people to meet, or a business relationship where I believed I could make a worthwhile contribution, I found it –

and I continue to find it – almost impossible to say 'no'. In the late 1960s and early 1970s, I hurled myself into this incredible lifestyle of racing commitments, in F1 and F2, in the CanAm (the sports car series in North America), and appearances for the Ford Motor Company, Elf, Dunlop and then Goodyear, and other promotions, and lunches and dinners to attend, speeches to make and photographs to be taken.

I know I was immensely fortunate – fortunate to be earning a fantastic living in a glamorous and exciting environment, fortunate to be emerging in an era as exciting as the 1960s and fortunate, above all, to have a wife who supported me unconditionally, provided a sense of stability and raised our children.

The rocket-ship ride sparked many incredible experiences, but it also created some major challenges in terms of where we would live and the amount of time I spent away from home. Every reward was balanced by an equal sacrifice. That was the reality, and I remember often being aware of the need to slow down, but the brakes on the rocket ship were poor. Sometimes, they hardly worked at all.

Max Aitken, the Second Baron Beaverbrook, the chairman of Beaverbrook Newspapers Ltd and a director of the Express Group, had phoned and said he wanted me to go somewhere and have a portrait photograph taken before the Daily Express Sportsman of the Year lunch at the Savoy hotel on the Strand.

'I'm sorry, Max,' I told him. 'There just isn't any time.'

'Jackie, it's for tomorrow's newspaper,' he persisted. 'You're going to win the Daily Express Sportsman of the Year Award, and we are planning a big spread with a photograph.'

'OK, look,' I said, 'I can maybe give it ten minutes.'

'He's a major photographer.'

'Max, that's the best I can do.'

So, I found my way to this cramped attic studio somewhere above Fleet Street and, as soon as I arrived, I told the photographer it would be helpful if he could be quick because

I was rushing. I assumed he was a snapper from the *Express* and, in retrospect, I might have seemed a bit impatient. The lighting and the reflector boards were already in place, and the photographer calmly set about his work. A couple of clicks later, he said that was all he needed, and thanked me for my time.

'No problem,' I said, as I scurried for the door, scarcely giving him a second thought because I was already late for another appointment I had squeezed in before the lunch.

The next morning, I picked up a copy of the *Daily Express* and quickly scanned the words printed alongside my photograph: *Today two greats from two different worlds come together. In front of the lens Jackie Stewart, behind the camera Karsh, who specialises in portraits of the more famous faces.* I felt like a fool. The humble man who had taken my photograph was one of the most famous and admired portrait photographers of all time, the genius who asked Winston Churchill to remove the cigar from his mouth and promptly captured the defining image of the British Prime Minister, scowling and defiant, which was published on the front cover of *Life* magazine during World War II and has been reproduced many times. In his time, Karsh had photographed everyone from Albert Einstein to John F. Kennedy, from Laurence Olivier to Muhammad Ali, from Princess Elizabeth to Princess Grace . . . and me. If I had only taken the time to find out who he was, I would have given him a full day, or as long as he wanted.

There was so much to do in the 1960s. Britain was emerging from post-war austerity and bursting out in a colourful blaze of music, fashion and social freedom. Everything seemed so new and, as a F1 racing driver with a growing profile, I was swept along in all the excitement, and the invitations kept coming.

It didn't take me long to learn the importance of looking the part. If I was the principal guest at a function, I recognised that I would need to be correctly dressed to make the right impression. That meant taking trouble to have the right suit, or blazer, or sports jacket, and the right trousers. So I kept my eyes and ears open and got to know the people who would help ensure I was presented in the best possible way, enhancing the value that I offered to the people around me, and to our sponsors and business associates.

In 1970, following a friend's recommendation, I visited the shop of Douglas Hayward at 95 Mount Street, London, and Doug and his colleagues have been making all my suits, jackets and trousers ever since. They know me, I know them; the quality of their work is outstanding, and Doug and his small team have looked after me tremendously well for more than thirty-five years.

If you're a sportsman with a reasonable physique, a fitted and well-cut suit will always look fantastic, but only if you have gone to the trouble to buy a properly fitted shirt that hangs correctly, without creases and with sleeves of the correct length. That may well look good, but to top it all off you are likely to find you have to buy a top-quality tie, which can mean you would have to spend, say, four times what you might expect but that is a small price to pay, given your likely income, for presenting yourself correctly. I am always amazed by the number of sports people who will invest in the right suit, but then ruin the overall effect by not bothering to find the best shirt, tie and shoes as well.

Nobody cares these days, some people might say. Times have changed, Jackie, you're out of tune.

Wrong, I would reply. Fashions change, of course – ties are no longer essential in many offices – although there's no harm in wearing one because, if it isn't needed, you can take it off; and there are prominent people who seem to take delight in deliberately 'dressing down', but it seldom serves them well.

In any function or business meeting, an individual is still instantly defined by the way he or she dresses. Dressing well doesn't get the whole job done, but it will start you off on the right foot. Dress badly and, very often, you won't get out of the blocks.

So, with a Doug Hayward suit, I set off in search of a bespoke shirt that would be comfortable around my neck and give me the right sleeves. Initially, I went to Turnbull and Asser at 71–72 Jermyn Street; later, I went to Frank Foster in Pall Mall.

'Jackie, you need to get yourself some decent shoes,' Doug noted one afternoon.

'You think so?'

'I do. Let me give you the name of somewhere to go.'

So, I made my way to George Cleverley, who was plying his trade in a quaint basement workshop at 27 Cork Street, Mayfair. What a craftsman he was. I felt extremely privileged to become a client of a man who had made shoes for Winston Churchill and some of the best-dressed men in the world. When we first met in 1970, he told me in no uncertain terms that he believed I should only have a pair of lace-up shoes and a pair of evening shoes. I'm still wearing both those pairs of shoes nearly four decades later. The leather is beginning to crack, but the distinctive, graceful and elegant form looks as good as ever, and they still wear like a pair of slippers. Cleverley shoes are not inexpensive, but such craftsmanship is rarely found. Over the years, I must have bought almost forty pairs of Cleverley shoes, and these included some slip-ons. George didn't like making slip-ons, and only did so with great reluctance.

'It's not the thing to do, Mister Jackie,' he would say, quite correctly. 'It's not good for your feet. Slip-ons don't give you the right support.'

He was still making shoes when he died in May 1991 at nearly ninety-three years of age, but by then he had decided that two of his apprentices, George Glasgow and John Carnera, shared his principles of shoemaking to such a degree that he was happy to give his permission for them to open a 'G. J. Cleverley and Co. Ltd' shop in the Royal Arcade, off Piccadilly. Whenever I need new shoes, for any occasion, this is still the place to go.

So, I hope, a properly dressed, long-haired Scottish motor racing driver took his place in the public eye.

There was something else I needed: some form of headgear to wear before and after my races, because my hair would typically get matted to my head. I looked around, and decided the image of a motor racing driver required something a little more trendy than a country gentleman's cap or a baseball cap, something different and maybe a bit more modern; in the end, I decided on a black corduroy cap, similar to the one worn at the time by John Lennon.

A recognisable brand was starting to emerge. Nobody planned it, and I would have been horrified by the thought of employing expensive consultants to create an image. It turned out to be a natural reflection of the way my life was evolving – sideburns, big dark glasses, black corduroy cap, long hair, cheeky grin.

If I look back now, and reflect on how I appeared to others and what I grew to represent in the late 1960s and early 1970s, I don't have any regrets at all. It was fun and inoffensive and, in many ways, I was having the time of my life.

My life was changing dramatically and, seemingly a million miles from Dumbuck, I suddenly found myself travelling and being introduced to people whom I had only ever dreamed of meeting. I was not seeking them, and they were not seeking me. Somehow, purely as a result of my status as a racing driver, doors opened, and I came into contact with some of the most famous, unusual and talented people in the world. It was an extraordinary privilege.

November 1966: in Las Vegas to race a Lola T70 Chevrolet for John Mecom, we go to see Frank Sinatra perform at the

Sands hotel. The 'Chairman of the Board' is backed by the Count Basie Orchestra, conducted by a young Quincy Jones, and his amazing renditions of 'Come Fly with Me', 'One for My Baby', 'It Was a Very Good Year' and 'Angel Eyes' make me a fan for life. I am bowled over by the sheer star quality of his performance, his perfect timing, the way he crafts every song so perfectly. We chat backstage after the show.

October 1968: in Los Angeles, between the US Grand Prix and the Mexican Grand Prix, I am spending almost every day with film director Roman Polanski and his beautiful wife, Sharon Tate. He says we should try a new restaurant with excellent music on Sunset Boulevard, so we go there and 'Hey Jude' is playing, and, suddenly, I'm dancing with Mia Farrow. It's amazing, and, fortunately, 'Hey Jude' is a quite a long number.

November 1968: still in Los Angeles, I'm getting my hair cut by Jay Sebring, hairdresser to the stars and a colourful character who drives a Porsche and revels in the high life. He is friends with both Roman and Sharon.

August 1969: I'm writing a condolence letter to Roman, after hearing the horrendous news that four followers of Charles Manson have burst into his home on Cielo Drive and murdered Sharon Tate, Jay Sebring, and two other people in the house at the time. Sharon was eight and a half months pregnant. The news had shocked me. In the early afternoon on the day after the incident, I had been sitting on the patio in our home in Geneva when the phone rang. I'd picked it up, and was taken aback to hear Roman's voice. He was clearly still in a terrible state, very emotional. I thought it was only other people who received calls like that. I commiserated with him. It's odd. I had had an early dinner with him and Sharon just a few weeks before, and that turned out to be the very last evening they ever spent together. Sharon left the next day, sailing alone to New York on the QE2, and then taking the train across America to Los Angeles. She couldn't fly. She was seven months pregnant.

March 1971: in the first-class lounge at Geneva airport, I am introduced to one of the greatest actors of all time, maybe the biggest name in entertainment. Charlie Chaplin lives in nearby Corsier-sur-Vevey and he is sitting patiently, waiting for a flight to Paris. Dressed in an impeccable overcoat, he is quiet and modest, and we talk for an hour. A photograph of us is taken, which I will cherish for years.

The rocket ship was soaring . . . without a safety net. Helen and I realised we were living an exciting life, but with no security. For all its glamour, my sport was also incredibly dangerous, and this reality forced us to make another hard decision: to leave Scotland and live in Switzerland. Our move was prompted by the reality that, as a top-rate tax payer in 1968, I was paying 93 per cent income tax. I was keeping seven pennies of every pound I earned. If I had been a high-flying business executive likely to earn a substantial salary for years to come, such high taxes would have been onerous but maybe sustainable. As a F1 motor racing driver with no cash reserves and maybe five or so good earning years ahead of me, there was simply no way I could make provision for my family if I was killed or involved in a big accident. This situation was untenable. In practice, the only way I could give security to Helen and the boys was to move and live in a place where we would keep more of my income. Neither of us wanted to leave. We had bought a lovely old house on top of the hill in Helensburgh. It was solid and typically Scottish, with five bedrooms, and was everything we had always dreamed of owning, but there was no option. The only choice we had was among the tax havens of the world.

Jim Clark had already gone non-resident to Bermuda, and that was a lovely place, but it wasn't going to suit us because I was spending much of my time racing in Europe. Another option was Monaco, which would have been fine for Helen and me, but we would have had to live in an apartment and we decided it would be easier for our young family to settle down in a rural environment with more open spaces, where the boys would be able to grow up and enjoy outdoor activities to the full.

'Jackie, have you thought about Switzerland,' asked Jo Bonnier, my fellow F1 driver, after a practice session before the 1,000 km race at the Nurburgring.

'No, I haven't,' I replied.

'Well, come and have a look next week. You can stay with us on your way down to Monaco.'

I accepted his invitation, arrived in this special part of the world, looked around and was instantly struck by the spectacular beauty of the villages on the north shore of Lac Leman, set on the slope with views across the water to the Alps and the magnificence of Mont Blanc. The quality of life seemed outstanding and the area where Jo lived was twenty minutes' drive to Geneva airport and from there it was a relatively short flight to almost everywhere in Europe. Jo introduced me to his lawyer, a man called Baron Andre de Pfyffer, who was able to make all the necessary arrangements for us to move to Switzerland, if we decided to go ahead.

There is no question my wife has had to put up with a great deal over the years, but I can't think of many occasions when her tolerance and support was more acutely tested than the time when I flew to Geneva and agreed to buy our new home before she had even seen a picture of it, let alone seen it for herself. As ever, the rocket ship was flying too fast. I had set aside one day in my schedule, and Andre de Pfyffer had arranged for me to view four properties. I arrived at a two-bedroom house just outside the village of Begnins, on six and a half acres of land, and immediately knew it would be perfect for the Stewart family. The building was 'Swiss solid', the elevated position was spectacular and surrounded by pretty woods, and there were two rectangular ponds in front of the house . . . they reminded me of the Palace of Versailles and were maybe a little pretentious, but, as far as I was concerned, everything looked just fine. I freely admit I didn't pay much attention to the kitchen, which turned out to be an unattractive vision in grey Formica with a wood stove, but Helen quickly put that right. In the years ahead, we built extensions, adding more bedrooms, a larger kitchen area and a family room, and we also filled in the ponds because they were not safe for small children. My first instincts proved to be pretty good, and the new 'Clayton House' turned out to be a wonderfully happy home.

News of our decision to leave Scotland was splashed over the newspapers in February 1968 and it provoked an angry response from people who reckoned I was turning my back on my country. Letters to the editor demanded to know why I thought I should not have to pay UK taxes like everybody else.

The reason, as I tried to explain over and over again, was that moving to Switzerland was the only way I could guarantee financial security for my family's long-term future. Some understood, others didn't. It was always going to be an emotional issue, but the resentment grew so intense at one stage that I took Helen away for a weekend at the Turnberry hotel, just to get away from it all. We even checked in under a false name.

'It's Mr and Mrs Smith,' I told the woman working at the hotel reception matter-of-factly.

'OK,' she replied, barely suppressing a smile.

We had been advised to move at the beginning of April, before the start of the new tax year, and this turned out to be the weekend when Jim Clark was killed, as I mentioned previously, so our spirits were desperately low on the Monday morning when I met Helen and the boys at Geneva airport.

It was not an easy time for Helen. As the young mother of a two-year-old boy and a three-month-old baby, she had had to leave her friends and family and move to a foreign country where she couldn't speak the language and where she would live in a house deep in the countryside, some distance from the neighbours; and no sooner had we arrived than I was waving goodbye, leaving to drive the Matra MS7 in the F2 Grand Prix at Pau. To say I owe Helen a debt is a massive understatement. While I was riding the rocket ship, attending glamorous events and meeting interesting people all around the world, she was making a home and bringing up our two boys.

Paul, our eldest son, was born in October 1965, on the weekend of the 200 mile race in Riverside, California. I happened to be relaxing by the hotel swimming pool when one of the staff called me to take an urgent telephone call. It was Anne Rennie, my secretary at the garage in Dumbuck, calling to give me the wonderful news that our first baby boy had been born at the Overton maternity hospital and safely arrived in the world. Helen had endured a very difficult pregnancy, being confined to her bed for many months, and there were times when we didn't know whether she would be able to keep the baby at all, so I was especially delighted to be told that my wife and her infant son were both doing well.

I flew straight back to Scotland after the race, together with Jim Clark, who also needed to get home quickly because his father was unwell. Having bought a soft toy at the airport, a big furry dog, I arrived at our house to greet our good-looking wee boy and Helen, who was looking remarkably well after giving birth.

In fact, she had made such an outstanding recovery that, on the evening after I got home, we decided to go out and celebrate. I took Helen up to Glasgow for a quiet dinner for two at what was a well-respected restaurant called '101'. There was a small orchestra playing throughout the evening, and, after dinner, we were dancing cheek-to-cheek to a slow, romantic number when we both overheard a woman indignantly complain to her partner that 'it was awful that that racing driver Jackie Stewart should be out on the town with another woman when his wife was still in hospital after having a baby'. Of course, Helen took the remark as a great compliment.

Our second son, Mark, was born at the same hospital in January 1968, and I wasn't present for that either. It wasn't the done thing in Scotland at that time, and, thinking back, I don't think I knew a father who was there at the birth of his child. I suppose we were all too old-fashioned. Times have certainly changed: both Paul and Mark were right in the middle of the action when their children were born many years later.

At least I was allowed to drive Helen to the hospital, and it was a dramatic trip because, on a wet and stormy night, we found the road blocked by a fallen tree. The only way I could get around the tree was to drive off-road, and we decided the bumpy ride would be no good for Helen or the baby. So, in pouring rain, we got out of the car, and I helped her clamber over the tree. I then drove round, picked her up on the other side and, with the mother-to-be looking a little wet and windblown, we resumed our journey.

We eventually arrived, and I waited until she was settled in before being told in no uncertain terms that I should go home and wait to be telephoned if anything happened. Naturally, I did as I was told, and waited, and waited . . . until the telephone rang. It was Malcolm McDougall, a journalist sent by his newspaper to keep sentry duty at the hospital.

'Hello, Jackie,' he said, 'it's Malcolm.'

'Yes?'

'It's a boy, and Helen's fine.'

'Wonderful.'

I put down the receiver, delighted by the news but thinking it was strange I had heard this news from the motoring correspondent of the *Daily Record* rather than Dr Gordon, the excellent specialist we had so carefully chosen. In any case, I drove straight to the hospital and found mother and child doing well. Helen was relaxed, and Mark looked great, but our Dr Gordon was clearly livid because it seemed that one of the nursing staff had leaked the news to some journalists, meaning the media knew I had become a father for a second time before me.

Moving to a brand new country with these two bundles of energy was far from ideal, even with the assistance of one or two wonderful Scottish nannies, notably Margaret Boag. I recall Paul and Mark had to sleep on the floor of the dining room when we first moved in because their rooms were not ready.

'OK,' said Helen, 'let's just get on with it.'

We began to settle down in Switzerland, making new friends like Doris Brynner, the ex-wife of Yul Brynner and an enormously effervescent lady who remains close to us today, a motor racing journalist called Bernard Cahier and his wife, Joan. The actor Peter Ustinov, who lived in the next village, followed motor sport keenly and used to delight the children with his imitations of a barking dog whenever he came over for lunch or dinner.

Even so, we looked forward to our regular trips back to Scotland, to see my parents and my brother Jim and to keep in touch with friends like John and Nan Lindsay, Gordon and Judy Hunter, Tim Morrison and others; and we used to go salmon fishing with Marjorie, James and Joe Walker, of the Walker's shortbread family, on the same stretch of the River Spey in Aberlour where my father and his friends had gone fishing.

Unfortunately, the garage at Dumbuck was not doing well:

it had comfortably supported the Stewart family when we were all living under one roof but, when Jim and I eventually left home and got married, the business as it was then was simply not big enough to sustain three families.

The books were not balancing, and I decided to buy the business because I certainly did not want the garage built by Dad, quite literally with his own hands, to be financially embarrassed in any way. Not long afterwards, I came to an agreement with my best friend, John Lindsay, and his wife, Nan, whereby they would take over the garage. They turned it into a successful Vauxhall dealership in the 1970s and they are still there, together with their son Damon, running it today.

Sadly, the health of both my parents started to deteriorate in the late 1960s. My mother suffered several strokes and was having physiotherapy at the Western Infirmary in Glasgow when she fell and damaged her leg. The wound somehow became gangrenous and her leg was amputated above the knee.

My parents continued to live at the family home, Rockview, and I made sure they received the special care they needed.

My father fell seriously ill at the start of 1972, and I was very concerned when I saw him the day before I flew to Buenos Aires to compete in the Grand Prix of Argentina on 25 January, which was, by coincidence, my mother's birthday. I returned to my hotel room immediately after the race and dialled the familiar number to see how he was doing. My brother answered.

'Jim,' I said. 'How's Dad?'

'Jackie, I'm so sorry,' my brother said. 'He died this afternoon.'

The end probably came as a release for my father, who by then had also suffered a series of strokes, but news of his death still came as a shock, and my mind flashed back to the moment just a few weeks earlier, when he heard I had been awarded an OBE for services to sport, and he said, 'Now, I can die happy.'

Jim was still on the phone.

'By the way,' he asked, 'how did you go in the Grand Prix?'

'Oh,' I replied, 'I won.'

Mother Stewart, as she was then known to one and all, stayed at Rockview for a while after my father's death, but she eventually said she wanted to move to an excellent nursing home in the village of Old Kilpatrick, two and a half miles from where we lived, and it was there that we used to visit her with her grandchildren.

With Paul and Mark at home in Switzerland, needing her attention, Helen decided to travel less frequently and she was soon attending mainly the 'local' F1 Grands Prix in Monaco, Britain, France and Italy. I didn't encourage her to come to the races in Germany and Belgium because I felt they were too dangerous. She was missed at the circuits, not just by me, because I had grown used to having her around ever since I first climbed into a racing car, but by the entire team because, with her time-keeping and her keenness to help whenever required, she had become an integral part of the Tyrrell operation. Helen had become a familiar presence in the pit lane, and, if I may be permitted to say so, it was a particularly beautiful presence as well. Photographers were often aiming their lens at her on the pit wall, and her picture was frequently published in newspapers and magazines around the world. She was also unfazed by the reality that many glamorous and undeniably beautiful women tended to flutter around the F1 racing world like moths around a light bulb and she handled potentially awkward situations with style and humour.

I remember one hot afternoon between practice sessions at the US Grand Prix at Watkins Glen, when a tall blonde beauty suddenly appeared, making her way down the pit lane. She was wearing nothing but a skimpy yellow bikini, and she was being followed by a mêlée of eager photographers. The Tyrrell team were at the end of the pit lane, and, as this girl approached, I noticed she was stopping and asking each of the drivers to sign their name on her naked flesh. I sensed the situation could become complicated so, noticing Helen had not seen what was going on and thinking quickly, I walked over and casually asked her if she would nip back to the garage area and fetch a new tinted visor for my helmet. It was the kind of thing she would do, and I calculated she would then be out of the way by the time the blonde reached our pit. She headed off; the plan seemed to be working.

The blonde duly arrived, said she would really like the world champion's signature and offered me her marker pen or 'sharpie' as they are known in America. I looked for a spare place on her body, which was by now not easy to find. Ken and Norah Tyrrell were looking on with interest, and, with the photographers getting excited, I decided there was no alternative but to sign my name in a space at the top of her thigh, slanting upwards. Everyone was laughing, and I was enjoying myself until, just as I finished, at the very moment that I completed my signature by writing a small circle right on the front of the blonde's bikini briefs, I felt a familiar hand on my shoulder. Helen had returned.

'Be careful,' she whispered. 'She's got dirty ears.'

The boys were soon heading to school, first to a kindergarten in the village of Gland, on the lake's edge, and then to a nursery school further up the mountain at St Cergues. As they grew older, we decided both Paul and Mark would be educated at a school where they would make friends of all nationalities, and they attended first the International School of Geneva at La Châtaigneraie before going to boarding school at the renowned Aiglon College, in Villars.

The reality is that, like so many fathers with business commitments, and even mothers nowadays, I was intermittently absent for the greater part of their childhoods. My motor racing and other commercial obligations all around the world meant I was only able to spend, as a rough average, maybe three or four days in every fortnight at home. It was, in the familiar phrase, 'quality time', but no sooner had I unpacked than it seemed time for me to start packing again. This situation was not easy for anyone, but I reckoned the window of time where I would be able to keep earning well would extend no longer than five years after I retired from motor racing – and it was not clear what I would do after that. So I was anxious to seize every commercial opportunity and achieve the financial security I believed was necessary over the long term.

Nobody needed to remind me that while sports people often thrive when they are at the top of their careers, life can become hard after they retire because, very often, they have not received the education or training to make a living elsewhere. If I had known then what I know now – that I would actually be able to extend my earning capacity for decades after I stopped 'driving in anger' – my priorities may have been different. However, it is also true that I learned a great deal during this period, working with exceptional people and gaining invaluable experience in media and marketing, gathering an understanding of corporate life and culture, preparing for what became my future careers in television and business.

The price to be paid was that, instead of having me with them, putting them to bed every night and attending their events at school, Paul and Mark had to be content with receiving the postcards that I religiously sent them from wherever I was working in the world, and with collecting the small model cars that I used to bring them every time I returned home.

When he was four, Mark suddenly announced he thought Daddy had another home and said I came to stay now and then but actually lived behind the 'big doors'. Helen and I were concerned by this and we wondered whether he was having nightmares but, after gentle questioning, it emerged young Mark had become so used to waving me goodbye at Geneva airport that he had started to believe I must live behind the large sliding doors that led to the departures lounge. As far as he was concerned, I suppose, I did.

However, there were many times when the rocket ship was parked at home, and we met people through sport who became friends not just of mine, but of Helen and the boys as well.

Sean Connery was one of the most recognised men in the world as the James Bond of the late 1960s and early 1970s but he has been a wonderful friend of our family for more than thirty-five years and he often came to stay with us in Switzerland. We first met in 1971, and I was instantly impressed by how comfortably he wore his fame. He seemed so modest and he was so relaxed when fans approached him in the street that I decided I should try to conduct myself in a similar fashion.

It was Sir Ian Stewart, the respected Scottish industrialist, who initially introduced us to each other at the Carlton Tower Hotel in London, and Sean asked if I would join him and Sir Ian as a trustee of the Scottish International Educational Trust. Sean was not only the co-founder of this organisation that provided scholarships to young Scots, he had also supplied its initial funding by donating his entire acting fee for playing James Bond in the film *Diamonds Are Forever* – around £600,000. I was subsequently appointed as a vice-president and have always tried to help where possible. SIET is still going strong today, still making a difference in the lives of thousands of Scots.

Sean and I soon became close and after I announced my retirement from racing, the four of us – Helen and I, Sean and Micheline – arranged to go skiing in the Alps. None of us had ever skied before, which seemed odd for 'James Bond', so lessons with a ski instructor were laid on all round. We all took to the slopes quite well until, on the third day of the holiday,

Sean somehow managed to fall over from a standing position, landing on his elbow and badly tearing the ligaments in his shoulder. He was in great pain when he went to the local medical centre and, in fact, he was told to return there for treatment every morning for the remainder of our stay.

We were thrown together in another sports environment some years later, when we were invited to take part in a charity golf match at Gleneagles. Sean and I were playing against Bing Crosby and a well-known American TV personality called Phil Harris and, to our amazement, 15,000 people turned up to watch. Bing was a serious golfer and clearly expected to win, so he didn't look too pleased when, playing off a sixteen handicap, I reached the first green in two and holed a 45-foot putt for a birdie three, which counted as an eagle because I received a stroke on that hole. The gallery went crazy, enjoying what was the highlight of my otherwise mediocre golfing life. That put us one up and we never trailed, eventually closing out a surprise 5 & 4 win on the fourteenth green. Bing wasn't happy, and, when I suggested we should play the last four holes because it was for charity and we ought to give the public some entertainment, he shook his head and returned to the clubhouse.

Sean and Micheline spend most of their time in the Bahamas these days, so we don't see them as often as we would like but we always keep in touch.

The rocket ship had just been launched when I first met Their Serene Highnesses, the Prince and Princess of Monaco, after I won the F3 race in 1964, and, as the years passed, we spent a lot of time with Prince Rainier, Princess Grace and their children, Albert, Caroline and Stephanie. Prince Rainer was gentle and kind, a motoring enthusiast who kept a superb collection of cars. Prince Albert has now become His Serene Highness Prince Albert II of Monaco, The Sovereign Prince, but I have clear memories of him as a wee boy, taking him down to the pits at ten o'clock on the night before the Grand Prix and showing him the F1 cars when the paddock and garage areas were quiet and peaceful.

Her Serene Highness the Princess of Monaco, formerly Grace Kelly, was aptly named twice; she was one of the most serene and most graceful people I have ever known. So glamorous, she was the image of a fairytale princess in a magic kingdom. I can still picture her attending the black-tie reception and dinner traditionally hosted at the Palace on the Saturday night before the Monaco Grand Prix. Amid a great assembly of people, including stars like David Niven and Peter Sellers, and the F1 drivers, all of whom used to attend in those days, the Princess would appear, bejewelled and beautiful beyond words. She died on 14 September 1982, aged fifty-three, when she suffered a stroke while driving in Monaco, and her funeral at St Nicholas' Cathedral was a huge and desperately sad occasion. I remember rushing home from Detroit, so Helen and I could attend.

The rocket-ship journey continued.

It was the last night of 1972, and Helen and I had been invited to a New Year's Eve dinner party hosted by Gianni Agnelli, president of Fiat, and his wife Mariella at their chalet in St Moritz. There were three tables of ten, as I recall, and we were intrigued to find ourselves sitting at the same table as Doris Brynner, shipping tycoon Stavros Niarchos, Prince Amin Aga Khan, the Begum Sally Aga Khan, Andy Warhol and his business manager Fred Hughes. It was clearly going to be an interesting evening when Andy placed a tape cassette recorder on the table in front of us all and said that, if we didn't mind, he was going to record the entire dinner. The originator of pop art told us this was a form of art and, every thirty minutes, he duly stopped to put in a new cassette.

At one stage of a wonderfully entertaining evening, Andy turned to me and said, 'Hey, Jackie, you know what? Why don't you come to my studio in New York and I'll paint you?'

I knew he had produced iconic works of Marilyn Monroe and Elvis Presley, and he seemed intrigued by my profile in the sport and was eager to paint a picture of me set within his perception of the exciting and glamorous motor racing world.

'That sounds interesting,' I replied. 'How would it work?'

'OK,' he said. 'Well, I'll give you the original if you give me all the poster and lithograph rights.'

'How long would I have to spend in New York?'

'A couple of weeks, maybe a little more.'

'Andy,' I said. 'I'm sorry, it's impossible. I just don't have that amount of open time.'

Big mistake: if I had been able to slow down and find the time to go to New York and be painted by Andy Warhol, I would today have owned a picture worth many millions of pounds.

I had decided in 1968 that it would be sensible for me to secure some help in steering the rocket ship, and handling my commercial activities more efficiently and effectively. Some observers have described me as the first professional and commercially orientated racing driver, with the implication that I somehow represented a new approach. It's true that, relatively early in my career, I saw the potential to earn a great deal of money from the sport, but I knew I would need to conduct myself in the most effective and professional manner possible. I remember reading a book by Arnold Palmer and being impressed by the way he had shaped his career as a genuinely professional golfer. It seemed a major factor in his success had been his relationship with a dynamic, innovative and driven sports lawyer and promoter named Mark McCormack. The sports world was evolving dramatically in 1968, and I decided this American was the perfect man to assist somebody like me.

So, in the autumn of that year, I arranged to have lunch with Mark in the Rib Room at the Carlton Tower Hotel, where he used to stay in London, and he appeared enthusiastic about my proposal that I become one of his clients. The following week, I signed with the International Management Group. Almost four decades later, I am still a client of IMG. Mark signed my contract and then promptly handed the task of assisting me to one of his employees who was in his first job, a youngster with glasses who was even shorter than me, named Martin Sorrell. He was good company and extremely bright, ambitious and as sharp as a needle, and he has since become one of the most successful British businessmen on the global stage. Sir Martin Sorrell founded the WPP Group in 1986 and has been the CEO ever since, guiding the company to become one of the largest communications services groups in the world, employing 97,000 people in over 2,000 offices in ninety-six countries. We remain close to this day, even if I find it hard to resist reminding him on a regular basis that he started as my first bag man, and that the period he spent with me represented ideal preparation for his subsequent career.

As my association with IMG evolved, I only met Mark McCormack now and then to discuss operational matters, but he would frequently call me with an idea. He became widely recognised as one of the most powerful men in world sport; in my view, he was perhaps, above all, the most phenomenal networker. Mark used to identify promising young people in major companies and then consciously contribute to their development and systematically ensure they were promoted within their own structures, even if that meant using his influence with the chairman or president of the company. By the time these individuals reached top executive positions, they would be eager to continue doing business with him, and of course the many exceptional people whom he brought to work at IMG. An ability to surround himself with high-quality individuals was another of his great qualities, and, over the years, I have been fortunate to work with many outstanding people at IMG: at first, there was Jay Lafave, Jay Michaels, Bud

Stanner and a wonderful Scot called Alastair Johnston in the United States, and Ian Todd, a very knowledgeable lawyer called Brian Clark, Andrew Maconie and Sarah Wooldridge in Europe, and then Andrew Hampel and, in most recent times, Rob Armstrong.

Mark died prematurely on 16 May 2003. His clients were the giants of their chosen sports. Arnold Palmer was first and was never anything but first in Mark's book, and rightly so. Jack Nicklaus and Gary Player were the next to join, and the list of exceptional IMG clients has now become too long to mention. Today it includes Tiger Woods and Roger Federer. Following his death, Mark's family sold the company to Ted Forstmann, who has been a friend of both Helen and myself for many years. Teddy is himself a great sports enthusiast, so it is no surprise the marriage is already proving to be a success.

With IMG aboard, there is no doubt the rocket ship handled more easily and began to travel in less turbulent air.

Around the same time, that statement could also have been applied to the manner in which my financial management was being sorted out. Making money isn't particularly easy, but looking after it is sure as hell a lot harder and more complicated. Too many high-profile sports people have failed in that regard. I was determined not to be one of them. So when, in 1968, I met up with a successful banker in Geneva, called Eli Zilkha, it was an important moment in my life. In fact, Eli also played a key role in my introduction to IMG, setting up the initial lunch at my request. Over the years, Eli's guidance and advice, and also that of his son Marc who took over the reins after his father died, and still looks after some of my affairs today, has been invaluable. The link between the Stewart and Zilkha families serves as another example of a happy, long-term business and personal relationship. Such connections, across a wide spectrum of activity, have underpinned much of my life, I am delighted to say.

CHAPTER 10

Tyrrell 003

No single chassis has won more F1 Grands Prix in the history of the sport. The Tyrrell 003 stands apart as the winner of eight *Grandes Epreuves*, the definitive terminology for a world championship F1 Grand Prix. It started with its maiden victory at the Spanish Grand Prix on 18 April 1971 and recorded its last win at the French Grand Prix on 2 July 1972. In the process, it came as close as any racing car I have known to assuming the kind of status more often enjoyed by a much-loved champion racehorse.

It was quick, it was robust, it was reliable.

The car was born out of adversity when, disappointed by his split with Matra after winning the F1 world title in 1969 and swiftly disenchanted with the indifferent performance of the replacement March chassis, early in 1970 Ken Tyrrell decided he would design his own chassis and build his own car.

'Ken, are you sure you want to do that?' I asked.

'We can't go on with the March,' he replied.

'I know that.'

'I'm tired of relying on other people and being disappointed.'

'Can you afford it?'

'I think so.'

The sheer courage of Ken Tyrrell's decision should not be underestimated. In 1969, he had become the first private entrant to win the world championship and now he was trying to repeat the feat with his own car. Still working out of the woodyard, and having run his plans past his bank manager, he prepared to become a F1 manufacturer and compete with the giants of the sport.

His first step was to arrange a meeting with Derek Gardner, a quiet, meticulous man who invariably wore a collar and tie and spoke particularly slowly, as if weighing every word. Derek had started his career in the aerospace industry and then worked for a company called Harry Ferguson Research, based in Coventry with the former Le Mans winner Tony Rolt as MD, where he developed the four-wheel drive systems for the Matra MS84, a car I tested at Oulton Park but never raced. Thereafter, he set himself up as an engineering consultant, transforming the bedroom of his house in Leamington Spa into a design office. Ken was impressed by his skill and thoroughness and now wanted to offer him a job as chief designer.

'I want you to design a car for us,' Ken told him. 'It must be able to do at least one full season. It must be easy to repair and, if necessary, to rebuild. Oh, and one other thing, it must be quick.'

'That sounds interesting,' Derek replied.

Ken continued: 'This project must be completely secret. You can start the design phase at your house. That will be perfect because nobody will suspect anything, and later you can come down to Surrey, and we can start the manufacturing process in the main hut at the woodyard.'

Derek agreed, and promptly set to work.

Several weeks later, Ken took me to one side after a test day and said he wanted me to take a trip to the West Midlands. I asked him what for. For the 'SP', he replied. I had no idea what he was talking about. It's for the 'SP', he repeated, and I then remembered 'SP' was the code name Ken liked to use for his 'Special Project', the clandestine development of the new car.

So on 23 March 1970, I flew from Geneva to Coventry, hired a car at the airport and eventually arrived at a quiet cul-de-sac in Royal Leamington Spa and knocked on the door of a semi-detached house. Derek Gardner answered and, with a smile, ushered me straight through to his wooden garage.

Standing there in front of me was a full-scale wooden model of the new monocoque. 'Go on, sit in it,' Derek said. 'We have to make sure that everything fits you.'

The car looked something like the Matra-Ford MS80, with the mock-up Hewland gearbox and a mock-up Ford Cosworth engine behind me. I had been aware that Ken and Derek had considered following the aerodynamic shape of the Lotus 72, but I was pleased to see they had decided to keep the fuel tanks in the centre of the car, as they had been in the Matra – the slightly bulbous tanks did give the car a 'pregnant' look, but the weight distribution was more well balanced and it instinctively felt right.

Derek then showed me the drawings, and we ran through a series of other issues: the placement of the pedal cluster and the foot rest, the amount of space and elbow room in the cockpit, the pitch of the seating position, the height of the steering column, the position of the gear shift and the alignment of the gear linkage, which had to be just right or you could easily miss a gear as the car rolled on the exit of a corner or pitched under heavy acceleration and, in that moment, you could be over-taken and a Grand Prix could be lost.

These were complicated and technical issues. Racing drivers of my era, in fact of any era, would have understood exactly what we were talking about, but I daresay many of them would not have wanted to get too involved in so much detail at what was still only the design stage. That wasn't my view. I believed that, if we could deal with these matters accurately and correctly in the car's concept design process and essentially pre-empt problems, we would save ourselves time and trouble down the line.

Derek and I had both learned a great deal from our respective experiences with Matra, and, in the end, this remarkable designer produced a car of strength and simplicity.

As I walked away from his house just an hour or so later, I looked around the cul-de-sac and saw the local people contentedly going about their business on this normal Monday morning, completely unaware that a piece of motor racing history was being created in their midst. At that stage, only five people in the world – Derek, Ken, his wife, Norah, Neil Davis back at the woodyard and me – were aware the 'SP' programme even existed.

I telephoned Ken that same afternoon.

'What did you think?' he asked.

'I think it looks good,' I replied, probably with less enthusiasm than he was expecting.

'Only just good?'

'Well, there's a long way to go.'

'I know, but it is looking good, isn't it?'

'It's exciting, Ken. I can't tell you more than that.'

I certainly didn't want to be negative, but there was not a lot to get very excited about when you were standing in a relatively primitive domestic garage, looking at a plywood mock-up in a fairly rough state that bore only the slightest resemblance to a racing car that might one day win the world championship. At any rate, Ken would never tire of reminding me in later years how, according to his version of events, I was not impressed by my first sight of the new car.

The project moved to the woodyard as planned, and work continued through June and July. In many respects, it may have appeared amateur, but as the world was to discover, it was anything but. Local firms supplied many of the parts. For example, a company called Morris Gomm Metal Development down the road at Old Woking cut the aluminium sheets for the chassis. Yet the level of technical expertise was genuinely exceptional.

Few of the Tyrrell mechanics had any experience of chassis construction but, under Derek Gardner's direction, they developed the required skills and became a team of people eminently capable of constructing their own car.

Still nobody in the close-knit racing community guessed what was happening; although a few people were surprised when, with a degree of extravagance that seemed wholly out of character, Ken decided all his mechanics would fly home after the Dutch Grand Prix at Zandvoort and then do so again after the French Grand Prix at Clermont-Ferrand. The usual practice in those days was for the team to drive back to England, but Ken was determined to keep his 'SP' on schedule, so he didn't mind paying for the air fares to get his men home and back to work as quickly as possible.

His financial commitment to the project soon rose past the £22,000 mark, and that was not a sum allocated from any kind of multi-million-pound budget of a large organisation; it was cash paid out of his current account. Ken was investing much more than just his fine reputation on the success of this car. For all that it was a vast sum for Ken to be personally shelling out, in reality it was a ludicrously small amount in terms of what he was aiming to achieve, which makes his success all the more incredible. Even accounting for inflation, it would be impossible today to put together a brand new F1 car for that amount.

Finally, on Monday 17 August 1970, the members of the motoring press were invited to attend a special event in the Ford exhibition room at the Dagenham Motors, Regent Street,

London and, to Ken's great delight, they seemed to be caught completely by surprise when the blue Tyrrell 001 was unveiled.

'This is our new car,' the proud owner announced, as the cameras flashed, 'and we will race it for the first time at Oulton Park on Saturday. Jackie Stewart will be driving.'

These were exciting times, and I desperately hoped the car would be quick straight out of the box. This wasn't just wishful thinking. Historically, over the years, this was the way it typically used to happen with very good new racing cars: reliability could be secured inch by inch over a period of time, but if a car was not fast from the moment when it first turned its wheels, the unfortunate likelihood was that it would never be fast.

I drove 001 for the first time at Oulton Park in the Gold Cup, a non-championship F1 race and, despite persistent problems with fuel surge during practice, I managed to come from the back of the grid and post the fastest lap. An engine failure forced me to retire towards the end but even so, when I brought the car in and removed my helmet, I looked up to see Ken grinning broadly.

'So what do you think now?' he asked.

'It's still good,' I replied, 'and it's quick.'

By now, I was grinning as well. The car had performed, and we both realised much more was in there. We were just scratching the surface, and the potential was obvious.

A fortnight later, we took the car to the Italian Grand Prix at Monza, but the fuel supply was still erratic, and a broken front stub axle meant I had to revert and drive the March 701 in the actual race. It was frustrating but, in this era before the extensive and expensive pre-testing of new models or computer simulations, everyone realised we would have to be patient and work through the teething problems before Tyrrell 001 could be considered fit to race.

I managed to put the car on pole position for the Canadian

Grand Prix at Mont Tremblant on 20 September and I led the race for some time. That felt good. It was wonderful to be competitive again after all the frustrations of the March. People were suddenly talking about us as genuine contenders again. However, we were not quite there. Race reliability was still elusive. My front axle stub broke on the thirty-second lap, with me over fifteen seconds ahead of Jacky Ickx's Ferrari at the time, promptly ending my challenge.

There was similar frustration in the US Grand Prix at Watkins Glen, when I secured second place on the grid and was leading until an oil leak forced me to retire. We had no option but to grit our teeth, keep faith in what we were doing and work harder to get the car right, but nobody could have foreseen what would happen to us at the Mexican Grand Prix in Mexico City.

Race day had descended into chaos as a reported crowd of 200,000 spectators gathered and, in the resulting crush, many thousands of people started breaking down fences and streaming on to the edge of the track. It seemed for some time that the race could not possibly go ahead and since I was the reigning world champion and recognised as 'Mr Safety', I was asked to go out with Pedro Rodriguez, the Mexican F1 driver, and plead with the crowd to move back behind the barriers.

The race started on a circuit, as *Autocourse* accurately put it, 'lined with human guardrails'. It was crazy.

I started the race second on the grid and was making progress until, on lap thirty-three, I hit a dog that had inexplicably strayed on to the track; it was large, but it had looked the size of an elephant from where I was sitting. The poor animal was demented, confused by the noise of the revving engines. Not knowing what to do or where to run, it suddenly swerved into the path of my car. The impact was severe. I must have been travelling at 160 mph down the straight. The dog disintegrated, and the car veered violently to the left, towards a bank where spectators were sitting cross-legged a few metres from the tarmac. I only just managed to regain control and prevent my car from ploughing into that area and scything through the crowd. It was hardly discussed afterwards, and nobody has ever said much since, but I know how perilously close I came to being at the centre of a major disaster, in which as many as twenty or thirty people could easily have been killed. I just exhaled deeply, and returned to the pits.

All of us were frustrated by our new car's continuing technical problems but we were far from disheartened: 001 was wonderfully quick and we felt sure it would soon demonstrate reliability to match its speed. Dunlop's decision to withdraw from F1 racing at the end of 1970 was a setback, but we reviewed our strategy and were able to enter into a new association with Goodyear. Their tyres suited the new car, and we remained on track, heading in the right direction.

Derek tinkered with the design during the winter months, altering the air box, remodelling the nose section, lengthening the wheelbase and slightly narrowing the monocoque. The new cars which he produced for us to drive in the 1971 F1 season thus became known as Tyrrell 002 and Tyrrell 003. Tyrrell 002 was going to be driven by my new team-mate, the handsome, promising young French driver by the name of François Cevert, and it was decided I would drive 003.

This was the plan. In reality, the new cars were not quite ready, and I drove 001 in my first three races of the year, including the South African Grand Prix, where I claimed pole position and then finished second behind Mario Andretti in a Ferrari. Our prospects for the rest of the year were undeniably good.

'What do you think?' Ken asked again.

'I think we can win,' I replied.

I looked across at this tall, somewhat lugubrious man and reflected on everything that had happened since we first met on the day of the F3 test at Goodwood seven years earlier.

In 1971, we didn't have any form of contract between us. There had been a simple signed agreement in 1968 but, since then, neither of us had felt the need to have anything written down on paper. It seemed unnecessary. Our association, our friendship, had become so profound that it was enough. Today, a F1 driver's contract can run to more than fifty pages and, in business, I am always adamant about having every agreement rigorously checked and signed. With Ken, it was just different.

Almost everything was different. At times, we were like equal partners, calmly discussing the merits of the car or our strategy for a particular race. Other times, we would be more like father and son, with him taking me aside and offering me guidance and advice. Still other times, we would disagree and argue, and Ken would get so angry that he would launch into one of his famous 'froth jobs', projecting saliva between his front teeth. Always, from the first day that we met until the last time we spoke just a few days before he died, I trusted Ken Tyrrell unconditionally, and I know he felt able to trust me.

003 was finally ready for me to drive at the Spanish Grand Prix in Barcelona and, although Jacky Ickx claimed pole position in his Ferrari, the Tyrrell showed its full potential, and I was able to secure victory in the car's first F1 Grand Prix. When I look now at the lap times over seventy-five laps, I am still amazed that I was able to achieve such consistency. The answer lay in the car. It was driver friendly. No matter what you do in life, whatever tools or equipment you may require, they should always offer you an invitation, never a challenge: 003 provided such an invitation for me. It was friendly, predictable. It didn't threaten.

If a young racing driver reads these words, he may find it difficult to appreciate the full meaning. In my era, with few exceptions, young drivers would drive by the seat of their pants. Blessed with a bucketload of God-given talent, they would instinctively drive on the limit and rely on lightning reflexes to get them out of trouble. Little has changed. When I attend a Grand Prix nowadays, I usually spend time in the Williams garage or pit lane area, wearing a headset tuned in to the communications between the two drivers and their engineers. So I listen to the drivers explaining the troubles they may be having out on the track, and seldom is something said that I have not heard many times before. Now, as then, everybody is seeking speed and the kind of consistency of performance that we were somehow able to achieve with 003 at the Spanish Grand Prix in 1971 – and, in my opinion, the key to our success was the ability and resolve of both driver and engineers to step back and analyse what may be going wrong with the car and clearly decipher what component may be causing the behaviour that was preventing the driver from delivering the kind of performance that everybody wanted.

Many young drivers are so consumed by driving as fast as possible that they are unable to recognise the subtle changes that can be made to improve performance. For them, it's all too much of a blur. They tend to overdrive, which means they bully the car into things it doesn't wish to do rather that handling it with finesse and coaxing the car through a particular situation, in such a way that they can feel what may be wrong. An overly forceful approach can yield results, and the hot-headed Young Turk can wring extra speed out of the car, but it usually doesn't last. In my experience, sustainable consistency is achieved by a driver who approaches his task calmly and smoothly, developing an ability to feel his car. Ideally, with experience, he becomes able to consume, securely bank in his mind and then accurately reiterate these dynamic motions in a vivid and precise explanation to his engineer of what is happening out on the track.

Jack Brabham was a master of this art. Combining a fine brain with great experience, he would only have to drive a car around one or two corners to decipher what component area was preventing him from making the car do what he wanted. I often saw him complete a single out lap and then come back to the pits to make the necessary adjustments, thereby saving time, preserving the tyres and brakes and keeping his mind fresh. His genius was a rare ability to cut through the nonsense, pin-point the core problem in a car and solve it.

This is the skill of accurate subjective analysis. In my day, that was all we had, but today it can be confirmed by the objective measurement provided by the sophisticated telemetry of more than 120 sensors attached to a modern Grand Prix car. Of course, such technology is welcome, but the objective analysis can never replace the subjective judgement and, for all the science, the driver still has a crucial role to play in maximising the car's performance and ensuring it meets his individual needs. These same principles, of being able to identify and solve problems, apply to almost every walk of life.

All Jack ever wanted, all I ever wanted, all any racing driver ever wants is a car that is quick and reliable, an exceptional team of mechanics and engineers to prepare your car, a designer or analyst to adjust it and a team director whom you can trust. In 1971, I was fortunate to have all three.

Even when things went wrong, they still went right. I crashed 003 in my next race, damaging the front left corner during the Daily Express International Trophy at Silverstone. The throttle had stuck wide open going into Copse Corner, and, taking one look at the car, I knew it would be difficult to have it repaired and ready for the Monaco Grand Prix two weeks later.

'Don't worry,' Ken said. 'I know 004 is in good shape, and you'll be able to drive that.'

That was not my first choice. Monaco was one of the biggest races of the year, and I wanted to drive 003 because it had a better sense of balance; for whatever reason, it just felt right.

'Please try and fix it,' I asked.

'We'll see what we can do,' Ken replied.

The car was loaded into the Tyrrell transporter and taken back to the woodyard in Surrey, where Roger Hill and his team of mechanics set to work. Within a week, I was called and told that, after all, 003 would be ready for Monaco. It was an amazing achievement and it reflected well on Derek Gardner, who had been briefed to create a robust car that was easy to rebuild. It seemed the new Tyrrells were exactly that.

Monaco 1971 was a picture; quite literally, because Roman Polanski arranged to bring his film crew to follow me around and shoot a fly-on-the-wall docu-drama called *Weekend of a Champion*, which was later given a full West End premiere and put on general release. Strangely, such has been the incredible pace of my life, I had not actually sat down and watched Roman's film from start to finish until the preparation of this book.

The opening scene shows Helen and me leaving the Hôtel de Paris and strolling down to the pit lane on the day of the race. I'm wearing my white overalls and a black corduroy cap, and Helen is wearing a black cap as well, and we're talking nervously about the weather. As we make our way through crowds, people are shouting my name, and we are both smiling and waving at them, and there are cameramen all around us.

It was an amazing time. Sometimes I think back and wonder why we put ourselves through the stress and danger. Then, I see images like these and I realise we did it because our lives were so exciting and so colourful.

It was a strange existence, and, before final practice on the Saturday, Roman captures two Jackie Stewarts: one was laughing, joking with everyone, the fashionably dressed, chirpy wee Scot with sideburns down to his jawbone; the other was a more intense, fractious character, quick to judge, quick to snap, always concerned by not sleeping well, anxious about the preparation of the car, incessantly worried about the weather. There is a scene in the film where I am getting dressed in my hotel room, while the Formula 3 cars roar past in the streets below our balcony, and one moment I am joking with Roman about not having sex for two days before a race and the next I am fretting again, saying the only thing that concerns me is whether we have left enough time to get down to the pits before practice. Maybe this was just the way I was able to function, living such a hectic life on such a glamorous stage, laughing one moment, frowning the next, driving fast, getting by, surviving.

In the pit lane, I am intense and demanding. First, I quiz Ken about the tyres, and he replies calmly, the image of a tall Englishman wearing his cloth cap and brown jacket dealing with his persistent Scottish driver. Next, I complain to Roger Hill that the car has not felt quite right going around Casino Square, working myself into such a state that I declare we were 'in real trouble' and 'in no state to compete'. Roger stands there, listening, head bowed, not knowing where to look, taking the ear-bashing. I then proceed to take the car out, equal the lap record and claim pole position for the race.

That was me, a typical double-sided Gemini: charming and laughing one moment, a pain in the ass the next. In mitigation, I would say I badly wanted to win in Monaco that year because I knew the car was good enough, and I didn't want anything to go wrong and ruin our chances. However, I freely concede that, throughout my career, even in the good times of 1971, I was always demanding, always concerned something would go wrong, always thinking somebody was going to go faster, always believing somebody had better tyres, always worrying, always hungry to win.

Just before the race, I remember, everything seemed in order. Then, on the warm-up lap, out of the blue, I sensed the brakes weren't doing the job. I stopped the car on the grid, and told Ken and Roger there was something not quite right with the brakes. Roger and Roy Topp started rummaging around, even though there was now no more than ten minutes to go before the race was scheduled to start. They noticed the brake balance bar had shifted, effectively leaving me with no braking power at the rear. There was no solution to the problem in such a short space of time, so I accepted the fact that I would have to drive without any rear brakes.

Even so, starting on pole, I held on to first place and gradually established a commanding lead over Ronnie Peterson. I missed the rear brakes on the demanding and unforgiving streets of Monte Carlo, but got by, adapted and was able to complete the victory.

I returned to the pit and collected my watch from Ken.

'Well done,' he said.

I was startled, because Ken never said 'well done'. That was not his way, but he clearly recognised how difficult it had been to finish the race without the rear brakes. In all the years I raced for him, this was the only time he ever said 'well done' to me. So far as I was concerned, that didn't matter. He was not a man who dished out compliments, and I was not someone who needed them. Some people may very well find that quite odd, but it was the way we worked together. Neither of us wanted any fuss.

There is a great shot in Roman's film, literally moments after the race has just finished and I have crossed the line with the legendary former driver Louis Chiron waving the chequered flag, and it shows Ken walking up and down the pit lane, telling the mechanics to be quick and get everything packed up. He is clapping his hands and rubbing them together in one unbroken movement, clapping and rubbing, over and over again. That was typical. As far as he was concerned, we had won the race, and the job was done. That was all behind us, and he really wasn't interested in any kind of celebrations because, a matter of minutes after I had crossed the finish line in Monaco, his mind was already moving on to the next challenge. It was almost as if he was prepared to give everything in pursuit of success – and he craved success as much as anyone else – but he was unable to sit back and enjoy it. That was his way. Ken used to insist on keeping all the trophies he won, but he put them all in his attic, where they were never seen again.

The team was buzzing. With a second place and two wins in the first three races of the season, I was well on the way to regaining the world championship and, with two wins in its first two F1 Grands Prix, 003 was flying, but we were both humbled at the next race, the Dutch Grand Prix at Zandvoort.

We raced in torrential rain, and it soon became clear that, while all the cars on Goodyear tyres, notably the Tyrrells and a few other teams, were slipping and sliding all over the place, the cars using Firestones were coping quite well and dominating the race. They had obviously chosen a very good soft compound and a good tread pattern, giving them better grip and a lot more speed. I tried to compensate, and pushed 003 to the absolute limit from start to finish, but could finish no better than eleventh, a result that I regarded as a total embarrassment. It was no compensation to be told I had finished first among the cars on Goodyears.

'Where is Leo?' I said, as I climbed out of the car at the end. 'What has he got to say for himself?'

'Go easy on him,' said Ken, trying to calm me down.

Leo Mehl was a delightful, easy-going American who had joined the Goodyear Tyre and Rubber Company in 1959 and made his name working with A. J. Foyt at the Indianapolis 500. He had then become responsible for his company's racing tyres in F1 racing. In my opinion, he owed us all some answers in Holland. I looked around the pit lane, and he was nowhere to be seen. Someone told me he had already left the circuit.

I was still not in the happiest of moods an hour or so later, when I arrived at Amsterdam's Schiphol airport to catch my flight home and I was walking through the terminal when I noticed a sudden movement to my left and saw a man jumping up from his seat and trying to hide behind one of the pillars. I walked over, peered round and grinned when I realised it was our very own Scarlet Pimpernel from Goodyear.

'No, no, no, please,' Leo babbled. 'I know we had the wrong compound. I'm sorry, I'm sorry.'

A frustrating weekend ended in laughter on all sides.

It was important for us to recover a fortnight later at the brand new Paul Ricard circuit, and we did. I led the French Grand Prix from start to finish, and François finished second to give Ken a notable one-two. In fact, the team's performance was so dominant and impressive that our opponents started to claim our engines sounded different, suggesting we were using illegal fuel or a bigger engine. They even went so far as to lodge an official complaint. The race organisers then conducted a technical inspection and gave us the all-clear, but still the rumours persisted because people could not understand how I had managed to establish a four-second lead by the end of the first lap, or how I had then posted a lap record on the second lap, or how 003 had been able to roar down the long Signe straight, easing away from the Ferrari. They wanted to know how this was done, and they found it almost impossible to accept the answer lay in simple, world-class, robust British engineering.

We were almost unstoppable. Even when our oil scavenge pump failed fifteen minutes before the start of the British Grand Prix at Silverstone, apparently ruling me out of the race, the Tyrrell engineers leaped into action. Neil Davis noticed a tiny screw was missing, Roger Hill found a replacement, and Roy Topp guessed the correct torque setting. Working under intense pressure, when many teams would have panicked, the boys got 003 to the starting grid on time, and I was able to reward their efforts by taking the lead on the fourth lap and going on to win the race.

We maintained a winning momentum at the newly renovated Nurburgring on 1 August, when we all returned to see how literally millions of pounds had been spent to resurface most of the track, widen a good many sections and erect Armco barriers where required and even create some run-off areas.

The German Grand Prix was run in dry weather, and I was able to lead from the second corner and, with François following, the Tyrrell Twins recorded another one-two finish.

In an era when so many cars were using the same Ford engines, when close contests were expected, it was almost unbelievable that 003 had won no fewer than five of the last six Grand Prix races. It was now possible for us to secure the world championship in only the eighth race of the season, the Austrian Grand Prix to be held at the new circuit in Zeltweg.

Either Jacky Ickx or Ronnie Peterson needed to finish ahead of me to keep the title race alive, and Jacky was forced to withdraw after thirty-one laps. I then had to retire only four laps later, after losing a wheel, and so found myself in the distinctly underwhelming position of sitting in the Tyrrell pit when it was eventually and officially confirmed that, with Ronnie finishing well down the field, I had become F1 world champion for a second time.

I was pleased for the mechanics because they had worked so hard to make this possible, and for Derek, who had designed such a phenomenally successful car, and, above all for Ken, who had invested £22,500 of his own money in building his own car and been rewarded with a place in F1 history – he had won the driver's world championship and the constructor's championship in his very first full year as a privately owned F1 manufacturer. I suspect that feat will never be repeated.

The remainder of the 1971 season threatened to ebb away, when I failed to finish the Italian Grand Prix at Monza, which Peter Gethin won by a margin of 0.1 seconds, or just a few inches, from Ronnie Peterson in what was then recorded as the closest F1 world championship Grand Prix finish of all time. However, the team rallied to win the Canadian Grand Prix at Mosport, giving us a remarkable sixth F1 win of the season, just one behind Jim Clark's all-time record of seven. It had rained as well, but we seemed to have learned the lessons of Zandvoort because the Goodyear tyres performed well. I was pleased to see Leo Mehl hanging around the pits after the race; this time, there was no need for him to make a quick exit.

The year ended in the best possible way when François recorded his maiden F1 victory in the US Grand Prix at Watkins Glen, becoming only the second Frenchman ever to win a *Grandes Epreuves*. I was delighted for my young team-mate because he had performed well all season, which is not easy as a No. 2, and was emerging as a fine driver in his own right.

A so-called 'Victory' race was arranged in our honour at Brands Hatch, and the joyful image of François and me, with garlands around our necks, and Ken standing on the back of an open truck, parading down the straight to the cheers of the British crowd seemed to set the seal on an almost perfect year.

Within an hour, the sport bit back. Another friend, Jo Siffert, the Swiss driver who had won the Austrian Grand Prix, crashed into the bank before reaching Hawthorn's bend and his BRM P160 burst into flames. I only saw the accident when I approached the crash scene on the next lap. The track was blocked, so I stopped and got out of the car. Someone told me that Jo was still in the car and, looking at the flames, I reckoned there was no hope. None of the trackside fire extinguishers could put out the fire, but Jo most probably died from the impact. What had started as a day of celebration ended as another day of mourning and anger at an unnecessary death.

'What happened, Daddy?' asked my six-year-old son Paul, who had been sitting with Helen and Mark in the grandstand and, with everyone else, had seen the smoke rising. I didn't answer, not just because I didn't really know what to say in the

circumstances but also because I was feeling physically
shattered, as exhausted as I had ever been.

A quick glance at my diary for the year would have offered
an explanation. Through 1971, I had essentially been doing
two jobs: driving for Tyrrell in Formula 1 and driving a Lola
T260-Chevy sports car for Carl Haas in the CanAm series in
North America. The F1 season was my priority, but CanAm
offered a second income stream that was hard to resist. So,
alongside several ocean-hopping racing drivers, I agreed to do
both: one weekend in F1, the next in CanAm, from June all the
way till the end of October. Starting on the weekend of 25 May,
my schedule took me on consecutive weekends from Monte
Carlo to Toronto to Amsterdam to Montreal to Marseilles to
Atlanta to London to New York to Frankfurt; then there was a
single free weekend before I jumped back on the treadmill and
travelled to Vienna to Chicago to Milan to Minneapolis to
Toronto to Edmonton to New York to San Francisco to
London, to Los Angeles on 31 October.

In addition to all this, I was fitting in dinners and cocktail
parties on the F1 circuit for Ford and Elf. When I was in
America, I had started to visit tyre dealerships for Goodyear
and to make public appearances for L&M cigarettes, sponsors
of the team, in shopping malls. I had also started to work
regularly for the ABC's *Wide World of Sports*, and there were
still the usual media dinners, press interviews and TV
appearances on the likes of *Good Morning America* and *The
Tonight Show Starring Johnny Carson*.

Unsurprisingly, the result was extreme fatigue, frequent
headaches, a persistent sore throat and total lethargy. In fact, at
one stage I was feeling so unwell that I was unable to collect my
award for becoming world champion, and Helen had to attend
the FIA annual presentation dinner at their headquarters in the
Place de la Concorde, Paris, on my behalf.

It was Helen who eventually pressed me to see a doctor in

Geneva, and I was promptly diagnosed with a severe case of mononucleosis. In layman's terms, I was utterly burned out because I was trying to do too much. The doctor told me to rest, which, for me, has always been the hardest medicine, but we spent a quiet Christmas and New Year at home in Begnins, and I began to feel better.

Tyrrell's domination of the 1971 F1 season had been so complete that some observers reckoned more of the same would keep us ahead of the pack in 1972, and this view gained credence when I jumped back into 003 and led the opening Grand Prix of the new season, in Argentina, from start to finish.

However, very little ever remains the same in motor racing, and it was not long before the Lotus 72, driven by the Brazilian Emerson Fittipaldi, emerged as a formidable rival.

I set a lap record in practice for the South African Grand Prix, but the gearbox seized after forty-three laps, forcing me to retire, and I began to wonder whether 003 might be wilting under the strain. I took the lead in the Spanish Grand Prix at Jarama, but was overtaken by Fittipaldi on lap nine and spun off.

Something was going wrong, and I was starting to go off the road more often than at any stage of my career. It was hard to tell whether the problem lay with the car or the driver.

I flew straight from Spain to the UK, because I had agreed to test the McLaren CanAm car with a view to driving it in the 1972 CanAm Series. I enjoyed working with Carl Haas in 1971, but the car had been a dog to drive, so I was keen to give myself the best chance of winning the series the following year, and I was sure the McLaren would be the best car in the field. So I tested this outstanding car at Goodwood and, for no apparent reason, I spun off the track, not once but twice on the same day, and was lucky not to hit anything. I was becoming quite alarmed, and decided something must be very wrong.

The season moved on to the Monaco Grand Prix, but again

I was feeling distinctly below par. In very wet conditions, I spun twice, and finished a disappointing fourth.

'What's wrong?' Helen asked.

'I don't know,' I replied. 'I'm constantly tired. I'm seeing stars. I'm seeing floaters dancing around in front of my eyes. I'm even having problems with my balance.'

'I'll arrange for you to see a doctor.'

A full check-up at a medical centre in Lausanne showed I was anaemic. Further tests revealed I had internal bleeding from a duodenal ulcer. The doctor left me in no doubt about the seriousness of the condition, and I immediately contacted McLaren to say I would not, after all, be able to drive for them in the CanAm series. I also called Ken to give him the bad news that I had been instructed to stop racing for a minimum period of between six and eight weeks.

I was given two options: either have an operation that would deal with the problem but require considerable recovery time and prolong my absence from racing, or take a course of extremely heavy medication that would, all going well, seal the ulcer and allow me to get back in the car significantly sooner, within the two-month period I'd mentioned to Ken. For me, that was no choice at all so I followed the doctor's orders, I started the medication, stayed at home with Helen and the boys, lay in the sun and slept, slept and slept. In fact, the sedation was wonderful, and I became so laid back that I could hardly bring myself to answer the phone, let alone make a call. In fact, ever since this horizontal phase of my life, my family have been suggesting I should get more of that treatment.

As a result of this inactivity, my weight ballooned from 63 kilograms to over 70 kilograms, and, as soon as the doctors were happy that the internal bleeding had stopped, I hired a personal trainer called Gunther Traube to get me back in shape. He actually came to stay with us at Clayton House and pushed me through a demanding schedule of running, pushing weights and stretching to get me fit and ready for my return to F1 racing.

'Stewart is finished,' people were saying. 'He's got two world championships, and he's had enough.'

It was the talk of the town. Everybody knew I had been ill, and almost everyone had started to wonder whether I had lost my appetite for racing at the highest level.

I'd been lucky with the timing. In the seven-week period between Monaco and my comeback race at the French Grand Prix, on 2 July, at the picturesque but demanding Charade circuit in Clermont-Ferrand, I'd only missed the Belgian meeting. Against every prediction, I belted myself into 003 in France, and won the race. It was a triumph of pure Scottish bloody-minded determination to prove the doubters wrong, but my revival proved to be the last victory for my beloved 003.

Ken had wanted me to drive Tyrrell 005 in the British Grand Prix at Brands Hatch, but François crashed the new car in practice, and I ended up driving 003. Again we tried to roll back the months and we fought hard to get within a second of Emerson in the Lotus before having to settle for second place.

The final curtain eventually fell for 003 in the 1972 German Grand Prix, when the car once again lost the ability to have any rear wheel braking, which meant it was almost impossible to exercise any late braking manoeuvres to overtake under braking at any of the 187 corners of the Nurburgring. I found myself stuck behind Clay Regazzoni, and, hard as I tried, it was extremely difficult to get past him. The situation was not helped when the Swiss driver started weaving on the straight, using questionable tactics to keep ahead of me. At one point, he moved across as I tried to pass him on the outside of a right-hand bend, forcing me into the guard rail and out of the race. I had never encountered anything like this before and I was so angry that, having caught a motorcycle pillion ride back to the pits, I then marched to the control tower and complained about Clay's conduct to the stewards of the meeting. This became a major issue but, in the absence of any video footage or TV coverage, and with no marshals or observers able to confirm what had happened, no action was taken.

I had a fantastic relationship with Clay when he was out of the car. He had wonderful charm and humour and he was an extremely nice man, whom I liked enormously. As soon as he climbed into the car, however, he often grew horns.

003 had been severely damaged in the accident. The left-hand front suspension was torn off. It was certainly repairable, but the German Grand Prix turned out to be 003's last race.

So, while Emerson Fittipaldi was being hailed as, at the time, the youngest ever F1 world champion, the celebrated Tyrrell was quietly taken back to the humble woodyard in deepest Surrey from where it had first emerged.

The statistics tell part of the 003 story: it won eight of the sixteen F1 world championship Grands Prix that it entered, finishing eleven times and putting me on the podium nine times. It claimed no fewer than six pole positions and recorded five fastest laps. On all the major circuits of the world, it proved itself to be fast and reliable, a well-principled thoroughbred.

Only one person ever drove this remarkable car in a F1 Grand Prix, and it remains one of the great privileges and pleasures of my motor racing life that that individual happened to be me.

CHAPTER 11

Final Lap

It is the one decision that so few sports people seem to get right: some decide to retire in the midst of a slump and later regret it, others hang on too long and outstay their welcome. Towards the end of 1972 and moving into 1973, I consciously resolved that I would do everything possible to be one of those people who got it right. I tried to step back, calmly assess the situation and identify the downside risks.

The greatest danger seemed to be that I would make a rash decision in one of the 'low' moments which are a feature of every sporting career, in fact of any career. These emotional troughs could be caused by loss of form, media criticism, sheer exhaustion or the pressure of having to maintain a reputation and fulfil so many people's expectations. Elite sport can be an exciting, glamorous and lucrative place to work, yet anybody who has worked in this world will have been exposed to the times when everything seems too much, when the travel feels endless, when there is no privacy, when you miss your family – and these are the moments when it can seem all too easy to decide you have had enough, and walk away from the sport that has made you what you are. You may initially feel better because a great weight has been removed from your shoulders but maybe a month or a year later, you may look back and wonder if you were a bit premature, and you may start to wish you had not made such an important decision when you were on a downer.

I understood how this could happen because there had been days during 1971 and 1972 when I was rushing to catch another transatlantic flight, feeling exhausted, and I had started to wonder whether it was worth carrying on. Each time, I told myself to calm down, take a few deep breaths, get a decent night's sleep and look at the situation when I was feeling better.

The other threat was that I would stay too long and become one of those sports people who seemed unable to accept the end and who kept convincing themselves they were capable of one more big win, of hearing the cheers one more time. In many cases, 'one more big win' never comes, and many distinguished careers have ended in disappointment, derision and even dismissal, and great pain for the person involved.

This was clearly a decision I needed to get right.

To her eternal credit, Helen never tried to influence me either way. There had been many distressing times over the years when we lost people who we cared about, and she might easily have asked me to stop racing, and I would have found myself in a genuine dilemma, but she never did.

'It's your career,' she would say. 'It's your decision. Whatever you decide, I'll support you.'

However, the nature of my profession was starting to affect our young son Paul, who seemed to have developed a nervous twitch, almost as if he was flicking invisible hair away from his eyes. His teachers suggested this could be a symptom of stress or worry, and it was not difficult to guess the cause.

Jo Bonnier had been close to me ever since he raised the idea of us moving to Switzerland. We raced together, worked together in the safety campaign and I even rented an office in the building he owned in Gland, on the banks of Lac Leman. His wife, Marianne, got along well with Helen, and his sons, Kim and Jonas, went to the same school as Paul and Mark. We became family friends, neighbours and an integral part of each other's lives. On 11 June 1972, Jo was killed in an accident at Le Mans, when his Lola-Cosworth collided with a Ferrari. The aristocratic Swede had raced in sixteen consecutive F1 seasons. It was a terrible loss, and a couple of weeks after the funeral, sitting in the bus on their way to school, young Kim Bonnier turned to Paul and said, 'Your father's going to be next.'

Paul didn't reply. To him, the observation was logical: first it had been Natasha's dad (Jochen Rindt's daughter also went to the same school); now it was Kim and Jonas's dad; and it almost seemed to follow it would be his dad next.

When he came home that afternoon, Paul approached me and explained what had happened. 'Kim says you're going to be next,' he said, innocently and calmly. 'Is that true?'

The question cut straight through me. There was no adequate response. I couldn't tell him that was not the case because, in reality, as long as I continued to go racing, week after week, I could easily have been next; but I could hardly have said that his young school friend might well be right. Instead, I told him that Daddy drove strong cars with good mechanics and that Daddy was going to be safe, that Mummy and Daddy loved him, and that Daddy would not leave him. It was very uncomfortable, and I switched his attention to something else.

Then, a few days later, I had to go back to Geneva airport to catch another flight to another city to drive another car in another race and I would try to blank out Paul's question and again immerse myself in the excitement and the glamour of the world in which my job and profession required me to live. This was the reality. For all the danger and risk, for all the concern it may have caused the people who were closest to me, I was still stimulated and exhilarated by motor racing. The sport had become the focal point of my life to a point where it defined me. I felt neither willing nor ready to walk away.

Moreover, the team was still indisputably competitive. We had proved as much at the end of 1972, when, in the closing weeks of a frustrating season spoiled by my illness and the superiority of the Lotus 72, we rallied to win the last two races. I drove 005 to victory in the Canadian Grand Prix at Mosport and then led the US Grand Prix from start to finish. François came second at Watkins Glen, and our one-two finish set down a clear marker for a powerful Tyrrell challenge in 1973.

'So you think you can regain the title next year?' a journalist asked me at the Glen.

'It will be difficult,' I replied. 'Fittipaldi will be strong.'

The talented Brazilian had become a major force, thriving under the guidance of Colin Chapman at Lotus, proving a capable successor to Jim Clark and Jochen Rindt and mobilising the passionate support of many millions of his compatriots. I had first met Emerson in 1969 when I presented him with the Formula Ford championship trophy in the Copacabana Palace hotel in Rio de Janeiro. Even then he was popular, but within a couple of years his profile had been promoted to a level where he was surrounded by the kind of hysteria usually reserved only for Pelé. He became one of the great trailblazers in the history of our sport, sowing the seeds of Brazilian ambition in what had historically been barren soil and becoming the first in a succession of wonderfully gifted drivers from that country to reach the highest level. Where he led, the likes of Carlos Pace, Nelson Piquet, Gil de Ferran, Helio Castroneves, Ayrton Senna, Rubens Barrichello, Felipe Massa and a host of others in the formative classes have followed.

In the early months of 1973, it was I who was following Fittipaldi. He began the new F1 season in irresistible form, winning in Argentina and then delighting his home crowd by storming to a comprehensive victory in the Brazilian Grand Prix.

Team Tyrrell had been competitive in Buenos Aires; in fact, I had led from the start but finished third after suffering a puncture with ten laps left, and François came second. However, we were no match for the Lotus on the bumpy, undulating Interlagos circuit in São Paulo and, amid Brazilian delight, I trailed in a distant second.

It suddenly seemed very important for us to win the third race of the year, the South African Grand Prix at Kyalami, although that hardly seemed likely when I crashed in practice. Travelling at 176 mph – I clearly remember the speed – I came off the throttle on the entry to Crowthorne Corner and pressed on the brakes with little effect. For whatever the reason, the front wheel brakes suddenly ceased to function. My car veered violently off the track and towards an eight foot high concrete wall, painted white and built to protect the grandstand on the outside of the corner. For the first and only time in my racing career, I thought this was going to be the end.

In these few milliseconds of crisis, when everything seemed to be happening in slow motion, I had one of the most unusual experiences of my life. I literally seemed to come out of my own body and I distinctly recall feeling as though I was looking down on myself as I fought to get the car under control. Even now, I can still hear the noise of the car going off the track and the noise of the car being torn apart as it ploughed through the three lines of chain-link fencing, which, ironically, in my role as GPDA president, I had asked to be installed to retard the velocity of the car in a situation exactly like this.

Then there was total silence, and, when I opened my eyes, all I could see was dazzling white. In that moment, I thought I must have arrived in heaven; it was only when my eyes focused that I saw that, with great good fortune, my car had come to rest right up against the high, white concrete wall. A high-speed collision had seemed inevitable, but I had been spared by the fencing.

Completely unhurt, I returned to the pits, where Ken decided I should immediately take over François' car and qualify it for the race in the few minutes still remaining. The track was closed while the chain-link fencing was replaced, and I then went out in a car not set up for me and secured sixteenth place on the grid.

After all this drama, the following day's race was all the more remarkable because I managed to work my way through from the back of the field, took the lead on lap seven and was able to complete a precious victory, albeit tinged with controversy. Clay Regazzoni crashed his BRM at the end of the straight on the second lap. Mike Hailwood had been following him, and almost certainly saved Clay's life by stopping and pulling him from the burning car. Both men suffered severe burns, and Mike was later awarded the George Cross for his act of courage.

As usual in those days, the race continued, and I was among the cars that passed the scene of the accident, building a lead and eventually winning the race. It was only after the podium ceremony that I was told McLaren had lodged an official protest about me, the team manager Teddy Mayer suggesting I had passed Peter Revson under a yellow flag. Nowadays, in the event of such a major accident, a red flag would be waved and the race would be stopped. However, back in 1973, the practice was for the officials to wave a yellow flag some distance before the scene of the accident, demarking a section of the track where drivers had to slow down and where overtaking was strictly forbidden. Teddy was claiming I had ignored the yellow flag and passed Peter in this section of the circuit.

This was a serious accusation, not just because I would have been penalised if found guilty but also because the charge undermined my credibility as an advocate for safety. A hearing was held, in which I said I was aware of yellow flags being flown and confirmed I had not overtaken any car in the accident zone or in any area where such a flag was displayed. I was absolved of any wrongdoing and, more importantly, Clay made a full recovery from his injuries, but the combination of another accident and the allegation took the shine off a fantastic team effort and left me feeling somewhat unsettled.

However feisty and combative I may have appeared out on the circuit and at GPDA meetings, I didn't enjoy any confrontation and, feeling a bit bruised, I started to wonder whether I really wanted the sport any longer, whether I still had the appetite for racing. There was nothing wrong with my form, and I proceeded to win the Daily Express International Trophy race at Silverstone but, as my mind continued to churn over, I seemed to find myself being drawn towards an important decision.

I was continuing to feel exhausted as in the previous season, but now, for the first time, I was experiencing considerably more aggravation than satisfaction from what I was doing. This was not an emotional low, this was not a peak and valley moment. It was a gradual and certain realisation.

Soon afterwards, I arranged a lunch in London with three of my most trusted friends: Ken Tyrrell and two executives of the Ford Motor Company, Walter Hayes and John Waddell. We assembled on Tuesday 24 April at Mark's Club in Charles Street, Mayfair, London, and none of my guests seemed to know why we were there. Even so, we ordered drinks and food and discussed the car and the encouraging performances of the past few weeks.

After a while, I said: 'Gentlemen, I have invited you here because I want you to be the first to know I have decided to retire at the end of this season. I won't say anything in public, and I know you will respect that, but I wanted you to know.'

I looked around the table and sensed the news was maybe not such a big surprise. Ken seemed to sum up the consensus reaction when, measuring his words, he said he wanted to try and talk me out of it and persuade me to carry on. 'But,' he concluded, managing a smile, 'I'm not going to do that. This was always going to be your call, and nobody else's. Now you've made your decision, that's fine. I would like to thank you for not just walking away and for saying you will complete the season.'

It felt as though an enormous weight had been taken off my shoulders, and I left the club, feeling light-headed, almost euphoric, because, deep down, after so many months of uncertainty, I categorically knew I had made the correct decision.

I decided not to tell Helen. That was difficult. I didn't want to place her in the awful position of counting down the races until the end of the season, effectively counting the green bottles standing on the wall and forever wondering if one of them, in the words of the rhyme, 'should accidentally fall'. Also, if I had told her, her logical mind would have asked why I didn't just stop there and then and not take any more risk. Then I would have had to explain why I promised Ken I would complete the season, and that would have been an issue. It seemed simpler and kinder to say nothing. So I didn't tell Helen and the boys and I didn't tell François Cevert either because the news could have clouded his thinking.

Nobody else needed to know. The decision had been made and now, I told myself, I needed to focus on my driving and look forward to the rest of the F1 season, my last. I was determined to enjoy it, maybe to take an extra moment to savour the atmosphere and the smells of each race and each circuit. In a sense, making up my mind early in the season created a precious opportunity for me, as the saying goes, to smell the roses.

Tyrrell 006 continued to run well, and only a brake failure

in the closing stages prevented me from winning the Spanish Grand Prix in Barcelona. Such setbacks are frustrating, but they happen. You have to accept it, resolve it, regroup and move on.

The weekend of the Belgian Grand Prix was always going to be awkward for me because, as I mentioned previously, I was widely regarded as the prime instigator of the GPDA's decision not to race at Spa-Francorchamps until the required safety measures had been applied. With the race having been switched to Zolder, as soon as I arrived at the circuit, I sensed resentment towards me among some officials. More hassle, I sighed. I just didn't need it.

The atmosphere deteriorated even further when parts of the newly laid track started to break up during practice and I became involved in the discussions that led to the majority of the drivers saying we would not start the race unless the track was repaired. I then proceeded to win the Grand Prix, with François coming second, but again, just as in South Africa, when we should have been celebrating another victory, I found myself caught up in conflict and controversy. My decision to get out and get away from all this started to look better and better . . . most of the time.

One moment, I was calm and clear. The next moment, I was waking up in the middle of the night racked by insecurity. I don't know how it happened but, out of the blue, I found myself overwhelmed by new doubt – I was planning to give up the one thing I could do well, perhaps the only thing I could do well. At the age of nearly thirty-four, I was walking away from all the opportunities, the money, the access and the privileges. And I was still winning regularly. Was I going too soon? What would I do after racing? Would I be able to earn a living? A thick, dense fog descended from nowhere and clouded my horizon. By the time my schedule took me back across the Atlantic to work for ABC in their coverage of the Indianapolis 500, I had become confused and bewildered. I checked into the

Speedway motel at Indianapolis and felt lost. There was nobody to turn to because I didn't want to share my thoughts with anyone I didn't know well and who might leak the story to the media.

In this moment of profound despair, an Anglican priest called Father Stan Easty appeared. One afternoon at the race track, I just turned around and there he was, in his vicar's collar.

'Hello, Jackie,' he said, 'how are you?'

We had met many times before and, not quite accurately, I told him I was fine. An eager supporter of motor sport, he was a familiar face at racing circuits in the United States and he explained how he had travelled from his home at Nag's Head, South Carolina to watch the Indianapolis 500. We were acquaintances, and we chatted for a while, and he seemed kind and sympathetic.

'Father Easty,' I said, 'this may seem an odd request, but I would be very grateful if we could get together at my hotel. There is something I would like to talk to you about.'

'No problem,' he said. A couple of hours later we were sitting in my room – it was room 109, I clearly recall – at the Speedway motel, and I was telling him about my intention to retire, my uncertainty, my confusion and my fears. He listened for some time and then asked if I had been confirmed.

'I'm not sure what you mean,' I answered.

He explained that it was the norm in the Church of England, and indeed the Church of Scotland, for people to be christened into the faith as infants and then to be 'confirmed' as a Christian at a later stage, when they were old enough to decide for themselves and make their own commitment. He added that, while most people were confirmed in their late teenage years, anybody could undergo the ceremony whenever they felt ready.

I told him I had not been through anything like that and explained that, although my family were not regular churchgoers, and I had never regarded myself as a particularly religious person, I did believe in God and I prayed on a regular basis.

'Maybe you might like to be confirmed,' he said.

'OK,' I replied.

'Well, would you like to be confirmed here and now?'

'Yes.'

I hadn't even been aware of the concept a few moments before but, at the age of thirty-three, I was suddenly kneeling on the floor of an American motel room, bowing my head before a priest whose church I had never visited and with whom I had only ever had this one substantial conversation. He conducted the confirmation and, when he had finished, he laid his hands on my head and prayed out loud, asking God to comfort me and help me.

In that moment, in that very instant, I felt an incredible release of pressure and tension. The doubts literally melted away, and for the first time in my life, I sensed the full presence of a loving God. There is no doubt in my mind that, kneeling there in that motel room, I was blessed with an extraordinary sense of peace, and I am convinced it was what the Bible describes as the 'peace of God that passeth all understanding'. The sceptics and cynics are entitled to their views, but I know what happened because I was there, and the facts are that I was confused when I walked into room 109 and I walked out an hour or so later with the certain knowledge I had made the right decision, I would survive the season, I would have a life beyond racing and I would be with Helen and the boys.

I met Father Easty many times at races over the years that followed, and was always grateful that he entered my life and gave me an awareness of God's grace. What an amazing gift.

Even after this awakening, I didn't start going to church on Sundays and I still don't do that today. However I did become, and have remained, an extremely frequent visitor to churches.

Wherever I have been in the world, I have got into the habit of walking into a place of worship, just sitting quietly, enjoying the peace and praying. It might be an Anglican church, but it could also be a Church of Scotland 'kirk', a synagogue, a Buddhist temple or a mosque. I am no theologian but, for me, they are all Houses of God with the same sense of spiritual power and presence, and, when I wander in and sit down, I always feel comforted.

I certainly felt comforted when I flew home from Indianapolis in 1973. The horizon was clear again, and I walked in peace into what, I knew, would be my last Monaco Grand Prix. Tyrrell 006 picked up where we left off in Belgium, and I started on pole position and established such a commanding lead over the rest of the field that, in the last ten laps, I started to ease off. The race seemed won. It wasn't. Emerson was charging, closing the gap and making me work hard for the victory.

It can often be difficult to get 'back in the saddle' in these circumstances and regain your timing and momentum but, with the Lotus looming large in my mirrors, I was relieved to see François ahead of me among the back markers that Emerson and I would soon have to lap. My team-mate had damaged a wheel on his car early in the race and was a lap down, but I fully expected him to let me pass and then be fast enough to hold up Emerson and enable me to re-establish a comfortable lead.

François duly let me through but then, unbelievably, he let Emerson through as well. This unnecessary generosity towards our rival earned him a froth job from Ken after the race, but I was still able to scramble across the line and secure the victory that took my total of F1 Grand Prix wins to twenty-five, one ahead of the great Fangio and equal with the all-time record held by Jim Clark.

Winning what I knew would be my last race on the streets of Monte Carlo was important to me. All right, I told myself, you're not going to pass this way again, so you may as well enjoy every minute of the slow-down lap. I took one hand off the wheel and started waving at the spectators in the grandstands. The reception was wonderful all the way through Casino Square, past the people watching from the balconies of their rooms at the Hôtel de Paris and down the hill towards Mirabelle. I stopped waving as I entered the tunnel, because there were no spectators to acknowledge, and relaxed. Holding the steering wheel with my thighs, I started to take off my gloves, raise my visor and loosen the strap of my helmet. I was delighted, and happy, and contented . . . and almost catastrophically casual.

Everything happened in an instant. Emerging from the dark tunnel into daylight, I glanced to my left and suddenly saw Emerson was driving alongside me. We were too close, much too close. Before I could do anything, he was driving over my wheel, ramping his car up into the air. It came crashing down on the tarmac, and he did well to regain control. The collision might easily have been very serious. I was shocked, and it had been my fault. Emerson and I were always the first to congratulate each other when either of us won a race, and this was all he was trying to do when he drew up beside me, but I was distracted by the emotion of my last lap in Monaco and lost concentration for a moment. We both returned to the pits, grateful for what had been a fortunate escape.

Three consecutive Grand Prix victories had consolidated my world championship challenge, but I then lost ground by finishing fifth in Sweden and then fourth in France, and the team was eager to improve in the British Grand Prix at Silverstone.

I was leading at the end of the first lap, but then a multiple collision behind me forced the race to be stopped, and, after the restart, 006 developed problems with the gear shift engagement. On the approach to Stowe Corner, the car slipped into second gear instead of fourth and spun violently into a cornfield. It was high summer and, when I came to a halt, all anybody could see above the corn was the top of the engine cover. Although 006 was not damaged, by the time I got it back on the circuit, I had lost so much time that I eventually finished back in tenth place.

Our season was beginning to drift, but the team worked hard, and we recovered with back-to-back victories.

Winning the Dutch Grand Prix at Zandvoort enabled me to pass Jim Clark's record of the most F1 Grand Prix victories, but the day was overshadowed by the death of Roger Williamson, a promising young British driver whose car dramatically turned upside down and burst into flames. David Purley had been driving behind and saw everything happen, so he stopped and tried to save his friend, at one point trying to lift the burning car. His amazing courage proved in vain, and he struggled to recover from the trauma.

As usual, the race had continued, and we had had to drive past the burning wreckage lap after lap, prompting a horrible sense of déjà-vu in those of us who remembered Piers Courage's accident at the same circuit only three years before.

We moved on to the German Grand Prix at the Nurburgring, where the two Tyrrells seemed in a class of their own, and Ken took great pleasure from another one-two finish.

1st Jackie Stewart (Tyrrell); 2nd François Cevert (Tyrrell) – it was becoming a familiar line in the results columns on sports pages around the world, and, on reflection, these days seem as happy and rewarding as any in my career. Why? I think it was because, within a F1 racing team that more closely resembled a family, I was able to enjoy success at the highest level with a team director in Ken and a team-mate in François, who both ranked among my closest friends. What more could anybody want?

François Cevert was the epitome of an ambitious, talented and well-mannered young sportsman. He had an amazing presence, with his big blue eyes, upright posture and incredible physique, and he had settled into the Tyrrell team with remarkable ease when he joined in 1971. He was one of those rare people who everybody just seemed to like and wanted to know. He was the son of wealthy parents, who would perhaps have preferred him to make a career out of his considerable talents as a concert pianist, but his great passion was motor racing and to his natural flair he added a cast-iron determination to work hard, to learn and become the best driver he could be. Some people tended to regard him as a playboy – he liked to dress stylishly, and at one stage appeared looking dynamite in a double-breasted, ankle-length fur coat with a shoal collar, and he was invariably seen with a beautiful girl on his arm, at one time escorting Brigitte Bardot to the Paris Motor Show – and yet he was always much, much more than that.

He showed his potential in winning the US Grand Prix at the end of 1971, taking both hands off the wheel and punching the air with delight as he crossed the line, and, even if he did struggle in his second season at the highest level, as many do in any sport, the consistent quality of his performances in 1973 certainly suggested he could one day become world champion.

For me, he was always more than a team-mate. He was my younger brother.

The relationship between the No. 1 and the No. 2 driver is important in every F1 racing team. In many cases, the No. 1 can demand preferential treatment and be intensely protective of his privileges, which often results in the No. 2 feeling like a second-class citizen and becoming increasingly frustrated. At the start of my F1 career, the reason I did not join Lotus in 1965 was that I knew Jim Clark was, quite correctly, so well looked after as the No. 1 that it would have been hard for me to progress as his No. 2.

François might have had similar misgivings about joining Tyrrell, but I always made a conscious effort to help him develop, and from the start we discussed everything. The relationship worked on both sides: on the one hand, he was a young driver who was open and receptive to advice and coaching – and surprisingly few of them are – and on the other hand, I never regarded him as any threat to my position within the team or the sport.

We drove essentially the same car in 1971, 1972 and 1973, and, in testing, practice, qualifying and before the race, I was happy to share everything with him, from my overall strategy to the gear ratios I would use, to the gears I was planning to take at each and every corner, and all my braking distances. There were no secrets. Why would there be? There was no need. François effectively became part of our family, as close to Helen and the boys as he was to me.

My win at the Nurburgring was followed by a second place in the Austrian Grand Prix, bringing me within reach of a third world championship. With just three races left in my last season, three races left in my career, I began to dare wonder whether I might just be able to bow out at the top. Even so, I resisted the temptation and still said nothing about retiring to Helen, or to anybody. Beyond Ken, John and Walter, nobody knew.

We approached the Italian Grand Prix at Monza with confidence. This was, after all, where I had won my first F1 Grand Prix in 1965, and claimed my first world championship four years later. A series of chicanes had been introduced to draw the teeth of the famously wide, fast, sweeping corners and yet, even so, Monza remained a circuit offering unmatched opportunities to overtake and maybe even to charge from the back of the field.

The weekend did not start well. I was suffering from flu and a sore throat and, after four practice sessions, I found myself back on the third row of the grid, with the sixth fastest time in qualifying, a full 1.5 seconds behind Ronnie Peterson.

On the Sunday, just over two hours before the race, the Ford

DFV engine that had carried me through the entire season suddenly blew, and our mechanics faced a desperate race against time to get a new engine installed for the start. As ever, Roger Hill, Roy Topp, Roland Law and the rest of the team rose to the challenge, but the day didn't get any better when I suffered a puncture on the seventh lap and, having been into the pits to get that repaired, rejoined the race way back in twentieth position, apparently well out of contention.

Now there was nothing to lose. Ken was not expecting a points result, and the crowd seemed to have lost interest in me, and so, for the first time in many months, I suddenly felt liberated from all expectation and pressure, free to try things: to take a slightly different line on a corner, to change up early, to ease the brakes on and off more gently. Completely relaxed, I rejoined the race and thought to myself: 'To hell with it, let's have a go.'

There were quite literally no other cars in sight because I was now so far behind the pack, which meant I effectively had Monza to myself. Whoopee! This was going to be fun.

My next lap was a second faster than anything I had done all weekend, even with almost a full load of fuel, and I started catching tail-enders and working my way through the field. In normal circumstances, the pit board is held out at the end of each lap to show a driver the time gap between him and the car in front, but there was nothing normal about this day, and Ken and Roger were soon having as much fun as me. Passing the Tyrrell pits, I looked up to see a pit board that read '–20 seconds Fangio'; next lap, it read '+10 seconds Ascari'. It was only when Ken realised that I was starting to make serious progress through the field – and I think he was amazed by the lap times I was producing – that he told Roger to start giving me the gap between me and sixth place where world championship points begin. Now, with the impossible starting to seem possible, this was all I needed to know.

After twenty-three laps, I had moved up to thirteenth position, still thirty-two seconds behind sixth place. Head down, totally focused, I was pushing myself and the car to the limit. After twenty-eight laps, I was ninth, gaining two seconds per lap on Mike Hailwood in sixth.

Freeze the frame.

Reflecting now on that exciting, warm, dry afternoon at Monza, when everything that could go wrong seemed to have gone wrong, with the man sporting the tartan band on his white helmet, hurling his blue car around the circuit, hungrily hunting down a third world championship, I have no doubt that I was a much better racing driver in 1973 than I'd ever previously been.

The reason? I never stopped learning. Perhaps it was a legacy of my terrible schooldays, but I had always been so hungry to learn about my craft and, over the years, I had accumulated a great deal of knowledge to a point where, in principle, I had a firm grasp of the basic skills. By 1973, I was entering a new zone, where, having banked the obvious stuff, I was able to focus on consuming the subtleties of driving techniques that would probably never have occurred to less experienced or less committed drivers. As a result, I learned more in my last year than in any other year. The more I learned, the better I became. I had matured into an analytical professor of information relating to the conditions of the track, my physical well-being and the car, to a point where I could clearly define issues out of a blur into crystal clear focus in milliseconds, better than at any stage of my career.

As a young driver, I reckoned there were three stages in a corner: the entry, the apex and the exit. That seemed simple, and I might have thought there was not much more to be said about getting through a bend as quickly as possible. However, I kept thinking, kept listening, kept learning and, by 1973, I had realised that, in fact, there were no fewer than eight specific segments in every corner. That meant there were eight specific tasks for me to complete if I was to coax and finesse my car through that bend in one fast, smooth and fluid motion.

The key to this progress was keeping my mind open. It often surprises me when I see people reach the top of the tree, whether it's in sport, business or almost anything else, giving the impression of thinking they know everything. Perhaps it is their status, power, fame or even their wealth that leads them to believe they can sit back because there is nothing more to learn. In my experience, there is always something else to learn and somebody else to study. Not a single day passes in anybody's life without something happening to them that has not occurred before and, by definition, that represents a piece of knowledge that will slip past a mind that is closed and complacent.

It is because I had always tried to keep learning that I believe so strongly that, at Monza on this particular day, I was driving at the very peak of my skills.

Play.

I caught Mike Hailwood on lap thirty-eight, moved into sixth place and kept pushing. After getting past Carlos Reutemann and being waved through by François, I glanced at the pit board and saw I was sixteen seconds behind third place with eight laps left.

Still relaxed, still having fun, I had set more than a dozen new lap records during my charge through the field, and I managed to set another on the fifty-first of the fifty-five laps, posting a time of 1:35.30, travelling at an average speed of 135.55 mph.

I eventually finished fourth, right behind Peter Revson. The Grand Prix was won by Ronnie Peterson, who remained ahead of Emerson and so denied his Lotus team-mate any chance of catching me in the race for the world championship. Many people wondered why Ronnie had not been instructed to let Emerson win and keep his title hopes alive, with the suspicion being that the decision may have been related to the fact the Brazilian had already announced he was leaving the team at the end of the season. I didn't know the ins and outs and, to be frank, I didn't really care.

As I pulled into the pits, it was Ken who walked up and gave me confirmation we had won the world championship, just as he had done at Monza in 1969 and at Zeltweg in 1971.

He smiled and asked, 'Why all the aggravation in practice?'

'Ken, I don't know,' I replied. 'I just don't know.'

It was a big moment – I had just driven one of the finest races of my life and clinched what Ken and I knew was going to be my last F1 championship – but neither of us were the type to make a big fuss. The removal of emotion may have been such a big part of the way we operated that, if we did win, we didn't have the time or inclination for a wild party. We celebrated quietly as a team that evening but, in typical Tyrrell fashion, were soon moving on to focus on the next challenge, the Canadian Grand Prix. Ken had decided to enter three cars in the race, with Chris Amon being brought in to drive alongside François and me, and a degree of misunderstanding followed.

My car was still running well, but, in heavy rain, we decided to use wet-weather tyres. It was while leading the race that I noticed a line on my front right tyre. Thinking it could be the start of excessive wear in the soft compound getting down to the canvas of the tread, which could have been dangerous, I was keen to get into the pits as soon as possible and decided to ignore the signal telling me to stay out on the track. I arrived to find Chris Amon and his car were already there and, in all the confusion that followed, I accidentally drove over a mechanic's foot.

Ken was livid, and even angrier when it turned out that the 'line' on my tyre was just paint. He subsequently launched into the mother of all 'froth jobs', demonstrating that even a

CLUB-HOUSE

Main picture: Belgian Grand Prix 1966. Graham in practice at the final corner of the Spa-Francorchamps track. In the following day's race he came to my aid after I span off. I was looking very 'second-hand' according to Graham.

Right: The car I was pulled out of. Eventually.

Right: Helen looks after me in hospital.

Below: Recuperating at a hill climb on the Rest-and-be-Thankful.

Bottom: After my crash I kept a spanner taped to the wheel until quick-release steering columns became standard.

STEWART
ASKS FOR
SOME POP

Below: Winning in the torrential rain at the Nurburgring in 1968. Arguably my greatest race…

Top left: … not that you'd know it from my expression.

Bottom left: Dutch Grand Prix 1968. First win in the Matra-Ford.

Bottom right: Gold Cup, Oulton Park 1968. The greatest racing driver of all time, Manuel Fangio, presented me with my trophy.

Championship Season 1969

Top: The Tyrrell woodyard.

Middle: Winning my first British Grand Prix.

Bottom: Starting a tradition of champagne celebrations, after winning in France.

Monza. World Champion.

Right: At the Nurburgring in 1969 we were a close-knit and happy group. But we paid a heavy price in the months and years ahead. Back: l-r, Bruce McLaren (deceased), Denny Hulme (deceased), Lucian Bianci (deceased), Jacky Ickx, Graham Hill (deceased), Chris Amon, Jo Bonnier (deceased), Jochen Rindt (deceased). Middle: Jean-Piere Beltoise, Piers Courage (deceased), Jackie Oliver, Jo Siffert (deceased), me. Front: Kurt Ahrens, Silvio Moser, Hubert Hahne.

Champion driver dies in 150 mph somersault

JIM CLARK CRASH MYSTERY

THE LAST LAP
PAGES 6 AND 7

JIM CLARK, motor racing's Flying Scot, died today in a 150 miles an hour crash

RACE STAR KILLED

Tragique Grand Prix de Hollande a Zandvoort

Nouveau double des ‹Tyrrell-boys›

Stewart triumphs and makes history

COURAGE HEIR DIES IN CRASH

By PATRICK MENHEM in Zandvoort, Holland
and MARGARET HALL in London

RACING driver Piers Courage, heir to the Courage brewery fortune, died in the blazing Grand Prix in Holland yesterday.

Cancelled

Flames

Zandvoort results

Tragedy mars Stewart's 26

Yes, I've got that record and a title lead now

By Jackie Stewart talking to David Benson

Death mars Stewart win

MOTOR RACING

Fittipaldi escapes in 140 m.p.h. crash

JOCHEN RINDT DIES IN 185 mph CRASH

From BASIL CARDEW - Monza, Milan, Saturday

JOCHEN RINDT, world champion elect this year and probably the most popular driver in the Grand Prix circus, was killed here today when his Lotus 72 car crashed at 180 miles an hour during practice for Sunday's Italian Grand

Helicopter dash

Left: With Jochen at Monza, 1970. He was dead within a matter of hours.

Top left: The season kicked off with a surprise meeting at Geneva airport – Charlie Chaplin.

Top right: With Roone Arledge, at Monaco…

Above: … and coming out of the tunnel, on my way to victory.

Right: I might have lost a wheel in Austria, but I was world champion again.

world champion could get a bollocking from the great team director.

It had been a frustrating weekend all round because I finished fifth in a race I could have won, and François injured his ankle in a collision with Jacky Ickx. That meant he would have to hobble around on a pair of crutches during the break we had planned to take before the US Grand Prix a fortnight later.

'Don't worry,' I told him, 'you can sit in the back of the car and rest your leg on the seat.'

'No problem,' he replied, grinning broadly.

The three of us packed into a Ford Fairlane – with me driving, Helen in the passenger seat and François behind – and we drove from the Mosport circuit near Toronto up to Niagara Falls. It was an impressive sight, even if my young French team-mate had insisted that I carry him from the car to the viewing point.

'I don't want the crutches,' he laughed. 'You carry me.'

'No way,' I replied, before being persuaded to put this grown man on my shoulders, as if he was Paul or Mark.

We then flew to Bermuda and checked into a beautiful hotel, where we could swim and go for walks on the beach; a doctor had told François that paddling in shallow water would be useful therapy for his ankle. These days remain vivid in my mind as one of the all too rare moments in my life when I could switch off the engines of the rocket ship and simply relax.

There was a fine restaurant in the hotel, and every evening we dressed for dinner in a collar and tie. The atmosphere was wonderful, the food was excellent and, while coffee was served, François would get up and walk across the dance floor to a large grand piano, where he would sit down and play Beethoven's Piano Sonata No. 8 in C Minor, commonly known as Pathétique. It was his favourite piece of music, and, as his fingers danced, I recall looking around and seeing how everybody, particularly the women, looked completely enchanted.

'Jackie,' he said to me one afternoon, as we lay beside the hotel pool, 'I have been talking to Ferrari.'

'Have you now?'

'Yes, you know, I have to be my own man one day. You and Ken have this fantastic relationship, and I don't think I will ever be able to beat you. Maybe I must find another team.'

He had no idea I was planning to retire after US Grand Prix, and that he would then become the Tyrrell No. 1.

'Well, I wouldn't do anything too hasty,' I said. 'You're good enough that you don't have to make a decision now. There is only one race left in the season, and Ferrari are not going to let you go for the sake of waiting another ten days.'

'Yes, but I must think about my future.'

'I know that, but be patient. It will work out well for you.'

Ken and I had been privately discussing succession plans for months and, by the time we arrived at Watkins Glen, Ken was clear that François would become his No. 1, and a talented South African called Jody Scheckter would join as a new No. 2. That appeared to be a promising combination and, now thinking how to make it work, the team director had another idea.

Early on the Friday on the weekend of the US Grand Prix, he took me aside and said he had a big favour to ask.

'Jackie, this is your last race, and you've already won the world championship,' he began.

'Yes,' I said, wondering what he was going to say.

'Well, our cars are going well, and if it turns out that you are leading in the closing stages with François in second place, it would be a fantastic gesture for you to move over and let him win the race. It would look as if you were passing the torch to him, and I was wondering what you think about that.'

'Ken,' I replied, 'that's asking a lot.'

'I know.'

'This could be my twenty-eighth Grand Prix victory, and that might be important. I would love to bow out with a win, and not many drivers have done that. You'll have to let me think about this one.'

'I understand.'

We discussed plans for the practice session, and I concluded the conversation by saying: 'Listen, Ken, I'll tell you what. It's not a bad idea about giving François a chance to win, but let's just wait and see how we go in practice, then you and I will make the final decision together before the race, OK?'

'That's fine,' Ken replied.

Friday's practice went well. Chris Amon was still in the third car, and the three Tyrrells were running so well that François and I returned to the circuit on the Saturday morning, confident that we could dominate the qualifying session and maybe even secure first and second place on the front row of the grid. Our main rival was Ronnie Peterson in the Lotus, but François was determined to be quicker and he said as much as he prepared to go out again on that bright, sunny morning.

Sitting there in his car, with his helmet on and his visor up, he caught the eye of Helen, who happened to be sitting on the pit wall, and he winked at her – one last, unforgettable wink.

What happened next?

Well, all three Tyrrells were out on the circuit with François, Chris Amon and me each working to put in fast laps. I was happy with the way things were going with my car but had no idea what was happening to the other two. I drove around past the pits at Watkins Glen, through the right-hander and a second right-hander, up to the fast left-hander at the top of the hill and there, on the brow of the rise, as I started to turn left into the section known as the 'Bridge', just at that moment, I saw a marshal frantically waving a yellow flag. In fact, he was waving double yellow flags, which was a sign to drivers that we should be prepared to stop. Oh no, I thought to myself, it must be a big shunt. So I slowed down to a crawl and started to see the debris strewn right across the track. It looked like the site of an air crash, but there were just enough pieces sufficiently large enough for me to realise it was blue debris; in fact, it was Tyrrell blue debris. It must be Chris Amon, I thought, and then I saw Chris walking along the side of the track. He glanced at me, and I pointed at him and gave him a quizzical thumbs-up sign. He shook his head and wagged his finger, as if to say 'it's not me'. If it wasn't him who had been involved in the accident, then it had to be François. My heart started to pound and I immediately pulled over, climbed out of my car and started running towards the wreckage.

The accident must have happened not more than a minute earlier, but there was nobody around. Several drivers, including Chris and Jody Scheckter, had stopped to help but, like the marshals, they just looked and walked away.

I arrived, and stared in disbelief and horror. I immediately realised there was nothing anyone could have done. The Tyrrell was wedged into the tangled remains of the metal barrier, its nose pointing down and the cockpit facing towards me. There was smoke and steam, and a stench of oil . . . and there, still strapped into his seat, was my team-mate, my protégé, my friend, my younger brother. He was dead.

I honestly don't know how long I stood there, less then two feet from this horrific scene, but I eventually turned away and walked back to my car. Should I have stayed with François? That is a question I have asked myself thousands of times over the past thirty-four years. Maybe he was unconscious, maybe I could have waited there and talked to him and maybe even been there when he breathed his last breath. I don't know. I'll keep wondering.

Whatever I might have done, I did return to my car and drive straight back to the pits, angered that this sport that we pursued with such passion could turn on us yet again and be so cruel and claim another young life in such a violent way.

A horribly eerie silence had descended on the whole pit area by the time I arrived. I turned off the engine, stood up in my car, took off my gloves and threw them to the ground.

Helen was there.

'What is it?' she asked.

'It's François.'

'Oh no.'

Ken walked over to me. Chris Amon had already returned to the pit, and I suspect he must have told Ken what had happened out on the track, but I didn't know for sure.

'François is dead,' I said, bluntly.

'Are you sure?'

'Yes.'

'How do you know?'

'Ken, I was there.'

'Did a doctor tell you?'

'No.'

'Well, how can you be so sure?'

As he questioned me, I wondered if I was absolutely sure. Was it possible to be 100 per cent certain that François was dead? I had been standing right next to him. From what I saw, I don't think he could possibly have lived.

'So you're not 100 per cent certain,' Ken persisted.

'Ken, please, I saw him. I think he's dead. That's all I know.'

It was too much for me. I walked away from our pit, through a sea of people who were now milling around outside because the track had been closed. I didn't seem to know anybody, and I just kept walking until I reached a small motorhome, where I found Edsel Ford and Cynthia, then his girlfriend and later to become his wife. Helen joined us soon afterwards, and the four of us sat there, neither moving nor speaking, in shock.

Confirmation François had died arrived some time afterwards, and I eventually returned to our pit area, where, even amid all the grief, the discussion had turned to what might have caused the accident. I wanted to know, and everyone, particularly Joe Ramirez, François' No. 1 mechanic, was fearful that an error might have been made that caused a mechanical failure and led to the accident. That would have been a terrible burden to bear. Ken and Roger Hill said they did not think François could have made a mistake in that particular section of the circuit, and, when the track reopened for afternoon practice, Ken came across to me and asked me what I wanted to do. I told him I wanted to go back out and work out precisely what happened. I needed to understand.

So I climbed into my car and headed out and, approaching the narrow Bridge complex at a speed of 130 mph, I noticed a small hump in the road. It was just past the apex and close to the exit of the left-hand corner and the disruption was enough to make the short-wheel-base Tyrrell feel pointy and nervous. Suddenly driving the car felt like riding a highly strung horse; it ran perfectly if you held it in a straight line but, if it was disturbed in any way, it could be unpredictable and react negatively. It was usual at Watkins Glen for the track to become cleaner and quicker as the weekend progressed, and my preference was to take this section in fifth gear, using the low end of the engine's rev range. This meant the car was more docile and able to cushion the nervousness of the car going over the hump. I was almost certain that François had chosen to approach the Bridge in fourth gear, at the top end of his engine's rev range, which might have made his car faster through the combination of corners but which also would have made the car's reaction to the hump even more nervous, twitchy and unpredictable.

It seemed to me that, on that fateful lap, his high-spirited thoroughbred car had hit the hump and responded in an overly nervous fashion, whipping on him as he came off the throttle at almost maximum revs, which would have made the car even more reactive. In those few milliseconds, he would have been unable to catch it and regain control. The car would have pointed itself towards the right side of the track, crashing heavily into the Armco barrier and then ricocheting at high speed across the track and colliding violently into the barrier on the left side, turning upside down in the process. Just to make absolutely sure, I decided to do another lap and to approach the Bridge in fourth gear as François had done, and the vehicle's reaction confirmed my view. Even though I was taking care and was prepared, it was not easy to keep control.

I drove back to the pits and related all this to Ken and the mechanics, saying that the decision to take that section in fourth gear had been the major contributing factor in the accident.

'There is no way that was a mechanical failure,' I told them, and the relief visibly spread across their faces.

Even as I spoke, I felt the pain and emptiness return. At that precise moment, towards the end of the day before a race, François and I should have been sitting together in that very pit, running through our gear ratios, and I certainly would have advised him to take the Bridge in fifth. It would have been impossible to know that before, but we would have learned that much from driving on the cleaner track. Now, it was too late for any advice.

Ken interrupted my thoughts.

'Jackie,' he said, 'my view is that we should not race tomorrow, out of respect for François.'

'I think you're right.'

He continued: 'There might be an issue with the circuit, because we are contracted to race here.'

'I think they will understand.'

'OK, I'll contact them now.'

The Tyrrell team's decision to withdraw from the US Grand Prix was accepted, and, amid the trauma, I suddenly realised my motor racing career had come to an end. At last, there was now no need to keep my decision to retire as a secret.

'Where's Helen?'

'She's gone back to the hotel with Norah,' somebody replied.

So, alone, I made my way back to the Glen Motor Inn and found her in our room. Helen was sitting on the edge of the bed, and I told her we had decided not to race the next day. Still standing and looking straight at her, I said, 'As of this moment, I am no longer a racing driver.'

'Now,' she replied, through her tears, 'we can grow old together.'

I have no idea how long we sat there on the bed, holding each other, crying our eyes out. It felt as if I had had to be so strong and clear-minded at the track, trying to make sure everyone was all right, working out how the accident had happened, but, finally alone with Helen in that hotel room, everything came pouring out – the agony and grief for François, whom we had lost, and the relief that I had somehow survived my racing career. My little pouch of precious fluid that had so successfully diluted my grief so often in past had now run dry, and my body was literally racked with pain and grief.

We returned to the circuit the following day and put on a brave face. As I recall, I was wearing a sports jacket with a black polo-neck shirt and grey flannels, and Helen wore an oatmeal trouser suit. It's strange how such details stay with you.

François' funeral was held in Paris, and Helen and I wept through most of the service. We travelled with his brave and stoic parents to the village of Vaudelnay, in Maine-et-Loire, where he was buried in the family mausoleum, beneath a piece of black marble with the image of his handsome face on the wall behind.

He had died on 6 October 1973, aged twenty-nine, and we arranged to send flowers to his mother and to his grave on that date of every year that followed, until she passed away. Ever since then, we have continued to send flowers to his grave.

Returning home to Begnins, we tried to look forward to the rest of our lives, but it is hard to exaggerate the impact of François' death on both Helen and me. Even now, so many decades later, we both find tears welling in our eyes when we mentally replay the tapes of what we saw and experienced.

I have sat down and tried to make sense of it all many times and my enduring view is that, as we arrived at Watkins Glen that weekend, everything was going almost too well in my life. After an idyllic week in Bermuda, I was one race away from retirement, and I felt entirely comfortable with the decision. In fouteen years of competitive racing, I had secured a high standard of living, enjoyed many privileges and been able to provide for my young family; and now, without spilling a single drop of blood as a racing driver, I looked forward to a bright and exciting future. Maybe everything seemed just too neat. The US Grand Prix was going to be the hundredth and last of my career, and I had won twenty-seven F1 world championship races, at that time more than anybody else in the history of the sport, and I had already secured my third world championship in five seasons. The Tyrrell team seemed dominant, Ken and I had resolved the succession plan, François had developed into a top-class driver, and I looked forward to watching him win the world championship I felt was within his grasp. My cup was not just full, it was overflowing. Looking back, maybe everything was too good to be true.

Then there was one small hump in the road.

That's life. However well things may be going, however much we plan and want to be organised and try to be considerate and caring, however successful we may seem, however much money we may earn, however clever and blessed we think we are, we are all just one small hump in the road from disaster.

Helen and I subsequently learned how, on that fateful Saturday evening, the Swiss TV news had mistakenly reported that I had been killed in an accident at Watkins Glen. Our seven-year-old son Paul was staying with some friends, the Chilcotts, and had happened to be watching TV at the time. He was ushered away to the playroom, and it was almost an hour before he was told that, in fact, I was fine. For that period of time, Paul had believed his father had been killed on the track, just like Natasha Rindt's father and just like Kim and Jonas Bonnier's dad. By deciding to retire from motor racing, I was making sure he would never, ever have to feel that way again.

'Daddy, please stop racing,' he had said, as soon as we returned home from Watkins Glen.

'OK, darling,' I replied.

'Yes,' he said, breathlessly. 'If we have to make pennies and if you really want to drive, you can drive the school bus that picks everyone up. You will be perfect.'

The media had started to speculate that I was about to retire – with roughly half the people thinking I would leave the sport, and the other half believing I would be back racing in 1974 – but nobody knew for sure, and arrangements were made that Ford would host a formal announcement at the Carlton Tower Hotel in London. We took the boys out of school, and the whole Stewart family flew across from Geneva to attend the event.

I was eager to stress that my decision to retire had been made many months ago in April, and that it was not an emotional reaction to François' accident. That was the absolute truth although the fact that one event had followed the other resulted in many people jumping to the wrong conclusion. That was beyond my control. However, I decided to make a particular effort to see one very important person and inform them in person of my decision – my mother.

She was living at the nursing home in Old Kilpatrick at the time, and I remember walking into a sitting room and finding her sitting in a chair next to a window, just as she had been at Rockview when, eleven years before, I had approached her with my brother Jim and told her I wanted to be a racing driver. In all those years, through everything that had happened, she had never once acknowledged me as a racing driver. She felt I had lied to her in my early years, when I raced as A. N. Other, so she didn't want to know. Motor racing was not discussed in her presence and, when F1 Grands Prix started being broadcast on television, my father went and watched at other people's houses. Of course, my mother knew what I was doing, and there was one notable occasion when she attended a dinner at the headquarters of the Royal Scottish Automobile Club in Blytheswood Square, Glasgow. In some ways, the saga became a family joke, but still she never uttered a word of recognition.

'Hello, Jackie,' she said, calmly, as I sat down beside her in the nursing home.

'Mummy, I have something to tell you. I've decided to retire as a racing driver.'

'You what?' she said, because she had started to struggle with her hearing.

'Mummy, I said I have retired as a racing driver. I'm not in racing any more.'

'You're well out of it,' she replied and, with that, she gave out this great screech of laughter.

The subject was not discussed any further or ever again.

My mother passed away in 1977, at the Cottage Hospital on the Cardross Road in Dumbarton. I had been with her for the entire day, and she had been slipping in and out of consciousness. Then, almost as if God had decided she should have privacy at the end, she died while I was outside the room taking a phone call.

As much as anything in this world, I hope that, from

wherever she is watching now, she feels proud of her younger son.

Following the final announcement of my retirement, various articles appeared praising my achievements as a driver and also my contribution to improving the safety of the sport. We also received many letters, including a handwritten note from Frank Williams:

Dear Jackie,
I am so happy for you and Helen and the boys, but quite sad for motor racing. I have always admired and respected everything you have done and realise full well the reasons, the emotions and the strength of character behind your decision. We are very much poorer now in our sport and I can tell you your absence will be greatly missed by Williams. I wish you every happiness and success in your future, plus personal fulfilment from whatever you turn to. Thank you for the times we had and thank you for what you gave.
Yours ever,
Frank

Ken told me he believed my greatest achievement was to retire at the top of the sport. Very few people leave motor racing, he said, before it leaves them.

Several weeks later, a gala dinner was held in my honour at the Savoy, attended by four hundred guests, including HRH Princess Anne and Captain Mark Phillips, who had only just returned from their honeymoon, and everyone in the room was given a black corduroy cap and a big pair of 'JYS' sunglasses to wear. Ken stole the show with a brilliant speech, in which he said he wanted to give me something so special that it hurt.

'I have decided against giving you my wife Norah,' he said, bringing the house down, 'but I would like to give you the car you drove to eight Grand Prix victories: 003.' Following its final race at the previous year's German Grand Prix, 003 had enjoyed a distinguished and fully deserved retirement, being exhibited around the world. Now Ken was giving it to me. It was a wonderful gesture, and I responded by saying I felt the car should be passed on to the next generation, so I duly gave it as a joint present to my sons, Paul and Mark. 003 was then put on public display at the Scottish Museum of Transport in Glasgow and was later moved to join the exhibition of single-seater racing cars at Donington, maintained under the expert care of Tom Wheatcroft and his son Kevin. It was extensively renovated by Roy Tropp in 1998, and remains in such immaculate condition that I was able to drive it at the Goodwood Revival in 2005, and then at the Scottish Festival of Speed at Knockhill in 2006.

People kept asking what I was planning to do next, and there was talk that I would star in a film based on the novel *Way to Dusty Death* by Alistair McLean, but, in reality, I had already started my next career by signing four major commercial contracts – with ABC's *Wide World of Sports* television show in America, with the Ford Motor Company, with Goodyear and with Elf Aquitaine. My view at the time was that these arrangements would keep me going for no more than five years, after which I would be well forgotten and would have to find something else to do.

We spent Christmas of 1973 as a family at home in Begnins, and Helen and I were touched when Mark asked if he could have some money because he wanted to buy us a Christmas present. He was only five years old, so Helen took him down to Nyon, where he decided he wanted to go to a record shop.

With Helen waiting outside, our young son walked in and, hardly tall enough to reach the shelves where the records were displayed, eventually picked out an album at random just because he liked the look of the glossy cover. He took it to the counter, had it gift-wrapped, paid for it with the money we had given him and emerged tightly holding the bag so his mother would not see the present.

François Cevert had been extremely close to Helen and he had told her that, if anything ever happened to him, wherever he was, he would make sure that somehow he would send us a message or some kind of sign to let us know he was all right. Imagine, then, how we felt when, on that Christmas morning, just eleven weeks after his accident, Helen and I opened the present from Mark, something chosen completely at random by a five-year-old child, and discovered it was a record of Beethoven's Piano Sonata No. 8 in C Minor, commonly known as Pathétique.

CHAPTER 12

The Thrill of Victory and the Agony of Defeat

THE OPENING SEQUENCE FEATURED A SKI JUMPER crashing spectacularly even before he had reached the end of the jump, his legs and arms flailing in the air. That image represented half of the slogan adopted by the most popular weekend sports show in America. 'The thrill of victory and the agony of defeat,' declared the announcer over the pictures. 'Welcome to ABC's *Wide World of Sports*.'

It was a broadcasting institution, created in 1961 by a ginger-haired genius called Roone Arledge, a giant in the American Broadcasting Corporation (ABC), who later became one of the most powerful media leaders in the USA when he combined the roles of president of ABC Sports and president of ABC News. Even as a senior executive, he maintained his basic skills. For all his achievements on the top floor and his influence in the White House, his natural habitat remained a live television control room, either in the studio or an outside broadcast unit, heading the production team at a big sports event, facing a wall of televisions, directing the feed, telling the story shot by shot. It was a magical experience to watch him in action, sitting in the hot seat at the Olympic Games, his eyes scanning across up to twenty-five screens receiving pictures from cameras placed around the venue, as he constructed the TV coverage that would be broadcast live to many tens of millions of viewers. This was an artist at work, punching the buttons as he constructed the broadcast, making inspired decisions in fractions of seconds. The amazing contradiction was that, away from the control room, Roone was one of the most indecisive men I have ever known. His many friends will remember he was also famously difficult to reach on the telephone: he always seemed to be busy and he very rarely returned calls. However, he was a truly creative thinker and innovator, interested not so much in what had always been done but in what could be done to make the product better and more exciting. It was Roone who created the role of a colour commentator accompanying the sports anchorman, offering expert insight and analysis, and it was he who first had the idea that a Scottish motor racing driver with a strange and different accent could have a career in American television.

'We've got O. J. Simpson and Frank Gifford in our American football coverage,' he told me, 'and I think you can do a great job for us in motor racing. What do you think?'

'It sounds exciting,' I enthused.

'Good,' he replied, 'now you need to meet Jim McKay.'

Jim was the established host of ABC's *Wide World of Sports*. A well-educated American with a wonderful command of the English language and perfect manners, he became highly respected for his emotional and sensitive coverage of the Israeli hostage crisis during the 1972 Olympic Games in Munich.

McKay was a stage name he created to protect the privacy of his family, who used his real surname, McManus. Jim's beloved wife, Margaret, was his business manager and she often travelled with him. Their daughter Mary and son Sean occasionally came along to motor racing events, and I was delighted to hear recently the young boy I remember has grown up to become Sean McManus, president of CBS News and CBS Sports. His father took me under his wing all those years ago and taught me the trade.

Jim McKay was unquestionably the biggest influence on my broadcasting career, and I was privileged to work beside him for fifteen years. Our lives then moved in different directions and we didn't see each other for a considerable period until I happened to meet Sean while I was in New York at the end of May 2008, and he mentioned his father had not been well recently. I gave Jim a call, and he sounded a bit weak, so I asked if I could come and visit him at his home in Maryland.

He and his wife Margaret lived at a beautifully kept farm, set in rolling hills, and we had a great lunch together, laughing and recalling all the times we had shared at ABC's *Wide World of Sports*.

Only three days later, Jim passed away. It was so hard to take in. Barely a week after our lunch, my son Paul and I were attending his funeral mass at Baltimore Cathedral, standing among a fantastic collection of people, recalling all those old stories all over again . . . only this time without Jim.

One of my first assignments for ABC Sports was the Monaco Grand Prix in 1971, when I was still racing. Jim McKay was in his element, and I pre-recorded a piece with him at the Monte Carlo golf club, positioned up high with a panoramic view of the Principality. That was used to open the show, and it was arranged that I would be interviewed by Jim as the last thing I did before I climbed into the car and the first thing I did after finishing the race. Fortunately, I won that afternoon, so he found me in good humour.

The broadcast worked well. It was remarkable for a broadcaster to use somebody as their colour commentator who was not only competing in the event but winning it, and it made for appealing television. We were thinking out of the box, and the twin role continued in 1973 when I was named ABC Sports Person of the Year while working for the network.

Most sports people don't move into television until they have retired, but I didn't see any point in waiting. I was being exposed to a new world, and it created more demands on my time, but it was exciting and in many ways as challenging as anything I was doing in motor racing.

The exposure I was receiving on American television eventually became a powerful currency. As my face and voice became known in homes across the US, my profile grew, my marketing value escalated and an increasing number of companies contracted me to endorse their products.

At one time or another, I appeared in US television commercials for Wrangler Jeans, Wheelhorse Tractors, Getty Oil and Fram Oil Filters. Taking into account my role in the regular TV and print campaigns run by Ford and Goodyear, and my work for ABC over a period of fifteen years, it's no wonder that a significant number of Americans have identified me as a television commentator rather than a racing driver.

ABC initially invited me to join their coverage of big motor racing events such as the Daytona 500 and the Indianapolis 500, where my role included interviewing drivers, explaining technical issues, offering insight into driver behaviour, highlighting safety issues and providing expert commentary on the races. I worked alongside true professionals such as Keith Jackson, Al Michaels, Chris Schenkel and Bill Fleming, and learned. It wasn't easy work, particularly for someone who had yet to be diagnosed as dyslexic, and I really struggled with long chunks of text. Working in a studio, I found it almost impossible to read from an autocue, or a teleprompter as they are known in America, but I largely got around the problem by writing out the script on a yellow pad, using words that came easily to me, and then memorising what I needed to say as best I could.

As I soon discovered, appearing casual and relaxed on television requires a vast amount of preparation and concentration. At their best, TV presenters are like ducks swimming on a pond: all you see is grace and elegance, but there is usually plenty of frenetic activity going on just beneath the surface.

My considerable experience of being interviewed as a racing driver wasn't a great help; working on the opposite side of the microphone proved much more complicated. In fact, preparing to deliver a piece to camera soon seemed as frightening and stressful as getting ready for the start of a F1 Grand Prix. My mouth would go dry, and my heart would feel as if it was about to beat out of my chest as I watched for the small red light on top of the camera and tried to work out what I was going to say; and, all the time, the director would be chattering away in my earpiece, telling me what he wanted me to do.

'OK, Jackie,' he would say, giving me the countdown, 'ten seconds to air, nine, eight, seven, six, five, four, three, two, one . . .'

The red light came on, and suddenly there was no turning back and no second take. We were 'live'. It was nerve-racking, but this was also fantastic training at the sharp end. I would start speaking, trying to appear neither too stressed and constipated nor overly relaxed and casual, and I soon learned how to breathe smoothly, in such a way that I filled my lungs and was able to reach the end of the sentence without gasping. I tried to come across as authoritative and knowledgeable, and yet also to convey a kind of easy charm that would make each of the viewers feel as if I were personally talking to them.

Interviewing was another challenge, because you had to do two things at once: listen to what the interviewee was saying, and also marshal your thoughts to formulate the next question. If I listened too intently to what he or she was saying, the interviewee could finish their answer and I would be stranded without another sensible or relevant question. But if I concentrated too much on what I was going to ask next, it was easy not to hear something of interest which required a follow-up.

In television, as in racing, as in everything, the challenge was to strike the right balance, to pick up knowledge, develop the required set of skills and accumulate experience. In colour commentary on motor racing, I had to provide the aficionados of the sport with the technical insight they wanted and yet to communicate this information in a way that was easily understandable to the uncles and aunties who were also watching but had a less profound knowledge of the sport. Even if we were discussing the merits of gear ratios and aerodynamics, we had to make sure the show engaged all the viewers.

'We must appeal to the broadest possible market,' Roone always used to say.

The next stage in the steep learning curve was to work at events outside motor racing, and it was a privilege for me to be part of the ABC productions at major occasions such as the 1976 Summer Olympics in Montreal and the 1976 Winter Olympics in Innsbruck, the Highland Gathering at Braemar, Scotland (when the entire production team turned up dressed in the kilt – even the locals were impressed!) and Ladies' Day at the Royal Ascot horse racing. I even worked for ABC News when the legendary Peter Jennings came to London to anchor their coverage of the Queen's Silver Jubilee celebrations in 1977, crossing to me as a roving reporter in front of Buckingham Palace, in the Royal Mews and in the Mall.

Each of these broadcasts was structured to tell a story as engrossing as any novel, and the production team was always encouraged to come up with new ways of looking at each event, and to find issues and personalities that would make interesting segments or revealing interviews. I enjoyed the work because I was bouncing ideas off creative, dynamic people, and imaginations ran wild, sometimes a little too wild.

Scheduled to join the commentary team at the bobsleigh world championships, I arrived in St Moritz to be told that the producer had made arrangements for me to be the third man of the four in the Switzerland fourth team.

'No way,' I said, without hesitation.

'Oh, come on, Jackie,' he begged. 'It will make great television. We're going to get you wired up with a throat mike, so you can actually talk us down the run while competing in a world championship. It's a real scoop.'

'Look, I have just survived a career in F1 motor racing and got away with amazingly few injuries. There's no way I'm going in that thing.'

'So you're chicken?'

'Absolutely!'

I sensed the production team were somewhat disappointed by my attitude, but they eventually persuaded a military man called Captain Eric Grounds to volunteer and 'make great television'. In fact, I knew him because he had been best man at the wedding of HRH Princess Anne and Captain Mark Phillips. The competition began, and my co-commentator started joking on air about how I had refused to get in the bobsleigh. Not long afterwards, while I was commentating on air, we watched as the bobsleigh that I was supposed to have joined suddenly turned upside down and skidded at breakneck speed along the icy run. Poor, brave Captain Grounds had to be taken to hospital with a broken nose, a badly cut cheek and heavy bruising. That left me looking like a smart cookie, and, as people who had heard the commentary congratulated me on my perceptive judgement, the ABC producer seemed very quiet.

Roone's overriding conviction was that ABC's *Wide World of Sports* should always include a wide variety of events, servicing the catholic tastes of its viewers and keeping everyone interested. So the show might break away from coverage of a motor race with the words 'we'll be right back' and switch to an off-beat segment on a log-rolling competition in Canada or a sheep-shearing contest in New Zealand, and then return to the race track. This unique mix made the show special and endeared it to an amazingly large average weekly audience of many millions, coast to coast, men and women, young and old.

Winston Cup stock car racing was a regular feature, and I was once sent to cover a race at the Darlington Motor Speedway in South Carolina, a place known as the 'Grand Daddy of Them All', and I thought it might be fun to interview some of the spectators who camped in the infield the night before the race. There were rough, tough southern boys who devoured huge steaks and barbeque chicken, washed down with significant volumes of beer and Jack Daniels. There was even a special compound, enclosed by barbed wire and high chain-link fencing, where women could go and be safe from men or, as they said, be 'unmolested'. We took our camera into that area and found it deserted, which said something about the good ladies of Darlington.

Like Ken Tyrrell, Phil Collins and Eric Clapton, Roone recognised the importance of surrounding himself with people of the highest quality. In my view, the team he assembled at ABC Sports in the 1970s and 1980s produced the best sports television coverage in the world in that particular era.

The senior producer when I joined was Chuck Howard, and the leading director was Chet Forte, an all-American basketball player in his prime during the 1950s. However, the ABC lifestyle eventually spread to Chet's waistline, which took Jesse Owens by surprise. 'Hey Chet,' the great Olympics athlete memorably said, 'what have you done to your body?'

Chuck and Chet were both leaders in their fields, genuine experts who made people like me look good.

John Martin was a key administrator, who dealt with the rights holders, and Nancy Dobi was Roone's secretary and gate keeper, an important person in the ABC Sports network.

Roone created a structure and a culture from which many exceptional professionals emerged: Don Ohlmeyer, who started as production assistant, became a director, then a producer and later went on to produce feature films; Bob Iger, who has become president and CEO of the Walt Disney Company; Ellie Riger, who became the first woman director and producer at that level; and others such as Larry Kahm, Doug Wilson, Bob Goodrich and Roger Goodman.

There was great camaraderie among these people. They enjoyed each other's company and consistently challenged one another to achieve the highest possible standards. They were professionals who thrived under pressure and delighted in meeting the expectations of their audience. At ABC Sports, they lived and worked in style, demonstrating again that if you give people first-class treatment, it will usually encourage them to perform at a first-class level.

Production meetings were often held in presidential suites, with enough food to feed several armies, and it was not uncommon for producers, directors and commentators to travel to and from events by private jet or helicopter. There were always cars and drivers on hand, and I once remarked, with a grin, that whenever an ABC sports producer has a child, the baby's first word was never 'Mama' or 'Dada' . . . it would always be 'limo'.

ABC headquarters on Sixth Avenue, Manhattan, New York City, was a hive of activity and style, and the excellence was carried through to the secretaries and administrative staff.

Inevitably, it was the presenters, commentators and colour commentators who became the famous faces of the organisation, upbeat, larger-than-life personalities who seemed to become woven into the very fabric of the sport they covered.

Howard Cosell was the voice of boxing in America. A friend of Muhammad Ali, he used to open the ABC coverage of the great boxing occasions of that era with tremendous showmanship, announcing: 'Hello and good evening, this is How-ward Co-sell, live at the Madison Square Garden.' Keith Jackson was the American football expert, known as 'the Horse'. Chris Economaki used to work at the major motor racing events and became famous for pushing a microphone under the nose of drivers after the race and asking his trademark question: 'So, how was it out there?'

Chris was a wonderful character and, one year at the Indianapolis 500, he came up with an idea of doing a segment explaining why the IndyCars had been converted to run on alcohol, rather than gasoline (or petrol as we say in the UK). He said the advantage of alcohol was that it was less likely to catch fire, but the problem was it could be dangerous because it burned without smoke or flame. He set up a demonstration in front of a small audience at the race track, which became rather too graphic when he swung a microphone cable and accidentally tipped over a metal pan full of burning alcohol. I happened to be passing by at this precise moment and was alarmed to see Chris hopping around apparently for no reason. He was in great pain, and I realised the invisible burning liquid had splashed over his polyester trousers. He was on fire, and nobody knew it. I rushed over, bent down and tried to suffocate the fire with some racing overalls lying nearby. Chris then decided the best option was to drop his trousers and take them off. So there I was – on my knees in front of one of America's best-known sports commentators with his trousers around his ankles. Thankfully, there were no press photographers present to record the moment for posterity.

Cosell, Jackson, Economaki, McKay – I studied these top names relentlessly, and learned from every one of them. However, there was one aspect of the *Wide World of Sports* operation where, modestly and quietly, I felt I had the edge.

Standard dress for an ABC presenter was a yellow jacket, made from double-knit polyester. They couldn't find one to fit me properly, thank goodness, so I got some beautiful, exceptionally comfortable Italian fabric of the same colour and asked Doug Hayward, my tailor in London, to make me a jacket. It fitted perfectly, and, even though I say so myself, I think it looked just great with my black corduroy cap.

Pursuing a television career in America while living in Switzerland could be a reasonable proposition today with advances in broadcasting technology, but, back in the 1970s, hard as it may be to believe, I used to fly from Geneva to New York to lay down a voice-over on a pre-recorded segment. The travel schedule was amazing. At one stage, I was doing something like twenty-five programmes per year, flying back and forth across the Atlantic more than eighty times in twelve months, and racking up a total mileage in excess of 450,000 miles, the equivalent of travelling eighteen times around the world. A typical week might have seen me flying to Atlanta on a Thursday to work at a NASCAR race and then leaving the track by helicopter to catch BA's Sunday-night flight to London. I would do whatever I had to do in Europe and get on the Wednesday-morning Concorde from London to New York, arriving at JFK airport at 9.30 a.m., rush in to the ABC dubbing studios on the west side of Central Park, finish the layover, get back into a limo to JFK and catch the overnight Swissair flight home to Geneva. Madness, people might say. It was tiring, but exhilarating, and it was just an extension of how I had led my life in my racing days. I really didn't know any different.

Every once in a while, perhaps unsurprisingly, the chirpy Scottish presenter strayed into controversial territory, and it's no surprise that the issue he put under the spotlight was safety in motor sport. One year, as we were preparing to cover the Indianapolis 500, I mentioned to Chuck Howard and Chet Forte that I thought the wall which separated the pit lane from the main straight at the race track was much too low, and I said I thought the issue merited an authoritative piece in the ABC's

Indy programme. They agreed, and I pre-recorded a piece to camera, outlining the issues that I felt needed to be addressed, showing the wall and explaining how, in my view, it was conceivable that two cars could tangle at speeds of 220 mph in the home straight and be launched into the pit lane, an area where several hundred people were working and where a large tank of highly flammable fuel was kept for each and every one of the thirty-three cars in the race. Officials of the Indianapolis Motor Speedway heard about the piece and asked to see the segment before it was broadcast. They felt it was damaging and asked Roone for it to be withdrawn.

He was not attending the race that year, so a tape of my piece was sent by courier to him, at home in Long Island, New York. The next day, he called me in my hotel room.

'Hello, Jackie, you having a good time up there?' he asked.

'It's getting quite hot,' I replied.

'Well, I've looked at the tape and I think it's a good piece. Are you 100 per cent sure you're right?'

'Roone,' I replied, 'there's no question. I'm comfortable with the facts.'

'OK, the easiest way out is just to pull the piece.'

'You can do that, but I feel the insert is worth broadcasting because, in the worst case, if something does happen, we would be on the record for having recognised the risk.'

'I understand. So you want to run it?'

'Yes, I do.'

'OK, Jackie, that's fine. I'll back you on this one.'

So the insert was broadcast; and the wall separating the pit lane from the straight was subsequently raised.

An even more substantial and awkward problem developed in 1986, and, though the outcome was not in my favour, Roone based his judgement on the same strong set of principles. The dilemma was created when a large motor manufacturer complained to Roone that a conflict of interest had arisen between my roles as an ABC presenter and as a contracted representative of the Ford Motor Company. They said I was appearing in so many Ford TV commercials being aired during ABC prime time that the *Wide World of Sports* shows on which I was working had started to look like an extension of the advertisement. Roone felt they had a point.

'It's probably not fair on them,' he said, adding: 'Jackie, we obviously very much want you to stay, but I think we would need you to stop appearing in the Ford advertisements.'

'I can't do that, Roone,' I replied, 'I have had a global contract with the Ford Motor Company for twenty-two years, and even if I did agree to leave them, you couldn't pay me what they pay me on top of what you are paying me already.'

'That would be unaffordable.'

'I know that.'

'Then we've got a problem,' he said.

I parted company with ABC and the *Wide World of Sports* after fifteen years, in which I had been exposed to a new industry, worked with exceptional people and been part of producing some of the best sports television coverage in the world.

By then, I was working for several other broadcasters in other countries, notably first CTV and then CBC as part of their teams covering the Canadian Grand Prix; and I was asked to join the team at Australia's Channel Nine working on the Australian Grand Prix, first held in Adelaide and later in Melbourne. Channel Nine was a bright organisation reflecting the dynamic leadership initially of Alan Bond and then of Kerry Packer, and they had assembled a sports production team of spectacularly clever and creative people such as David Hill and Tony Sinclair.

Others might differ, but my view is that *Wide World of Sports* began to lose its soul when ABC merged first with ESPN and then with Capital Cities, prompting severe headcount cuts and reduced production budgets. By the 1990s, Channel Nine was emerging as a new world leader in sports television.

I enjoyed the relaxed and informal but extremely committed Australian way, and, when Channel Nine started allocating proper resources to their F1 production, it felt as if I had been transplanted back to the halcyon days at *Wide World of Sports*.

One of my Channel Nine inserts brought me into conflict with one of the greatest drivers in F1 history. Since moving from the starting grid to the commentary box, I had always tried to be as honest, factual, objective and colourful as possible and, in all my observations, to enhance the broadcast by telling the viewer what he or she could not see. If a driver made a mistake, I felt it was my job to point it out.

Towards the end of 1989, Ayrton Senna needed to win the last three races of the season to pip his McLaren team-mate, Alain Prost, at the post and become world champion, and he started with victory in the Spanish Grand Prix. This contest between the top two drivers of their generation captured everyone's imagination as it moved on to the Japanese Grand Prix at Suzuka. With Alain leading, Ayrton tried a risky late braking overtaking manoeuvre at the entrance to a chicane. Alain held his line, as he was entitled to do, but the two cars collided, started sliding and came to a stop on the edge of the track. Alain climbed out of his car, believing he had become world champion, but Ayrton called the marshals to push him out of the danger zone. He rejoined the race, took the lead and was first to cross the finishing line, only to be disqualified later because he had missed out part of the course after the collision.

The incident provoked intense debate throughout the sport. My view was that Ayrton had intentionally tried to put Alain out of the race, but nobody in the media had been prepared to say so by the time the F1 teams arrived in Adelaide to prepare for the Australian Grand Prix, the last race of the season. Every media outlet wanted a one-to-one with Ayrton but, after pressure was put on the organisers and the McLaren team, a date and time was arranged when the driver at the eye of the storm would give an interview to Channel Nine, host broadcaster of the Grand Prix. It was my job to ask the questions, and I decided there was no point in beating about the bush.

There was great interest in what he had to say, and a large group of photographers and print media had gathered at the appointed time in the pit area; and they were all still there in the pit garage when Ayrton finally turned up, two hours late.

I opened up the interview with a statement of fact, to see how he would respond, and to gauge his attitude to driving, in light of the Prost incident. 'If I were to count back all the world champions, and totalled up the number of times they made contact with other drivers, and compare that number with you in the last thirty-six or forty-eight months, you have been in contact with more cars and drivers than they might have done in total.'

The charismatic Brazilian allowed a slight smile to play on his lips before he fixed me with a furious stare and replied: 'I find it amazing for you to make such a question, Stewart. You are very experienced and you know a lot about racing. You should know that being a racing driver means you are racing other people and if you no longer go for a gap that exists, you are no longer a racing driver. We are competing to win.'

The interview didn't last long and, as soon as it ended and the cameras were switched off, Ayrton told me that I should not ask for another interview because he would never speak to me again. I wasn't pleased that he was so upset, but I had regarded it as my job to raise these difficult issues.

Two years later, still working for Channel Nine and back in Adelaide for the 1991 Australian Grand Prix, I received a telephone call out of the blue. It was Ayrton, asking if I would meet him at his hotel to discuss his increasing concerns about safety in F1 racing. I went along and we chatted for a couple of hours about what he could do to raise awareness and create change.

'You're bullet-proof,' I told him. 'Even if some of the media are against you, with your record, you can go on television and speak with authority about safety on behalf of the drivers and F1 community.'

He phoned me several times over the next couple of years, usually from his home in Portugal, and we would speak for an hour or so. Ayrton was frustrated that very few people in F1 were taking safety seriously and he felt that a dangerous complacency had set in because no current F1 driver had been killed since Elio de Angelis during testing in May 1986.

'I really want to say something in public,' he told me.

'Ayrton,' I replied, 'you have the power to do that, and it's your duty to speak up. I have been through exactly this situation, and you're certainly the right man to do it.'

We spoke on the telephone a few weeks before the 1994 San Marino Grand Prix, when Austrian driver Roland Ratzenberger died during practice on the Saturday, and Ayrton crashed into a wall and was killed during the race on the Sunday. I was not at Imola that weekend, instead attending a F3 race at Silverstone, where the Paul Stewart Racing team were competing. A group of us saw the accident on television and I remember the sense of shock that descended on the paddock area when the news came through that Ayrton had actually died. So many people seemed to have forgotten such things could happen in our sport.

I decided to attend Ayrton's funeral and flew to São Paulo, where his family had arranged for a helicopter to meet me at the airport and take me to the church. We flew over his cavalcade, and it was incredible to see 200,000 people lining the streets, mourning the loss of this great Brazilian hero.

As we gathered before the service, I was asked if I would join Emerson Fittipaldi, Alain Prost and Ayrton's great friend Gerhard Berger, among the pallbearers, and we duly carried Ayrton to his last resting place, where his coffin was lowered into the ground. Each of us then threw a handful of soil into his grave.

Ayrton was undoubtedly the fastest of his generation, but, while many devoted Senna fans will disagree, in my view, Alain was a more complete racing driver. The 'Professor', as he was known, was able to analyse precisely what he needed to do to get the car set up in such a way that it never seemed necessary for him to extend either it or himself beyond the limit. In contrast, Ayrton always stretched the elastic as far as it would go. The Prost–Senna rivalry was captivating, and I observed it as a television commentator, trying to draw the viewers' attention to details like the images of Alain provided by POV (point of view) camera, attached to the engine cover behind the driver's head. These showed how little he worked the steering wheel during the race, which was another indication of the extraordinarily calming influence that he had on the car. Senna, on the other hand, would have been working the car more aggressively. Alain was such an expert on vehicle dynamics that I would suggest his contribution to the McLaren team when Ayrton was his team-mate was more significant than most people recognised; in fact, I would respectfully suggest that, if Alain had not been there to set the cars up as well as he did, Ayrton would not have enjoyed as many F1 Grands Prix victories as he did.

I also used to talk on air about my observations at qualifying sessions, when I would stand around the pits and study how every driver reacted during those first moments after he came in from a quick lap when he was still sitting in his car. That was when you saw the real essence of Senna. He was typically so gentle and measured out of the car, but in those few seconds, when the adrenalin was still pumping and his eyes seemed to be on fire, his pupils enlarged, he looked every inch the daring genius, full of intensity and nervous energy.

In those telephone conversations I had with Ayrton before his death, and in my general observations of the man through my television work and through attending F1 race meetings, I had begun to form the impression that he was seriously considering retirement. His whole demeanour, his concerns over safety issues, indicated to me that he was a little less in love with the sport he was once so passionate about. Of course we will never know if I was correct or not, but if he was considering leaving motor racing, I suspect he would have been one of those sportsmen who retire and decide to walk away from the sport without a backwards glance. That certainly wasn't my approach in 1973 when I stopped racing.

Despite all the tragedies I had witnessed, and the battles with the authorities and track owners I had been through, I still loved motor racing. I still do today. I was fortunate that, over the next twenty-five years, Roone Arledge and many others gave me the opportunity to experience the sport from another perspective in the commentary box and so stay close to 'the thrill of victory and the agony of defeat'.

CHAPTER 13

Adding Value

Sporting superstars in their prime are often hideously spoiled, and the lavish adulation and attention they receive can blind them to the realities and the pitfalls of their lives beyond sport. They are smothered in privileges, ranging from free meals at the best restaurants to the use of private aircraft and yachts, exotic holiday homes and even islands, and they earn such vast amounts of money that almost anyone's values would be spoiled; it becomes easy for these pampered heroes to start believing the world owes them a living, to think the five-star treatment will last forever.

It doesn't. In fact, it usually ends pretty soon after they retire from their sport. As the spotlight moves to the next hero, the now 'former' superstar is swiftly relegated to the 'B' list and before long returned to the real world, where they come to realise that, indeed, there really is no such thing as a free lunch. Only when the high life becomes a memory do they start to consider and plan their lives beyond sport. By then, it may be too late because it is certainly harder to build the kind of commercial relationships that can provide long-term security when you are no longer an active frontline achiever. I have always been an advocate of taking preventative medicine and thinking ahead: taking action to avert a problem is always preferable to waiting and only acting when the problem actually materialises. If the sportsman or woman is wise, they will recognise the key to success beyond sport lies in changing their approach, being able to stop being a taker and start being a giver. If they don't, they can fall into a once unimagined void where their light no longer dazzles and where comfort is often found only in alcohol abuse and drugs. Fallen sporting heroes are many.

This seems such a waste of human potential. If an individual has had the ability to become the very best in the world at his or her chosen sport, then there is no reason why he or she should not be able to take that same talent and commitment and learn to add value and be successful in another field. The challenge for any superstar retiring from the world of sport, entertainment or any high-profile activity is to recognise the dangers, clean up their act and embellish their assets. In many cases, the reward can be a long-haul journey of extraordinary access and privilege, sustained respect and financial gain. At the peak of their sporting career, it may have seemed that winning was enough to provide all the wealth and benefits they could ever want. As soon as they retire, it very often becomes clear that, in fact, winning is not enough, and it becomes necessary for them to adapt their skills to a new challenge.

In my case, the realisation that I could add significant value to companies providing products or services to motor sport dawned on me long before I thought of retiring as a racing driver. So I was able to prepare myself to meet the new needs and, when the time came, move seamlessly from the cockpit into servicing a series of long-term commercial associations with several large multinational corporations. These contracts have proved wonderfully stimulating and sustained me and my family ever since.

In my experience, the crucial factor has always been a desire and determination to provide more value than the contracting company or individual perceives they are paying for.

Early in 1974, my first year back in the real world, Helen and I decided we would take the boys on holiday to Disneyworld in Florida, and we were driving in the outskirts of Orlando, along one of those wide, typically American streets with car dealerships to the left and right, as far as the eye can see.

'Look,' said Mark, aged six. 'There's Daddy's autograph.'

We didn't know what he was talking about, but we turned to see our young son was pointing at the instantly recognisable blue oval-shaped emblem of the Ford Motor Company. He had so often seen me wearing racing overalls with the Ford insignia, or appearing at Ford events, or featuring in Ford advertisements that he had grown to assume their logo also represented me.

In fact, I was first contracted to the company in 1964 and I would remain so until 2004. First as a racing driver, then a public affairs representative, a sales and marketing spokesman, a vehicle dynamic assessor, a concept design consultant and lastly a strategic adviser in training engineers, my forty years with Ford represented the most significant commercial association of my life.

It began in October 1964 when I turned up at the British Motor Show at Earls Court, London, as a young racing driver hoping to make some contacts in the motor industry. These were early days, and I had decided to drive south from Scotland through the night because I didn't think I could afford to stay in a London hotel. Even so, I had three names written on a scrap of paper – Dick Jefferies from Dunlop, Geoff Murdoch from Esso and Walter Hayes from Ford – and I hoped that if I could meet any of them, they might be able to help develop my career and hopefully improve my financial situation.

The Motor Show was paradise for an enthusiast like me, and

my attention was drawn to the Ford stand and a creamy white Ford Zodiac with red upholstery and chrome wheels. I can still see it now, displayed on a rotating turntable behind a red leather-cushioned balustrade, and I just stood there, staring at it.

'Do you like it?'

A complete stranger was standing beside me.

'Yes,' I replied.

'It's lovely,' he said. 'Would you like one?'

'Of course, but that's unlikely to occur.'

'Well, if you drive for me, I'll give you this car and a bit of money as well.'

I looked at this small, dapper man and wondered if he was for real.

'You don't know me, but I know you,' he said. 'My name is Walter Hayes.'

We started talking, and that evening I phoned Helen to tell her about my new contract with the Ford Motor Company. In return for driving a Ford Lotus Cortina in a few touring car races and making the odd appearance, they would give me £500 per year and a creamy white Ford Zodiac with red upholstery for my own use.

Walter Hayes became an enormously significant man in my life, not just because he remained my contact point at Ford for many years but also because he taught me so much about the art of presentation, the skill of communicating and the value of paying attention to detail. I learned so much from him.

'If you are going to make a speech, always take the time to be properly prepared,' he used to tell me. 'Make sure you have a good sound system with enough speakers in the right places for the audience to hear and always check the position of the microphone and the height of the podium. Oh, Jackie and one other thing – a golden rule – do it all yourself.'

Walter Hayes worked at the *Daily Mail* and became editor of the *Sunday Dispatch* before, at the age of thirty-seven, he made the move from journalism into public affairs and joined the Ford Motor Company. Before long, he became a confidant of Henry Ford II, the grandson of Henry Ford the founder. 'Henry II', as he was known, served as president of Ford from 1945 to 1960, and as chairman and CEO from 1960 until 1980. So a polished, soft-spoken, pipe-smoking Englishman rose to become one of the most influential executives in the Ford Motor Company, rising though various posts in Europe and North America and contributing as much to the brand as any individual outside the family whose name stood above the door.

Walter's stroke of genius was to recognise the commercial link between major motor manufacturers and motor sport at all levels, from the formative classes through to F1; and his great achievement was to develop an association between Ford and F1 motor racing, which effectively transformed the global image of Ford vehicles from cars for blue-collar workers into something glamorous and powerful that professional people would want to drive. He recognised that, unique among sports, motor racing was joined at the hip to an enormous, booming industry; and, as such, the sport could become an effective marketing vehicle for so many car, tyre, fuel and oil companies and many others supplying parts and expertise, all of whom would want to be associated with the prestige and high-performance technology.

'The sport can drive the industry,' he used to say, 'and the industry çan drive the sport.'

He proceeded to put Ford in pole position on the commercial grid by developing their involvement in the formative classes of the sport and then commissioning Cosworth to develop a revolutionary F1 engine, the DFV, which went on to power more than 150 F1 Grand Prix victories.

His strategy became amazingly successful: millions of people all around the world watched F1 motor racing, saw Ford engines beating Ferraris and went out to buy Ford cars. In America, they used to call it 'Win on Sunday, sell on Monday'.

In December 1979, Walter was appointed head of corporate affairs worldwide. He moved to America and started work in Dearborn, Michigan, where he collaborated with Henry Ford II and Bruce Blythe, treasurer of Ford of Europe, in the company decision to buy first Aston Martin and then Jaguar. He subsequently returned to Europe and, in 1990, played an important role in the rescue of Aston Martin. Four of us – Walter, Bruce, Ford executive Jacques Nasser and I – became directors of a company that was producing only ninety cars per year. That was not viable, but, by launching new models such as the DB7, the company was able to make giant steps forward in technology and also increase production to a healthier 700 per year.

Walter also served as a BBC governor in what was, by any measure, a very full and remarkable life, shared with his beloved wife, Elizabeth. He died on Boxing Day 2000 at the age of seventy-six, and I was privileged to be asked to speak at his funeral, which was held at the Chapel Royal, Hampton Court Palace on the banks of the River Thames.

I can still hear his voice now. 'Even diamonds have to be polished, Jackie,' he would tell me, speaking softly. 'Rough diamonds don't have the same appeal. If you want to be successful in life, you need to have polish and a little bit of style.'

It was Walter Hayes who first introduced to me to members of the Ford family, notably Henry Ford II, a real buccaneer of a man with a glint in his eye, whom I got to know quite well, going for dinner several times at his home in Grosse Pointe, Michigan.

In 1966, Walter brought a seventeen-year-old young man to

the German Grand Prix at the Nurburgring, and introduced him to me as Edsel Ford II, the son of Henry II. Edsel was a keen follower of motor sport, and we became extremely close friends, meeting often at races and elsewhere in the years that followed. He ran Ford Australia towards the end of the 1970s, became chief operating officer of Ford Motor Credit in 1991 and has served on the main board of directors since 1988. I remember when he started seeing a young lady called Cynthia Neskow and I was delighted to be an usher at their wedding. Today, Edsel and Cynthia have four fine sons – Henry III, sometimes known as Sonny, who also works for the company, Calvin, Stewart and Albert, and they live in Grosse Pointe Farms.

The Ford family is widely renowned and respected as one of the most prominent families in America, and I have always been tremendously impressed by the serious and profound manner in which, collectively as a group, they feel a sense of responsibility for the company and all its employees.

In four decades with Ford, I worked for six chairmen, starting with Henry II. He was followed by Phil Caldwell, who presided over the launch of the successful Ford Taurus, and he was succeeded in 1985 by Don Petersen, who introduced an inclusive, team-oriented management style. Harold 'Red' Poling served as CEO from 1990 to 1993, having been regarded as the saviour of the company when, as executive vice-president for North America, he cut costs and returned the unit to profitability. He was followed by Alex Trotman, born in Yorkshire, brought up in Scotland and blessed with a Scots accent, who took over in 1993 and tried to unify Ford's manufacturing, marketing and product development forces worldwide. William Clay 'Bill' Ford, a cousin of Edsel, was appointed chairman and CEO in 1999 and made giant strides in the area of fuel efficiency and environmental matters.

I first came across many of these people when they were

rising through the ranks, and I took care to develop a relationship with each of them because I realised it would be easier for me to add value if I was able to deal and interact at the highest level of the company; that was where the important decisions were made, even if the chairmen, presidents and CEOs were rarely the most technically skilled and knowledge-able about cars. This was because the corporate culture on either side of the Atlantic, and specifically within Ford, seemed to carry generalists rather than specialists to the executive positions. It was widely held that the most effective preparation for a prospective senior role would be to work for a period of, say, no longer than three years in each of the important cells of the business and gain a broad, but not deep, degree of experience and knowledge. I could understand the logic, but, in my view, the world needs more specialists and fewer generalists. The problem is that many of these talented people never stay long enough in one place to become a specialist. The same is true of cabinet ministers in the United Kingdom: they seem to be shuffled from department to department with such regularity that they very rarely have time to master a brief and they typically end up as parrots repeating what their advisers tell them.

I remember one occasion when I was trying to persuade a senior executive of the Ford Motor Company that money needed to be spent on improving the door handles on the Lincoln Town Car. I dragged him from his office down to the car park and tried to show him the exact problem that needed to be addressed.

'Look, Jackie,' he replied, exasperated. 'I don't know what to say. I don't know about door handles.'

Whether they understood or not – and, to be fair, many did – these men made the decisions, and I always kept in contact, even if it meant just taking the time to stroll down the two corridors on the twelfth floor of Ford's world headquarters at

Dearborn, near Detroit in Michigan, popping my head around a door, just saying hello and keeping in touch, passing on an idea or an observation. Many people are often hesitant to converse with those in the higher echelons of a multinational company, but, for me, this channel straight to the top became an important way of getting things done, and therefore continuing to add value.

At first, while I was driving competitively, my main role with Ford was to make public appearances, although the precise number was never stipulated in writing. Whenever we sat down to negotiate a new contract, Walter Hayes used to say we should just leave that particular detail blank, and that was fine with me because I knew he would never abuse the situation.

Walter was an expert at planning these dos, and I vividly recall a three-day event in 1965 at the Bristol Street Motors Ford dealership in Birmingham, run by Harry Cressman, a remarkable and energetic American entrepreneur in the British motor industry. His concept was that Jim Clark, Graham Hill and I would attend, participating in Q&A sessions with the public, doing media interviews and signing autographs. More than 20,000 people passed through the showrooms over the duration.

Ford began to develop a reputation within the British motor industry for staging the best product launches and media events, and I enjoyed being a part of Walter's show. As the years passed, he consciously nurtured a team of high-quality people, such as John Waddell and Harry Carlton in the UK, and David Scott in the United States – in fact, David succeeded him as head of corporate affairs worldwide. With Walter, and subsequently with each of his protégés, nothing was ever second rate or left to chance. At every event and public appearance, I was content to watch and learn.

From the late 1960s through to the late 1980s, an important

element of my work for Ford was to make regular appearances in advertising campaigns, both in print and on television, initially in the UK and Europe, and then in America. The relationship worked well, and the J. Walter Thompson advertising agency, which had been working with Ford since 1943, produced a series of TV commercials that broke new ground in explaining complex technical advances in a graphic manner to a broad audience. In one US commercial, describing how the styling technology of the latest Ford Taurus would improve fuel efficiency through the use of improved aerodynamics, I was shown driving at 50 mph with my left arm sticking out of the open window. At first, I held my hand with the fingers pointing up and the palm facing forward, and I showed how it buffeted and shook against the wind resistance. Then, I moved my hand so the fingers were pointing forward and the palm was facing down, and demonstrated how it glided and cut through the air smoothly and without any resistance. It may sound unsophisticated by today's standards, but it got the message across in a simple, graphic and successful way.

Once I had retired as a racing driver at the end of 1973, my role at Ford extended into vehicle assessment, and I began to work as a research and development consultant on future vehicles, assessing performance, recommending improvements to everything from accelerator pedal function to door handles, from engine characteristics to transmissions, steering and brakes.

I began travelling around the world on behalf of the company, visiting associated companies and testing vehicles at Ford testing facilities in such far-flung locations as Lommel in Belgium, Cologne in Germany, Geelong in Australia, Warley and the MIRA facilities in the UK, Hiroshima in Japan, road routes in Brazil and on a frozen lake in Norway.

The largest facilities were in the United States, at Naples, Florida, and Dearborn, Michigan. At least, I thought they were large until I worked at the 4,500-acre testing facility in Romeo, Michigan; and I thought that was impressive until I saw the 7,500-acre site near the small town of Kingman, in Arizona.

In essence, I was creating a new career for myself by taking the analytical skills I had gathered during my racing career and deploying them in the development of road cars. This knowledge and experience turned out to be the cornerstone of the value I added to the Ford Motor Company.

'There's too much stiction on roll,' I would tell a group of engineers, after testing a vehicle.

'Huh?' they would reply.

'Too much stiction,' I would say. 'It's not helping the feel of the car, and I'm not happy with it.'

'What is stiction?'

'Look, stiction is different from friction. When a car enters a corner, there is "dive" as the weight moves to the front of the car under braking. Then there is lateral "roll" under steering input as it goes around the corner. Then there is a "pitch" change under acceleration as it exits the corner. If everything is set up correctly, this critical sequence of "dive-roll-pitch" movements will be silky smooth, gentle, linear, controlled and consistent. Do you follow me?'

I would look at them, checking they were still with me, and then I would continue: 'However, what you often find is that the car gets hung up or sticks on one of these stages, and that can cause discomfort to the driver or the passengers, or both. Maybe it sticks at a certain point of the roll and then suddenly snaps to another point, and then to a third. Instead of a single smooth linear progression from zero lateral loading to maximum lateral roll, it can go in three stages, jolting and disturbing other component functions and negatively affecting the ride.'

'So, that's stiction?' an engineer said.

'Exactly.'

'What do we do about it?'

'Well, it's sometimes a puzzle, and the answer could lie in a number of component areas that need to be examined and checked. It could be created by the shock absorbers, roll bars, suspension bushes, rose joints or suspension links, and it could be something to do with the deformation of certain materials, which might be caused by a myriad of variations in the directional stresses connected to the compliance of the components. You got that?'

'Erm . . . yes.'

It was often complex stuff, but it was my job to try and make them understand exactly what I meant. In fact, 'stiction' turned out to be one of the simpler problems to identify and solve.

Often, I would take a vehicle on an intensive three-day R&D ride and drive, all the time dictating my thoughts and observations into a tape recorder. Then I would get home and try to distil the subtleties of what I had discovered. 'Subtlety' is not a word often used in America, where almost everything tends to be regarded as one thing or the other, on or off, black or white. So, in my efforts to explain to the engineers what I had felt, I started to create my own phraseology.

A 'silent debit' was something that didn't feel quite right in the car. It might be associated with the steering, the braking or the transmission, or it might be partly this and partly that. It would be hard to pin down, but it would categorically be there; and it mattered because a potential customer taking the model for a test drive might have no idea what was causing him or her to feel a certain lack of confidence, but it would be enough for them not to go ahead and buy the car. A 'silent asset' produced the opposite effect and enhanced the feel-good factor, but it was equally hard for a member of the public or an engineer to explain why they got that positive experience.

Accurate identification of silent debits and silent assets – and working out what is causing the subconscious feeling and, if necessary, what is required to correct the problem – lies at the heart of subjective vehicle dynamic assessment, and, in my view, it is what I do best. It seems to be my core talent.

'Every function must be an invitation and never a challenge,' I would tell the Ford engineers. And every time I said it I thought of the 003.

'OK.'

'And that goes for the passengers as well as the drivers. A driver wants a car that makes him or her feel good and look good, so he or she doesn't need problems with an accelerator pedal that feels too sharp or a brake pedal function that is too fierce. If Granny is sitting in the back seat, she can get dislocated vertebrae in her neck if the acceleration is too abrupt; equally, if the brake pedal is too fierce, poor Granny would immediately have her dislocation put back in place. That's not a good feeling. And no one wants to upset Granny.'

I was trying to be as graphic as possible.

'So, we must be mindful of producing a car that feels right for the driver and each of the passengers, whether they want to read a book, look out of the window or sleep. That is why four of us should go testing in each vehicle, so we can each sit in each seat, rotating and monitoring the ride in the driver's seat, the passenger seat and on the left and right seats in the back.'

In due course, I introduced Static Vehicle Evaluation Days at Ford, where the engineers and I would analyse the touch and feel of almost everything in the car – door handles, bumper assemblies, mirror adjustments, seat comfort, pedal feel, luggage compartment, interior finish – by using a simple technique.

'Any of you could do this at home,' I would tell a group of engineers. 'Just roll up your shirt sleeve and remove any watch or ring that you may be wearing on that hand.'

One of them would be wearing a jacket.

'You'll have to take that off,' I would say.

'It's OK. I'll take that into account.'

'No, you must take it off because the buttons on your jacket can make a noise and that would interfere.'

So he would take off the jacket, muttering, but this was only going to be worthwhile if he did it properly.

'Right,' I continued, 'now make a fist with that hand, and go round the entire car, banging your fist against every part of the car, listening carefully to exactly what you hear.'

I would tap the fleshy part of my clenched fist against the wing mirror.

'How does that sound? Is that a solid, high-quality sound that makes you feel comfortable or is that a twangy, fragile noise? If it's not right, all we may need to do is insert a small rubber grommet or maybe use a screw with a nut instead of a self-tapping screw. That's all, but it would make a huge difference.'

Then I would ask each of the engineers to go round the car, tapping everything – the bonnet, front grill, door handles – listening intently, noting good sounds and identifying bad noises that needed to be corrected.

'Don't just hit it once,' I would say. 'Hit each component and each area of the car with your fist sixteen times. That's a good number, because you'll only hear one sound for the first ten times and only then will you start to hear secondary sounds as well. Don't go to twenty, because that's boring.' Well I had to let them off at some stage . . .

So all these engineers would be walking around, banging not only Ford models with their fists, but also competitor cars which had been brought in for the sake of comparison. This was the wonderful world of Static Vehicle Evaluation; and it worked.

I would conclude: 'My instructions are that I must not sign off on any model until I am absolutely happy, and I will not be happy until every single component and function looks, feels and sounds exactly right. That's why I am here.'

Some of the Ford engineers probably started to wish I was not there because demanding high standards and attention to detail was nothing less than exhausting. However, this is what I felt was required for our cars to become the best in their class.

At one stage, one or two engineers tried to get around the 'Jackie problem' by finding out when I was due to visit and then prepare a prototype vehicle they hoped I would assess and pass. I used to find pieces of Elastoplast being used to stop things rattling under the all-knowing fist, and to discover elastic bands wrapped around a component to keep it from vibrating.

'It's no good,' I would say, causing yet more consternation and irritation. 'This car has been tarted up. This is not the actual car we can mass produce, so I can't pass it.'

I would seldom compromise. At one stage, Jac Nasser called me 'the critic from hell' and he meant that as a compliment because that's exactly what he paid me to be.

Probably the biggest face-off occurred during the development of the Ford Mondeo in the early 1990s. As I conducted the vehicle assessment, I started to realise it was a truly exceptional car, one which would sell extremely well across Europe but, but . . . but . . . but there was a wee problem with the steering. It was not giving the driver a confident feel, and I raised the issue with Richard Parry-Jones, the exceptional engineer in charge of the development of the car.

'There's a problem with the steering,' I said.

'What exactly are you feeling?'

'When you turn into a corner at medium speeds, there is a sense of unease that makes you feel as though you have to induce more steering angle. No sooner have you increased the steering input, than you feel you have to take it out again. It's really uncomfortable, and it's the only weak issue in the car.'

'I agree it needs to be fixed, but they're not going to like it, Jackie,' he replied.

'We will have to try and fix it.'

'I'm not sure they can feel the problem.'

'It would not be a good idea to go to Job 1 as it is.'

Job 1 was the term for full production.

Richard continued: 'Jackie, I agree it needs fixing but I'm not sure the team know how to put it right. We have only a certain amount of available time.'

'Well, we need to at least improve the issue because I would not sign off on the car as it is now.'

The following week, I was asked to attend a meeting at the then European headquarters at Warley in Essex and I found myself invited to share a sandwich lunch with William H. Fike, then president of Ford Europe, in his office, together with John Oldfield, the chief engineer and the head of engineering.

Bill Fike said, 'Jackie, we have a problem here. You're saying you're not signing the Mondeo off, and we don't think there is a real problem with the car. We're going to go with it.'

'Well, that's fine,' I replied. 'It's your decision, not mine. I don't want to go with it.'

'We need your signature, Jackie.'

'Well, I'm not signing it. It's not good enough.'

'You've got to sign it.'

'I don't.'

'It could cost $500 million if we hold up production.'

'We can put it right for a lot less than that.'

'But that would mean delaying Job 1.'

'Look,' I said, firmly. 'You can't be a little bit pregnant. It's either right or it's wrong. This Mondeo has the potential to become the best car of its size ever produced, but it has a flaw; and it's a big flaw because the driver's hands are on the steering wheel from the time he or she gets into the car until the time he or she gets out of the car. It doesn't matter whether you are a former world champion or you're a first-generation driver, there is a very good chance that you're going to get into that car and be aware of a distinct lack of confidence with the steering. The design might have looked good on a drawing board or a computer screen, but it isn't feeling good in the car.'

'Fine,' he said. 'We're going to override you on this one. I'll call Red Poling in Dearborn and tell him what has happened, and my recommendation will be that we go ahead.'

'That's your privilege,' I said. 'The Ford Motor Company contracts me to tell them what is good, bad or ugly with the cars, and that's exactly what I am trying to do.'

'OK.'

'Well, there's nothing more to say.'

It was not an especially enjoyable lunch, and that had nothing to do with the ham sandwich. The executives had expected me to roll over under pressure, but I had held out. And I was sure I was correct to do so. Some of the very best, most talented designers I have ever known don't have attuned sensory skills to recognise good from bad. That is what I was trying to help them with. I was driven back to the Grosvenor House hotel in London and had sunk into a hot bath when the phone rang. It was the chairman and CEO.

'Jackie, I hear you were in Warley today,' Red Poling said.

'Absolutely.'

'And I hear there's a bit of a logjam.'

'Red, I'm sorry, but the steering is not right. There is a problem. It has to be found and it can be found. To go to Job 1 now is going to be less than good for the company because you are going to get criticised in the media. The steering is one of the vital organs in the vehicle. Either it makes somebody feel good or it creates a lack of confidence. The steering and the brakes are things you can't play with. You have to get them right, and this fault must at least be improved, if not eliminated, as soon as possible.'

'Can you compromise on it?'

'Red, I can't. It's not right for me to sign off the car as it is.'

'Are you absolutely sure?'

'Red, I'm absolutely sure.'

'Well, I have to make a decision on this.'

'Look, Red, there's nothing in it for me to create a problem here. Everyone thinks I am a pain in the ass over this, but I am just giving you my honest opinion, that's all.'

'OK, I will go with you.'

The decision to readdress the steering issue was correct. Richard and I agreed it would be good to get some fresh eyes to help look at the issue and we invited Adrian Reynard, a designer of racing cars, to join Richard, me and the rest of the engineering team on a trip to our preferred drive evaluation route starting at Gleneagles, where we all focused our minds on this single problem. Together, as a team, we improved the issue to a point where it was almost imperceptible. I signed it off. The Ford Mondeo was launched in 1993 and it became an enormous success. As far as I am aware, nobody complained about the steering.

Many of the Ford engineers were exceptional, most notably Richard Parry-Jones, who was starting out when I first met him but who became Ford's chief technologist worldwide. Ulrich Eichmann left BMW to join Ford and rose through the ranks, before eventually being poached by Volkswagen; he has since become the chief engineer at Bentley, with a seat on the board. Joe Buckeye worked on the Focus and Fiesta before moving to the US, where he worked with Ford Truck and was seconded to Mazda before returning to Ford. I met Neil Ressler when he was in middle management, but he was promoted to become the head of engineering at Ford North America. Each of these men was, in my experience, a professional of the very highest quality and integrity.

Several years earlier, Walter Hayes's tentative suggestion that I should be used to assist the product development of Ford vehicles in the United States had met with little enthusiasm. The

American engineers didn't want a foreigner. So far as they were concerned, I was a former F1 racing driver from Europe who wasn't going to tell them anything they didn't know already. In their minds, I might as well have come from another planet. To be honest, in my mind, their cars may as well have come from another planet. It constantly amazed me that the Americans continued to produce huge, unattractive, gas-guzzling vehicles that, as I used to say, looked and felt like a pregnant elephant as they wallowed their way down the road. It did not seem a promising match, but Walter persisted and he eventually arranged for me to pay a visit to a man called Dan Rivard and test drive some cars together.

Dan started by taking me around the handling track at the Ford Motor Company's proving ground at Dearborn, and, although he was obviously fast and had a certain touch, he was quite coarse and aggressive with the car.

'That's good, Dan,' I said. 'Can I have a turn now?'

He seemed a little tentative as he handed me the keys, but he did move into the passenger seat, and I took the car around the circuit a little more smoothly and quickly.

'That was amazing,' he said. 'You hardly seemed to be pushing the car at all.' Dan was a convert and he invited me to work with him in the Ford Light Truck division, where we developed trucks like the Ford F150, which became one of the best-selling pick-up trucks in the world, laying down the engineering base from which Ford eventually produced a successful generation of SUVs (sports utility vehicles) such as the Explorer.

The testing facilities at Dearborn were fine, but, as time moved on, I began to test more and more Ford cars at the drive evaluation route closer to my roots, where we were to resolve the problem with the Mondeo. It was Malcolm McDougall, a fine motoring correspondent with Scotland's *Daily Record* newspaper, who first told me about this particular loop starting at Gleneagles, and the next time I was in the area, I went to have a look for myself.

Following Malcolm's instructions, I made my way from Gleneagles along the A9 to Dunblane, then on the A820 to Doune, along the A84 to Callander, up past Kilmahog to Strathyre, on to Lochearnhead, east on the A85 along the banks of Loch Earn to St Fillans, before heading south to Comrie, along the B827 across some barren moorland that was used as an army gun range, to Braco and then back to Gleneagles. The circular route took approximately an hour and twenty minutes to complete and, remarkably, it included almost every category of road and every kind of road surface.

I telephoned Malcolm that same evening.

'What did you think?' he asked.

'Well,' I replied, 'that is the best vehicle evaluation drive route in the whole damn world.'

I was serious, if maybe a tad biased, but the route was perfect for what we required, and we regularly used that run to test a series of Fords, Jaguars, Mazdas, Range Rovers and many other vehicles over the next twenty years; at one stage, we even arranged for a Ford Thunderbird to be flown over from America to be tested there before it was launched in the US market. The beautiful, rugged scenery was an added bonus, especially for the Americans who came over. I even got Jac Nasser there, and he immediately understood the route's appeal.

In the later years of my association with Ford, I began to educate the senior management in the same way I had coached the engineers, showing them how to identify and to feel both the good and the bad characteristics of a car. The point was that, just as the engineers had needed actually to feel what was wrong before they could start to fix it, so the executives needed to feel what was wrong before they agreed to pay for the solution.

There were days when the invitees would arrive for a testing session, and I sensed some of them were excited by the prospect of driving with a three-time F1 world champion. If that was the case, and they were expecting a burn-up and a few lap records, the day was going to prove a terrible let-down.

I would welcome them, and say, 'We won't go any faster than 50 miles per hour today. That's an ideal speed to evaluate the total vehicle. If we went faster, we wouldn't be able to consume much information, and we would miss almost everything.'

'No faster than 50 miles per hour?' they would say, amazed.

'Look,' I would reply, 'if I took you to God's country, to Scotland, and we drove at an average speed of 130 miles per hour, all you would see out of the window is a green blur. But, if we drove on the same route at thirty miles per hour, you would be able to look out of the window and see a grouse tucked in among the heather, or a salmon leaping on a river, or even a stag standing majestically on the side of the hill, and the country would look magnificent. The whole point of this testing session is to hear and feel everything that may need to be corrected, and you will only be able to do that if we drive slowly.'

They almost always understood, and we would tootle along the test route at around 50 mph, and sometimes even slower so we could bank in our heads exactly what we were feeling, and I would get the driver to focus on feeling the issues and idiosyncrasies of the vehicle. If we were driving any faster, he or she would have to concentrate on their driving and they would not have been able to consume what was going on with the car.

'Focus on NVH,' I would tell them. 'The "N" is for noise, which is different to sound because, while sound is often pleasing, noise is usually irritating. "V" is for vibrations, which can typically be isolated but, if not dealt with correctly, can cause irritation. "H" is for harshness, which means you can feel every pebble you drive over, and that will create discomfort.'

At various stages, Ford leaders such as Alex Trotman, Don Petersen, Red Poling, Jac Nasser and Bob Rewey all attended what became known as our Executive Vehicle Evaluation days, and I would take them out in our latest Ford model and then its nearest competitor to try and make them feel what was good about our vehicle and, maybe, what needed to be put right.

I remember one day when Jac and I were in a Ford Explorer with him driving, and I asked him to ease on the gas pedal, and pull away from a standing start to a speed of 20 mph.

'What's more,' I told him with a smile, 'I'll give you $100,000 if you can do that smoothly and gently without me feeling anything. And I'll give you six attempts to get it right.'

He couldn't do it.

Then we got out of the Explorer and got into what I rated as the model with the best-in-class gas pedal function, a BMW X5 and I asked him to do the same thing, adding: 'But I'm a canny Scot, so there's no money at stake this time.'

He executed the manoeuvre perfectly.

'What's going on, Jackie?'

'Well, you felt the difference for yourself. The point is that, in too many instances, we're using poor-quality components, and the engineering is not good enough to allow the driver to execute the most basic of tasks.'

'Can we put that right?'

'Of course we can, but you're not finished yet.'

I asked him to get back in the Explorer and told him to drive at 30 mph, then to start braking at the first marker cone beside the road so he would come to a halt at a second marker cone, as if it were a pedestrian crossing, and I said he had to brake so evenly and smoothly that, as his passenger, I did not feel disturbed. 'And the money's back on the table,' I added.

Hard as he tried, he couldn't do it.

'You've made a complete cock-up of that,' I told him.

Then we would get in a Range Rover, and he would be able to complete the task with ease.

'Why can't we fix the braking system, so it's like that?' he asked, becoming just a little agitated.

'We can.'

'Really? The Explorer could do that?'

'That's what I've been telling the company for the past six months, and we won't do it.'

'Well, I think we should do it now.'

The executives didn't always say go ahead and solve the problem because every improvement came at a price and inevitably there were times when the incremental advantage was not worth the additional cost. Then, it made perfect sense to compromise and do what we could within the budget. However, I did find it harder to accept a certain mentality that seemed to be developing within the company from the mid-1980s and into the late 1990s, which amounted to a certain tolerance of the mediocrity that started to characterise most of the vehicles that were being launched in the domestic US market.

At one stage, I completed the assessment of a future model and told a senior executive the behaviour of the car suggested it was well below what was regarded as best in the class.

'It's OK, Jackie,' he told me. 'We're not competing with brands like BMW and Mercedes-Benz.'

'That's wrong,' I replied. 'In continental Europe, many taxis are Mercedes, and there are plenty of small farmers who drive a BMW. Those cars are your competition.'

'Oh, Jackie, don't worry,' the executive said, just a little too comfortably. 'We're the Ford Motor Company.'

'Well, I think we should be careful,' I said. 'There's an old Scottish saying that goes, "big trees blow over, it only depends on the strength of the wind". I remember some giant shipbuilders who thought they were impregnable. Nobody ever is.'

Times were changing at Ford, and, when the R&D budgets were severely reduced, I started to wonder whether I was still able to add value. Towards the end of 2004, I decided to resign, bringing to an end forty years of continuous contracted service.

It would be wrong for me to pretend I did not leave with mixed feelings. Of course, I felt enormous gratitude for all the good times I had enjoyed and the friends I had made, but there was a measure of sadness that the ethos of the company seemed to have changed. I had always believed that, just as estate agents spoke about 'location, location, location', the key to success in the motor industry was 'engineering excellence, engineering excellence, engineering excellence'. Perhaps I was old-fashioned.

Edsel Ford II generously hosted a wonderful Ford dinner in my honour at the Detroit Athletic Club on 7 January 2005 and he went to the trouble of inviting not only Helen but also Paul and his wife Victoria, and Mark and his wife Anne. So, surrounded by my family and so many great friends and colleagues, I was able to drink a toast to forty years with Ford and gently close the door on a major part of my life.

Ford has had its difficulties in recent years, but the product is competitive in Europe and I believe all the company needs to do is to produce a strong range of cars in America. As soon as people start believing in the brand again, the company will turn itself around.

It won't be easy, especially in a recession. Perhaps the problems facing the 'Big Three' motor manufacturers in the USA can be traced back to what seemed a general reluctance to change the product line. In recent years, General Motors, Ford and Chrysler all appeared to go to sleep and they failed to provide the levels of quality, economy, ride and handling increasingly being demanded by the youth of America. Even the more mature generations were starting to realise it was easier to park a Toyota, Honda or a Lexus than it was to handle a Lincoln Town Car or a Cadillac. Top management didn't seem to notice. It was almost as if they had simply assumed they would always be there, doing what they had always done, and they overlooked the reality that people no longer wanted to buy those colossal, gas-guzzling engines. You could say the Big Three kept producing apple pie and ice cream models, while the American public was developing a taste for crème caramel.

Demand has nose-dived and, as a result, the city of Detroit and much of the state of Michigan may well end up in mourning. If one of the Big Three does go under, the total number of jobs lost in that company, and associated suppliers and partners, could easily reach a million.

During my racing career, as part of my strategy to seek out long-term commercial relationships where I could use the skills I had learned as a driver beyond my time on the track, I realised I could add value to the Goodyear Tyre and Rubber Company, the third-largest tyre manufacturer in the world.

The relationship started at the end of 1970 when Dunlop withdrew from F1 racing, and the Tyrrell team went in search of a new tyre partner. The choice lay between Firestone and Goodyear, and, while I knew the people at Firestone and had used their tyres at Indianapolis and in big sports car racing in America, Ken Tyrrell wanted to develop a relationship with Goodyear, who were relatively new to F1 racing, and asked me to make the approach. I duly arranged to visit the company's world headquarters at Akron, Ohio, to meet with Larry Truesdale, the man responsible for all Goodyear's racing activities worldwide.

In preparing for the presentation, I had been uncertain what to wear and, in the end, I settled for a dark, well-cut sports jacket, with a white shirt, a solid-colour tie, dark-grey trousers and a pair of black slip-on shoes. It looked all right, but, standing in the hotel elevator on my way to the meeting, I glanced in the mirror and abruptly decided I looked too casual for an important business appointment. So I rushed back to my room and changed into a pin-striped Doug Hayward suit with a white shirt, dark tie and lace-up shoes.

As I've said, first impressions are always important, and, properly dressed – or so I hoped – I sat down with Larry and started to outline what Tyrrell would require in 1971. Having won the world championship the previous year, I felt we had a good deal to offer, but the meeting was not going particularly well. Then, Chuck Pilliod, the president of Goodyear International, walked into the room.

'Hello, Jackie,' he said, 'how's it going?'

'Not that well,' I replied, frankly. 'I think Larry is having a few budget problems.'

'Well, the board is meeting today. Why don't you come and have lunch with us. I'm sure everybody would like to meet you, and then we can try and sort something out.'

I accepted his invitation and promptly walked into an executive dining room full of Goodyear directors . . . all of whom were wearing dark-blue or pin-striped suits, white shirts, dark ties and lace-up shoes. My instinct in the lift had been spot on, and, feeling correctly dressed, I concluded the deal later in the day. The right suit won't always clinch the deal but, on that day, if I hadn't been properly dressed I wouldn't have even been in the boardroom.

The following year, Goodyear asked me to start promoting their road vehicle products and corporate image, and I entered into a commercial and technical association that lasted for seventeen years.

As a racing driver, I had always taken a keen interest in tyre development programmes, particularly when I realised there were greater gains to be found by improving the tyre performance than almost any other area of the car – better tyres could often give you a full second per lap. So, while some drivers seemed indifferent to their tyres, preferring to turn up and drive, I was more than eager to spend long, tiring days testing various new compounds, new constructions and exploring the latest developments, always seeking to maximise the performance of the car.

The F1 tyre war that broke out between Dunlop, Firestone and Goodyear in the 1960s triggered my interest in the industry, and it was the knowledge and experiences that I consumed during this era that later enabled me to add value to the exhaustive subjective and objective testing of road vehicle tyres within the R&D operations at Goodyear.

My status as a F1 world champion was also well used by the company, and they arranged a series of public affairs programmes for me around the world. At various times, I flew the Goodyear flag at tyre plants, dealerships and distributors in places as diverse as India, Thailand, Hong Kong, Malaysia, Indonesia, Australia, the Philippines, throughout Europe and throughout North, Central and South America. Hopefully, somewhere along the way, I played a part in the remarkable growth of worldwide sales from $3.6 billion in 1971 to more than $9 billion in 1981.

The inspiration of this growth was Chuck Pilliod, who became chairman and CEO in 1973, and was later appointed by President Reagan to be the US Ambassador to Mexico. He was succeeded at Goodyear by Bob Mercer, with whom I developed an excellent working relationship. In fact, the quality of people working at the company was exceptional, most notably Mo O'Reilly, Leo Mehl, who was responsible for racing operations, and Trevor Hoskins, who started as the public relations director of Goodyear UK and was then appointed to head the international PR department at Goodyear headquarters in Ohio.

My association with the company ended in 1987, during a

restructuring of the company in the wake of a hostile takeover bid by Sir James Goldsmith and the Hanson Group.

I later spent five years as a consultant to Bridgestone, where I was reunited with Trevor Hoskins, who had also left Goodyear in their troubled times. The position afforded me the opportunity to learn the ins and outs of Japanese culture.

In any assessment programme, whether for tyres, cars or anything else, I have always believed the most useful conclusion is reached by combining hard objective evidence with the subjective analysis provided by a suitably qualified human being. When I realised that Bridgestone attached very much more importance to the objective electronic measurement of lap times than to anything somebody like me felt or said, I recognised my potential to add value would be limited, and there seemed no point in renewing my contract after the initial five-year term.

Alongside the relationships with Ford and Goodyear, the third commercial relationship that I established while I was driving and sustained after my retirement was with Elf Aquitaine, where I was featured in various public affairs and advertising programmes under the guidance of François Guiter.

In many respects, François was the French equivalent of Walter Hayes – a communications expert with an eye for detail and a commitment to quality. His contacts with media around the world were remarkable, and his network of photographers produced many of the most striking and elegant images of the sport. Men like Just Jaeckin, who later became world famous for creating *Emmanuelle*, and Manu Zurini, who became a leading sculptor, were always great company and wonderful fun to be around. Like Walter, François groomed his protégés: most memorably Jacques de la Béraudière, a stylish young aristocrat who dressed well, shot well, rode well and suited the Elf image and has since become an art dealer in Paris, and

François Xavier Dehaye, who became adept at handling the media throughout the world.

In the years after I retired from driving, François was always open to new ideas and together we developed the concept of driving journalists around the circuit on the Thursday before a F1 Grand Prix. We had passenger seats put in a couple of GT race cars. A talented French female race and rally driver called Marie-Claude Beaumont drove a Renault 5, and I drove a race-prepared Ford Capri, and the programme became a great success and earned a great deal of goodwill and media exposure for Elf.

My relationship with the French company matured to a point where I was appointed Elf's vice-president of marketing in the UK, taking on added responsibilities for organising product launches and visiting dealerships around the country. It was the sheer pressure of other commitments that forced me to conclude my formal association with this fine company in 1986.

Each of these commercial relationships originated directly from my career as a racing driver, but I was also fortunate to be able to launch, nurture and develop additional associations with two universally respected companies that seemed content to connect their brands with whatever I was growing to represent.

The first is Rolex, perhaps the purest and most pristine brand in the world. The name has become so synonymous with quality, prestige, style, dignity and exclusivity that, when someone refers to the 'Rolex' of any category, everybody instantly realises they are talking about the very best. Hans Wilsdorf, a German who took British citizenship, founded the company in 1908, in London, and remarkably he guided its growth right through until his death in 1960. Two years later, André Heiniger was appointed as director general.

I was first introduced to Rolex by Mark McCormack, of IMG, in 1968, and contracted as a global ambassador at the same time as the legendary American golfer Arnold Palmer and Jean-Claude Killy, the great French skier who won three gold medals at the 1968 Winter Olympic Games in Grenoble. Each of us remains contracted to this day, and, in 1998, a wonderful photograph of the three of us together was taken to celebrate our thirtieth anniversary with Rolex and subsequently used in advertising around the world.

I bought my first Rolex watch in Houston, Texas in 1966, when I was driving for John Mecom, who arranged to have the dial encrusted with diamonds, and I have never worn another brand since. It remains a magnificent product with universal appeal: sportsmen value its ruggedness, adventurers enjoy its reliability and just about the entire world appreciates its elegance. It certainly appealed to me. I remember seeing one advertisement in a magazine that showed a picture of the General Assembly of the United Nations, with the words, 'If you were speaking here, you would be wearing a Rolex'. In my mind, my contract with Rolex was a passport to respectability.

André Heiniger was a wonderfully distinguished man who always ensured the company stayed true to its guiding principles of excellence and quality. He passed away on 3 January 2000 and was succeeded as director general by his son Patrick, whom I have known for a great many years and has also become a friend. He is a dynamic leader who travels extensively, nurturing company-owned subsidiaries and distributors across the globe. His uncanny ability to ensure the company changes with the times, very often in the most subtle ways, and yet remain true to its founding principles is the hallmark of his leadership.

Even after all these years, I am still filled with wonder and awe whenever I visit the company's headquarters in Geneva and I take a moment to observe the craftsmen wearing white laboratory smocks and sitting at their worktops in near silence as they set about the task of producing the finest watches in the world. Each component of every tiny movement is sculpted by hand, and every angle is rounded and polished to a pristine shine. This work is not visible, but it embodies the purity of the brand.

For my part, as a global ambassador, I have sought to add value to Rolex by wearing the watch in a way that reflects positively on the company. This involves arranging for my shirts to be made with a slightly wider sleeve cuff on the left side than the right, to ensure the watch moves freely and is always visible. In the same vein, if I happen to be in New York, I will try to call on Alan Brill, general manager of Rolex Watch USA Inc., to see if there is anything I can do, and I try to maintain frequent contact with Roger Maingot, MD of Rolex UK.

The second world-class company is Moët & Chandon. As I described in an earlier chapter, my association with the best-known champagne house in the world began on that warm day in 1969, when I celebrated winning the French Grand Prix at Clermont-Ferrand by spraying the contents of a double magnum of Moët & Chandon champagne 30 feet into the air. Count Frédéric Chandon de Briailles, then a vice-president of the company, often attended F1 races, and I met him soon afterwards. We became friends, and, as celebrating with champagne soon became a feature of Grand Prix victory podiums, Fred asked me to serve as a Moët & Chandon ambassador. The company merged with Hennessy Cognac in 1971 and with Louis Vuitton in 1987, becoming LVMH, one of the world's largest luxury product groups. I was appointed as a member of the UK board of Moët in 1986 and I continue in that capacity to this day, still trying to add value wherever possible.

Add value – that is what I tried to do when I signed a contract with Walter Hayes at the British Motor Show in 1964, and this is still what I am trying to do in my commercial relationships. Nothing comes from nothing and there really is no reason to expect any company, large or small, to pay somebody over an extended period of time unless that person is able to bring something tangible to the business. Adding value – in fact, by working hard to add more value than the company expects, and to over-deliver – has always been my goal in developing long-term relationships.

Through forty years with Ford, seventeen years with Goodyear, eighteen years with Elf, thirty-nine years with Rolex and still counting, and thirty-seven years with Moët & Chandon and still counting, I hope that somewhere along the line I have made a worthwhile contribution.

CHAPTER 14

Staircase of Talent

IT WAS THE CONVERSATION I DREADED. My seventeen-year-old son Paul found me sitting on the patio beside the swimming pool at our house in Switzerland, and declared: 'Daddy, I want to be a racing driver.'

Oh no. No. No. No.

I was shocked. I hadn't seen it coming. By nature, I always try to be very well prepared. I prefer to plan everything and I work relentlessly to minimise downside risks. Some people might say I overdo it, but I simply want to do everything possible to ensure that, in my life, things tend to go right rather than wrong. Now Paul was saying he wanted to be a racing driver. He had not seemed particularly interested in cars or motor racing when he was younger, and when his early teenage years passed without any mention of wanting to try karting or anything like that, Helen and I started to think we might just have got away with it. Now, he had declared his ambition, and he was serious.

'Paul, I can't help you,' I replied, agitated.

'Why?' he said.

'Because I don't want you to be a racing driver, and your mother would hate it.'

I stood up and walked away towards the house.

Paul followed me. 'I just want to go to a racing drivers' school and see how things go,' he persisted.

'Oh Paul,' I said, exasperated.

Arriving in my study, I glanced at a shelf and what happened to catch my eye was the name JO SIFFERT, written in capital letters on the spine of a book. Jo had been just another one of my many friends who had also once said they 'want to be a racing driver', who had pursued that most glamorous and exciting career, and had then paid the ultimate price.

'Look at Jo,' I said. 'He was another one.'

Paul knew exactly what I was talking about. He had come to watch me race that day at Brands Hatch, together with his mother and his brother Mark, and he had been sitting in the stand when the ominous column of black smoke had suddenly appeared from behind the trees at the end of the straight, and the news filtered through that Jo had been killed in his burning BRM.

'I would really like to try this,' he continued.

'Paul, I can't support that.'

He left me sitting at my desk, my mind swirling. I had been a racing driver and, somehow, I had got away with it. So many of our friends were killed on the track, and it sometimes felt as if I had been blessed. Now Paul wanted to get into it, and I couldn't help feeling the law of averages was against us. Could one family have another run of such good fortune? Surely that was too much to ask. It was tempting fate. On the other hand, I wondered if I was overreacting. Times had changed, and motor racing was so much safer. Even so, why did he want to go racing? Of all the careers he could have chosen, why this? I couldn't get my head round it. There again, maybe I had no choice. If I refused to help, the chances were that he would simply find somebody else to help him; and, if I did get involved, at least I would then be in a position to ensure he had the best mechanics, machinery and equipment to help minimise the risk of anything going wrong.

I didn't know what to do, so I went to speak to Helen. She was taken aback and as concerned as me. After enduring more than a decade as a wife of a racing driver, she was far from excited about the prospect of getting aboard that emotional rollercoaster all over again as the mother of a racing driver.

Paul and I spoke again later in the day.

'I don't like it,' I said. 'I think you should finish school and go to university, as we have planned. That's important. If you still want to be a racing driver after you have finished your degree, then I'll do what I can to help. If you insist on going to racing drivers' school now, you're going to have to do it on your own.'

He was still at Aiglon in Switzerland, but we had decided he should attend university in America rather than the UK, because that would give him a more rounded education, and I was pleased when he agreed to stick to that plan.

'You never know,' I told Helen later that night, 'there's still time for him to change his mind.'

In truth, that was not likely. Once decided, Paul was not easily swayed. He was a particularly determined young man, as we saw when he set his mind on securing a place at the highly respected Duke University, in North Carolina. Not content with delivering the standard application, he armed himself with personal references from Don Petersen, chairman of the Ford Motor Company, and two friends of our family – a Texas oil man called Oscar Wyatt and Bud Schaefer, a Duke Alumnus and benefactor – and arranged to meet Anthony Duke, himself, at his home on Long Island. Paul explained to Mr Duke why he thought that he, as an international student, should be admitted, and he was duly given a place.

It seemed entirely within character when, during the spring break of 1987, he turned down invitations to join his friends at the beach and planned to enrol for a week at the Racing Drivers' School at Brands Hatch. He had even taken a job with a firm of New York stockbrokers so he could get enough money together and pay for the course himself.

As Paul and I were mapping out his plans, I made the point that he should maybe consider using a pseudonym: if the course organisers realised he was 'Jackie Stewart's son', they could be tempted to give him a favourable report for all the wrong reasons. It was just a thought, but Paul took the point. He wanted to stand or fall on his own merits and, showing commendable initiative, he signed up to the course as Robin Congdon, having borrowed both the name and the driving licence of his friend and former roommate from Aiglon.

Everything seemed to go well and he impressed not only his instructors but also Stirling Moss, who had happened to be spending some time at Brands Hatch and who had noticed a young American driver – or so he was told – going quite quickly. Paul told me he had seen Stirling at the circuit, but that he didn't think the British motor racing hero had recognised him.

I gave Stirling a call a few days later and, after a while, I said: 'And I hear you were down at Brands the other day.'

'That's right,' he replied.

'Anything much going on?'

'Well, there was a young American who looked fast.'

'I tell you what, I think you're talking about my son. He was down there, and he said he saw you.' That surprised him.

That same summer of 1987, Paul decided to drive for Ralph Firman's Van Diemen team in the British Formula Ford 1600 junior championship. His aim, as he explained it to me, was to find out (a) whether he would enjoy the motor racing life and (b) if he was any good at it.

'Is that all right?' he asked.

'That's fine,' I said. 'Ralph knows what he's doing.'

His first race at Snetterton attracted a blaze of publicity, with the media eager to report on the exploits of the son of a three-time world champion. I decided to stay away, because my presence was only going to increase the hype, expectation and pressure on Paul. In the event, Paul was unlucky to get tangled up in a collision on the first corner, and his misfortune was mercilessly featured in the following day's newspapers, being covered on the front page of *The Times* and splashed over the *Daily Mail*.

Constant comparisons with his father were the cross he would have to bear throughout his racing career, and Paul accepted that reality, but the fact was his family connection brought a series of considerable advantages as well: sponsors were more easily found, and various doors were more quickly opened.

By the end of his season with Van Diemen, in August, Paul appeared to have decided that (a) he did enjoy the life of a racing driver and (b) he could be competitive. His main challenge, it became clear, was to get as much experience as possible as quickly as possible and catch up with those competitors who had been karting since they were ten and followed the prescribed route into the sport.

Everyone seemed to think he had potential, and I heard that Stuart Turner had asked him if he had thought about becoming a rally driver – Stuart was a friend for many years and head of motor sport at Ford of Europe, and that option might have given Paul more space to be his own man. Then, I heard somebody I didn't know was offering him a drive in a Formula 3 car, which seemed premature for a driver still learning the business. I sensed the moment had arrived for me to get more involved.

'If we're going to do this,' I told him, 'let's do it properly.'

'Which team should I join in 1988?' Paul asked.

'How about your own team?' I replied.

'That could be an option.'

'You and I can start our own racing team, and we'll call it Paul Stewart Racing.'

It had occurred to me the best way for me to ensure he was surrounded by high-quality people, and therefore more likely to stay safe, was to help him create his own team, with his own car and mechanics. At least, we would have a degree of control, and Helen and I would have more peace of mind.

I knew the majority of accidents were caused by mechanical failures, so my first call was to a top mechanic with a thorough and professional attitude, the kind of man who would never let a car go out when it was underprepared. Roy Topp had worked with me at Tyrrell in 1972 and 1973 and he was still active in the sport. I explained what we had in mind with Paul Stewart Racing and was delighted when he agreed to join the team.

The project quickly began to gather momentum. We agreed the fledgling team would be based in a workshop not far from Roy's home in Hampshire. The aim was to enter one car in the 1988 British Formula Ford 2000 series, with Paul as the driver, and we put together a neat and tidy commercial programme to fund the venture. Camel signed up as the main sponsor, with the Carphone Group and Elf also coming to the party. Hugo Boss joined as our team apparel suppliers, which meant that right from the start our team members looked immaculate and well turned out. The business was up and running, and we always ensured our expenses were covered by our income. It was, and it remains, a matter of great pride for Paul and myself that PSR made money every year, which we reinvested in new equipment and people.

With the workload swiftly increasing, it was not ideal that

Paul was still completing his studies at Duke in North Carolina, and I was based in Switzerland and still committed to so many obligations around the world, but we got the job done.

'Come on, Paul,' I would say, 'if it's worth doing, it's worth doing properly. You can't be . . .'

'I know,' he would say, mimicking my well-worn phrase. 'You can't be a little bit pregnant.'

Helen and I visited the United States as often as possible during this period, particularly when Mark started attending a school in Boston. We owned an apartment in New York City, on the corner of 54th Street and Sutton Place, and there were many happy times when the four of us met up in the Big Apple.

Paul scheduled another visit back to the UK in the spring of 1988, and I planned to make this a trip he would not forget. Helen met him at Heathrow and drove him to the Trust House Forte Post House hotel just a ten-minute drive from the airport, where, as they came around the corner, there in the hotel car park, before his eyes . . . was the Paul Stewart Racing team brought to life. Our new raised-roof Ford Transit van and the new trailer unit, with the racing car inside, each emblazoned with the Paul Stewart Racing insignia and our sponsor logos – all painted in the yellow and blue Camel livery. It was a tremendously exciting day, and another milestone in our young team's development.

On his next visit, we staged an official media launch. Helen attended, but once again I decided it was sensible for me to stay away because I didn't want to be a distraction. This was Paul's team, and he needed to be centre stage. Much better.

Paul graduated in June 1988, becoming the first member of our family to receive a university degree, and he returned to the UK in time for the start of the motor racing season. I remember how excited and exhilarated he was by the prospect; as for his mother and father, we were the nervous parents. One comfort for Helen and me was that Paul would be staying on the doorstep of some good friends of ours, Lord and Lady Romsey. We'd met many times through shooting and it had been arranged that Paul would rent a house on their Broadlands estate, near to where the team's workshop was located.

After considerable thought, I had reached a decision that, as a rule, I would continue to stay away from his races – quite apart from the other reasons, as I used to say, nobody takes their father to work. However, I kept in touch and, whenever he was racing, wherever I was in the world, whatever I happened to be doing, I took steps to stay abreast of his progress.

'Hello, is that the press room?'

'Yes,' came the reply.

'I'm sorry to bother you,' I would say, 'but can you tell me how Paul Stewart is going?'

More often than not, the person at the other end of the line would recognise my voice and be able to let me know precisely how Paul was going in the race. I realised that phoning the press room was a much better option than phoning anywhere else, such as the track manager, because the journalists were usually on the ball and they had instant access to all the information. So I made a point of finding out the phone number of every press room at each circuit where Paul happened to be competing. I used to phone four or five times during the race. I hated it. I hated calling. I hated hearing the ring tone and wondering if I was about to be told there had been an accident.

My suspicion is that other fathers dealt with this ordeal much better than I did, maybe because they had been following their son's racing careers for several years since early karting days. Such men were experienced troupers. I was not. As a racing driver, I was consumed by the challenge of trying to win the race; as the father of a racing driver, I was consumed by fear. It became a weekly hour of anguish – yes, it really was as bad as that – and, as I suffered, I could hear the shrieking voice of my late mother saying, 'Now you know how it feels.'

Our small company continued to grow, and, in 1989, we moved to larger premises in Egham, Surrey, and entered two cars in the British Formula 3 championship, with Paul and a talented young German called Otto Rensing, as drivers.

Just a year later, we were on the move once again, to an even larger factory in Milton Keynes. The number of full-time personnel required to run the team had risen to twelve, including our efficient and dedicated technical manager, Andy Miller, Angela Buckland, who handled most of the administration as well as media and PR (and later married Gil de Ferran, one of our racing drivers), and two top-class mechanics – Bruce Jenkins, who came from McLaren, and Tony Fletcher, who moved across from Lotus.

In 1990, PSR entered not two cars in one class, but six cars in three classes: Paul and Derek Higgins drove in the Formula 3 series; Andrea Chiesa, an Italian, and John Jones, a Canadian, drove in Formula 3000; and, competing in two different series on alternate weekends – the Formula Vauxhall Lotus series in Britain and the Opel Euro series in Europe – we found a pair of promising youngsters: a talented Brazilian called Gil de Ferran and an eager young Scot named David Coulthard.

I first saw 'DC' drive at Snetterton and immediately sensed something special in the way he exited the corners and generally managed his car. Talented, young, keen to learn and Scottish – he seemed a perfect match for PSR, and I invited him to visit me in Switzerland, together with his father, Duncan, and 'Father' David Leslie, the well-respected Scotsman who had run his car in Formula Ford, so we could discuss whether he would drive for us. It turned out to be an interesting discussion. I started by explaining how, in my experience, many young people reach a moment quite early in their career when they need to make a move away from the environment and people who started them on their journey. Whether it is in motor racing or anything else, if they are to develop, it almost becomes necessary for them to experience new challenges and new influences. Maybe the best analogy is of a small bird one day having to fly away from the nest where it has been fed and nurtured for as long as it can remember.

'If you think David has reached that point in his motor racing career,' I concluded, 'then perhaps PSR could prove the ideal team to take him to the next stage.'

My visitors seemed to agree, and David spent the next three seasons driving for PSR, making confident strides along the road that led to him becoming such an admired racing driver. Everyone connected with PSR has always felt enormously proud of what 'DC' has achieved in a career in which he has scored more than 500 points in the F1 world championship, more than any other Briton. I remember days when, with his car set perfectly, he looked virtually unbeatable; he really was that good. There were other days when a strange drop-out in concentration would cost him dearly, but his status as one of the finest British F1 Grand Prix drivers of all time is engraved in the history of our sport.

As the team kept growing, so did our staff. David Stubbs arrived from Brabham to be manager of the Formula 3000 team. Caroline Goodacre left her job at the Gleneagles hotel to join PSR and handle sponsor and corporate hospitality, a role that she continued to play at Stewart Grand Prix (SGP) and Jaguar Racing and she is still working for Red Bull Racing. Ian Cunningham left Williams to handle our press and sponsor liaison. The fact that many proven, talented and respected people were leaving F1 teams and joining PSR suggested we were on the right track.

My role was to provide counsel and find sponsors, many of whom I still have a close relationship with. By dipping into my well-thumbed contact book, I was able to make the pitch and gain the support of people and companies. In no particular order, these included Sir Peter Burt at the Bank of Scotland, Sir Tom Farmer at Kwik-Fit, the Walker family of Walker's Shortbread, Jo Beesden of Highland Spring Mineral Water, Sir Rocco Forte of Trust House Forte Hotels, Wilson Marshall of Marshall Foods, Boyd Tunnock of Tunnock's Caramel Wafers, Robin Barr at Irn Bru, Gordon Baxter at Baxter's Soup in Fochabers, Willie McLucas of Waverley Mining, Jim McColl of Clyde Blowers, Sir Fraser Morrison of Morrison Construction, Lord Laidlaw in his personal capacity, Duncan Coulthard of Hayton Coulthard Road Transport Contractors and Crawford Beveridge of the Scottish Enterprise Board. The enthusiastic support of so many Scottish companies gave us the capacity to create opportunities for a succession of talented Scottish racing drivers such as David Coulthard, Dario Franchitti, Andrew Kirkaldy, Peter Dumbreck and Alan McNish. We even sustained the model by persuading Labatt Breweries in Canada to sponsor the car driven by their compatriot John Jones.

A certain Paul Stewart was putting together an impressive CV as well, recording several notable victories: in a Formula Ford 2000 race at Caldwell Park in 1988, at the Rolex 24 Hour of Daytona as part of a four-man team in 1989, and at a British F3 championship race at Snetterton in the same year. He was driving and thriving, and I was still phoning press rooms.

'How's Paul going?' I asked.

'He's had a shunt,' came the reply.

'Is he OK?'

'Yes, he's fine. I can see him in the pit area.'

Paul had a big accident during a F3 race in Japan in 1991, and my heart was thumping again when his brakes failed during a F3000 race at Enna, Sicily, in 1993, and his car collided with a tyre wall and was launched into the air before crashing down heavily on the tarmac and hitting another tyre wall. Luckily he was totally uninjured.

By the end of 1993, Paul had established himself among the leading drivers in F3000, and had started negotiations with two F1 teams, Arrows and Minardi, about whether he might consider making the logical step to the highest level. However, the reality was that hardly anybody secured a F1 drive unless they brought a $2 million package to the table. Paul was not in that position and so, after six seasons behind the wheel, he retired as a racing driver at twenty-eight. It was probably on the tip of my tongue to give out a screech of delight and tell him he was 'well out of it'. Instead, I agreed with his decision to focus all his attention on the business.

PSR was a remarkable organisation in many respects, notably and maybe uniquely because it was clearly structured and run as a kind of academy of motor sport. Our declared aim was to identify and recruit promising talent in every area of the industry, which we would then seek to nurture to its full potential. This was much more than some vague notion of collaring a bunch of gifted youngsters at entry level and throwing them in at the deep end. It was a determined programme to instil experience, knowledge and wisdom; and it worked.

The team won more than its fair share of titles and trophies, but the most rewarding measure of our success was not the silverware on the shelf, it has been the outstanding careers so many ex-PSR staff have carved out in the sport. It is wonderfully pleasing to track the progress of, for example, someone like Barry Mortimer, who started with our F3000 team and is now the test team chief mechanic at Renault F1. We called it the 'staircase of talent', and it carried not only the best young racing drivers but also the best young mechanics and truckies, the best young sponsor liaison representatives and the finest young managers. Nobody was excluded; everyone had the chance to grow.

To list every programme and every individual would require

a book on its own, but we did invest a substantial amount of time and effort in our corporate hospitality programme to a point where it matched anything on offer even in F1. Our approach was that our off-track performance was just as important as the on-track performance of the drivers and their cars, so we ensured our sponsors and guests, and sometimes members of the media, were consistently well looked after. Outstanding hospitality enhanced the general perception of our team, and, even on days when a mechanical failure or an accident involving driver error might have represented a poor performance on the track, our 'back-up' corporate hospitality team would step in and make certain that everyone went away not disappointed but hugely impressed by what they had seen and how they had been treated. So we bought a 32-foot Winnebago motor home, painted it in PSR livery and drove it from race to race: with its awnings extended the vehicle could cater for as many as a hundred people.

We didn't stop there. An ordinary sound system was not going to do the job because of the exceptionally high level of noise at the circuits, so we worked a little harder and spent a little more to make certain every guest could hear every word. The speeches were given by the PSR drivers, who addressed the gatherings before their race, outlining what they intended to do, and then after the race reflecting on what had happened. Each and every driver was obliged to take part, and those needing assistance were sent on public-speaking courses.

The drivers needed to look the part, so we negotiated a deal with DAKS Simpson, and each driver was provided with a well-fitted blazer, grey flannels, shirt, tie, shoes and even socks. Some of the young men had never worn a tie before, let alone learned to tie a knot, but, without exception, they looked very elegant. All our efforts and attention to detail seemed so worthwhile on the occasions when we stood at the back of the venue and watched a young driver looking so smart and speaking so well, projecting such a positive image of himself to the very people whose financial support was enabling his progress in the sport.

As a result, so many individuals learned skills that would help them secure senior positions in the sport, and PSR developed a reputation for high-quality presentation that we felt would stand us in good stead if and when we started a F1 team.

Inevitably among the team managers, engineers, commercial officers and many others packed on to PSR's 'staircase of talent', it was the racing drivers who got the most attention.

David Coulthard heads the list, because nobody wins thirteen F1 Grands Prix without being an extremely good racing driver.

Then, in alphabetical order . . .

Helio Castroneves was another talented Brazilian who raced for PSR. His father used to sprinkle holy water on the nose of his car before each race and, one famous day at Donington, I happened to notice these drops of water, looked up to see if it had begun to rain, tut-tutted the mechanics for not keeping the car perfectly clean and then took out my handkerchief and wiped it dry. Helio and his father were kind enough not to point out my mistake. Having moved to America in 1998, Helio proceeded to win the Indianapolis 500 in 2001 and 2002 and continues to be admired as one of the top drivers in American open-wheel racing.

Gil de Ferran was intense and methodical, the son of a highly respected Ford engineer at home in Brazil. He won the British F3 title in 1992 and later advanced to become the 2000 and 2001 CART Champ Car world champion with the Penske Honda team, and then to win the Indianapolis 500 in 2003. He retired from racing at the end of that season – but not before achieving the remarkable feat of winning his very last race, the Chevy 500 Mile event on the Texas Motor Speedway high-speed oval. That really is going out at the top.

Dario Franchitti was a charming young Scot from Whitburn

who won the 1993 Formula Vauxhall Lotus championship with PSR and moved on to the German Touring Car championship before making his mark in American open-wheel racing with Hogan Racing and Team Green, with whom he is still racing today. In 2007 he realised the ultimate success in American racing by winning the Indianapolis 500. He married the beautiful and talented American actress Ashley Judd in 2001.

Ralph Firman Jr, the son of the constructor who gave Paul his first drive, won the British F3 title for PSR in 1996 and then went on to drive for Jordan during the 2003 F1 season.

Alan McNish drove in the 1995 Formula 3000 championship for PSR and has gone on to become one of the most successful and highly rated sports car drivers, becoming one of the few Scots to have won the 24 Hour of Le Mans.

Juan Pablo Montoya was a young Colombian eagerly looking for a break when he contacted us and asked for a test drive. Having agreed to pay the going rate of £1,700, he was looking good until he went off the track and wrote off the car. When we discovered the accident had been caused by a mechanical failure, we offered him a full refund. He declined. Good move. We appreciated his attitude and offered him a drive in Formula Vauxhall. He was signed to drive for the Williams F1 team in 2001 and finished third in the F1 world championship in 2002 and 2003 before moving to McLaren and then to America, where he had previously won the premier CART title and the Indianapolis 500 at the first attempt. He went on to achieve the same feat at the 24 Hour of Daytona in 2007.

Johnny Mowlen drove for PSR in Formula Vauxhall and F3 and has turned out to be an extremely polished individual, in the car, as a driver in Europe, and out of the car, where he has become an accomplished television presenter.

Tomas Scheckter, the son of my contemporary Jody, drove for us in F3 and has enjoyed success in America.

Justin Wilson competed in Formula Vauxhall with PSR and went on to secure F1 drives for Minardi and Jaguar Racing in 2003 before continuing his career in US Champ Car racing.

Each of these young men seemed to recognise the truth that, whatever you are doing, there is always somebody with relevant experience who might be able to offer something that could just make all the difference to your performance, but they tended to be the exception. Over the years, I have seen many drivers, notably in F1, who appeared to think they had little to learn. I have often wondered why there is such a minimal culture of knowledge transfer in motor racing. Even dominant world-class sportsmen like Tiger Woods and Roger Federer utilise coaches, but, to date, F1 drivers don't recognise the same need. In my view, each F1 team should employ a driving coach with experience and knowledge who can talk to the drivers, analysing both their mental approach and their performance. It doesn't have to be a former world champion – one of the most successful golf coaches is David Leadbetter, and he never won a Major title – but it does need to be someone who has a deep understanding of what the job requires and of the pressures faced by every F1 racing driver. Such people exist in and around the sport but, inexplicably, they are seldom called upon to help. The same attitudes prevail in business, where you often find chairmen, presidents or CEOs behaving as if nobody can tell them anything. Wrong!

Some people will say great motor racing drivers are born, not made. I'm not so sure. Almost by definition, every F1 driver has achieved significant success in the formative classes of the sport, winning championships in their own country or continent before being given an opportunity at the highest level. They all have exceptional natural ability, but, in most cases, the drivers who become multiple world champions are the drivers who enhance that talent by learning the skill of mind management, in and out of the car; and this is the area where, one day, I'm sure coaches will make an enormous contribution.

In almost every walk of life, wise counsel takes away much of the static electricity in a situation; and it is static electricity that can cause sparks; and it is sparks that can lead to uncontrollable fires. However, wise counsel is only received by open minds.

PSR continued to grow, and the combined efforts of an exceptional group of people – as much a close-knit family as a business – translated into success on the track, most notably in the British F3 series, where the team celebrated six titles within the space of eight seasons: through Gil de Ferran in 1992, Kelvin Burt in 1993, Jan Magnussen in 1994, Ralph Firman Jr in 1996, Johnny Kane in 1997 and, lastly, Mario Haberfeld in 1998. The record shows that, from its formation in 1988 until the team was bought at the end of 1999, PSR claimed no fewer than 136 single-seater race wins, 222 podium finishes and 10 championships.

'Why don't we run a F1 team?' suggested Alan Maybin, one of our engineers, during the middle of 1995.

'Don't be ridiculous,' I replied, dismissing the idea. 'We'll never be able to afford that.'

CHAPTER 15

A New Way of Doing Business

THERE IS ALWAYS A NEW WAY: a new way of solving a problem, a new way of climbing the mountain. The ability to identify that 'new way' is a valuable asset because most people won't see past the way things have always been done. The confidence to pursue that 'new way' and look at an issue from a new angle is rare enough because most people will obstinately refuse to change. The desire and drive to execute the 'new way' lies at the heart of every great innovation.

As a schoolboy who was humiliated in front of his class-mates because he could not read or write, there was no alternative for me but to find another way. Just to keep up. It became a habit, and, ever since, in whatever I have been doing, in clay pigeon shooting, motor racing or corporate life, I have always tried to get ahead by looking for a new way of doing business.

'Why would you want to do that, Jackie?'

If I have heard it once, I've heard it a thousand times. Maybe it *will* work, I reply. It might be easier to seek comfort and security in doing things as they are usually done, and in conforming to the consensus. However, following my instinct to seek an alternative, more often than not, there has indeed been another way, and it has proved to be more successful.

'How do we get into Formula 1?'

That was the question starting to exercise the minds of people at Paul Stewart Racing in 1995. The consensus was we would need either $35 million in the bank, which we didn't have, or the support of a major motor manufacturer, and most of the likely candidates were either already committed or had been involved in F1 and had withdrawn. We needed to find another way.

'You're doing well in Formula Vauxhall, F3 and F3000,' somebody told me. 'Why on earth would you want to get involved with F1? It could be the end of you.'

It was a fair question. Many people were seriously concerned I would lose whatever money I had amassed and also jeopardise the reputation I had worked so hard to earn. For my part, I felt confident that what we had achieved at PSR could be extended into F1. Par for the course for start-up F1 teams was that four out of five failed – I knew that, but we had developed a structure with a strong financial foundation and, I firmly believed, we could avoid the same pitfalls.

In recent memory, most new entries to F1 have chosen to buy and rebrand an existing team. In this way Tyrrell became BAR, SGP became Jaguar Racing and then Red Bull Racing, Minardi became Toro Rosso, Jordan became Midland and then Spyker. The advantage of this route was that you usually inherited a factory, machine tools, assembly shops, personnel and, above all, a series of existing rights and financial benefits from the company owning the commercial rights of F1. We preferred to start our F1 team from scratch, effectively to build on a greenfields site, to be independent and free to create our own culture, unencumbered. To be frank, we didn't want the baggage of an existing team. When you buy somebody else's business, you take on people, facilities and often liabilities, all or any of which can bring problems not of your making.

Our strategy was bold, but we were determined to reach F1. It made sense for us and it made sense for our staff members on the 'staircase of talent' so they could sustain their development and have a chance of reaching the top floor. In fact, as our plans gathered momentum, we felt a strong sense of moral responsibility towards people within our business and those working for our outside suppliers. If we were prepared to start a F1 team, it seemed as if they would be prepared to go along with it as well. For whatever reason, they trusted our integrity and our judgement to make sound, sensible decisions.

For all its glamour and wealth, the reality within the F1 world was then, and remains now, that many individuals and companies are vulnerable and financially fragile. Some of our staff had joined SGP from F1 teams simply because they had complete confidence that we would pay them at the end of each month; as everyone knew only too well, that didn't always happen.

So we stood there, still thriving at PSR in the green valleys of our sport, and still gazing up at the F1 summit that seemed at once so close and yet so far away, wondering how we could possibly find another way to climb the mountain.

I mused: 'If we could find a developing country eager to project itself as a centre of high technology, maybe we could get them to fund and brand our F1 racing team . . .'

'Why would you want to do that, Jackie?' came the reply.

Undeterred, I looked towards south-east Asia, a part of the world where dynamic governments were looking for new ways to develop their people and countries. Singapore was already well packaged, but Indonesia, Thailand, the Philippines and South Korea offered real potential . . . and then there was Malaysia, with an annual growth rate around 9 per cent, a national commitment to technology and a well-developed motor industry, including a motor manufacturer in Proton and a petrol company in Petronas.

I mentioned the concept to Lord King, then chairman of British Airways and a long-time friend, and he replied: 'You've got to talk to the top man. I'll write to Prime Minister Mahathir and ask him to see you.'

The Prime Minister's office was impressive, but there was no time to enjoy the view. I had been granted a one-to-one twenty-minute meeting with Dr Mahathir bin Mohamad, so I came straight to the point and explained how his country could benefit from an association with F1 racing. He liked the concept and seemed to see the opportunity to project Malaysia worldwide. We ended up talking for an hour and a half and, running well behind schedule, the Prime Minister concluded by asking me to take the project forward with his Minister of Science and Technology. On the way back to my hotel in Kuala Lumpur, I sensed we may have found another way to climb the mountain.

A series of meetings followed, and I was grateful for the counsel of two successful British businessmen with experience of making things happen in Malaysia: Sir Charles Masefield, who had started in the private sector and become head of defence export services for the UK Government, and Alex Roberts, chairman of Short Brothers. Both helped me climb a steep learning curve.

The process took another step forward when a high-powered Malaysian delegation visited England to look around our factory in Milton Keynes and also the facilities at Cosworth, the company that produced the Ford F1 engine. They seemed to be impressed, and soon afterwards we received a fax, giving us provisional permission to start designing a F1 car.

Paul and I began to identify people to recruit and we had started sounding out candidates when, three weeks after the first fax, the office machine whirred into action once again and rolled out another letter from Malaysia, informing us they had decided to cancel the entire project. Although they had made no firm commitment, we were surprised and disappointed, but it seemed the Malaysians had decided £24 million per year was too much to spend on a F1 team that could take some time to reach a level where it was consistently competitive. They wanted to get involved in the sport, but they were looking for a swifter dividend.

'How long till we start winning?' Dr Mahathir had inquired.

'It could take as long as five years,' I had replied. That was my standard response to prospective sponsors, the media and anyone who asked. I had decided to be frank and not raise any false expectations. 'Of course it could be sooner,' I would add, 'but five years is generally how long it takes.'

The Prime Minister felt he didn't have that amount of time, but we kept in contact, meeting now and then when I was in Kuala Lumpur or when he was in London; some months later, I arranged a meeting between him and Bernie Ecclestone to discuss whether Malaysia could host a F1 Grand Prix. Bernie was already having discussions with various people in Malaysia, but, in that country at that time, Dr Mahathir was the only man able to take a decision of that magnitude. On the appointed day, I collected Bernie from his office at Queen Anne's Gate and took him to the Prime Minister's residence in Kensington, where the CEO of Malaysian Airlines, the president of Petronas and other leading lights from government and the private sector had gathered. Dr Mahathir asked me to sit in on the meeting, and he and Bernie agreed a deal that very day.

I grew to know and admire the Mahathir family. The Prime Minister's achievement in transforming Malaysia into a stable and prosperous country was a matter of record, and his faultlessly courteous, mild-mannered and relaxed manner in private belied his reputation for ruling with an iron fist.

This friendship became a very good example of how a brief

business meeting can launch another long-term relationship that has matured to a level where our families holiday together. Helen and I have remained close to the former Prime Minister and his son Mokhzani, who is now the chairman of the Sepang International motor racing circuit in Kuala Lumpur, and we have also got to know and admire the current Prime Minister Abdullah Badawi, his son Kamal and his family.

The Malaysian F1 project may not have proceeded as we had hoped, but the close relationships we had forged would stand us in good stead in years to come, so we banked the knowledge gained and started looking for another way of starting a F1 team.

It was proving difficult. That was no surprise. I understood the complexities of the business and was under no illusions that our journey would be anything other than tough. Even so we were undaunted, and our destination remained F1.

On Sunday 11 June 1995, I spent my fifty-sixth birthday working as a CBC TV commentator at the Canadian Grand Prix in Montreal. The race was won by Jean Alesi in his Ferrari, and, coincidentally, it happened to be his birthday as well. That same evening, it had been arranged that I would join three senior Ford executives on a Falcon 900 corporate jet, owned by the company, which would take us down to Detroit, where I had meetings to attend the following day. This turned out to be one of the more significant flights of my business life.

There were two pairs of seats facing each other at the front of the aircraft, and I found myself sitting with Bob Rewey, group vice-president of marketing and sales, Neil Ressler, vice-president of advanced vehicle technology, and Dan Rivard, my friend who had helped me get into vehicle assessment in the US and had since taken on a dual role as director of special vehicle operations and head of motor sport in the United States. They were not happy.

Ford had developed an impressive record in F1 racing since 1967, with their engines winning 174 F1 Grands Prix and 13 drivers' world titles, including all 3 of mine. However, the company was disappointed with the first 6 races of 1995. They had celebrated the previous year when a young Michael Schumacher had won the world championship in a Benetton-Ford, but it looked to me as though someone had then taken their eye off the ball and, as can happen in a large multinational organisation where nobody has the authority to make a swift decision, a deal to renew the association with the Benetton team was left lying on the table. During this delay, Benetton went off and agreed a deal with Renault, leaving Ford to search for a new team; they eventually agreed to supply engines to Sauber, but the Swiss F1 team were struggling with only a fifth place and two sixths in six races to show for their efforts. Both Sauber-Fords had retired that afternoon in Montreal, prompting the downbeat mood in our aircraft as we took off and headed into the clouds.

Bob Rewey asked me what could be done. Feeling free to give my honest opinion among senior executives who paid me to do just that, I told them Ford should get out of F1.

'Bob, Ford doesn't seem committed to F1,' I said. 'Honda and Renault have come in and made a big impression, and now Peugeot and Mercedes-Benz look like doing the same, but it feels as if Ford have let the flame go out. The company doesn't even publicise its successes properly: when Ford does do well, it seems to remain a well-kept secret in the global marketplace. Many people in F1 are starting to wonder if Ford is really serious about Grand Prix racing any more.'

My travelling companions understood what I was saying, and their frowns were getting deeper.

I concluded: 'You know, I've heard you talk about getting out of F1 often enough. Now, I think you should do it.'

'It's not so easy, Jackie,' Bob replied. 'We have so many

commitments at so many levels, especially in our international markets where F1 is big. We can't just walk away.'

'OK, then,' I said. 'You need to stop the bus and rethink your entire strategy. There's no point carrying on as you are, hoping someone is going to wave a magic wand and make everything better. That's just not going to happen.'

'So what's the solution?' Bob asked.

'I don't know,' I said, 'but I would like to think about it.'

There was a pause, before Bob said: 'Can you put together a proposal of how we should go ahead?'

'No problem,' I replied.

Easily said, not easily done.

I immediately contacted my son Paul, Rob Armstrong, a New Zealander who had worked for IMG and joined PSR as commercial director in 1994, and the board of trustees who ultimately owned the company, in order to let them know about this latest development. Paul, Rob and I then set about preparing a document that – I think we all realised – would make or break our F1 ambition. Over the next three months, we put in an enormous amount of time and effort into developing a detailed proposal that offered Ford exactly what they were looking for. The inch-thick dossier covered every detail, ranging from the technical input we would require from Ford to a comprehensive financial breakdown with all our projected outgoing and incoming monies on a monthly, quarterly and annual basis. We did our homework, even going so far as to contact Ford's long-term advertising agency in Detroit, J. Walter Thompson, and find out what style and format of presentation would be most appealing to the Ford executives. Martin Sorrell put us in touch with the right people, and Peter Stroh and Frank Brooks, both from JWT, were generous with their time and their informed advice.

Correctly dressed and well prepared, I stood in one of the meeting rooms at Ford's Design Center in Dearborn, cleared my throat and began the presentation. My audience included my three fellow passengers in the Falcon 900, Bob, Neil and Dan, together with Jac Nasser, then chairman of Ford Europe, and Bob Transou, vice-president of manufacturing worldwide. Sitting beside me was my son Paul, as MD of PSR, and Rob Armstrong.

Aware Ford had suffered some bad financial experiences in motor sport and eager to strike the right tone, I started by saying, 'Gentlemen, the Ford Motor Company requires a reliable and trustworthy long-term partner in Formula One . . .'

That was exactly what we were offering: a highly professional racing team with a proven track record of success headed by a person who they had known and trusted for thirty-one years, pledging transparency in every respect and guaranteeing delivery.

When I had finished, Jac Nasser asked directly, 'So you can run the F1 team for £24 million in your first year?'

'Yes,' I replied. 'We've done the figures.'

'So you want us to supply the engines at no cost and an extra $6 million in set-up costs?'

'That's right,' I said, 'plus 50 per cent of the drivers' fees.'

'And you're looking for a five-year deal?'

'Correct.'

They didn't baulk at the terms, and the meeting ended on a positive note with an agreement we would reconvene in due course. Ten days later, back in Dearborn on product development work, I received a message from Jac Nasser, asking if I could go to see him on the twelfth floor of world headquarters at the end of the day. We met for dinner in an executive dining room.

'Jackie,' he said, 'is there an alternative structure?'

I paused, and replied, 'Well, you could finance everything and own the team yourselves. I would find the sponsors, and we would run the team for you at cost plus 10 per cent.'

That was a reasonable option, but Jac said the board would be unlikely to approve the amount of money and liabilities associated with a fully owned F1 team. We chatted for a while and agreed to pursue the structure we had initially proposed.

Paul, Rob and I flew back to Detroit for the follow-up meeting, and we seemed to be making progress until Bob Rewey asked what they should do about Sauber. I said their unhappiness with Sauber was the whole reason we were sitting there.

'I know,' Bob replied, 'but maybe we could keep supplying them with an engine and then, if your team doesn't work out, we would still have them in reserve. Would that be OK?'

There often comes a point in a negotiation when you have to draw a line in the sand and be firm, and that moment had arrived. There was no point doing a deal at any cost, especially if the terms of the deal would prevent us from succeeding.

'Bob, I think that would be a deal breaker,' I said. 'If you keep supplying Sauber, there will always be a division of effort at the engine manufacturers and elsewhere. If this thing is going to work, we need total focus and total commitment.'

I looked around the room. It seemed touch and go for a while, until Jac broke the silence. 'OK, Jackie,' he said, 'you've got a deal.'

We were suddenly in business, and I clearly recall leaving the meeting and returning to our car and seeing the elation on the faces of Paul and Rob. They had worked so hard on the project, and it seemed as if their dream had come true. I sat in the front of that Lincoln Town Car, with very different emotions. Oh my God, I thought to myself, what have we done? I sat there fretting quietly, worrying the F1 project would become not a dream, but a nightmare for us all. I knew what lay ahead and I felt sure the workload and pressure would be enormous.

Somewhere in that car, as we drove towards the Ritz Carlton hotel in Dearborn, I could hear the voice of my father, saying,

'A small fire can warm you, but a big fire can burn you.' PSR had been a typical small fire: neat, successful and moderately profitable. Was Stewart Grand Prix going to burn us? I was well warned.

The following week, I phoned Ken Tyrrell to tell him what had happened. My old friend was still running his team in F1, so he knew the business. He was pleased for us, but he added: 'You know it won't be easy to find sponsors, but the hardest part will be getting the engineering right.' There would be many occasions in the months ahead when I recalled these wise words.

Nothing came easy.

First, the message didn't get through to Sauber about Ford's decision, which put us in the awful position of having to tell Peter Sauber, a wonderful man, that he would not be using the Ford engine in 1997.

Then, there were delays in getting the contract processed and signed, even to a point where people wanted to postpone the official press announcement. I have always been a firm believer in what I call 'closed loop procedures' where you reach agreement, ensure every activity and intention is clearly understood, sign the contract, pay the money, put the matter to bed and move on. That is the way I like to do business: it's clean, transparent and effective. However, large organisations are often very bad at closing the loop, thinking that once the terms of a deal have been agreed, then that is it done and dusted. In fact, very often, there are still a bunch of loose ends flying around, which need to be clarified, committed to paper and signed off. Delaying the press conference would send the wrong message so, eventually, I contacted Jac Nasser, and he helped ensure the paperwork was processed.

So it happened that, on 4 January 1996, we appeared at the Detroit Motor Show to announce that Ford and the newly created Stewart Grand Prix had agreed to form a new F1 team for 1997, to be called Stewart-Ford. Just fourteen hours and a frenetic dash across the Atlantic later, together with Albert Caspers, president of Ford of Europe, we walked on stage and made the same announcement at the Autosport International Show in Birmingham, England. Media interest was extraordinary, and it amused me that, even in the close-knit world of motor racing, the news of our venture seemed to have caught everyone by surprise. Just as Ken Tyrrell had wanted to be discreet, and put his trust in the right people, and managed to keep the development of 001 so quiet twenty-six years previously, so we had managed to maintain a cloak of secrecy around our car.

With Ford on board, we launched two parallel processes to get the team ready: Paul took charge of the expansion of the factory and development of the car in Milton Keynes, while I launched the global quest for sponsors, ideally five or six companies each buying a commercial package at £5 million per year.

Nothing came easy. In Milton Keynes, the requirements of a F1 team meant we had to treble our floor space in the factory at Tanner's Drive, which we did by leasing the property next door. This period of remarkable growth was handled by an impressive management team led by Paul as MD, with Rob Armstrong as commercial director, David Stubbs as team manager, Andy Miller as technical team manager, Colin McGrory as production manager and Nigel Newton as the financial director who policed every departmental budget. Our first-choice technical director was Alan Jenkins, then working for Arrows. His decision to join us was a major boost, and he and his design team set to work on creating the new car – not by building a plywood model in the garage at home, as Derek Gardner had done with the Tyrrell 001, but by tapping their keyboards and designing the car on the latest computers in a room with soft blue lighting and climate control.

Meanwhile, I was racking up the air miles, travelling around the world, making presentations and seeking sponsors.

Mapping out my plans, I realised that until then motor racing had been quite primitive in seeking support from the same circle of sponsors: fuel and oil companies, tyre companies and above all cigarette companies. We took a decision not to approach cigarette companies because tobacco advertising was in the process of being prohibited in many countries. Then we discovered the fuel and oil companies were no longer investing large sums of money; they had all been in and around the business for almost too long. I had assumed Elf would be an obvious candidate as petrol supplier, particularly in view of my long association with the giant French company, but they came back and said '*non*' – no to being a sponsor, no to being a supplier. I was amazed. In the end, we secured deals with Texaco and Havoline as our petrol and oil suppliers, and with Bridgestone, our first-choice tyre manufacturer, but I realised we would have to cast our net wider and seek sponsors in untapped areas of commerce.

My first move was to contact my friends in Malaysia. Tan Sri Arumagam was an extremely successful businessman whose name I had been given by Lord King and whom I first met with Sir Charles Masefield in London. 'Aru' came with me to another meeting with Dr Mahathir, at which I proposed that Malaysia become a sponsor of our F1 team. The Prime Minister agreed with the concept that the country would take space on the car at a cost of £5 million per year, and it was Aru who coined the slogan 'Visit Malaysia', which was eventually emblazoned across the car.

Continuing my search, I sensed an opportunity in the ongoing globalisation of the financial services industry. The major banks were still visible on the high street but they were also expanding their commercial interests across national borders into areas such as public services and providing financing and insurance in the world of transportation. Formula 1 racing was an ideal platform to project a brand to a global audience.

I approached the Bank of Scotland, who had sponsored PSR, but they said they had no real global ambition at the time. I approached the Royal Bank of Scotland, but they said they were not yet big enough to make such an investment. I approached Standard Chartered, and they were excited by the prospect of tapping into the popularity of F1 racing in the Asia-Pacific market but, after serious consideration, decided it was not for them. I then approached ING, who had recently bought Barings, the bank whose image had been tarnished by the reckless activities of one trader in Singapore, and suggested an association with our F1 team could help restore their image and credibility. Nobody wanted to touch Barings at the time, but I saw an opportunity there because companies at a low ebb can often be more open and receptive to concepts with the potential to turn around their standing in the marketplace. It could have worked, and I was disappointed when they declined.

As it turned out, ING did invest in the sport eleven years later, when, in 2007, they invested in excess of $40 million annually to support their sponsorship of the Renault F1 team.

HSBC was another option, and they had already declared their ambition to be a global bank. In planning how to approach them, I recalled a chance meeting a few months earlier. I had been invited to attend a cocktail party in Edinburgh followed by a dinner in Glasgow where the then Prime Minister, John Major, was speaking, and I had been told that Sir William Purves, chairman of HSBC and a fellow Scot, would be on the same flight. I introduced myself, and we were talking in the British Airways Executive Club at Heathrow when it was announced over the PA system that our flight to Edinburgh had been cancelled.

'That's it,' said Sir William, 'I'm going to pack it in.'

'Wait a moment,' I replied, 'let me call my office and get them to reschedule for both of us.'

Within fifteen minutes, new arrangements had been made for us to fly directly to Glasgow, be met by a car and driver and be taken to the hotel at 1 Devonshire Place, where two rooms had been reserved for us to change. We would then skip the Edinburgh cocktail function and instead attend a drinks party in Glasgow hosted by Peter de Vink, who was hosting us at his table for the black-tie dinner where the Prime Minister would speak.

'That's all done,' I told Sir William.

Everything had worked out, and he had seemed pleased. Now I gave him a call and reached his secretary, who recognised my voice and put me straight through.

'Hello, what do you want?'

The no-nonsense, Scottish accent unmistakably belonged to Sir William, and he was clearly not in the mood for chit-chat, so I said I would like to come and see him.

'Yes, but what do you want?'

'I have a proposal I would like to discuss.'

'Is it sponsorship? If it's sponsorship, I'm *no* interested.'

'No, it's a business opportunity, which I would like to communicate to you in the fullest sense. I think it would be best if we could sit down and talk to each other.'

'Well, it sounds like sponsorship, so I'm *no* interested.'

I clearly wasn't getting anywhere, so I took a deep breath and said something that turned out to be perhaps the most important few words of my entire business life.

'Sir William,' I said, 'I am very surprised a man of your calibre would actually say no to something when you haven't even heard what I'm proposing.'

There was silence on the line.

'Well, you'd better come in, then,' he said.

I duly arrived for a meeting in his office and discovered he had also invited Mary Jo Jacobi, a communications specialist who had worked at the White House before joining HSBC. Sir William gestured for me to settle into his comfortable, low sofa while he sat on a particularly high armchair. He was much taller than me already and the combined effect of that and the seating arrangements meant that Sir William was looking down on Mary Jo and me from a dizzy height.

'OK,' he said. 'What have you got to say?'

I outlined the concept, and he responded by saying it wasn't a likely starter, but I could send a proposal if I wanted. I did exactly that and then arranged a further meeting with Mary Jo, where I took her through the various aspects and subtleties that I believed would offer significant benefit to HSBC.

Another meeting with Sir William and Mary Jo followed, which the chairman ended by saying he didn't think there was any chance the bank would be interested, but that it might be worth my while to meet John Bond, the CEO. 'He won't want to do it either,' he said, 'but he's the man who runs the company.'

This fourth meeting seemed to be going well, and John Bond was starting to show interest, when Sir William interjected and said it really didn't matter what he or the CEO thought because a deal of this size would require board approval.

'And I have to tell you I doubt the board will want it,' Sir William added. 'We don't do sponsorship. The only things we are involved in are the Hong Kong Sevens rugby and some opera – and, to be frank with you, I'm not an opera fan.'

A time and date was set when I would be able to make a full presentation to the HSBC board and, recognising the importance of this pitch, I left nothing to chance. If we were going to fail, I decided, it was not going to be for the lack of good planning, good structuring and good preparation. So I worked on my speech with Lee Bowman, an American who owned Kingstree Communications, the company that ran the public-speaking courses for PSR drivers; and, the day before the meeting, I asked if I could visit the HSBC boardroom at their head office to acquaint myself with the layout so I could work out how I could make the best impact on the twenty-three members of the board who would be sitting around the horseshoe-shaped table.

The next day, I walked in to address this impressive gathering of people, including chairmen and CEOs from companies like Cathay Pacific, Jardine Matheson, Goldman Sachs and British Airways, and Sir William greeted me in what had become familiar style. 'Hello,' he said, 'we don't have much time, so you'd better get on with it. In fact, you've got fourteen and a half minutes.'

My task was to ensure that was long enough.

'Ladies and gentlemen,' I started, 'I don't believe many people understand what HSBC stands for. They may know it in Hong Kong, but that's not the case in many other countries around the world, certainly not in Britain. I understand you want to be regarded as a global bank, and I believe there is only one major activity that can project your brand and guarantee you the global exposure to help you achieve that goal. That's F1.'

I ran through our plan to develop a F1 team and described the benefits they would receive from putting their corporate identity on our cars and team livery. As soon as I finished, Sir William said he didn't suppose there would be any questions, but if anyone had something to ask, they should speak up.

'Thank you, Jackie,' said Baroness Dunn, deputy chairman. 'We all know F1 racing is a dangerous sport. My concern is about the negative impact if one of the cars gets involved in an accident, and our logo was photographed on the wreckage.'

I replied: 'Baroness Dunn, if I gave you £10 million, could you 100 per cent guarantee me a healthy return on my investment?'

Lydia Dunn smiled.

I continued: 'As you know, it is difficult to 100 per cent guarantee anything in banking, and it's hard to give a 100 per cent guarantee in motor racing. However, I can tell you F1 motor sport has probably the best risk-management system in the world because it attracts probably the largest capital investment of any sport, and there are many large global companies involved.'

Worried that Sir William was about to close the session, not knowing whether he would allow any other questions and eager to make all my points, I kept talking: 'Another thing is that F1 motor sport is both completely classless and socially acceptable, and that also makes it particularly attractive for HSBC.'

Sir William allowed the Q&A session to continue for another forty-five minutes and then declared it was time for the board to move on to 'more important' things.

'I'll call you at three o'clock,' he announced.

I thanked the board members for their time, thanked Sir William and made my exit. I didn't know which way the decision was going to go. The presentation had been well received but I had never known a large company to make a quick decision, and when he said they were going to call that very same afternoon, I started to believe the answer would have to be 'no'.

I was sitting in an office at IMG when, on the dot at 3 p.m., the telephone rang.

'Hello?'

'Hello, Jackie, it's Willie Purves here.'

'Good afternoon, Sir William.'

'I can't believe this, but the board approved your sponsorship proposal, subject to contract. So you had better prepare something and send it through as soon as you can.'

'Thank you, Sir William.'

'OK, goodbye.'

Bang . . . down went the telephone.

For all Sir William's apparent severity, there is no doubt in my mind that he picked the ball up on the first bounce. Right from the start, I believe he recognised the benefits offered by an association with F1 racing and a partnership with Ford, a company that, incidentally, banked with HSBC at the time. I believe he liked the freshness of our ideas and my personal commitment, and he realised that my return to F1 as a team owner almost twenty-four years after retiring as a driver would create major interest. As I subsequently learned, he had done his homework and he was aware I had won a F1 Grand Prix in almost all the countries where we would be racing and that, in itself, would guarantee a high level of media visibility for HSBC.

Sir William's office received the draft contract within a few days, and the ink was soon dry on a deal that started at £5 million per year. As the bank agreed to take even more branding space on the car, it reached £12.5 million per year.

HSBC's decision represented an enormous and decisive act of faith in what was still an embryonic F1 team, which at that stage had not even designed a car, let alone turned a wheel. The support of such a well-respected financial institution left everyone in the team feeling more than flattered; we were proud.

Ford were also impressed, to an extent that Mac MacDonald, the company treasurer, travelled from Detroit to share the platform with Sir William, John Bond, Paul and me at the press conference where we announced the sponsorship.

Willie Purves has since become a friend, and Helen and I see him and his wife Becky as often as possible. A dour, down-to-earth Scot with a well-disguised sense of humour, he emerged as the banker of the nineties, earning great respect around the world.

Not every campaign ended with success. In the same window of time, we started discussions with a major global sports footwear and apparel company and developed a concept where clever artwork would make our F1 car resemble one of their running shoes. It was innovative and exciting, a new way if ever there was one, and we attended a series of meetings with their marketing people in North America and Europe. Eventually, on Saturday 29 June 1996 – I won't ever forget the date – I met the chairman of this large company in a suite at the Hilton hotel at Hyde Park Corner, London, and we shook hands on an incredible five-year deal worth £60 million.

'The great thing about people like you and me, Jackie,' he said, smiling warmly as he gripped my hand, 'is that we don't need contracts.'

'That's lovely,' I replied. 'Shall I get our lawyers to draft the contract, or will your people prefer to do that?'

'You go ahead,' he said. 'It won't be a problem.'

The contract was sent promptly but it remained unsigned for a fortnight. Then another week passed, and another, and another, until I eventually called him on his mobile phone and found him at the Olympic Games in Atlanta, where the company had assembled its entire marketing management team.

'Oh, Jackie,' he said, clearly embarrassed. 'I've run into a major problem with my marketing people here. We're not going to be able to go ahead with your project.'

That was that.

Paul and I were devastated – there was no other word. The deal that would have provided an amazing boost for our team, and broken new ground for F1 racing, simply collapsed, and the old adage of never counting chickens before they are hatched was never more vividly or painfully demonstrated.

Not every success required a campaign. We secured Hewlett Packard as a sponsor with a single phone call to Lew Platt, the chairman and CEO; there was no need to fly across the world and make a presentation to the HP Board in Palo Alto,

California because, in the course of a fifteen-minute conversation, Lew saw the opportunity to project the brand, be associated with other premium sponsors such as Ford and, specifically, to play the key role in designing a F1 car solely with computers. That had never been done before. We had taken a decision to dispense with the drawing board, and replace it with forty or fifty computers in a design office. Alan Jenkins led this pioneering project with consummate skill and enthusiasm, but it would not have become reality without the active and committed support of Hewlett Packard, and the man whom Lew Platt designated to implement the project, Alex Sozonoff.

This was certainly a 'new way of doing business', and far from everybody welcomed the move; in fact, we lost a few people who, quite literally, preferred to go back to the drawing board. However, I believed our minds were working correctly – the new technology had many advantages, not least complete accuracy in measuring parts to be ordered from outside suppliers. People often hesitate to buy the best new equipment because it is often substantially more expensive. However, used correctly, it invariably pays for itself in the long run. The SGP design office took the design of F1 racing cars into a new era and, when it had been decorated in HP's company colours and insignia, it looked magnificent.

Alex Sozonoff also played a key role in helping us secure EDS as one of our software suppliers, through his association with Jim Duncan, the EDS head of sales and marketing in Europe and another Scot. We were also helped by Tony Affuso, then working for a US company called Unigraphics Solutions, in which EGS was a majority shareholder; he was an expert in the CAD/CAM technology and committed himself completely to the project. Today, he is chairman and CEO of UGS PLM Software.

Hewlett Packard were also alert to all the incremental opportunities arising from being part of the same project as

Ford, and they duly secured a chance to bid for the rights to supply computer equipment to the motor manufacturer; the contact was developed, and business was duly done. SGP played a soft role in such arrangements, but we never guaranteed preferential treatment. It simply became clear that the quality and prestige of the companies in our programme offered genuine opportunities for sponsor networking. Where Ford and HSBC had led, others were eager to follow.

This was an important factor for MCI Communications, the American telecommunications company, who joined the SGP programme at the end our first season in 1997. I had called Bert Roberts, the chairman, on his mobile while he was attending the 'MCI Classic – The Heritage of Golf' tournament, as it was then known, at Hilton Head Island, South Carolina, and outlined our proposal. We spoke on the phone again a week later and agreed a £5 million per annum deal before we had ever met face to face. As an SGP sponsor, MCI gained access that enabled them to bid for part of Ford's telecommunications business, which was then exclusively held by AT&T; and, in due course, they did secure a substantial 10 per cent slice of that very attractive cake.

It was clearly important for us that Ford would be receptive to the approach of a fellow SGP sponsor and at least allow them to bid for business, and, in this area, we were indebted to Carlos Mazarin, the Argentinian in charge of Ford's commercial purchasing, and the hardest-working man I have ever met; it was amazing how much he could pack into a very long working day. Carlos was later succeeded by Tony Brown, who was equally helpful in providing guidance on how to handle possible partners in our team who wished to do business with Ford around the world.

Two further pieces slotted into the jigsaw: Sanyo were an ideal sponsor because they were one of the few consumer product companies with global reach; and an association with the Lear Corporation made sense because they were one of Ford's suppliers of vehicle interiors, seats and instrument panels.

The completion of the SGP commercial programme ranks as one of the significant achievements of my life. It is in the nature of human reflection that the highs linger longer and more strongly in the memory than the lows; similarly, this account of what was a difficult and exhausting year has dwelled on deals done rather than proposals rejected. In reality, for every company that said yes, there were ten who said no. This might sound like the predictable observation of someone in their late sixties, and I realise it's not something people like to hear, but the cornerstones of our success were hard work, focus and perseverance. None of these seem fashionable today, but there is no substitute for them. I found it amusing when people described me as a kind of wizard at finding sponsorship, because there was never any magic spell and I never owned a wand. Any success was earned by knuckling down to prepare convincing presentations, making phone calls, developing relationships and never giving up. This was not a triumphant tour of the world's boardrooms by a three-time F1 motor racing world champion, picking up so many millions of dollars along the way. It was bloody hard work.

Ask Helen to reflect on this period of our lives, and she will tell you the stress and pressure made it a nightmare. We gave up our home in Switzerland when it became clear that, if we were going to make SGP work, I would have to live on the job; so we moved from our lovely spacious house overlooking Lake Geneva into an apartment in Sunningdale, west of London – all in the name of Stewart Grand Prix.

I had imagined it would be an easy commute to the factory in Milton Keynes, but, in fact, the journey took ninety minutes early in the morning and almost three hours on a wet evening, but I put up with it, and so did my driver, Gerry Webb, who started and ended his day in London – all in the name of Stewart Grand Prix.

Companies would stall on signing contracts, and I would have to call the chairman or CEO and ask him to hurry things along, and these discussions were often not pleasant, but they would have to be done – all in the name of Stewart Grand Prix.

At various stages of the process, Paul was seriously worried we would not secure the sponsors and would have to abandon the project. In fact, he phoned me and said as much on his way with the PSR team to the prestigious F3 race at Macau in 1996. I tried to reassure him that everything would work out well, as I always believed it would. In fact, Ralph Firman gave PSR a notable victory in Macau, and the clouds of doubt drifted away.

Paul was also genuinely concerned about my state of health, and I suppose there were days when I looked like a prime candidate for a heart attack. However, over the years, I had become well used to the rigours of international travel, jet lag, feeling exhausted, attending a lunch, being knocked back in a meeting, doing a press interview, having to attend a cocktail party in the evening, then going to a separate dinner somewhere else, getting a few hours sleep and being up early in the morning to appear, bright-eyed and bushy-tailed, for another day of convincing people. That had been the pattern of my life for as long as I could remember, so although the treadmill of finding sponsors for SGP was tough, it was nothing new. I had learned to cope.

I was immeasurably helped in the process, not only by my office first in Switzerland and then at SGP, but also by the remarkably efficient Donna Wise. In search of a personal assistant in the US, I had contacted Rod Campbell, a PR expert who had worked for me during the CanAm series of 1971, and he seconded Donna to be contracted by Ford and to work for me. She did a fantastic job. Today she is married with two little girls, and Helen and I still keep in touch.

Meanwhile, Alan Jenkins and the design team had completed the task of designing the car from scratch. If we had bought an existing F1 team, they would simply have had to update last year's model. Instead, they had started with a blank computer screen and designed and manufactured more than 3,500 individual components that made up the total SF1 racing machine.

We needed to find somebody to drive the cars, so Andy Miller, David Stubbs, Paul and I sat down and drew up a shortlist of individuals who could meet our three key criteria: they needed to be (a) desirable, (b) available and (c) affordable.

First choice was Damon Hill, the son of my late friend Graham Hill and the reigning world champion. Paul and I flew to meet him in Dublin, and he seemed interested by our offer. He did request a substantial salary, but, with Ford's support, it was affordable.

In search of a No. 2, we approached Jan Magnussen, a young driver who had driven for PSR and been on the staircase of talent before competing in a single F1 Grand Prix for McLaren at the end of 1995 and driving in the US CART series in 1996. At one point, I had gone on record saying I thought the twenty-three-year-old Dane was the most promising driver I had seen in F3 since Senna.

Jan signed, but, when Damon came back to us and said he felt that, as the world champion, signing with a new team was a bridge too far, our search for a No. 1 moved to Rubens Barrichello.

'Not another ABB,' I laughed.

That was a term we used for 'Another Bloody Brazilian', because there seemed to be so many talented racing drivers from that country. Rubens' talent had never been in doubt since he came to Europe and won consistently in the formative classes. We saw him up close as he raced against us at PSR. He began his F1 career with Jordan in 1993 and finished sixth in the drivers' championship in 1994. However, the relationship within his team had soured, and, by the end of 1996, he was eager for a new start. He seemed ideal for SGP: with four F1 seasons behind him, experienced enough to cope with the frustrations and unreliability of a brand new car; and yet, at twenty-four, young enough to have potential to grow with the team. Rubens duly signed.

At last, on 10 December 1996, with everything ready – the cars, the drivers and the sponsors, some of whom had only signed their contracts literally hours before – we, along with Ford, hosted a full-scale press launch in London. The media and guests arrived at the venue to find a racing car hidden beneath tartan . . . but not just any tartan. It had been Paul's idea to create something new and unique, and he worked with Kinloch Anderson in Edinburgh to create a new Racing Stewart tartan, based on Scottish blue incorporating the Royal Stewart tartan that I wore around my racing helmet and the Hunting Stewart tartan that Paul had on his helmet. It turned out well, and was registered with the relevant authorities. I suppose the moment when Paul and I stepped forward and drew back the tartan to reveal the new car was about as good as it gets for a father-and-son team. We hadn't even started a race but, as the cameras flashed at the new car, it was impossible not to feel a considerable sense of achievement.

Most people had expected SF1 to be the same royal blue as my racing cars had been, and there was some surprise when we unveiled a pure white car decorated with a trail of Racing Stewart tartan. We had worked with a design company called Carter Wong, and the overall look was impressive. I took a step back and looked at the car. In a holistic sense, it was exactly what we had wanted – there was nothing that took your eye and made you wonder why it was there, there was no pimple on the cheek, and that was always a good sign. Alan Jenkins and Eghbal Hamidy, a top aerodynamicist who had joined SGP from Williams, had produced a clean, sleek, smooth racing car. There were some nice touches. Paul had arranged for the steering wheel to be made from blue leather with white stitching, providing an echo of the Scottish flag. It may have been a small detail, but it mattered to Paul and to me because it showed our ambition to be an organisation prepared to do that little bit more to be that little bit special and gradually develop a profile to match the premium brands of our blue-chip sponsors.

After I had thanked everybody who needed to be thanked, it was Paul's turn to stand at the podium and outline the team's plans for our debut F1 season in 1997. He was doing just fine until he reached the part of his speech where he wanted to thank me for, as he put it, giving him 'this incredible opportunity'. At that moment, his voice cracked, and he appeared to be overcome by emotion. My instinct was to get up from my seat, walk over and put my arm around him, as any father would do. However, just as I was getting up from my seat, he recovered his composure and duly completed the speech.

After all the ups and downs, after all the design meetings and the sponsorship proposals, after all the work with scarcely a free weekend or a holiday, Stewart Grand Prix was a reality.

CHAPTER 16

Building the Business

A SMALL GROUP OF US HAD GATHERED AT BOREHAM AIRFIELD, a few miles outside Chelmsford, Essex, on the morning of 16 December 1996. It was cold, wet and misty, but, at last, we were going to see SF1 move under its own power for the first time. Far from the glamour of the public launch, this was the place where our F1 car was going to roar into action. Rubens Barrichello climbed in and, within a few moments, he was driving the white racing car, away from us, into the mist, down the disused runway. I recall there was a lump in my throat.

This was just a 'shakedown', where the car accelerates in a straight line to check for oil, water or fuel leaks. We started a more comprehensive testing programme at the Jarama circuit, near Madrid, soon after Christmas, and the initial signs were encouraging. In fact, I started to sense there was some optimism flying around but, as a brand new F1 team in its first year, it was unrealistic to expect we would be consistently competitive.

So our early results proved.

Australia: Rubens qualified in eleventh place, and Jan in

nineteenth place, and both retired from the race . . . kind of OK.

Brazil: Jan had an accident on the first lap, and Rubens had to withdraw with a suspension problem on lap twenty-two . . . disappointing.

Argentina: Rubens qualifies in fifth place, but he retires with an engine problem on lap twenty-four, and Jan's engine fails with just six laps to go . . . a very much better performance.

San Marino: Jan spins off on lap two, and Rubens retires with more engine problems on lap thirty-two . . . disappointing again.

As the team headed to Monaco for the fifth race of the year, I hoped for a performance to announce our arrival as team owners at the same circuit where I had first made my mark as a racing driver when I won the F3 race thirty-three years before.

It was dry on the morning of race day, but the first few drops of rain started to fall about half an hour before the start, and we took a quick decision to go with 'wet' tyres from the off. Most of the other teams looked up and reckoned the shower was only temporary, so they went with 'drys' or 'intermediates', which was intriguing. Such decisions could be decisive.

Rubens produced a fantastic start, erupting from tenth place on the starting grid, apparently overtaking at will, storming into fifth place by the end of a frenetic second lap, and then into second place by the end of lap six, with only Michael Schumacher ahead of him. It was an extraordinary drive.

There were some exciting moments: Michael locked his front tyres on lap fifty-three and skated up the Ste Devote escape road; then Rubens also went off the tarmac, but he didn't hit anything and was able to rejoin the race, still in second place.

With twelve laps left, Rubens ran into trouble.

'The hydraulic pressure is dropping,' David Stubbs said,

looking anxiously towards Dave Redding, our chief mechanic. 'Do you think he will make it to the finish line?'

Dave couldn't be sure. Nobody knew. The entire pit crew stood in the pit, on tenterhooks . . . Paul was chewing on his nails . . . Rubens kept going . . . a few more laps . . . nobody spoke . . . two laps to go . . . one lap to go . . . come on . . . and he finished . . . second!

Rubens crossed the line fifty-three seconds behind Schumacher to claim second place at the Monaco Grand Prix. Fantastic! In that moment, the vast reservoir of pressure and expectation built up over the previous year came flooding out; and, right there in the pit, Paul and I fell into each other's arms, him holding my head, both of us in floods of tears.

For a start-up team to finish second in only its fifth F1 Grand Prix was remarkable, all the more so since it was the first time SF1 had actually finished a race. Helen and Mark were watching from the paddock, so they shared our excitement.

We rushed down to witness the presentation ceremony at the Royal Box and, after the three placed drivers had received their trophies and sprayed the champagne around, I was approached by François Mazet, a friend and one of the race officials, who told me Prince Rainier would like Paul and me to join him on the podium. It was a very nice touch, because he obviously knew our history and appreciated the significance of the moment for our team.

After such a high in Monaco, the rest of the season unfolded as a frustrating series of mechanical problems. The statistics don't lie, and the reality was that, in seventeen F1 Grands Prix, Rubens finished the race only three times and Jan only five times. The Ford Zetec-R V10 engine appeared to lack power and it seemed fragile in the SF1 chassis. A series of meetings was held with people from Ford and from Cosworth, as we urgently sought a solution to provide that elusive reliability.

This was not our only concern. The European Commission

had created some turmoil in the sport by launching an investigation into the administrative and commercial structure of F1 racing. Rumours were running through the pits that each of the F1 teams would be asked to give evidence to this inquiry, and it was being said that, as new boys in the class, Stewart-Ford were more likely to 'talk' than others, and this would not meet with the approval of some concerned. In the event, we were not approached at all, but the paddock talk had created tension between our team and various individuals and organisations. We were happy the matter somehow blew over and it was ultimately not required for us to appear before the Commission.

Then, out of the blue, in October 1997, our name appeared on the list of accepted entries for the forthcoming 1998 F1 season with an asterisk, indicating FIA, the governing body, wished to see evidence that we had sufficient sponsorship to compete.

'What's going on?' I asked Paul.

'They're just having a laugh,' he replied.

'It's ridiculous,' I said. 'We're backed by Ford, the second-largest car manufacturer in the world, HSBC, one of the world's biggest banks, and Hewlett Packard, one of the leading IT companies in the world, our other sponsors are robust multinational companies, and they question our viability? For goodness' sake, we've never even had an overdraft. If they question us, what about everyone else? There are no secrets in F1. At least we have never had to borrow from anyone so we can pay salaries at the end of the month.'

Our auditors, Rawlinson & Hunter, supplied documents to FIA which confirmed our guaranteed income of £21.5 million for 1998, and the asterisk soon disappeared. We then wrote letters to our sponsors to reassure them and to confirm, at least, our business integrity. The storm passed.

It had been a warning shot across the bows, just to remind us who were the ringmasters of the F1 circus. We were like a young circus lion that had been told to keep quiet and get back on its perch with a short, sharp crack of the whip. It was quite funny, really. Our status as an independent team somehow seemed to have left us outside the inner circle of F1, and this may have resulted in a loss of privileges.

The Concorde Agreement is a confidential document setting down the terms by which F1 teams would compete in the races and then take their share of the television rights revenues and other sources of income, and its latest renewal had been signed on 5 September 1996 by all the existing F1 teams, except McLaren, Tyrrell and Williams, who had each refused to accept the conditions. SGP was not party to this deal, as we did not enter F1 until 1997, so we received no money for all the effort we put into our first year. These were serious issues, but I had been around long enough to understand such machinations went with the territory and they were nothing we couldn't handle.

In my own mind, I sensed 1998 could prove a tough year for the team. There were signs of progress in our quest for reliability, but our task had been complicated by two factors.

First, very late in the off-season, regulations were introduced that forced all F1 teams (a) to revert to using racing tyres with a tread and (b) to narrow the 'track' of the car. The FIA was eager to reduce the cornering speeds; to this end, treaded tyres would mean there was less rubber on the road, reducing the car's ability to grip the surface, and a narrower 'track' – the distance measured from the centre of the tyre on one side to the centre of the tyre on the other, both front and rear – would have the same effect of reducing cornering speeds. Their reasoning was beyond reproach, but it was the timing of the late changes that caused problems since the cars had been designed many months before. The cars would need to be adapted and, while the larger and richer teams could afford to make the adjustments and find speed elsewhere, it was going to be much more difficult for teams like us.

Second, we had decided to introduce a revolutionary carbon-fibre gearbox to save weight in the car. It was a calculated gamble and maybe ahead of its time.

'The cars could come right,' somebody said.

'Of course, they can,' I replied, 'and I'm not being negative. I am being realistic. If this is a year when things don't go well on the track, then we must over-deliver off the track.'

My thinking was straightforward. If we accepted it was going to take time for our cars to start performing consistently, producing regular podium finishes and challenging for the world championship, there was no point sitting in the corner and sulking – we had to get out there and find a new way to project a successful image to our sponsors, the media and the public worldwide.

'How can we do that? If our cars are retiring from every race, there's not much you can do.'

Wrong. To a great extent, the effects of a poor season on the track could be countered and compensated for by producing a truly outstanding performance off the track:

- SGP sponsor networking could be the most focused and efficient, promoting business-to-business opportunities;
- SGP launches and promotional events could be the best in the industry, raising all the standards;
- SGP corporate hospitality packages could build on the strong PSR foundations and be the best in F1;
- SGP garage and pit lane tours could be the most graphic, exciting and informative;
- SGP media relations could be the most effective;
- SGP personnel could be the best presented;
- SGP cars and transporters could be the cleanest and most immaculate in the paddock.

So we poured human resources into these areas. We knew we would not get by forever on just looking good, but this strategy would enable us to maintain our reputation for a season or two until the on-track performances began to improve.

The engineers were starting to grumble that they needed more space; the commercial staff were beginning to complain that they needed more offices. For some time it had become clear that, as a fast-growing F1 team, SGP would very soon have to move to larger and better-equipped premises. My mind was ticking over. Maybe such a move could become another way of proving SGP's quality in 1998; it would give us a reason to put on a bit of a show and stage a really impressive, high-quality official opening function.

People often talk about moving house as one of the most stressful experiences, and it's even worse for a F1 team. The operation is horrendously complex: everyone needs a new desk, a new phone and a new computer, and then there are vehicle jigs and machine tools and the rest of the manufacturing equipment to deal with, and then you have to dismantle the entire workshop and put it back together somewhere else. It can be chaos. Such change is incredibly disruptive, and it will lead to a drop-off of performance even today. However, by moving in 1998, SGP could turn something that people had always seen as a negative into a genuine opportunity. We made the decision and arranged to move from the factory in Tanner's Drive to much larger premises at Bradbourne Drive, just a few miles away. By doing so we could show all our sponsors that even if our racing results weren't what we all hoped for, we had total confidence in the future – and therefore, so should they. Under Andy Miller's direction, the logistical planning went smoothly, and the move was set for the end of March and the start of April, when the racing team were away for a fortnight, at the F1 Grands Prix in Argentina and Brazil.

We then prepared to stage an impressive opening of the new

factory, with HRH the Princess Royal as the guest of honour and an unprecedented procession of six competitive race cars, from our F1, F3 and Formula Vauxhall teams, moving through the streets of Milton Keynes from the old factory to the new. Securing permission from the traffic and police authorities was a major task, but the media response was very positive. The function was impressive in every respect, from a guest list that included Edsel Ford, Sir William Purves and Lord King to the pristine surroundings of an immaculate factory, and our sponsors seemed proud to be associated with SGP. Not for the first time, nor the last, paying attention to what might have seemed a relatively insignificant detail made all the difference.

'What sound system are we having?'

'A microphone and speakers,' came the reply.

'Have you thought this through? Are you sure everybody will be able to hear every word that is spoken?'

'We think it's OK.'

'Let's be certain. Can we get Roger Lindsay?'

Roger had packaged the sound systems at major pop concerts and events around the world and was recognised as one of the best in his industry. He would get the job done. Excellent sound is always a silent asset at a function: hardly anybody says anything if it's right, but everyone notices if it goes wrong. Paying a little more to get it absolutely right was always money well spent.

The season was turning out to be every bit as frustrating as we had feared, with neither car managing to finish the race in either Australia, Brazil or San Marino. There was an improvement at the Canadian Grand Prix in Montreal, where Rubens finished fifth and Jan came sixth, but we remained off the pace.

Our back-up plan came strongly to the fore on the weekend of the British Grand Prix at Silverstone. We had invited a group of VIP guests to attend the qualifying session on the Saturday, and they were standing by when the engines of both our race cars and also the spare car all blew up while still in the garage. Not one of the Stewart Fords had even got as far as the track.

'Oh well, these things happen,' I said cheerfully, trying to peer through the smoke which made it impossible to see one side of the garage from the other, and ushering our guests away. 'Shall we take a walk through the paddock?'

Working hard, I took them past every team and then guided them around the SGP transporter, where the rubberised floor was spotless and everything was neat and tidy.

'Look at these cabinets,' I told them. 'They're made by Lista in Switzerland, and they're the best in the world. You could say they are the Rolex of cabinet makers. That's craftsmanship of the highest quality. Feel how that drawer opens and closes.'

Each of them would try it, and they would be impressed; and each of them would be shown all the washers, nuts and split pins, in their allocated places. Then we would visit our truckies Paul Singlehurst and Drew Miller who had made sure the tyres were stacked, all impeccably aligned with the manufacturer's name at the top of the arc, highlighted in white.

You might read all this and think: so what?, but the combined effect of this careful presentation was to create a series of positive memories for our guests to take away. I would spend time with them, looking after them, relating stories from the past, and we would go to great lengths to make sure their travel plans worked well, bringing them in and out of the circuit by helicopter, and the food and drink in our motor home would be top class. We did all this to ensure our sponsors and their customers went home talking not about the engines blowing up but about the wonderful SGP hospitality.

By then, we had decided to release Jan Magnussen. It was unusual to replace a driver halfway through the year, but he was struggling to adapt to F1, and the blunt reality was that part of each team's income was, and remains, based on the total number of world championship points earned, so both drivers needed to deliver for sound financial reasons, and that wasn't happening. Jan was understandably not happy, but it was the right decision for the team. We signed Jos Verstappen, who had been released by BAR at the end of 1996 and was one of the very few experienced F1 drivers available in mid-season. The Dutchman tried hard, but we later decided to sign Johnny Herbert to partner Rubens in 1999. We hoped the experienced British driver, preparing for his eleventh season in F1, would bring maturity and consistency to our efforts.

There were other changes within the team at the end of 1998, notably the departure of Alan Jenkins. He had successfully designed SF1 for 1997, updated the car for 1998 and was well on the way to completing SF3 for the 1999 season. At all times, he gave heart, body and soul to the project, and he has since successfully deployed his design expertise in the diverse worlds of America's Cup yacht racing and Ducati motorcycles. Alan was replaced as technical director by Gary Anderson, a sound, practical designer with considerable experience.

We approached the 1999 season with renewed optimism and an updated car which appeared quick out of the box. Both Rubens and Johnny had qualified competitively at the Australian Grand Prix in Melbourne, the opening race of the year, and Paul and I were standing in the pit, just before the start.

Suddenly, I noticed smoke from the grid.

'There's a car on fire over there,' I said.

'It's your car,' said someone with a clearer view.

They were right. Moments before the start, Johnny's engine had burst into flames. Just as we were cursing our bad luck, exactly the same thing happened to a second car on the grid, and this time we didn't need anyone to tell us it was Rubens. The fire marshals dashed out to extinguish the flames, and it was announced that the start of the Grand Prix would have to be delayed.

It transpired the cars had had to wait longer than normal on the grid, following the warm-up lap, and this had caused intense heat, which split an oil line running along the side of the Cosworth engine. The oil had leaked on to the exhaust pipes, causing the fires. In the limited time available, the Cosworth engineers, assisted by our boys, did well to find a solution to the problem, which enabled Rubens to line up for the restart. He took the opportunity with both hands and finished fifth, which eased our team's embarrassment.

Rubens sustained his form in the Brazilian Grand Prix a month later and briefly led the race in front of his home crowd at the Interlagos circuit in São Paulo. It was a remarkable experience to hear the entire grandstand chanting his name, and then to see the white SF3 appearing over the crest of the hill. Sadly, there was no fairytale victory, and his engine blew on lap forty-two.

We were clearly making progress and starting to perform with genuine consistency: Rubens finished third in San Marino, Johnny came fifth in Canada and Rubens qualified on pole position in France, eventually finishing third. He then came eighth at Silverstone and took fifth place at the Hungarian Grand Prix. I had told Dr Mahathir and everybody else it would take five years for our team to be competitive, but it was starting to look as if we were reaching that stage sooner than planned. The spirits in the team were high, and people were smiling.

John Lindsay, my best friend, joined the team for the Belgian Grand Prix at Spa-Francorchamps and, dressed in full SGP regalia, he took himself off to watch a qualifying session from a particular corner at the back of the circuit. He has been a great enthusiast of motor sport ever since we worked together serving petrol at Dumbuck garage all those years ago, and he knows his stuff. On this particular Saturday at Spa, John returned to the pit after the qualifying session and eagerly started to explain how he had been listening to the throttle and he felt Rubens was lifting off too early on the entry to that particular corner.

'It's costing him close to a second on each lap,' he claimed.

'Well, go and tell him,' I replied.

So John walked over to Rubens and, without beating around the bush, told him exactly what he was doing wrong. The Brazilian driver listened politely and, even though he did not immediately recognise this animated Scotsman as a legendary F1 driver of the past, he accepted the advice in good heart and, to the amusement of everyone in the garage, said: 'Thank you so much, John. From now, I will call you Mr Driver!'

Rubens was once bitten, twice shy and, at subsequent races, he always made a point of asking which corner John was going to be watching. In fact, the quality of his driving through 1999 was such that he was recruited by Ferrari in 2000.

Our team was maturing to a point where the reliability issues were under control and we were performing with consistency. By the time we arrived at the Nurburgring to compete in the Grand Prix of Europe on 26 September 1999, we had earned the respect of the aficionados of the F1 motor racing press. Intermittent rain turned the race into a frenetic contest, with the various teams and drivers having to decide when to use wet tyres and when to use the 'drys', when to come into the pits to change and when to stay out.

David Coulthard took the lead on lap thirty-three, but then slid off; Ralf Schumacher took the lead, but then had a puncture; Giancarlo Fisichella took the lead, but then spun out . . . and all of this left Johnny Herbert in the Stewart-Ford coming through to take the lead with seventeen laps remaining.

They proved to be a very long seventeen laps. The fast-changing weather had turned the track into a bit of a lottery, and we were constantly looking at the sky, trying to judge whether the track would continue to dry out or whether another shower of rain would necessitate another tyre change, back to wets. We had to stay one step ahead of the game, whatever the conditions. At one point, I walked right down to the end of the pit lane to a place where I could get a clear view of the sky. Johnny kept the lead, and Rubens was soon pushing Trulli hard for second place. We were all on tenterhooks, glancing from monitors, to circuit, to the sky, and half hoping we may clinch a remarkable one-two finish. In the end, we settled for Johnny as the winner and Rubens in third.

Our first F1 victory may have had an element of good fortune, but the team had made the right decisions at the right time, the drivers had stayed on the track in very difficult circumstances and it seemed just reward for our steadily improving performances during the year. We were ecstatic; there is no other word.

As the winning constructor, I stood on the podium at the Nurburgring – the same place where I had stood twenty-six years before after my last F1 Grand Prix victory – and was presented with a large round glass plate. What a thrill it was to be back there, standing to attention and hearing 'God Save the Queen' play again. That trophy now sits on the table in the entrance hall at our home. I like to have it there where I see it every day because it has come to represent the collective achievement of a remarkable group of people.

The bare facts were that we had created a brand-new F1 team, and reached the victory podium within thirty-one months. Johnny and Rubens jubilantly drenched Paul and me in champagne at the end, but we didn't mind. In fact, after all the hard work and tough times, the bubbly had never tasted so good.

However, in the true Tyrrell-Stewart tradition, we didn't hang around long after the race and were soon all packed up and on our way to the airport to catch the flight home. The mobile phone rang in the car. It was Norbert Haug, the Mercedes-Benz Competitions Director, wanting to know where we were.

'You won,' he said to Paul. 'It's time to party.'

'I'm sorry, but we've already left the circuit,' he replied.

Old habits die hard, and that was just our way, but Paul and I were every bit as thrilled by our maiden Grand Prix victory as any other fledgling team would have been.

Not one ounce of the joy was taken away by the fact that, by then, we had negotiated the sale of Stewart Grand Prix, together with Paul Stewart Racing, to the Ford Motor Company for a handsome sum. The seeds of this deal had been sown as far back as the weekend of the Italian Grand Prix of 1998, when the concept was raised in informal discussions, and Paul, Rob Armstrong and I sat down and considered the pros and cons and relayed them to the board of trustees. Until then, I had been focused on building a strong business, and the thought of it being sold to anybody had not even crossed my mind.

'Would part of the business be up for sale?' asked somebody from Ford.

'You can buy up to 49 per cent,' I replied.

'No, we would want a controlling interest.'

'I know that won't work for us. If you want to control the company, you would have to buy the whole thing.'

Somebody connected to Ford subsequently mentioned a price that was way below our valuation, and nothing more was said.

In March 1999, I was in Dearborn working with Jac Nasser on a vehicle development project when he suddenly turned to me and, almost as a casual aside, mentioned Ford might be interested in buying the entire SGP business.

'Are you serious?' I asked.

'Sure,' he replied.

My mind flashed back to the discussion four years before, at the start of the project, when he asked if there was an alternative structure and I had said Ford could own the business and we would find sponsors and run it for them at cost plus 10 per cent. He had said the board wouldn't agree. It was maybe a sign of how far we had come that we were now talking about a cash sale.

'All right,' I said, 'let me think about that one.'

The idea that Ford should own, rather than just supply, a F1 team appeared to have been prompted not so much by one big decision but by a combination of factors.

First, Ford had entered a phase where it was buying companies that offered new capacity: they had bought Aston Martin and Jaguar, as premier vehicle manufacturers; they had bought a large percentage of Mazda, as a mass production vehicle producer; they had purchased Cosworth as respected experts in creating and producing high-performance engines. So it seemed to follow that they might wish to buy a F1 team.

Second, Jac Nasser had attended the Hungarian F1 Grand Prix and been impressed by the way Ferrari owned their own team and used the platform to market its expensive consumer sports cars. He felt there was no reason why Jaguar should not be able to do the same and, looking at all the Ferrari red caps in the crowd, he declared: 'Next year, we will make this a sea of green.'

I understood the logic. Ford's brand identity in motor sport seemed to have become muddled, and Jac was proposing to clean up the strategy by aligning Ford of America with NASCAR racing and Ford of Europe with rallying, and then to promote luxury brands such as Jaguar in F1 Grand Prix and, potentially, Aston Martin in world championship GT racing.

Third, one or two people within Ford had started to develop certain reservations about our team, both in the way it was being branded and in the way it was being run: there was muttering that the 'Stewart' name was being over-promoted to a point where it put Ford in the shade, but they didn't seem to appreciate that Stewart and Ford had been complementary, not competitive, in the sport for almost thirty-five years; and there was also some grumbling that we seemed unable to produce a reliable car, but these sentiments emanated from people with very little knowledge and even less experience of running a F1 team.

At various levels, for various reasons, the concept of owning a F1 team gathered momentum in Dearborn.

My response was cautious, because the team was moving in the right direction, and we were starting to compete on the fringes of the leading pack. On the other hand, I had become increasingly aware the task of taking the team to the next level, where we would challenge for constructors' and drivers' world championships, would require a large injection of money, to fund new technology and additional personnel. I believed I would be able to raise the funds from sponsors, but I knew it would not be easy. Paul and I discussed the matter with the trustees, and together we reached a tentative view that, if the price was right, we would sell.

That same March, Wolfgang Reitzle was appointed as head of Ford's new Premier Automotive Group. He arrived with a strong reputation from BMW, and it appeared he had been given the task of pulling the SGP deal together. Still no formal meeting was arranged, and it was one afternoon at Dearborn, again when I was working on other business, when Wolfgang turned to me and asked if we would accept an offer that was almost 50 per cent greater than the original sum mentioned.

Instinctively, I replied, 'That's still not enough. We haven't built the company to sell it, so the answer would be no.'

In the meantime, Ford were exploring the option of buying another F1 team, but their discussions with Benetton had broken down when Luciano Benetton said he was prepared to sell only half of the team, and Ford wanted all or nothing.

A couple of weeks later, I saw Wolfgang again and mentioned we would perhaps consider a higher offer for SGP. I named a price, but he responded by saying Ford would never pay that kind of money. However, the negotiations seemed to be gathering momentum.

Paul and I had been monitoring the issue on a regular basis in order to be able to report back to the trustees, and along with Rob Armstrong and Nigel Newton, our financial director, we had even given the matter its own secret name, Project Hilton, because we didn't want the rest of the SGP team to be destabilised or distracted by rumours. We also secured the help and guidance of Charles Milner from KPMG. When the stakes are so high, it's important to have experts at hand.

For their part, Ford assembled a cluster headed by the chief financial officer, John Devine, and including three senior executives: Neil Ressler and Richard Parry-Jones, both of whom I had known very well for many years, and Wolfgang Reitzle. They proceeded to conduct due diligence on SGP, which didn't take long. It had always been our policy to give Ford open access to our books, and the Ford analysts soon confirmed the business was transparent and squeaky clean.

Other discussions took place, and, at one stage, John Devine said he felt Ford should pay a wholesale price for SGP as opposed to a retail price, because they had helped build the company. I said the terms of Ford's involvement had been discussed, agreed and set down in a written contract. This made no mention of preferential terms to buy SGP, and therefore none existed.

A formal meeting was eventually arranged, and Paul, Charles Milner and I travelled across the Atlantic to meet John Devine, and another Ford man called George Joseph, at the Four Seasons hotel in New York City, a couple of blocks from Central Park. Our discussions lasted for several hours, with good spirit and good manners on all sides. We trusted John Devine as a man of considerable integrity, and, in the end, he said, 'Jackie, we can't pay what is being asked for SGP.'

'All right, John,' I replied. 'To make it happen, I think the owners would be prepared to include Paul Stewart Racing into the deal as well, and keep it at the price discussed.'

If SGP was going to be sold, there was no point keeping PSR and running a racing team in the formative classes.

John thought the proposal made sense and, after more discussion, said he would seek board approval.

The decisive meeting was set for 8 June 1999, and Paul, Helen and I arranged to be there in Dearborn, on our way to attend the Canadian Grand Prix in Montreal five days later. We agreed Paul would remain at the Ritz Carlton hotel with Helen, as he would more easily be able to start making calls from there, while I made my way down to world headquarters.

I was sitting in John Devine's office with Neil Ressler when the news arrived that the deal had been accepted by the board and I immediately phoned Paul and Helen. Paul then began calling the trustees, Rob Armstrong, Nigel Newton, the lawyers and accountants and the whole list of their people who needed to know what had happened. It was a strange feeling: on the one hand, there was a great degree of satisfaction in being part of completing what was a big deal, but there was also a measure of sadness at reaching the end of a journey that had started a decade before when we formed a small racing team to accommodate Paul as a driver.

Our main concern was that our staff should hear the news from us, so Paul travelled back to Milton Keynes to make the announcement at the factory, and I flew to Montreal to tell the race team, who were preparing for the Canadian Grand Prix.

'This is the best possible news for everyone,' I declared. 'Your jobs are safe, and Ford has the will and the resources to take this team to the next level. There's no downside.'

I also contacted each of our major sponsors, some of whom were not best pleased because, as one said, 'we invested in a family business'. However, we reassured them about the future and were later able to transfer every contract to the new owner.

Some of the Ford executives could scarcely contain their excitement. They seemed completely intoxicated by the glamour of F1 motor racing, and thrilled beyond words that they now owned a part of this world in which they had been just a guest. In fact, one or two of them turned up in Montreal and reckoned they should take over the running of the team there and then. I felt that was amazingly naive.

I called Jac Nasser, and it was agreed that we would continue running the team until the end of the 1999 F1 season, when a new management structure would be introduced and the name would change from SGP to Jaguar Racing. The period of transition was not entirely stress-free. Ford personnel began to hang around the pit during practice, shaking their heads.

'Unbelievable, unbelievable,' one of them kept muttering.

'Excuse me,' I would say. 'What is unbelievable?'

'The way this team is run is unbelievable.' And this from someone who knew nothing about the sport, as far as I was concerned.

Even so, we reached the end of the year with our win under our belts and, by 25 January 2000, a new management team moved in. It was an auspicious day – my mother's birthday and the first Burns Night of the new millennium – and I was more than ready to hand over the reins. Neil Ressler took my place as chairman and team principal, and Paul continued, working as the chief operating officer. It was agreed I would remain on the board, with specific responsibility for servicing sponsors and helping to find new commercial partners for Jaguar Racing.

Neil was a fine man, whom I had liked for many years, but he had only been in the Jaguar Racing job for eight months when he was forced to return to America when his daughter fell ill. His departure started a series of appointments that denied Jaguar Racing any sense of direction or stability. A revolving door seemed to have been installed in the CEO's office.

Neil was succeeded by Bobby Rahal, who had run various racing teams in America but had no experience of working in an environment as complex as F1. He was eventually succeeded as CEO by Niki Lauda, and the three-time world champion might have got it right, but other commitments meant he was unable to give the team his full and undivided attention.

Richard Parry-Jones had since become chairman and, in due course, he appointed as CEO Tony Purnell, a man with experience in electronic technology, sensoring devices and software, but who had never run a racing team, let alone a F1 team.

I continued to sit on the board throughout this period, and made a contribution by renewing the HSBC sponsorship and tying up various other deals, but it was not an enjoyable experience. From 2000 onwards, Jaguar Racing lost its way and its competitive edge, and it was starting to devour budgets larger than SGP had ever seen. There was never a lack of money, but there was a lack of direction, brought on, I am sure, by the constant changes at the top. Any organisation is bound to suffer from such a lack of continuity.

Somebody once noted that Ford's handling of Jaguar Racing was typical of a large multinational organisation trying to run a corner shop, and failing because successive CEOs simply did not appreciate the ins and outs of the business. It summed up the increasingly disappointing situation quite well.

Eventually, in August 2004, I resigned from the board of Jaguar Racing. Nick Scheele, then president of Ford worldwide, asked me not to make the decision public because he feared it could prompt concern, and I agreed.

Looking back, I believe that Stewart Grand Prix rates, by any measure, as an extraordinary success. In motor racing terms, we started a brand new F1 team from scratch, secured a second place within five months, won a Grand Prix within thirty-one months and finished fourth in the constructors' world championship within thirty-six months. In financial terms, the company made money in every single year and never, ever went into overdraft at the bank. If Paul and I were proud of our financial achievements at PSR, this, to us, was something even more exceptional. To have run a F1 team and to have stayed out of the red, and for the company not to have any equity partners, that may well be unique. In human terms, the project brought together a group who collectively started something special at PSR and then created something almost unprecedented at SGP. It would be impossible to name and thank all the people who made a contribution, but, I hope, each and every one of them continues to feel proud of what we achieved.

CHAPTER 17

Living and Dying

Iᴛ ᴡᴀs ᴛʜᴇ ꜰɪʀsᴛ ᴡᴇᴇᴋ ᴏꜰ Aᴘʀɪʟ 2000, and, by any measure, the Stewart family was thriving. Such times should always be enjoyed to the full because, in an instant, everything can change.

I remember it was early in the morning. Having just woken up in the Dorint hotel in the Dutch town of Eindhoven, I was starting to get ready for a day's work at the Ford of Europe testing ground in Lommel, across the border in Belgium. I recall precisely how the room was decorated and that I was sitting on the left-hand side of the bed when the telephone rang.

'Hello.'

'Hello, it's Paul.'

'Hello, darling, how are you?'

'I've got cancer.'

I literally froze on the bed. Such moments are engraved on your mind forever. My eldest son proceeded to explain how the doctors in America had called him at 11 o'clock the previous night and said the tests showed he was suffering from a very rare form of non-Hodgkins lymphoma. He and his wife Victoria had been up all night, coming to terms with the news.

'OK, darling,' I said. 'Don't worry. We'll sort this out.'

I didn't know how. My head was numb.

Paul had not been feeling well for some time. He had spoken to Professor Sid Watkins, who had arranged for him to see some doctors in London. He hadn't said anything to me because he didn't think the condition was too serious and he didn't want to worry me. Then, one day, Sid and I were chatting.

'I'm worried,' he said, out of the blue. 'It's being going on for too long.'

'What are you talking about?' I asked.

'This problem with Paul.'

'What problem?'

He told me the whole story. My immediate response had been to call Paul and suggest he get himself to the Mayo Clinic in Rochester, Minnesota, where they had the people and resources to give him a more profound examination. So he had flown there and had all the tests, and now we knew: it was cancer.

My first instinct was to phone Helen and talk things through, but then I thought again: maybe I ought to wait until I had spoken to the doctors at the Mayo; also, it would certainly be better to tell her in person. So I decided not to call.

The person who would be able to give me the full story on Paul was Professor Ian Hay, our family's point of contact at the Mayo, but it was early morning in Holland, the middle of the night in the US, so I was going to have to wait until late afternoon, which seemed a hideously long time. Trying to stay composed and calm, I headed off to start work at the test track.

There is a high-banked circuit in the facility at Lommel, and we were in the middle of a fast lap when my mobile phone rang. I answered. It was Ian Hay. I asked my colleagues to stop the car immediately, so we pulled over and came to a halt at the bottom of the banking. I climbed out and walked into the relative peace of some woods to take the call, just to get away from the noise of the other cars roaring around the circuit.

'Hello, Ian.'

'Jackie,' he said, 'we've got a problem with Paul. It's in the colon, and we'll have to get on with it.'

'Will he be OK?'

'I can't say until we've run some more tests, but I do think he should get back here as soon as possible.'

'He can do that, but will he be OK?'

'He's a strong, young man. I think we've caught it early enough.'

Almost without thinking, I found myself slipping into the same calm, clinical management mode that had always been my standard response when a friend was killed on the track. I tried to eliminate the emotion and be practical, working out what needed to be done, how to get it done, who I needed to contact. What could I do? When I was a F1 driver and something went terribly wrong, there was plenty to do, like making sure the driver's wife was looked after, helping to sort out the delicate issues and then getting involved in the wider campaign for safety. They were difficult days coping with the loss of people who mattered to me, but this felt so much harder because this was my son. This was Paul.

What could I do? I couldn't fight the cancer in his body. Only he could do that. The counsellors at the Mayo would help, but it seemed such a massive and unfair challenge for a thirty-four-year-old who had worked so hard to develop the racing team, a young man who was happily married, a father of three young children.

What I could do, I decided, was to make sure Paul was treated by the very best specialist in this field on the planet; not the second-best or the third-best, the very best. After seeking advice from qualified people, we arrived at the conclusion that his entire treatment should be handled at the Mayo Clinic. It was, in my experience, the most outstanding medical facility anywhere in the world, an opinion which was reinforced when I heard how his condition had been diagnosed. It transpired that Paul had arrived at the Mayo and had explained how the doctors in London reckoned he was suffering from good, old-fashioned chronic ulcerative colitis (CUC). Routine X-rays, a computerised tomographic (CT) scan and numerous blood tests performed at the Mayo revealed nothing sinister, but then, instead of booking another colonoscopy, Ian Hay decided to take a different approach and had arranged for another look directly at the colon, this time with a sigmoidoscope. The results of this study were then examined by a senior colon specialist, who considered the issue and eventually agreed with the diagnosis made in London.

'Don't worry, Paul,' he said. 'This is normal colitis. I'm so sorry you have had to come such a long way, but I'm going to put you in touch with a friend of mine who is based in Oxford. He's very good, and he'll look after you.'

So Paul left the Mayo at the end of the day and flew back to Europe, still believing there was no real problem, although he knew that the biopsy slides were still to be carefully examined.

Ian Hay wasn't entirely satisfied. He often says the Mayo Clinic is at its best when a doctor says, 'I know what I know, but the guy next door knows more,' and, adhering to this principle, he revisited the case with Dr Roger Dozois, the professor of surgery who had supervised the sigmoidoscope and taken a biopsy of the tissues.

'Roger, something seems not quite right.'

Dr Dozois was well respected on both sides of the Atlantic, and his wife was from Perthshire in Scotland. 'I know,' he replied. 'The appearance seems most unusual for ulcerative colitis.'

It would have been easy for Ian Hay and Roger Dozois to conclude their report and move on to the next needy patient but both men had seen many cases of colitis and, deep down, they sensed something was different. So they kept looking and asked six expert pathologists at the Mayo to examine Paul's biopsy and give an opinion. Finally, they made the diagnosis – it was not colitis, it was a very rare form of non-Hodgkins lymphoma, and it was life-threatening.

I have often wondered what if . . . what if Ian Hay had not persisted and asked for somebody else to look at the biopsy, what if Roger Dozois had not believed something was unusual, what if the cancer had gone undetected and been left to grow and spread through Paul's body. It's not an exaggeration to say that Ian and Roger effectively saved my son's life.

Paul immediately flew back to the Mayo Clinic, where it was decided he would need a potent dose of chemotherapy every three weeks for a period of six months. Our decision that he would be solely treated at the Mayo meant he was going to be incessantly flying back and forth across the Atlantic. Some people reckoned this travelling was unnecessary, and they told us so.

'The drugs are pre-prepared,' they said. 'It's like Scotch whisky, and it won't make any difference whether he gets the chemo here in the UK or over there in America.'

That wasn't true. The hassle of flying to Rochester, Minnesota for each session was a price worth paying because, on every visit to the Mayo, he was going to be treated by the same oncologist, Professor Tom Witzig, who would constantly analyse the blood counts and therefore be in a position to adjust the cocktail of drugs as and when necessary. So far as we knew, this kind of personal treatment was simply not available in the UK. If this was what we wanted, we had to go to America.

A week passed before I found the right moment to sit down and break the news to Helen. I remember we were sitting in our London apartment when I told her. She was shocked, but she was also strong – it was almost as if, like me, she had been thrown back three decades, back to the days when she used to sit on the pit wall and have to cope with the consequences of a racing accident. 'We'll deal with this,' she said. 'At least, this explains why you've been acting so strangely over the past few days.'

It was a tough time. At one point, Paul's chances of recovery were put at no better than 50/50, and I began to understand what people mean when they say cancer is a disease that affects not just the patient but the entire family. We were all suffering, and each of us dealt with the crisis in our own way. I started wandering into places of worship even more often than usual, to sit and pray my son would get well. And my fear or superstition of looking at cemeteries, held in check for thirty years, returned. At other times, when nobody else was around, when I didn't have to be strong for anyone, I would sit and think about what was happening, and tears would fill my eyes, and a lump would grow in my throat. It was a terrible period, and I hated feeling so helpless and unable to control something that was so critical to Paul, to Victoria and the children, to Helen, to Mark and to me.

Paul had been losing weight for some time, and this prompted some wild rumours in the F1 community: one said he had become addicted to cocaine, another suggested he had AIDS. When this gossip percolated into the Italian media, I contacted Sir Tim Bell, the PR guru, and asked him what we should do.

'Just tell the truth,' he advised.

So we sat down together and prepared a press release, which announced Paul's illness, confirmed his resignation as chief operating officer of Jaguar Racing and included a statement from Jac Nasser, president of the Ford Motor Company, as the team owners, supporting his decision and wishing him well for a swift recovery. The public response to the news was overwhelming, and the avalanche of support and good wishes from the F1 community and beyond took us all by surprise. I remember a banner was held up at the Monaco Grand Prix reading 'GET WELL PAUL'. Wherever I happened to be in the world, but especially in Scotland, strangers would come up and ask me about my son. In fact, even now, years later, it's amazing how many people still ask.

Hair loss is a common side-effect of chemotherapy, and, early in his treatment, counsellors at the Mayo advised Paul to get himself a very short haircut, so the children would be less shocked when he went bald. This proved sound advice, but it was the loss of his eyebrows and eye lashes that seemed to have the greatest impact, making him look so haggard and so gaunt.

On one occasion, we took Paul to watch the horse trials at Gatcombe Park, and I sensed friends were genuinely shocked by the way he looked. For many cancer sufferers, dealing with the actual disease is only part of the challenge because they also have to deal with the way people react to their appearance. The day at Gatcombe was not easy. We had bought a couple of fleece-lined bomber jackets for Paul and me to wear, just to make sure he kept warm because the chemotherapy made him vulnerable to infection, but, even so, he became weak and tired, and he was physically sick. At one stage, I looked across at him and saw he had fallen sound asleep in his chair.

However, day by day, flight by flight, Paul worked through his treatment and, thank God, made a full recovery. We will always be grateful to the staff at the Mayo Clinic.

I first became aware of this remarkable institution in 1978, following the death of Gunnar Nilsson. He was a tall, athletic and handsome Swede who drove for the Lotus F1 team in 1976 and 1977 but was then diagnosed with testicular cancer and suddenly, brutally reduced to a shadow of his former self. He fought the disease with courage and, even though he was already seriously ill, he made a special effort to attend the funeral of his compatriot Ronnie Peterson, who had died following an accident in the 1978 Italian Grand Prix at Monza. Gunnar was too weak to be a pall-bearer, but he was determined to walk beside his friend's coffin and pay his last respects. Five weeks later, he died at the Charing Cross Hospital in London.

Typically, his last wish had been that a group of his friends should raise money to buy a new MRI scanner for the hospital. It was going to cost £450,000, so a trust was formed with art dealer David Mason as chairman, and Prince Bertil of Sweden, Mario Andretti and me as the three patrons. We set to work, staging a series of fund-raising events, including a race and demonstration day at Donington Park in which Juan Manuel Fangio took part and a tennis challenge between Björn Borg and Vitas Gerulaitis at the National Exhibition Centre in Birmingham. We also received a large donation from the proceeds of the F1 Race of Champions at Brands Hatch, and we exceeded our target. In the end, we raised almost £3 million, which was enough not just to buy the MRI scanner, but also to build an extension to house it and to pay the specialist staff required. HRH the Princess Royal duly opened the Gunnar Nilsson Wing at the Charing Cross Hospital, and the Gunnar Nilsson Cancer Foundation is still going strong in Sweden today.

Helen and I attended the funeral in Helsingborg and then flew back to London, from where I had to catch the Concorde flight to New York. As I settled into my usual seat, 1A – securing the same seat was one of the benefits of flying so regularly to the US, as many as forty-three times in one year – I was not in the mood for chatting, but the man who happened to be sitting beside me was a motor racing enthusiast, and we started to talk.

He turned out to be a professor of pathology, an Englishman based in Oxford who had strong connections with a cancer research programme in the USA. It transpired his unit in America had just received a large contribution for cancer research from the US Government, and they were deciding how to spend it. I told him how I had just come from burying a friend who had died of cancer and I explained how Gunnar had been struck down in his prime.

'How can somebody avoid that?' I asked. 'I don't want to check out unnecessarily early.'

'Regular and extensive check-ups,' he answered, without any hesitation. 'That's your best option.'

'At any hospital?'

'No,' he said. 'I'm British, but I don't know of any medical facility in the UK that gets sufficient funding to create the kind of infrastructure that is required to offer the level of analysis that I am talking about. So far as I know, there are four in the US: the Memorial Sloane Kettering Cancer Center in New York City, the Johns Hopkins Hospital in Baltimore, the Massachusetts General Hospital in Boston and the Mayo Clinic in Rochester, Minnesota.'

He went on to explain how a comprehensive annual check-up can provide substantial peace of mind for a mature person because the human metabolism often slows down beyond the age of forty, and, if anything does appear during the examination, it would very likely be at an early stage and be entirely treatable.

He continued: 'You need to find a torch bearer at one of these institutions, and he or she will then manage your case and make sure you see the right people in every area of medicine. If any problem crops up between your annual check-ups, this person could arrange for tests to be done in Geneva or London, and the results would then be sent electronically to the US and be considered by specialists who are intimately aware of your medical history.'

'It sounds impressive,' I said. 'So how do I go about finding myself a torch bearer?'

'Well, let me give you the contact details of someone I know at the Mayo Clinic. His name is Professor Richard Reitemeier. Give him a call, and he'll be pleased to see you.'

I booked my first check-up at the Mayo Clinic in 1979, and

Helen and I have returned religiously each and every year. Professor Reitemeier provided us with an outstanding service, and, when he retired in 1988, we were passed into the care of Professor Ian Hay, who was maybe not completely aware of what he was taking on because he has looked after not only the Stewart family but also more than 600 of our friends and acquaintances, whom I have referred for treatment at the Mayo. Ian Hay is a tremendously hard-working Scot, an expert in his field, a consummate professional and always available at the end of a telephone when you need to speak to him. He is a living embodiment of the Mayo Clinic, and the quality of service it provides.

As time has passed, I have come to realise preventative medicine is considerably less painful and less expensive than corrective medicine, so Helen and I strive to stay healthy by eating well and taking regular exercise. I worked out in public gymnasiums for many years and knew how much I benefited, physically and mentally, from maintaining a reasonable level of fitness. We have recently built a gym at home, and installed the equipment that suits the needs of people at our mature stage of life. I use weights, but not heavy weights because I'm not interested in building bulk. Gerard Gray, my trainer, has introduced me to the benefits of stretching and three ninety-minute sessions each week usually does the job.

Aside from eating well and keeping fit, Helen and I make sure we schedule our annual visits to the Mayo. These check-ups take two full days, from 7 a.m. to 6 p.m., and they include blood tests, electrocardiograms, lung and chest X-rays, ultrasound scans of the heart and abdomen, stress tests, a full body examination by a dermatologist and almost certainly an MRI or CT scan. In addition, we discuss any ailment that may be causing us concern, however minor it may seem, and the issue is investigated by an appropriate specialist. All tests are taken in the morning, and the results come back that same afternoon, so we return to Professor Hay's office at around 4 p.m. each day to be told the outcomes of all our tests and examinations and, importantly, how they compared with our results in previous years. Such prompt and efficient analysis means that, if any treatment is necessary, it can be started without delay.

We have had a few anxious moments over the years. In 2002, our check-ups produced the shattering results that Helen needed treatment for breast cancer and that I could be suffering from a heart problem. Again slipping into crisis management mode, I sat down with Ian Hay to locate the top specialists in the breast cancer unit and, within a few hours, Helen and I were attending a meeting of four Mayo professors as they discussed every aspect of her case and debated whether or not she would need an operation, whether she would then require radiotherapy or chemotherapy, and finally what follow-up drugs ought to be prescribed. In my case, an echo-cardiogram had suggested there could be a blockage in an artery at the back of my heart, and the professors said open-heart surgery may be necessary.

It was a Friday afternoon and, after much scurrying around, it was arranged that I would have my operation, if it was required, on the Monday, and Helen would have hers on the Tuesday. It had been an eventful and stressful day, to say the least, but we trusted the Mayo and we felt completely comfortable that everything was in hand.

'OK,' I told the doctors, 'we'll see you on Monday morning.'

'What?'

'We'll be back here on Monday. I have an appointment at Ford in Detroit tomorrow.'

'There's no way you can fly.'

'I'm sorry, there's no way I can miss this meeting.'

They could hardly believe their ears, but the fact was I had planned to have dinner with Jac Nasser at the Ritz Carlton hotel in Dearborn on Saturday night, and it was important because we were going to agree a new three-year contract with Ford. I felt absolutely fine and said I didn't see any reason to cancel the trip. In the end, the doctors agreed to let Helen and me go, but only on condition that I take beta blockers to keep me calm and regulate my heartbeat.

All went well, at least until the Sunday morning, when we decided to take a stroll around the Somerset mall, outside Detroit, before flying back to the Mayo. I was walking up a broad staircase in the shopping centre, when the beta blockers suddenly kicked in and I found myself struggling to reach the top. I just ran out of steam.

At any rate, we completed the return trip without further alarm and, by Sunday evening, on schedule, we were back at the Marriott hotel in Rochester, which is conveniently connected to the clinic by an underground walkway. I reported on time early on Monday morning, and was taken away to be prepared for my coronary angiogram and a possible cardiac surgical procedure. The next thing I recall is waking up from the general anaesthetic and instinctively running through a meticulous routine that racing drivers are advised to follow after an accident, where they take time to feel each limb, finding out exactly what hurts and what doesn't. First I moved my hands . . . no problem; then my arms . . . still no problem; then my shoulders . . . fine; feet, legs, stomach, chest and head . . . all fine. It was very odd. After what I thought had been open-heart surgery, I was feeling absolutely fine, which put me in a state of considerable confusion until Professor Tajik arrived and explained that, before cutting me open, the doctors had decided to put me through a thorough coronary angiogram to confirm the diagnosis.

'We were just putting on our belt and braces,' the professor said, borrowing one of my favourite phrases.

The angiogram had provided them with a much more

reassuring picture. I definitely had coronary disease but, fortunately, there were only 40 per cent obstructive lesions, and they therefore felt there was now no need for either a stent or a bypass. Nothing had needed to be done, except stricter medical management (a baby aspirin, a cholesterol-lowering drug, weight loss, and even more regular exercise!).

'Hello, darling,' I said, bouncing into Helen's room.

She was shocked to see me, but then relieved to hear what had happened. I was particularly pleased because I would be able to remain with her through her own ordeal the next day.

That operation went well and, when her doctors prescribed a course of radiotherapy, we had to decide where Helen was going to be treated. One option was to stay at the Mayo and have everything done there, but she preferred to return to the UK, where she would be surrounded by our dogs and her home comforts. No problem, I thought. The front door of the Royal Marsden hospital in London was no more than 60 yards from our apartment. It was not so simple. The Marsden turned out to be fully booked for the next four months. They offered treatment at their sister hospital in Surrey, but Helen would then have had to make the three-hour round trip almost every day for six weeks.

We eventually arranged for her to be treated at the Cromwell Hospital in London, but even that was not completely satisfactory because they could not guarantee she would have the same technician on each visit. I was disappointed and frustrated, but these seemed to be the realities of the limited facilities and resources available for cancer care in the UK – and Helen had private medical insurance; I suspect that organising treatment would have been even more difficult and more stressful if we had been relying on the National Health Service.

Helen made a full recovery, which was a great relief to us all. However, nobody is ever bullet-proof, and, like Paul, she continues to be regularly monitored. For all the exceptional medical advances in recent years, cancer remains a formidable foe.

It may seem unusual for two members of the same family to be diagnosed with cancer within the space of two years. In 2003, the Stewarts made it three cases in three years.

In the course of my 2003 check-up, a dermatologist found traces of a malignant tumour in my cheek. There was no scab, lump or roughness, but he spotted an abnormality on the skin, took a biopsy, placed the suspicious area of my cheek under an intensive magnifying lamp and was able to make the diagnosis. The mass was removed within a week, and I was left with thirty-five stitches inside and out and a slight scar. I didn't think anybody would notice, but a press photographer then took a photograph of me during a media conference to announce the arrival of Niki Lauda as CEO of Jaguar Racing, and there was no hiding from his zoom lens. People began asking questions, and I was forced to issue a brief statement clarifying what had happened.

Inevitably, the seriousness of the problem was exaggerated in some of the media coverage that followed. In truth, the vigilance of the Mayo Clinic staff had dealt with a minor problem that, left unnoticed, could have become severe.

Once again, I felt our rigorous approach to getting the best possible medical treatment had been vindicated. Few people go to the trouble of having regular check-ups. Instead, they only see the doctor when they have symptoms. Then, by the time the problem is properly diagnosed, it may have spread to other areas and reached a stage where it can no longer be managed. The mathematical reality is that a high proportion of us will encounter cancer at some stage of our lives, and it is surely better to face up to the risk, identify a problem as soon as possible, use the latest treatment to stamp on it and move on.

'Oh no,' people sometimes say to me. 'If there is something wrong with me, I would rather not know.'

What good is that to the people who are left behind?

I realise, of course, that regular health checks are not generally available to those who can't afford to pay for them privately. But it is always worth checking with and pushing the local health centre – check-ups may well be provided for those with hereditary problems. It is certainly worth making the effort to find out.

The core concept of the Mayo Clinic is to assemble the best doctors and specialists, provide them with the best equipment and so stimulate a continuing quest for excellence. This structure produces established geniuses in each field, and everyone respects and admires them. However, over the years, I have learned to keep an eye out for 'the coming man'.

In medicine, as in F1 motor racing and in business, it often happens that the acclaimed 'big name' is past his peak, and, to find the very best, you need to look further. For example, if I needed a quadruple bypass in the 1970s or early 1980s, most people would have said I should see Christiaan Barnard because the South African heart pioneer was universally admired. However, by then, he may have been out of practice because he was spending less time in an operating theatre and more time travelling, addressing conferences and informing people about the latest advances. Reputations, by definition, are built on past performance and, so, at any given moment, being the most famous is not always the same as being the best. If you want to find the top person, it's often not a bad idea to peer beyond the limelight, to look past the name in lights and try to identify the coming man.

The Mayo Clinic attracts the top medical minds, of today and tomorrow, not by offering the highest salaries – a specialist with a private practice in Harley Street, London, could earn more – but by providing its 2,500 consultants, including about 500 professors, with a unique environment that incorporates:

Championship Season 1973

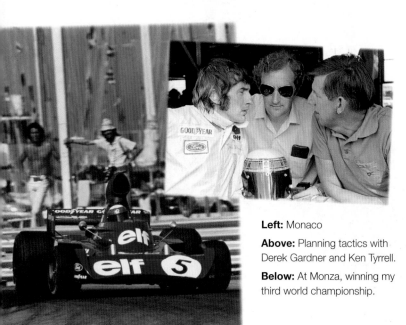

Left: Monaco

Above: Planning tactics with Derek Gardner and Ken Tyrrell.

Below: At Monza, winning my third world championship.

François Cevert

Above: A Tyrrell 1-2 in the 1971 French Grand Prix.

Right: Watkins Glen, US Grand Prix 1973. The day before François died.

Jackie's torment

By Philip Finn

JACKIE STEWART yesterday quit the U.S. Grand Prix—for the sake of his wife Helen.

And because another of his nine friends was dead.

Now there seems little doubt that world champion Stewart will not drive in a race again.

He may quit for Helen after racing partner dies

Nine friend

SPARE from Frances Cevert, Jackie Stewart had two other special friends the would like also be around by racing travelling.

They were Jochen Rindt, who died in September 1970 in the cockpit practice for the Italian Grand Prix, and Piers Courage, also

THE AGONY OF JACKIE STEWART

He quits big race after his friend is killed

From SYDNEY YOUNG in Watkins Glen

WORLD champion racing driver Jackie Stewart pulled out of the US Grand Prix yesterday for the sake of his wife Helen.

Clockwise from top left: Edsel Ford; François Guiter; Working for ABC at the Braemar Gathering; Henry Ford; Helen and I with Lord King on his 80th birthday.

Paul Stewart Racing

Left: Snetterton 1989. Paul Stewart, winner of the British F3 championship race.

Below: David Coulthard on the PSR staircase of talent in 1991. I'm sure he is listening to my every word...

Stewart Grand Prix

Above: The beginning

Left: Monaco 1997. Schumacher led Barrichello in practice. And that's the way i finished on race day. Our first podiun in only our fifth Grand Prix

Top-bottom: Nurburgring 1999. On the podium again, 26 years after my final F1 victory, as winning constructor. With SGP scoring a remarkable first (Herbert) and third (Barrichello)…

…we had a lot to celebrate.

Frank Williams: 'If your team ever wins a Grand Prix I'll wear a pair of your tartan trousers.'

Japan 1999. The end.

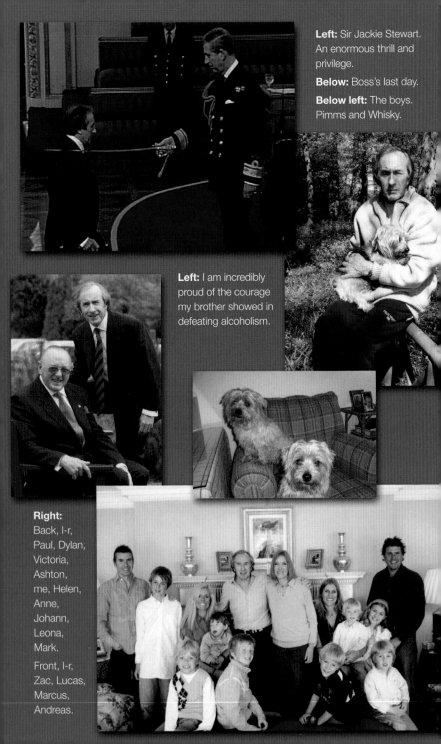

Left: Sir Jackie Stewart. An enormous thrill and privilege.

Below: Boss's last day.

Below left: The boys. Pimms and Whisky.

Left: I am incredibly proud of the courage my brother showed in defeating alcoholism.

Right:
Back, l-r, Paul, Dylan, Victoria, Ashton, me, Helen, Anne, Johann, Leona, Mark.

Front, l-r, Zac, Lucas, Marcus, Andreas.

- outstanding administration and technical support,
- the very latest equipment,
- the opportunity to focus on one specific field,
- the time and resources to conduct research, and
- the prospect of addressing conferences worldwide.

It's easy to understand why so many high-quality people work at the Mayo, and why so few leave. The clinic in Rochester offers nineteen floors of investigative medicine, and is connected by walkway to two fully equipped hospitals. Such service does come at a significant price for international visitors, but the Mayo is far from an elite institution for Americans, where the availability of health care plans means you will very often find the farm worker sitting beside the millionaire farm owner in the waiting room.

My enthusiasm for the institution, and the number of people I have referred to it, has prompted some people to suggest I am on some kind of commission. That's not true. All I have ever taken from the Mayo Clinic is outstanding treatment, for which I have been extremely happy to pay. Why do I refer people? Simply because, in that terrible, devastating and often very confusing moment when you learn that either you or a loved one is suffering from a life-threatening illness, I believe there is no better place to be treated than the Mayo Clinic.

The effort I put into staying alive might suggest I am overly concerned about the prospect of dying. On the contrary, after living through a motor racing career where the sight and smell of death seemed to lurk at every corner, perhaps, like a soldier in war, I have seen so much that I am almost immune to the shock. Of course, I want to live as long as possible because I feel I still have so much to do and I want to see our eight grandchildren grow up, but I am not afraid of dying. In fact, I believe death is nothing more than a transition because the human soul endures. When a friend or loved one passes away, we don't see them any more, but they don't just disappear into thin air. Their spirit remains among us. Not a day passes without me feeling the certain physical presence of someone who has died, whether it's my mother or my father, or Jim Clark, or Jochen Rindt, or François Cevert, or Graham Hill, or Allan Jones. They're all around me, and it's not a hunch – I have no doubt.

Whenever my mind turns to the question of living or dying there is one man who often comes to my mind.

I first met Nando Parrado during practice at the 1972 Grand Prix of Argentina. This 19-year-old, who looked very much the worse for wear, had been a member of the Uruguayan rugby team whose plane crashed in the Andes and who had survived for more than nine weeks in arctic conditions. Only ten days previously, he and a fellow survivor, Roberto Canessa, had walked to safety and raised the alarm. 'Walked to safety.' Those words do not encapsulate what they endured. You don't just walk out of the Andes. They had mountains to climb and suffered the disappointment of more than one failed attempt. Their extraordinary tale rightly attracted worldwide attention, in the book *Alive* and as a feature film.

His ears and eyelids were severely damaged by the torturous reflection of the sun on the snow and ice and the incredibly low temperatures, but nothing could quench this remarkably mature young man's enthusiasm for motor sport and his inspiring passion for life. He spent most of that weekend with the Tyrrell team, and impressed everybody he met.

A year or so later, Nando gave Paul the very chain and cross worn by his mother when she died in the air crash. Today, I would not only count his recently published book, *Miracle In The Andes*, as one of the best I have ever read, I would also count Nando, Veronique and their two daughters among the closest friends of the Stewart family.

In the words of the song, there is a time to live and a time to die, and this is my time to live. For as long as I can remember, I have been intensely driven by a need to succeed, and prove over and over and over again that I'm not as stupid as I was made to feel at school. At stages, I have wondered if this urge has made me so focused on my work, my schedule and the next project that I have never been able to relax and sit back. I feel as if there's an engine inside me, relentlessly propelling me to the next meeting or public appearance and, after all these years, I haven't found the 'off' switch. Clearly there is a balance to be struck between time spent working in the garden and time spent smelling the roses, and I don't think I have ever quite found it. Even so, organising my life at the 'work' end of the spectrum has not stopped me getting along with people who function at the other end.

One example is Bob Longhi. He was a successful insurance salesman in Washington, DC, a man of 'average height' who cut a dashing figure in a collar and tie, three-piece suit and Homburg. In 1976, he decided to give his employees the bonus of a holiday on the island of Maui, the second-largest and most beautiful island in Hawaii, and he decided he would go along with them just to make sure they all had a good time. In fact, he enjoyed himself so much that he stayed an extra week, and another, and another. More than thirty years later, he's still there. He simply fell in love with the place and decided there was more to life than rushing around a big city. Bob opted out of all that and opened his own restaurant on Front St, Lahaina. Longhi's was soon doing such a roaring trade that today he owns no fewer than three thriving restaurants on the island.

Helen and I well understood Maui's appeal. In fact, together with Mark McCormack, we co-owned a condominium there for fifteen years. It was beautiful but it was a twenty-five-hour trip from home, so we didn't visit as often as we'd have liked. Whenever we were in town, we ate regularly at Longhi's, and I used to sit there, and see what he had created and admired the choice he had made.

I was introduced to Bob Longhi by his friend George Harrison, another remarkable man who appeared to live his life at the more relaxed end of the spectrum. We had been talking about our respective ideas of paradise, when George said that he had bought a 250-acre property on Maui. 'It's an amazing place,' he said. 'You must take Helen there as soon as you get the chance and, when you arrive, make sure you go to meet Bob Longhi and eat at his restaurant.'

So we did, and we kept going back.

George was an extraordinary musician and the sweetest of men, and, over the years, I grew to adore his gentle nature, his music, his deep spirituality and his friendship. We first met when The Beatles turned up at the Monaco Grand Prix in 1969, then we saw each other at subsequent F1 races. From the start, we got along: he visited us in Switzerland, we visited his home near London and we spent a lot of time together. George enjoyed motor racing, and he got to know several of the racing folks quite well; that was his way – he seemed to move so comfortably among any group of people. In 1979, he wrote and released a single called 'Faster'. The chorus ran:

Faster than a bullet from a gun
He is faster than everyone
Quicker than the blinking of an eye
Like a flash you could miss him going by
No one knows quite how he does it but it's true they say
He's the master of going faster

Recalling these lyrics still brings a smile to my face because I can just see George sitting somewhere, taking it easy, getting an idea in his head and then scribbling the words on the back of a cigarette packet. That was his genius.

The legend on the cover of 'Faster' explained the record was 'inspired by Jackie Stewart and Niki Lauda and dedicated to the entire F1 circus' and noted that all proceeds would be donated to the 'Gunnar Nilsson Cancer Fund', which just went to show how close George felt to our world.

We had some fun shooting the music video for 'Faster', in which I made a cameo acting appearance as George's driver, wearing a chauffeur's hat with a tartan band, in the same style as my old racing helmet. I drove the Daimler while, on the other side of a glass partition, George sat in the back, strumming on his guitar and singing the song.

As time passed, we became close, which seemed to confirm the old saying that opposites attract. While I liked to organise my life with military precision, George took a more laid-back approach. I remember one time when we were at an airport and I was starting to worry whether we were going to get to the boarding gate on time. George just smiled and said he wanted to get a cup of tea.

'OK,' I fretted, 'but I don't think we have time.'

'There's always time for a cup of tea,' he said.

'Well, it's getting late.'

'Don't worry, we can get the next plane.'

'No, we can't.'

'Jackie, why would you want to spoil a cup of tea?'

If we had been dropped from the same height, George would have been a feather, drifting this way and that on the breeze, and I would have been a lead weight plunging straight down: the point is we would have both got there in the end.

There were times when we could have been living on different planets, times when George was procrastinating over what to do and I would be decisive and all action, or wearing amazingly casual and way-out clothes when I would be more traditionally dressed. Yet there were many other times when we seemed so similar, paying the same fanatical attention to detail.

He could be amazingly fastidious, keeping his cars immaculately clean and taking such care and time over his gardens, both at his home near Henley, England and in his tropical paradise on Maui.

This determination to get things exactly right extended to his music. George would work and work until the song was totally as he wanted it to be – not just right, but precisely right, so precisely right that it would almost sound as if it had evolved naturally, out of nothing, dreamily and effortlessly.

We shared many wonderful times. On one occasion, when he was staying with us in Switzerland, we decided to go and watch the French Grand Prix in Dijon. It was not far, so we drove there and back on the same day, and it was a fantastically clear and warm evening when we arrived home. Helen had prepared a barbeque, and Paul, who was twelve at the time, brought out his guitar. George seemed so completely at ease and he just started to play, running through all the great Beatles hits, singing parts of the songs and explaining what the lyrics meant to various members of the band. I remember sitting there and thinking this had to be one of the greatest privileges anybody could have, to enjoy such a perfect evening at home with such a remarkable man.

George had such a great soul, full of understanding. His instinct was always to forgive rather than to condemn and, when people behaved badly, he would make excuses for them. I learned so much from him, and all of us – Helen, Paul, Mark and I – grew to love him; and, I think, he loved each of us.

Another time, we were together at the 1985 Australian Grand Prix at Adelaide, and, after the race, on the spur of the moment, I asked him if he wanted to go to Queensland.

'A friend of mine owns an island near the Great Barrier Reef,' I said. 'We're going to fly up there privately and relax for a few days. Do you know Keith Williams?'

Almost everyone in Australia had heard of Keith Williams,

as dynamic and charismatic an entrepreneur as that country has ever produced. We first met in 1964, when he attended a motor race at Brands Hatch. I later drove at his circuit during the Tasman Series and won a Surfers' Paradise twelve-hour race there. He had been the Australian waterski champion, and I admired his energy in creating first the Cypress Gardens waterski resort on the Nerang River, and the Sea World resort on the Gold Coast of Queensland. His new project was to develop Hamilton Island, and he had suggested that a few of us fly up there and see what he had in mind. George agreed to join us and, together with Barry Sheene, the British motorcycling champion, our group boarded a Falcon 20 aircraft and flew to an airfield at a place called Proserpine, from where we travelled by boat and finally arrived at Keith's paradise island.

Keith outlined his plans to construct a fully serviced resort, with its own marina, condominiums and private homes. At a later stage, he reclaimed land from the sea to build a runway large enough for wide-bodied jet aircraft because he believed this would be crucial to maximise the potential for tourism. The resort proved a great success, and, even though he took a hit during the recession of the early 1990s, Keith has bounced back and is now developing a new resort at Port Hinchinbrook, further up the coast, between Townsville and Cairns. Helen and I always take time to visit Keith and his wife Thea when we are in Australia.

On that particular week in 1985, George was so smitten by the beauty of Hamilton Island that he decided to buy a piece of land, on which he later built a wonderful house.

We saw more of George, his wife Livy and their son Dhani in the late 1990s, when we started to spend an increasing amount of time in England, and we always enjoyed our visits to their home at Friar Park. It was an extraordinary mansion built by the eccentric Sir Frank Crisp, with small friars' heads everywhere from the light fittings to the window frames, some laughing, some scowling. The house was variously used as a school, a hospital and a home for Catholic nuns until it was bought by the Harrisons. George took great pride in restoring the magnificent house and garden to its original state, reviving the underground canals and restoring a 60-foot mountain modelled on the Matterhorn in Switzerland, complete with its own alpine flowers and streams. He spent endless hours contentedly tending to the plants. 'I'm a gardener,' he would say. 'The gardener is the ultimate creator, spreading beauty and colour, giving order to the living world, his feet planted squarely on earth.'

George was diagnosed with lung cancer in 2001 and he fought the disease bravely, travelling around the world and trying many different kinds of treatment in search of a cure. He spent some time in Lugano, in Switzerland, and it was there that he was once visited by Ringo Starr. Ringo later told me that even though he was by then very weak and confined to bed, George listened intently as his old friend told him about some problem he was facing.

'Anyway, I'll have to go and sort it out,' Ringo said. 'That's a trip I'm not going to enjoy.'

'Well, look,' said George, trying to sit up in bed, 'would you like me to come with you?'

That was typical.

On the morning of 29 November 2001, Helen and I were getting ready for the day, standing in our suite at the Gleneagles hotel, where we had attended a dinner the previous evening. A news flash was broadcast on the television: George Harrison had died in Los Angeles. Paul rushed in a few moments later. We had known he was seriously ill and feared the worst, but the news was still a shock. We stood arm in arm, in tears.

Six months later, the entire Stewart family – Helen and I, Paul and Victoria, Mark and Anne – attended an unforgettable memorial service held in a sunken area of the garden at Friar

Park, where George had installed a sandstone gable end rescued from a Glasgow church that had been damaged during the war. The service was led by Brother Mitrananda, a monk from the Self-Realisation Fellowship, a spiritual organisation of Eastern origin founded by Paramahansa Yogananda in 1920. He spent a great deal of time with George in California, and handled the occasion with great depth and dignity. It was a beautiful day, so simple and so perfect.

We have stayed very close to Livy and Dhani, who has grown up to bear such a striking resemblance to his father, both in his appearance and his mannerisms.

For me, George was a true friend who opened my eyes to so much that I would otherwise not have seen, and who in his calm, gentle way gave me a new perspective on living and dying.

CHAPTER 18

Shooting Days

THE IDEAL CHARITY EVENT IS A GATHERING where a substantial amount of money is raised for good causes, and everybody enjoys themselves. With this basic concept in mind, a small team of us set about organising a series of high-profile clay pigeon shooting competitions called the Rolex Jackie Stewart Celebrity Challenge.

In many ways, the project simply evolved. I was keen to promote clay pigeon shooting to a wider audience; then the new owners of the Gleneagles hotel wanted to stage a prestigious event; and, in due course, very many well-known people decided it was something they would like to support. As a result, the guest list for the Rolex Jackie Stewart Celebrity Challenge began to compare favourably with that of any 'celebrity' charity event anywhere in the world. Over the years, the following people attended.

Royalty: HRH The Duke of York, HRH The Earl of Wessex, HRH The Princess Royal, Peter Phillips, Vice-Admiral Timothy Laurence, Captain Mark Phillips, HRH Princess Alexandra, The Right Honourable Sir Angus Ogilvy, HM King Hussein of the Hashemite Kingdom of Jordan, HM Queen Noor, HRH Prince Hamzah bin Al Hussein of Jordan, HRH Prince Hashim bin Al Hussein of Jordan, HM King Constantine of Greece and HM The Queen of Greece, HRH Prince Hakim of Brunei.

Aristocracy: Duke of Argyll, Duke of Atholl, Duke of Somerset, Duke of Roxburgh, Duke of Westminster, Earl of Airlie and Countess of Airlie, Earl of Normanton, Lord Montagu of Beaulieu, Lord Romsey, Lord Stafford, Marchioness of Northampton, Lady Fairhaven, Lady Jane Grosvenor and Lady Romsey.

Entertainment: Anthony Andrews, Frank Bough, Chris de Burgh, Sir Sean Connery, Billy Connolly, Tom Conti, Ronnie Corbett, Harrison Ford, Barry Gibb, Gene Hackman, Dame Kiri Te Kanawa, Mark Knopfler, Cheryl Ladd, Nick Mason, Kenneth McKellar, Suzi Quatro, Andrew Ridgeley, Steven Spielberg, Pamela Stephenson and Olivia Yu (Miss Hong Kong).

Business: Dame Vivien Duffield, Edsel Ford, Sir Rocco Forte, Lord King, Arne Naess, Sir Evelyn de Rothschild, Johann Rupert and Sir Jocelyn Stevens.

Sport: Derek Bell, Ian Botham, Martin Brundle, Jack Charlton, Kenny Dalglish, John Francome, Bernard Gallacher, Wayne Gretzky, Gavin Hastings, Imran Khan, Rod Laver, Nigel Mansell, Ivan Mauger, Colin Montgomerie, Tessa Sanderson, Jody Scheckter, Kevin Schwantz, Peter Scudamore, Stan Smith, Alberto Tomba, Derek Warwick, John Watson, Jim Watt and Ian Woosnam.

Royal gamekeepers: Sandy Masson, Bill Meldrum, Graham Cummins, Stephen Cuthbert, John Stubbs and Gary Coutts.

The remarkable turnout made it possible to secure sponsors such as Rolex, British Aerospace, British Airways, Ford, Hewlett Packard, Land Rover, Barbour, Irn Bru, Champneys, Walkers Shortbread and Moët & Chandon, which enabled us to generate large sums for charity. Hopefully I have not omitted from the above lists any guests who attended or sponsors who supported us – if I have, such omission is entirely inadvertent and please accept my apologies. At the event in 1995, we raised £650,000 – that would have been a reasonable return in the United States, but it was exceptional for a relatively small event in the UK.

The calibre of people attending was truly remarkable – but it wasn't always easy. One year we were struggling, as a result of prior commitments, to find four dukes to make up a team. I had heard that the Duke of Montrose may be a possibility and so I asked my PA to find his number. He duly did and I called.

'Good afternoon. I'm looking for his Grace. I wonder if he is available to speak?'

'Eh?'

'My apologies. I said I'm looking for his Grace. I wonder if he is available to come to the phone?'

'Who?'

'His Grace. The Duke of Montrose. This is Jackie Stewart speaking.'

'Oh hi there Jackie. How you doing? Nice to speak to you,' said an unmistakable Glasgow accent. 'This is the Duke of Montrose pub.'

The mighty oak grew from a humble acorn. After retiring as a racing driver in 1973, I wanted to resume some involvement with clay pigeon shooting, the sport that had given me so much pleasure and confidence in my youth. So I called up Allan Jones, and we created a one-day celebrity clay pigeon shooting competition to be staged at the North Wales Shooting School, near Chester, created by Allan's father Glynne.

I enjoyed returning to this familiar environment, and, after some debate, we decided our competition would include the standard sporting clay pigeon shooting disciplines, with the target being fired to simulate the flight and behaviour of birds and ground game. So, one after the other, the competitors shot at clays that resembled a high pheasant, a driven grouse, a bolting rabbit, a settling duck and a rising teal.

Rolex agreed to come on board as the title sponsor from the start, and, in those days at the North Wales Shooting School, we used to raise a few thousand pounds for charity. It gradually became clear to us that the better known the celebrities we were able to attract, the more money we would be able to raise. With this in mind, we worked hard and negotiated various supplier arrangements with companies such as Barbour wet weather coats, Hugo Boss and Hunter wellington boots, and we concluded an arrangement with the Grosvenor Hotel, Chester, owned by the Duke of Westminster, that they would accommodate our VIP guests.

Year by year, we managed to raise the profile of the event, and, into the early 1980s, the likes of Prince Albert of Monaco, England rugby captain Bill Beaumont and top British jockey Willie Carson came to join us for a day's clay pigeon shooting in this particular corner of North Wales.

Meanwhile, I had agreed to assist the new owners of the Gleneagles hotel with their worldwide marketing campaign. A consortium of businessmen had bought this beautiful property from British Rail and they were looking for a Scot with an international profile to help project a global image. Alastair Johnston, of IMG, developed the contact, and the deal was done.

Peter Lederer, whom I had met when he worked at the Carlton Tower Hotel in London many years before, had been appointed general manager at Gleneagles and he was eager to outline his goal to make it a 'year-round hotel'. That was not going to be easy. Scotland is a beautiful country, partially because the countryside is so green, and the reason everything is so green is that it rains quite a lot. In fact, I was aware that, in previous years, the Gleneagles hotel had closed from the end of October until the weather improved in April.

'What we need to do,' Peter continued, 'is to offer our guests something to do apart from play golf, and ideally it would be something they could do even if the weather was unkind.'

'I see.'

'Have you got any ideas?' he asked.

'Well,' I replied, 'I don't think we can build a motor racing circuit around Gleneagles, but have you thought about creating a shooting school?'

'Shooting?'

'That's right. It could be the perfect package.'

I explained how a shooting school could be constructed on the grouse moor beside the hotel, how it could offer clay pigeon shooting tuition, how we could provide a top-quality experience for men and women, both young and more mature.

'There isn't a high-quality shooting school anywhere in Scotland,' I continued, 'and it's a popular sport. We could kit out the guests in Barbour jackets and Hunter wellington boots, so they'd be ready to face all four seasons of Scottish weather. In any case, they would shoot from sheltered areas, so if the weather was unfavourable, it would be a way for them to be able to get outdoors without getting too cold or wet.'

Peter seemed interested, but asked, 'You don't think it would be too specialised?'

'I don't think so,' I replied. 'We would have qualified instructors, and they would make the experience as enjoyable for complete beginners as it would be for accomplished shooters.'

'It could work,' he said.

My first call was to Allan Jones, because of his family's experience in setting up a shooting school in North Wales, and he was immediately enthusiastic about the venture. In fact, it was soon agreed that he and his wife Shan, together with his brother Noel and his wife Susan, would be prepared to drive up to Gleneagles on a regular basis, maybe twice a month, and help me turn the concept into a reality.

We negotiated an arrangement where we would manage and run the school at the hotel, and the Jackie Stewart Gleneagles Shooting School was created. Our strategy was to offer quality in every respect, so we built a comfortable lodge where we would be able to serve the guests excellent lunches and dinners, and we ordered our consignments of Barbour jackets and Hunter wellington boots, as well as thirty brand-new over-and-under guns from Beretta, some 12 bore, a few 20 bore, fewer 28 bore and a couple of 410s for young customers.

I had first been introduced to Beretta guns in 1970, when Ugo Gussalli Beretta asked to meet me at the Villa d'Este hotel on the banks of Lake Como, where I was staying for the Italian Grand Prix. He explained he would like to give me a matching pair of 12 bore Beretta EE LL guns to celebrate my world championship success, which I had secured at Monza the previous year.

'We have been making guns since 1526, and we're the oldest gunmakers in the world,' he told me, 'and I know you enjoy shooting.'

It was a wonderful gesture, the guns were beautiful. Ugo and I became friends and ever since I have chosen to shoot with Beretta guns, all crafted under his direction.

So the school became established, and we swiftly developed a strong team of people, headed by Allan and Noel Jones, with Shan and Susan working with Anna Duncan and Nicola Hodge in our thriving wee shop. In due course, we appointed Allan's son Justin to become the full-time manager.

The concept worked, and our shooting school became one of the busiest in the world, welcoming no fewer than 12,500 visitors per year; and approximately 60 per cent of these were first-time clay pigeon shooters, which meant we were promoting the sport as well as building a successful business. Our instructors were often retired gamekeepers and they gave expert guidance in the key disciplines of the sport – safety, etiquette and gun handling. As time passed, a trend emerged that may have surprised a few people – our female visitors very often proved more successful than the men. This is not a sexist observation, and I am aware it may not be politically correct, so let me simply record the facts.

For novice shooters, the loud bang when they pull the trigger can be quite frightening, and the recoil can be not only alarming but also quite painful if the gun is not mounted and held correctly; add to this the fact that a gun is an inherently dangerous object, especially when incorrectly handled, and it was no surprise that many of the women who arrived at the school seemed a little wary. However, if a novice listened carefully to what the instructor told them and held the gun correctly – in the right place in the shoulder, with the head and cheek addressing the stock – and wore the proper ear protection, then there was a very good chance that he or she would be able to hit the target. Our experience was that, in general, the women listened more carefully, proved quick on the uptake and emerged as accurate shots in this introductory period.

For their part, many of our male customers swaggered on to the shooting ground, giving the impression that they truly believed they were direct descendants of Wyatt Earp, the famous gunslinger from the Wild West.

'Never mind the chat,' they would say, paying little or no attention to what the instructor was trying to tell them and joking with their friends, 'let's just get on with the shooting.'

In their macho haste, they usually held the gun in the wrong way and missed the targets, much to the glee of their wives and girlfriends, who had recorded higher scores. The men would stomp off to play golf, but the women would then come back to further develop their skills – our statistics showed that more than 40 per cent of our visitors were female.

By 1985, the annual celebrity challenge was thriving in North

Wales, and the shooting school was becoming established at Gleneagles – maybe, I thought, we could combine the two ventures and create something really big that could generate substantial sums of money for good causes. Thus, the Rolex Jackie Stewart Celebrity Challenge at Gleneagles was born.

'If we're going to do this,' I said, 'let's do it properly.'

We sat down and agreed the ground rules:

1. The event would meet all costs relating to travel to and from Gleneagles, and we would provide all meals, drink and accommodation at the hotel; in addition, all our visitors would be given a Barbour jacket, cashmere sweater, gloves, hats, boots, socks . . . and T-shirts because, in Scotland, you need to be prepared for any weather;
2. Every guest would be treated in exactly the same way;
3. Nobody would charge expenses against the event, and that included me;
4. Appearance money was out of the question.

As we had learned over the years in North Wales, success was going to rely on the quality of celebrities we could persuade to come to Scotland for two days of shooting and fun, so I started to trawl through my address book, personally sending out invitations to people from a wide variety of fields. Fortunately, most of these invitations were accepted.

Organising such an event was, in many ways, a logistical nightmare, and an exceptional group of people heroically rose to the challenge of coordinating complex travel arrangements, gathering clothing sizes, planning the accommodation and organising a series of lunches, cocktail parties and dinners.

Ruth Kinnear, my secretary based in Switzerland, and Chris Bliss, my accountant at Rawlinson & Hunter, provided support to the team at Gleneagles, which included Ian Ferrier and his secretary, Audrey Walker, Caroline Pyle, Anne Parker (who later moved to the Grand Prix Mechanics Charitable Trust), Caroline Goodacre (who later worked for Paul Stewart Racing and Stewart Grand Prix), Steve Jarvis and Tony Gorst, who ran the scheduling and the scoring of the shooting.

David Burnside also provided invaluable counsel and support. Then head of public relations and a member of the main board at British Airways, he facilitated arrangements for many of our guests to travel to Gleneagles on the 'world's favourite airline'. David subsequently became an Ulster Unionist Member of Parliament, and now runs his own international PR company.

Through the efforts of all these people, we were able to gather an extraordinary group of royalty, film stars, entertainers, sporting legends and the aristocracy in one place. Life was rarely dull.

Keeping such a galaxy of stars content might have seemed an almost impossible task, and there were a few well-developed egos on the guest list, but it was extraordinary to see how even the most notoriously demanding celebrities caused no trouble at all as soon as members of the Royal Family arrived. In general, anybody acting 'big time' was quickly cut down to size by those around them.

On one occasion we arranged for Terry O'Neill, the famous photographer, to take a group picture, which was to be published on the front cover of *Hello!* magazine. Everyone was in their appointed place on time, all except Alberto Tomba. I was making calls on my mobile, desperately trying to track down the handsome, wonderfully charismatic Italian alpine ski champion, when he suddenly appeared.

'Hey,' declared Tomba la Bomba, grinning and waving his hands.

'Just sit on your f— arse,' thundered the unmistakable voice of Sean Connery. 'You're late!'

Generous laughter erupted and Alberto did as he was told –

well you would, if 007 was telling you what to do. Although, perhaps surprisingly, it was at the Celebrity Challenge that Sean first shot a gun.

Nobody took themselves too seriously, and everyone seemed to enjoy the informality. We had decided to put a group of four well-known, successful and extremely high-powered business-men in a team, sponsored by Hewlett Packard, which we had intended to call 'The Winners'. However, it wasn't long before, by general consent, they were renamed 'The Rich and Bossy'. They were delighted to receive such recognition. 'We're surprised anyone noticed us,' they liked to say. 'In this crowd, we're only businessmen.'

Accommodating such a group in the same hotel was a challenge in itself, particularly since so many of our guests were used to being given either a suite or the best room wherever they stayed. In the end, we decided to allocate the suites to the royalty and the best rooms to the gamekeepers.

That was the solution. Nobody complained. People just seemed to relax and enjoy themselves. As the years passed, the event developed a reputation as a worthwhile and enjoyable couple of days, and, one year, we were delighted when two of the biggest names in Hollywood accepted our invitation. Steven Spielberg and Harrison Ford arrived at Gleneagles, and I was there to welcome them. As the three of us chatted, I noticed that both the famous film director and the star actor kept peering over my right shoulder, where something had clearly attracted their attention.

After a few minutes, Steven Spielberg said, 'Excuse me, I don't want to be rude, but there is somebody over there who looks exactly like King Hussein of Jordan.'

'That is His Majesty,' I replied. 'Queen Noor is also here.'

Steven Spielberg seemed surprised and taken aback and he proceeded to explain how he had been trying to get permission to film part of his new movie, *Indiana Jones and the Last*

Crusade, on location in Petra, the ancient city where many of the buildings have literally been carved out of the stone.

'We've been talking to the authorities in Jordan for some time,' he added, 'but we haven't got very far and, in fact, we've been trying to contact King Hussein for months.'

'Well,' I said, 'I'm sure Their Majesties would love to meet you both. Let me take you over.'

Permission was granted that very day at Gleneagles, and the scene where the characters played by Harrison Ford and Sean Connery go in search of the Holy Grail was partly filmed at Petra.

As the scale and stature of the event grew over the years, so did the total amount we were able to raise for charity. In 1985, we generated more than £200,000 for the Scottish International Educational Trust and the Save the Children Fund, which seemed a reasonable effort, but we raised more in 1988 and 1990. In 1995, which proved to be our final year, we were able to reach that figure of £650,000, which was excellent. By then, the Jackie Stewart Rolex Celebrity Challenge seemed to have assumed its own profile but, for me, it remained what it had always been since the early days in North Wales: an opportunity to raise funds and to spend a couple of days with some exceptional people, many of whom were friends.

HRH The Princess Royal stands in both categories. I have always admired her integrity and work ethic and, through ups and downs, she has been a very good friend for a very long time. We met as fellow sports people, and I remember the occasion clearly. The *Daily Express* always used to host an annual awards lunch, and, in 1971, when the votes of the newspaper's readers were counted, the Princess emerged as the Daily Express Sportswoman of the Year following her victory, on Doublet, at the European Eventing Championship in Burghley. After winning the F1 world championship, I was voted Sportsman of the Year, and we were seated together at the top table.

As I recall, I was particularly struck by her hands. The Princess conducted herself with great dignity and she certainly had a royal aura, but her hands were working hands. In fact, as she told me, she had spent that morning mucking out the stables. She clearly liked to be totally involved in whatever she was doing and to be part of getting things done. We chatted very amicably over lunch, and then met again and again at a series of similar sporting functions to celebrate what had been, for each of us, a very successful year.

As soon as I realised she was an enthusiast of driving, I asked if she would like to come and spend a day at Silverstone, watching a Tyrrell F1 testing session. She eagerly agreed and she appeared to enjoy herself. When the two F1 cars had finished, I drove her around the circuit in a race-prepared Ford Escort.

'May I drive myself now?' she asked.

'Ma'am, I'm sure that could be organised,' I replied.

I was slightly apprehensive because I was not sure whether the Princess had previous experience of driving at a circuit, so I felt it was right to give her a quick briefing on some of the pitfalls that may lie ahead.

'Ma'am, please be careful,' I said. 'It is sometimes difficult to know quite how fast you are driving on a racing circuit, because there are none of the points of reference for speed that you have on a public road, such as telegraph poles and parked cars. So many people drive too quickly into the corners and then they brake too late and, before they know what's happened, everything ends in tears.' She was listening intently and she nodded. 'So, Ma'am, please be careful.'

I need not have worried, because the Princess handled the car remarkably well.

In my experience, top sports people are typically very quick to pick up the basic skills and techniques of any other sport; and, as she drove the race-prepared Ford Escort around

Silverstone, she seemed to be drawing on the same touch that she used to ride Doublet around a cross-country course.

'Maybe you should try three-day eventing some time,' she said afterwards.

'No thank you, Ma'am,' I replied. 'I've always thought anything under 500 horsepower is dangerous.'

The Princess's trip to Silverstone had been a private visit, and, even though she had been seen by some of the media, who were always present at F1 testing sessions and a few lines did appear in several newspapers the next day, I was relieved to see there were no photographs in the press, just because I didn't know how such publicity would be received.

Two days later, Walter Hayes of Ford telephoned me and asked, 'Jackie, have you seen the picture?'

'What picture?'

'The one of the Princess sitting in the F1 car with you and Ken Tyrrell standing behind. It looks fantastic, and it has even got the Ford oval in the frame as well.'

'Don't tell me it's in the newspaper.'

'No, not yet – some photographer is trying to sell it to me.'

'Walter, I'm sorry, we can't do that.'

I explained my concern, and Walter agreed to deal with the problem by buying all rights to the photograph and making sure it was never published. It was a really nice picture, and I eventually got a print, put it in a frame and displayed it on the piano in our drawing room; it's still there today.

In the years that followed, Helen and I often used to have dinner with the Princess and Captain Mark Phillips, before and after they were married, and I have clear memories of the great excitement when their son Peter was born in 1977 and then again when their daughter Zara followed in 1981; and Helen was very touched when she was asked to be a godmother to Zara. Peter is now married. How time passes.

The Princess Royal has been and continues to be widely

admired for the enormous amount of work she has done for charity, notably for The Princess Royal Trust for Carers and the Save the Children Fund. Her response to being asked to become president of the latter organisation was entirely typical: yes, she said, as long as I'm not just a figurehead. In fact, she has rolled up her sleeves, travelled the world and done a fantastic job. Her trips to Africa have been more numerous than most people would imagine – in fact, it has been reported that the Princess Royal has made more visits to that continent than the combined total of the trips of Princess Diana, Bono and Bob Geldof. And they've all been there a good few times. I was co-opted to sit on the Save the Children board for a couple of years and I remember being tremendously impressed by the way she chaired the meetings, brought focus to the work and got things done.

As a family we have stayed friends with the Princess and Vice-Admiral Tim Laurence, as well as with Peter, who now works for the Royal Bank of Scotland servicing their sponsorship in sport, and with Zara, who has emulated her mother's success in the equestrian world.

One of the most memorable occasions we shared took place on 2 November 1997, when the Princess invited Helen and me to have dinner and spend the night aboard Her Majesty's Yacht *Britannia*, which was docked on the River Clyde in Glasgow. This was a very emotional period for many people, particularly the Royal Family and the long-serving crew, because the much-loved Royal Yacht was about to be decommissioned and was undertaking one last clockwise circumnavigation of the country. I had never been aboard *Britannia* before, and was hugely impressed. It was immaculate: every brass fitting was perfectly polished, everything was done with style and dignity.

When Her Royal Highness returned from a full day of official engagements, the three of us enjoyed a wonderful spoiling dinner, and conversation drifted towards the yacht. The Princess told us how *Britannia* had been built on the River

Clyde and launched in 1953 and that, only the previous evening, she had invited Dr John Brown, the original designer, now ninety-six years of age, and his son to come aboard for dinner. It was an unusual coincidence, the Princess explained, that Dr Brown had the same name as the shipyard at which *Britannia* had been built.

Over breakfast the following morning, the Princess asked about our plans for the rest of the day.

'We will just fly back to Luton,' I replied.

'Well, *Britannia* is due to sail down the Clyde today,' she said. 'I have some engagements, unfortunately, but if you can delay your flight, you are welcome to remain on board.'

'That would be lovely,' I said.

The Princess immediately telephoned the Queen to secure her approval, and Her Majesty said she thought it would be a wonderful idea if we were able to change our plans and stay a little while longer.

A considerable crowd had gathered on the dock in Glasgow to see the Royal Yacht pull away from its berth and turn her bow to head down the Clyde for the last time, and, with the crew standing at their stations, the Royal Marines band took up their positions on deck and played a wonderful selection of Scottish music. For Helen and me to find ourselves in the middle of such ceremony, in the heart of our own country, was a rare privilege. *Britannia* made her way down the Clyde, as thousands of people gathered on either bank of the river to see her pass, just as, half a century earlier I had stood with my friends and watched the likes of the *Coronia* and the *Vanguard* sail by. It was becoming a profoundly nostalgic day.

Commodore Anthony Morrow had kindly invited Helen and me to join him on the bridge and, as we approached the site of the former John Brown & Co. shipyard, he was surprised to see two solitary figures standing on the selfsame slipway where the Royal Yacht was launched forty-four years before. 'Good

Lord! That's Dr John Brown and his son,' he told us, looking through his binoculars.

At that moment, Commodore Morrow asked Helen to sound *Britannia*'s horn and to keep sounding it for forty-five seconds in salute to her birthplace. The crew had gathered on the starboard deck, and the RM band played 'We'er No Awa' Tae Bide Awa' ('We are not away to stay away'). Commodore Morrow saluted the figure standing on the shore. John Brown waved back.

The combination of *Britannia* shortly to be decommissioned, the yacht's history, the music, the designer standing at attention and the significance of the slipway created an extraordinarily emotional moment and so far as I could see there was not a dry eye on the yacht. Both Helen and I certainly had tears running down our cheeks.

We cruised on and caught a glimpse of Rockview, the house where I was born, and then the Dumbarton Rock and the Castle and so many of the old familiar places of my childhood and youth, and we were soon passing Helensburgh and we saw Dino's Café in the distance, where Helen and I first met.

Eventually we disembarked at Gourock, at the mouth of the Clyde, and returned home with a series of memories to last a lifetime. It had been a truly remarkable day, made possible by the Princess and Her Majesty the Queen.

Another enthusiastic supporter of the shooting event at Gleneagles was Lord King of Wartnaby. His strong reputation had preceded him, and I was initially concerned whether our small operation would be able to handle the formidable and much-admired chairman of British Airways; in fact, we discovered he was the perfect gentleman, who was the first to send a thank you letter after the event, written by hand. We got along like a house on fire from the moment we met, and I admired him tremendously. Like me, he had left school without any qualifications but had then built up a business to be the third-largest manufacturer of ball bearings in Britain. In 1981, he was asked by the then Prime Minister, Margaret Thatcher, to lead a restructuring programme at British Airways. It was far from painless – staff numbers were cut from 52,000 to 37,500 within two years – but Lord King's relentless focus on improved customer service and smart advertising effectively transformed the business from a national embarrassment into the 'world's favourite airline'. The figures speak for themselves: in 1981, British Airways reported a loss of £140 million on a turnover of £2 billion. By 1992, after a remarkable decade with Lord King at the helm, the company had doubled its turnover to more than £4 billion and was able to report a profit of £434 million. Lord King eventually retired as chairman of BA and he was given a title of life president, but he seemed to miss being at the sharp end of the business. This was a man who yearned to be on the field, in the midst of the contest, directing the team's strategy, urging them forward; he found precious little satisfaction in merely standing on the touchline and offering advice.

As our friendship developed, we began to meet on a regular basis. I greatly appreciated his experience and wise counsel and enjoyed his sharp perception. I remember one occasion when I told Lord King over lunch that I had met an impressive person.

'Really?' he replied. 'What was his name?'

'Er . . . you know I'm not good with names. I don't remember.'

'Don't remember his name, eh? That's not a good sign. He couldn't have been that impressive.'

He also had a good 'nose' for people, and that can be a valuable asset. Almost as soon as he met somebody for the first time, he would have a good idea whether he wanted to be associated with them, or not. He always used to say he trusted his 'nose', and it rarely let him down.

We shared a love of the countryside – he was a keen

shooting and fishing man – and we spent many happy days at various shoots all over the country. John King passed away on 12 July 2005, at the age of eighty-six, and was rightly hailed as one of the outstanding business leaders of his generation. Lord King never got around to writing his memoirs, which was a pity because he had so much to say. I didn't want to leave any such regrets, which is why these words have been written.

I have continued to pursue my interest in shooting all over the UK, and all around the world, and have enjoyed many wonderful days with a wide variety of friends.

Patrick Lichfield was always terrific company. One of the outstanding photographers of his generation, he was the epitome of a good-looking, elegant and well-dressed host, and one of the most incredibly loyal friends I have ever had. To stay with the fifth Earl of Lichfield and Lady Annunziata Asquith at Shugborough Hall in Staffordshire was always a great pleasure. The guests were looked after with such care, and I admired the attention to detail – a portable radio was placed beside every bed, always tuned to BBC Radio 4. It was, I always used to say, the most beautifully run house in Britain. Patrick was an outstanding shot, and, if I was hosting a shoot at Hambleden or Gatcombe, I always tried to invite him with Lord Stafford and Andrew Parker-Bowles, because the three of them were so competitive on the very high pheasants and they all shared a great sense of humour and a love of the countryside.

Arthur Brealey and Brendan McGuirk were two members of his staff, who often came along as loaders. They had grown and developed with Patrick and were organised and efficient. In many ways they were the bookends of his life.

One of the most enjoyable shoots I have attended took place not far from Madrid. All the guests were elegantly and immaculately dressed, and the most wonderful lunch was served in a marquee on the shoot, by waiters wearing white gloves and white tie and tails. Such events were generally hosted on a grander scale in Spain than in Britain. In Scotland, England, Ireland and Wales there is somehow an informality about shoots which doesn't exist in other places. That is not to suggest that respect between the land owner and the land worker – be it the gamekeeper, beater, dog handler or those who manage the estates – does not exist. It does, but it cuts both ways. There is a deep understanding about how all the pieces of the countryside jigsaw fit together, and how essential each party is to every other party if the rural economy is to survive. It is that mutual understanding that brings the informality and the fun and remains something unique and wonderful about the countryside in this part of the world. It is certainly something I cherish.

At this particular shoot outside Madrid, I was a guest of His Majesty King Juan Carlos of Spain, whom I have known well since we first met at the Spanish Grand Prix in 1966. That was nine years before the Spanish monarchy was restored. We remained friends during the years when he worked tirelessly to establish the monarchy in Spain. He managed to align himself with the people in a most humane way, not least through his great interest in sport – he is an excellent shot, an accomplished yachtsman and a keen driver – and the way he has managed to earn first acceptability, then respect and genuine affection has been remarkable.

I remember one day at the Jarama circuit near Madrid, when His Majesty the King and several other members of the Royal Family attended a driving day that I had put together for them. He brought along his rare Porsche 959, and we all enjoyed a relaxing and hopefully informative day, where I hope they learned something of driving safely at the limit of themselves and the cars they drove.

The Jackie Stewart Gleneagles Shooting School continued to thrive through the 1990s and beyond, I hope, adding substantial value to the hotel. At the end of 2001, with the management contract up for renewal, I decided it was the right moment to move on. For Allan and Noel Jones, and indeed for me, travelling back and forth was tiring, and each of us had reached an age where we ought to be doing less, not more. In fact, Allan was suffering from cancer, and sadly he died in December 2004. I spent time with him before he passed away, and we were able to recall many of the wonderful times we had spent together: driving our Austin Healeys in the snow at Oulton Park, buzzing around Paris on the back of a scooter and shooting together all over the world. He was a shooting and motor sport enthusiast who became a farmer, and, over the course of fifty years, there was a real depth to our friendship.

One of the trials of living to a good age is you find yourself too often having to bury your greatest friends.

CHAPTER 19

A Remarkable Man

ONE OF THE GREAT BLESSINGS OF MY LIFE has been the opportunity to meet and become friends with many remarkable people, some who were famous during a particular era and others who have been giants over decades or even their entire lifetimes.

Sport, like entertainment, captures the imagination and inspires the passion of millions of people across the globe; and it seems that for many of us the chance to meet a well-known sportsman or woman or a top entertainer becomes a deeply intoxicating experience, one which often seems to prompt what can almost be described as a chemical reaction. In motor sport, the added chemistry of danger and probable loss of life magnified the appeal, particularly in an era when the sport was more guilty of causing the death and destruction of so many young and charismatic drivers.

My life has long since moved on from the horrid accidents and the flaming wreckage, but I have never strayed far from motor racing and, even today in many people's eyes, I have somehow remained closely associated with the sport – in fact, even in my late sixties, when I am travelling in various parts of the world, it is not unusual for complete strangers to walk up to me and say, 'All the best for the weekend.' I am too embarrassed to tell them I haven't driven a racing car in anger for thirty-four years.

Over all this time, I have often asked myself how some of the relationships with the remarkable people I've met have blossomed into genuine friendships. I know I was very often impressed by their talents and achievements, but I'm not sure what they saw in me – in all honesty, I have never regarded myself as anybody special – but it does take two to tango, and it is the case that these friendships lasted.

One such friend was His Majesty King Hussein of Jordan. We first met at Daytona Beach, Florida, where I was working at the famous 500 mile Stock Car race for the ABC's *Wide World of Sports*. The King was attending the event with Jim Kimberley, heir of the Kimberley Clark empire, which produced Kleenex tissues and many other products. Jim had been a prominent racing driver in the late 1940s and 1950s and he was a great enthusiast of motor sport, but one of his more unusual interests was in making sure he was a passenger on the maiden voyage of every great ocean liner. He later moved from the sea to the sky and booked his seat on maiden flights of all the great aircraft, like the Boeing 747 and Concorde. He was a man who could afford an extraordinary lifestyle but, as importantly, he knew how to live life to the full and thoroughly enjoy it.

His Majesty and I chatted amicably in Daytona, but the infrequency of our meetings over the next few years meant our friendship matured slowly, like good wine. However, as time went on, we saw more and more of each other.

During the 1990s, the years of Paul Stewart Racing and later Stewart Grand Prix, Paul and I saw King Hussein on a regular basis, just to talk about motor racing and bring him up to date with the latest developments in the sport and our team. He was always knowledgeable, enthusiastic and supportive. However, on one particular visit in the spring of 1995, we turned into the driveway of his house, near Ascot, west of London, with a barely concealed sense of excitement and anticipation.

Elizabeth Cork greeted us at the front door, as usual. Apart from being his goddaughter, she worked as the King and Queen's private secretary in the United Kingdom, and, ever unflappable and efficient, she said she would lead us through to the study where King Hussein was waiting. We chatted for some time until, at an appropriate pause in the conversation, adopting a formal tone, I said to His Majesty that Paul had something particular he would like to say.

My son said, 'Sir, you may recall how, three years ago, you told us how you would like to see me compete in the Formula 3000 season of 1992, and you made that possible by providing us with the very generous sum of money, in your private capacity. It was an amazing gesture of kindness towards our family.'

'Yes, I remember,' HM said, smiling.

'Well, as you know, our company has progressed since then, and today we want to thank you again for your more than kind gesture and to tell you that we would very much like to repay your kindness.'

'Really?'

'Absolutely.'

I turned to the King, and saw there were tears in his eyes.

In fact, all of a sudden, each of us was struggling to contain our emotions. I had the strong impression that our gesture caught His Majesty by surprise; it was as if he had never contemplated or expected any form of repayment, as if it was not something that happened very often in his life. Our pledge seemed every bit as unprompted as his had been three years before. This was an intensely significant moment because, I'm sure, it affirmed the integrity of our bond and, as the years passed, it came to represent the very core of our friendship.

His manners were impeccable. Manners maketh man, goes the saying, and this was true of King Hussein, who showed the same courtesy to every single person he met. He once came with me to test drive some new prototype Jaguars at the Motor Industry Research Association (MIRA) track in Oxfordshire, and, since we had decided to travel by helicopter, I took my usual precaution of ensuring a full fire crew was on hand both when we took off and when we landed. As we were preparing to leave, HM noticed the group of firemen standing to one side and took the trouble of walking over, thanking them for their time and shaking each and every one of them by the hand. Likewise, on the occasions when the King visited the Paul Stewart Racing factory in Milton Keynes, or when he came to the pit lane before or after a race, he always made a special point of greeting every member of staff and showing them his respect. He became a revered and popular visitor.

Another time, we were travelling through Amman, the capital of Jordan, in an armoured Mercedes-Benz 500 SEL. His Majesty had insisted upon driving himself, I was sitting in the passenger seat, and Helen was in the back. We came to a halt at some traffic lights, adjacent to where an old man was standing. The man was unshaven, toothless and racked with age but he took a step towards the car and, breaking the golden rule of travelling in an armoured vehicle, HM nonchalantly opened his window. The elderly man's lined face broke out into the most exhilarated of smiles as he recognised his monarch. I glanced in the mirror and saw the policemen in the back-up car behind us starting to panic, but there was no cause for alarm, and the King pulled over to the side of the road so he and his subject could continue their conversation for a few more minutes.

King Hussein was a keen sportsman. Despite being what I like to call a 'man of average height', he was fit and muscular and, whether he was riding a motorcycle or a horse, driving a racing car or a speedboat, waterskiing or flying a plane or a helicopter, he pursued his interests with boundless spirit, energy and enthusiasm.

On one of many happy visits to Jordan, Helen and I were invited to join a helicopter trip over the Dead Sea. His Majesty took the controls of the Super Puma, and we were soon skimming low over land and water. After a while, the King turned and called me forward to sit in the jump seat and then gestured for me to check the altitude. I looked and was alarmed to see that, according to the altimeter, we were flying below sea level. HM was smiling at me, enjoying my brief moment of anxiety, until I cottoned on and remembered that, in fact, the Dead Sea lies below sea level.

The King always enjoyed driving interesting cars, and, one day during 1988, we managed to organise a day of driving at the Donington circuit for the King, his son, Prince Abdullah, who was destined to succeed his father to the Hashemite throne, and his friend, King Constantine of Greece. Paul and Mark came along, and I invited Martin Brundle, then a current F1 driver who had just won the world sports car championship, because it was helpful to have somebody else with the experience to keep such a large group occupied and to provide expert driving advice as and when required. The event was a success, with HM relishing the precise agility of the Paul Stewart Racing single-seater Formula Ford 2000 car.

Two years later, we managed to organise an even more stimulating day. Once again, we returned to Donington and the hospitality of Tom Wheatcroft, legendary owner of the track and also of probably the finest collection of single-seater motor cars in the world. His Majesty arrived at the circuit in style, flying his own Sikorsky 76B helicopter, with Her Majesty Queen Noor and King Constantine as passengers. His co-pilot was Richard Verrall, a fine pilot in his own right with experience of flying Boeing 777s.

We had gone to some trouble to ensure the King was

properly kitted out for the day, and he looked pleased when he emerged wearing his made-to-measure thermal racing overalls and carrying his new full-face Bell F1 racing helmet. Organising the helmet had been an adventure in itself because, while most men would take a size 6 or 7, or maybe even a 7½, the King's head was extraordinarily large. He took in excess of a size 8, so the helmet needed to be made especially for him, complete with the Jordanian flag and his royal crest.

We spent the morning driving a variety of cars, among others a single-seater Austin 7 racing car from the Brooklands era of the late 1920s, early 1930s, an ex-factory F1 Ferrari once driven by Clay Regazzoni, the Tyrrell 006, which was my car when I won the F1 world championship in 1973, and a selection of race-prepared GT and touring cars. Everybody was having a good time, driving one car after another, and even Queen Noor appeared to enjoy driving, and being driven around the circuit at up to 140 mph in the latest Ford GT car, so there were plenty of tales to be told during a relaxed lunch in Tom Wheatcroft's suite overlooking the track.

Early afternoon, we travelled by chopper to a place called Bruntingthorpe, then a little-used airfield with the longest and widest runway in Britain; and there we were met by the then current Benetton Ford F1 team complete with transporter, F1 car, mechanics and driver, primed and ready for action. It was an exciting and extraordinary sight, made possible by the cooperation of Walter Hayes, of the Ford Motor Company, and the help of Benetton team director Flavio Briatore, who had brought along his F1 driver Alessandro Nanini to set the car up in good order.

'What's the top speed?' the King asked.

'In excess of 220 mph,' Flavio replied.

Planning an opportunity for a world leader to drive a F1 car is no easy matter. We had decided Donington was probably too tight for a driver with no previous experience of handling a

1,000 horsepower single-seater racing car, but Bruntingthorpe was perfect, more than three miles long and wide enough for three Concordes to take off or land at the same time. Our other concern was ensuring the drivers would be able to see when to brake at either end of the runway. This may not sound like an issue but, in a F1 car, the driver's head is barely 24 inches off the ground, meaning even the slightest undulation in the runway would look like a blind rise, making it even more difficult to judge distance and increasing the risk of braking a few seconds too late and overshooting the end of the runway. The solution was to station cars with headlights flashing at the correct braking points and, based on the evidence of Nanini's dry runs, the vehicles were parked in position.

His Majesty stepped into the Benetton Ford, mastered the complicated starting procedure with ease and, in a burst of raw mechanical power and noise, accelerated into the distance.

Everything had gone well, but getting the King into the F1 car proved to be the easy part. It soon became clear that getting him out of the car was going to be much more difficult, as he drove down the runway, turned at the end, drove back towards us, turned again and drove back to the other end again.

'How many laps is he going to do?' Queen Noor asked me.

'Oh,' I replied, 'I think he'll do three or four trips.'

In fact, His Majesty did a fourth trip, and then a fifth. At that point, on his sixth run, we decided to hold out a pit signal board, which indicated he should come in. The King ignored it and turned in preparation for his seventh run. The Queen was starting to become more than a little anxious.

'Jackie,' she said, firmly. 'I think you've got to put a stop to this.'

'Absolutely,' I said, not really knowing what I could do.

Thankfully, after we had made even bolder 'IN' pit board signals, His Majesty came in after his ninth trip. As he climbed out of the cockpit, he took off his helmet and gave one of his wonderful smiles, a grin so broad it seemed to consume his entire face, an expression of delight so uninhibited that he suddenly looked twenty years younger. What a moment!

King Constantine and Paul also took their turns at driving the F1 car on this rare afternoon, and, at the end of the day, I remember standing on that runway, watching the Sikorsky take off and feeling a great sense of relief that the occasion had passed off without incident and that everyone seemed to have enjoyed themselves so much.

There are other days that endure in my memory . . . the day when His Majesty and I tested his latest Mercedes-Benz competition touring car on a hill climb at Tel Al Rumman, near Amman, and we managed to set a record time; the day when we took the King, Queen Noor and the young princes, Hamzah and Hashim, shooting pheasants at Hambleden. Wherever we happened to be, whatever we were doing, I felt genuinely privileged to be in the company of a man of such intelligence, such integrity, such courtesy and such infectious enthusiasm.

On another occasion, attending the European Grand Prix at Donington in 1993, we were walking down the starting grid when, all of a sudden, the national anthem was played over the public address system. Ever aware of protocol, the King and Queen stopped and stood to attention. We walked on a few paces, enjoying all the anticipation and excitement of the grid experience, when another national anthem began, and, again, we stopped and stood until the music was finished. This turned out to be the one and only time, so far as I could recall, that the national anthems of each driver competing in the Grand Prix was played on the PA system prior to the start of the race, and, even as rain poured down, His Majesty stood still and respected every single anthem. This process took such a long time that, in the end, we were scrambling off the grid as the cars pulled out on the warm-up lap.

I knew His Majesty as a friend and, although he often spoke

frankly about Jordan and his quest for peace in the Middle East, others are better qualified than me to assess his place in history.

However, I heard him enthuse about the youth and the importance of education, and I am aware the literacy rate among the people of Jordan rose from 33 per cent in 1960 to more than 90 per cent in 1996. I also heard him speak about improving his people's quality of life and I know that, while only 10 per cent of Jordanians had access to water, sanitation and electricity in 1950, this figure rose to 95 per cent by the turn of the century. By general consent, he guided his country through the ongoing turbulence of the Middle East with such skill that, even without oil, it became an oasis of stability in the region.

We also spoke about driving, and my philosophy of handling a car smoothly and progressively and with finesse appealed to him to such an extent that, at one stage, he asked me if I would be prepared to fly to the Far East and share some of my theories with his friend and fellow enthusiast, the Sultan of Brunei. The visit was duly arranged, and I found the Sultan to be an extremely charming, shy and modest man as we talked about driving and motor sport and drove some of the cars in his extraordinary collection. Our drive finished when we arrived at a polo ground with the beautifully appointed and impeccably furnished pavilion, where I sat and watched the Sultan and other members of his family enjoy a few chukkas.

King Hussein led such an active life that news of illness in the late 1990s came as an enormous shock, but he fought the cancer with typical courage. He decided to be treated at the Mayo Clinic, and Helen and I were able to visit him there on several occasions during that difficult time. I became aware of the profound impact he made on the team of specialists fighting to save his life and was not surprised to see this extraordinary man once again having a remarkable effect on the people around him. By the sheer strength of his personality, he seemed to bring out the best in everyone.

In the end, the vast esteem in which he was held around the world was amply demonstrated when he flew home for what seemed very likely to be the last time. His wide-bodied Tri-Star aircraft was escorted by six fighter planes of the air force in each major territory that he crossed, all the way from Minnesota in the USA, across the Atlantic, to the UK, across Europe and back to Amman.

Helen and I were sitting in the conservatory at home on the evening of 6 February 1999, when Elizabeth Cork phoned to tell us the King was very seriously ill and weakening. She said Queen Noor had suggested we travel to Amman to see His Majesty as soon as possible.

We flew the next morning, arrived in Jordan, checked in at our hotel and were preparing to be called to the hospital when Elizabeth phoned to say the King had peacefully passed away. I immediately called Paul and Mark to tell them the news and, with all the commercial flights fully booked, made arrangements for them to fly privately to Jordan, so they could join us for the funeral.

King Hussein's funeral surely ranks among the most extraordinary events of modern times. I doubt whether so many powerful and influential people have gathered in the same place at the same time. More than forty heads of state and four former presidents of the United States, a host of Arab leaders and the entire Israeli Cabinet stood among the group that assembled in a courtyard and then formed an orderly line that led up some wide stone steps, through a double door leading into one of the palaces, up another staircase and into the throne room, where the King lay in state, his coffin draped in the Jordanian flag. The line moved slowly, with the protocol officers admitting each group of mourners to the throne room one after the other to pay their respects, so everyone moved a few steps, then waited for a minute or so, moved a few more steps, then waited again.

I was standing with Paul and Mark, because the tradition was that women did not attend the funeral, and Helen was with Queen Noor and some of the other wives of those at the burial. So, when our turn arrived, we three Stewart men walked in, turned to face the coffin together, bowed our heads and, I am not ashamed to say, we shed our tears. As I stood there, my head was full of all the times we had spent together and all the experiences we had shared, of how privileged I had been to know him, and of how close the King had grown to our family, even to the point where, in 1995, he agreed to become a godfather to Paul and Victoria's eldest son, Dylan.

Several months after His Majesty's passing, Paul and I were standing on the starting grid of the British Grand Prix at Silverstone when Victoria called Paul on his mobile. She told him a parcel had just arrived at their home from Jordan and that it contained a set of King Hussein's rosary beads as a present for Dylan. It was an amazingly touching moment, for Paul and me to find ourselves in the middle of such frenetic activity and excitement, just minutes before the start of a Grand Prix, with our two Stewart Grand Prix cars on the grid, and to learn that Her Majesty Queen Noor had thought of this unexpected and wonderful gesture. Not for the first time in our relationship with this remarkable man and his family, we found ourselves struggling to contain our emotions.

Simply put, King Hussein of Jordan was the most impressive man I have met in my life, nothing more and nothing less.

CHAPTER 20

Part of My Soul

THE SOUL IS NOT EASILY DEFINED BUT, TO ME, it feels like something in my core, a mass which is fused with my background and my values. It has nothing to do with money, material success or any form of achievement; it goes much deeper than that.

It relates to places which have meant a lot to me, like the top of the glen at Rest-and-Be-Thankful or on the slopes of Ben Dhu overlooking Loch Lomond, but it also lies in the countryside; since I was young, I have always felt at peace on a moor or in woods, surrounded by wildlife.

In addition, my soul seems profoundly attached to my family and friends, and, without a doubt, to our dogs. When our Norfolk terrier, Boss, passed away in 2005, I certainly felt a part of my soul went with him, and his loss created a void and a sense of emptiness that has not been properly filled. It is said that you can replenish the soul by keeping in regular contact with whatever means so much to you, and I certainly do get great pleasure from spending time with people and dogs that are close to me, and from just being in the countryside.

Media coverage of my motor racing career has for many years referred to my continuing interest in shooting and fishing, and this prompted a series of invitations to many of the finest shoots and rivers in the country and around the world, enabling me to be reintroduced to the people whom I had grown to admire so much in my youth: the gamekeepers, deer stalkers and ghillies. These folk are the salt of the earth and the backbone of many rural parts of the country, where the local economy often relies on the revenues and jobs created by the sporting estates. They are often fascinating characters, not least because in the course of their work they often spend considerable periods of time in the company of heads of state, presidents and prime ministers, captains of industry, leaders from the armed services and religion, and well-known personalities from the worlds of sport and entertainment. It would be almost impossible for even an executive from a major multinational corporation to secure just a thirty-minute meeting with such prominent people, but this select band of gamekeepers, deer stalkers and ghillies spend hours in their company, all the while gaining wisdom and experience because everybody seems to fall into conversation while waiting for the fish to bite, the birds to fly or the stags to pause.

One such individual is Monty Christopher, who was head gamekeeper for Her Majesty the Queen at the Sandringham estate, and another is Bill Meldrum, his successor.

Monty is a remarkable man in many ways: a keen churchgoer with a great command of the English language, a fine sense of humour and a superb singing voice. He is into his nineties now, but we get together whenever I am in Norfolk and recall the times we have shared over the years. I like to remind him of how, when we first met, he used to keep the shooting guests in order. I was first invited to shoot at Sandringham by the then HRH Princess Anne and her husband at the time, Captain Mark Phillips, along with a very jolly and somewhat noisy group of their equestrian friends. On one occasion, we were getting out of the vehicle – in fact, it was called 'the Jumbo', a unique, extended long-wheelbase Land Rover specially designed by HRH the Duke of Edinburgh to meet all the needs of a shooting party – and we were in an area where the game crop was holding the pheasants and partridges. Monty Christopher was anxious for us to stay quiet, so his beat keepers and underkeepers would be able to go through the fields while the birds were still settled. If any of the shooting party, no matter who they were, made a noise, he would tell them in his inimitable manner, speaking softly but firmly: 'Gentlemen, it would be to all our advantage if we were to keep quiet. Please don't make a sound.'

I first met Bill Meldrum when he was breeding and working the dogs for Her Majesty at Sandringham, before he was appointed to succeed Monty as head gamekeeper. I have always admired his profound knowledge of dogs and the land, his frankness and his extraordinary humility and integrity. He worked for the Queen for a total of thirty-eight years, and, as he approached his retirement, the land agent at Sandringham, Marcus O'Lone, advised Bill he was going to be given a party.

A typically quiet, dour Scotsman, Bill replied: 'I din'na want a perty, and I din'na want any fuss. I din'na have a lot of friends and I would'na know who to ask anyway.'

The land agent said he would get back to Bill on the subject and, a few days later, he revealed it was the Queen who wished to give the party in Bill's honour to recognise his length of service to the Royal Family, and furthermore the party was to take place not in Norfolk, but at Buckingham Palace. Bill was still reluctant, repeating he wouldn't know who should be invited, but the land agent pressed him and said there must be many people who he had worked with over the years and who Bill would like to come along.

'Oh well, I suppose so,' Bill conceded.

He was expressly told he should invite whoever he wanted and whoever he felt was important to him and he started to put together a guest list of the dog breeders he knew, all his keepers and underkeepers, and the farmers who had made his job that much easier, and one or two of the guns who he had got to know and enjoyed over the years. The land agent was relieved to report to Her Majesty that Bill had accepted the fact there would be a party and, in the end, the guest list for the man who had not wanted a 'perty' at all reached an extraordinary 600 people, which meant the venue had to be switched from Buckingham Palace to Windsor Castle.

One autumn evening in 2000, while Helen and I were sitting in front of the fire at home, watching television, Bill phoned and asked me what I was doing on 24 February 2001.

'Oh, I've got no idea, Bill,' I replied.

'Well, it's important,' he said.

'Wait a minute, I'll go through to the study and get my diary.'

I went to look at my long-range planner and reported back that I was scheduled to be in Melbourne on that particular day, preparing to do some work with the Ford Motor Company before the Grand Prix of Australia.

'Oh, that'll no' do,' he said.

'Well, how's that, Bill?'

'I am having a *perty*,' he said.

'Oh, Bill, that's lovely, and I would have loved to be there but, as I say, I have to be down there in Australia'.

'Oh, no, no, no, that'll no' do at all.'

'Well, what's the story behind the party, Bill?'

'The Queen is giving a *perty* for my retirement, and I've been asked if you would say a few words about me.'

'Look, leave it with me, Bill. I'll see what I can do.'

'You'll have to be there.'

'I'll call you back, Bill. Give me a couple of days.'

In the end, I managed to move the Ford commitment to the week following the race, and I was able to be with Bill on his special occasion. What a party it turned out to be. Her Majesty provided buses for all those coming from Norfolk, and an amazing collection of people gathered in St George's Hall at Windsor Castle. Many members of the Royal Family were present, with members of royal families from other countries, and dukes, viscounts, peers and knights of the realm, and all the farmers, keepers, dog breeders and country folk who had known Bill so well. HRH the Duke of Edinburgh stood on the most wonderful oak podium, originating from the fourteenth century and standing on wheels so it could be moved in and out like a huge wheelbarrow, and welcomed everybody on behalf of the Queen; he then invited me to propose a toast in Bill's honour.

I began by suggesting, with my tongue firmly in my cheek, that everyone present had something in common because we all knew Bill as a hard taskmaster. 'And,' I added, 'there is probably nobody in this assembly who has not at one time or another been shouted at by Bill Meldrum.' That brought an outburst of laughter and once it had subsided, I followed it with, 'That's to say . . . with the possible exception of one.'

There was another burst of laughter and, when that died down, an unmistakable voice declared: 'Not true!'

Her Majesty was laughing, Bill was laughing, and everybody was laughing.

I went on to relate various tales of Bill's life and times and noted his retirement as head gamekeeper marked the end of a remarkable era in his life. 'As from today,' I said, 'all that is in the past, and you must look forward to the next stage.' In conclusion, I said, 'Bill, I know how incredibly proud you are to have served the Queen, the Duke of Edinburgh and other members of the Royal Family over such a long period of time and how much you have enjoyed all these years of such privilege, such fulfilment, such relationships, such loyalty and such respect. In fact, my own grandfather would have understood exactly how you feel tonight, because he had similar emotions when he retired as head gamekeeper for Lord Weir. I can imagine him looking down on us right now, together with my father and my mother, being so amazed and so pleased that a fellow gamekeeper should be honoured at such a magnificent occasion as this, and maybe also feeling so proud that his wee grandson should be standing here and addressing such a company of people at Windsor Castle.'

It was an emotional moment for me, for Bill and for others, but I composed myself and duly proposed the toast.

Bill made his way to the podium to respond and, although speaking to such an audience must have been daunting, he carried it off with honesty, style and emotion, and there was scarcely a dry eye among all present as he spoke of his pride at having served Her Majesty for so many years.

This extraordinary event unfolded as a wonderfully relaxed and enjoyable evening, which later seemed all the more remarkable for the fact that the occasion was never even mentioned in any newspaper or magazine. Media interest would certainly have been significant, but each of the 600 guests completely respected the integrity and privacy of the occasion. Bill and Annie Meldrum had been given an unforgettable send-off, the like of which I doubt has ever been given to somebody in Her Majesty's service. They still live on the Sandringham estate, and Bill still looks after Her Majesty's dogs when required.

The Queen is a knowledgeable handler of dogs, keeping spaniels and Labradors as well as the famous corgis, and her skill and experience is widely respected in the gun dog world. In the late 1970s, Helen and I were delighted when Her Majesty gave us a Labrador puppy, fathered by the famous Sandringham Sydney. The Queen likes to name each of the new puppies and she gave this sweet little black bitch the name 'Snare'. A good many months later, over lunch during a shooting day at Windsor, I found myself sitting on one side of the Queen with Trevor Banks, a horseman from Yorkshire, on the other. Trevor was a great friend, with a fine sense of humour.

'So how's the dog, Jackie?' Her Majesty inquired.

'Very well, Ma'am,' I replied. 'She's really going well.'

'What did I call the dog, Jackie?'

'Well, Ma'am, you may recall you called it Snare, but I have to admit we have changed the name.'

'Oh?' the Queen said.

'Yes,' I said, stumbling over my words, 'er . . . the children thought "Snare" sounded a little too much like a trap. She is such a sweet dog they wanted to change her name, Ma'am.'

'What have you called it?'

'Blossom, Ma'am.'

'Is the dog healthy?'

'Yes, Ma'am, but she has a slight speech impediment.'

'What do you mean?'

'Well, Ma'am, it doesn't bark quite like other dogs.'

Her Majesty has a keen sense of humour, and I was starting to get the distinct impression that I was being set up.

'So what does it sound like, Jackie?'

'Well, it sounds a bit like a seal, Ma'am.'

'And what does a barking seal sound like, Jackie?'

Imitating Blossom's peculiar bark was not going to be easy, but I had no option but to give it my best shot, and I made a noise that sound something like: 'Ahwaaah! Ahwaaah!'

Trevor Banks had not been listening to the conversation, but this unusual noise attracted his attention and, ever eager to engage in any banter that would embarrass me, he leaned across, smiling self-confidently at the Queen, and said, 'Knowing Stewart, Ma'am, he'll have got the dog cheap from a poor home.'

The entire lunch party erupted in laughter, causing such a commotion that members of the Royal Protection Group rushed in to see what was happening. When the laughter had subsided, the Queen turned to look at Trevor, then turned back to me and, keeping a completely straight face, said, 'Jackie, does Mr Banks know from whom you got the dog?'

That prompted another explosion of laughter. It was wonderful, and Trevor never lived it down.

Even with her 'speech impediment', Blossom became a much-loved member of our family. I have always loved animals. Ever since my first day at school, when I found a stray cat on my way home and was allowed to keep it – we called it Fluffy – there has hardly ever been a time when we haven't had a pet in the house. What joy they have brought. What companions they have been. In fact, they have been more than companions. In a frenetic and demanding life, my dogs have been a sanctuary. Far away from the spotlight, removed from the world where you must be properly dressed and carefully prepared, far from any kind of judgement and expectation, they offer unconditional love – and I seem to mean as much to them as they mean to me. The times in my day when I take the dogs for a walk or just get down on the floor and play with them, giving them kisses and cuddles and tickling their tummies, have always been important to me. In some respects, it's a kind of therapy.

Anybody who has felt the remarkable bond that can develop between a human being and a dog will understand precisely what I am talking about. However, I realise some people may be surprised, and a few might even mock the suggestion that these four-legged friends can be so important. I don't mind. Dogs have played a hugely important part in my life, providing countless hours of joy and pleasure. I have cared about them so much and, in one or two cases, their loss has plunged me into the depths of despair and grief. The old saying runs that 'you can judge a person by the way they treat dogs'. It may seem a bit simplistic but, in my experience, it's not far from the truth. Show me a person who meets a dog for the first time and can put them instantly at ease, and the chances are that individual will be pretty decent.

I got my first dog when I was nine. Prince was a Springer spaniel, and he became a loyal friend to me throughout my teens and into early adulthood, right through until the day in 1962 when he was off his food and seemed a bit off colour. My memory is absolutely clear – I took him to see the vet in Helensburgh and, standing in the small room, I thought Prince was being given some medicine to make him better. In fact, without saying anything to me, the callous man in the white coat had given him a lethal injection and put him to sleep. I was shocked. At that time, I was twenty-three years of age, about to be married and an established international clay pigeon shooting competitor just starting a motor racing career, but I was deeply affected by the loss of Prince, and the fact his life had been ended in such a casual and cold manner. Even now, it upsets me.

Helen has always shared my affection for dogs, and, when we moved to live in Switzerland, we had first a wonderful Boxer and then a Pekinese. Next, there was the sweet black Labrador bitch from Sandringham, whom we grew to love as Blossom. She always seemed so at home at Clayton House, in Begnins, and became such a gentle presence in the years when our boys were growing up. Blossom lived until she was fourteen and a half, when she developed a tumour. Helen and I took her to an animal hospital in Berne, but we soon found ourselves facing that terrible day, which every dog owner will recognise, when a decision has to be made. We stayed with her right until the end, holding and comforting her while the vet ended her life in the most peaceful way.

By this time Paul and Mark were studying in America, and I felt a couple of Labradors would suit us well, but Helen said she would prefer a lapdog. I wasn't keen on the idea, but she looked through some books, and set her heart on a Norfolk terrier.

'I don't know why you want a wee dog,' I said. 'You can't give them a good clap on the flank like you can with a big dog, and they're always yapping.'

'Well,' she said. 'I suppose I would just like something for me that I could pick up and cuddle.'

The compromise solution was to get a Labrador and a Norfolk terrier, and to hope they would get along.

I contacted Bill Meldrum at Sandringham, and he said that he would look into it. He made some inquiries and came back to let me know that he felt sure that one could be made available to us. 'Bugsy' duly arrived as a fully fledged two-year-old gun dog.

In search of a Norfolk terrier, I contacted John Stubbs, the head gamekeeper at Windsor, and a man with a great knowledge of who was who in the dog world.

'You're in luck,' John said. 'There's a breeder in Rugby who has some puppies.' Since we were living in Switzerland at the time, John suggested he would choose one for us, take it home and get it house trained. He said we would then be able to pick it up from his house when we were next in the UK.

'That sounds perfect,' I replied.

It was a beautiful summer's day when we eventually drove to Windsor, and I arrived at the house to find the door ajar. I rang the bell and, knowing John and his wife Pat well enough, made my way into the house. In that instant, a small dog appeared running along a corridor directly towards me, in full flight, barking his head off. This was 'Boss': from the moment we met, a tremendous wee dog, always rushing around, constantly on the move, full of personality.

We made arrangements to take the two new additions to our family back to Switzerland and, realising they would have to be put in a box in the hold if they travelled on a commercial flight, we decided to take them in the Jet Stream 31 that I owned at that time. In years to come, when 'passports for pets' started, we flew in private aircraft whenever we took the dogs.

'The dogs always fly privately,' I used to joke, 'but Helen sometimes flies commercial.'

Bugsy and Boss settled quickly at Clayton House and they had the run of the place once we had installed an elaborate fence around the entire property, even reaching several feet underground because Norfolk terriers are renowned diggers. Almost immediately, quite remarkably, it became clear that Helen's dog had become Jackie's new best friend. Boss and I seemed to be glued together. Where I went, he went. Where I slept, he slept. Helen started to say we even began to look the same and behave in the same way. He had such character. At times, he would sit, look up at us and almost seem to talk. Moving his head and opening his mouth, he would make sounds with an intonation that resembled human speech. He wasn't barking and he wasn't asking for food or to go outside but he was certainly communicating. Maybe he had picked up our mannerisms from watching us. In any event, he would just sit there, chatting away to his heart's content.

In 1996, when it became clear that I needed to be in England to create and develop Stewart Grand Prix, our F1 team, Helen and I reached a decision that it was necessary to leave Switzerland for a while to carry out this development. It was a terrible wrench for both us because we had been so happy there, and it was a decision made even more difficult by the knowledge that UK law meant that, upon arrival at Heathrow, both Bugsy and Boss would have to spend six months in quarantine.

I was desperately worried how they would cope with living in a confined space with a concrete floor, surrounded on each side and above by metal fencing. At least, they were allowed to stay in the same kennel, so they had each other for company. Helen and I visited them twice a week every week – very little took preference in my diary – and, day by day, they and we endured the trial.

It has always seemed to me that, as humans, we have only a basic understanding of a dog's inner senses, and this suspicion was confirmed during our visits to the quarantine kennel. We would be sitting there, playing with Bugsy and Boss, when all of a sudden the Rhodesian Ridgeback in the next kennel would start jumping up and down, barking and obviously getting very excited.

'What's all that about?' I would wonder.

Sure enough, about twenty minutes later, the owner arrived for a visit. It was uncanny, but it happened over and over again during the six months. I would happily declare under oath that somehow these dogs were able to know their owner was on his way twenty minutes before his arrival, and that period of time represents a fair distance in a car. Quite amazing. I have no idea how they did it, but they categorically did. Human beings may be quite clever, but we certainly don't understand everything.

The vet who used to do his rounds at the quarantine centre was Martin Watson, a Scot, whose surgeries was not far away in Windsor, Egham and Ascot. He is a complete professional with a wonderful manner and he would become an important person in our lives.

A long six months eventually passed, and it was pouring with rain on the much-anticipated day when we were able to collect Bugsy and Boss from the kennel and bring them to their new home in Sunningdale, where we were living at that time. We walked the boys to the kennel's car park on the lead, with both dogs stopping at every tree along the grass path. They were so excited to be out and about.

'I'm going to take them for a walk,' I told Helen when all four of us were in the car.

'In this weather?' she said.

They had suffered long enough and, before we had even gone to the apartment, we drove straight to the golf course. We were not going to be put off by a bit of rain, not even by this torrential downpour. Sunningdale is one of the few major golf courses in England where dogs are permitted to run free, and, as we reached the side of the eleventh fairway, I opened the rear door of the car and let them off the lead. What joy. The dogs burst out of the blocks like 100-metre runners, and were just so delighted to be free of confinement, sprinting in figures of eight, Boss chasing Bugsy and Bugsy chasing Boss. Helen and I watched in fits of laughter and joy. Four drenched souls eventually returned to our apartment. It was still raining hard, but it had been a memorable moment of supreme happiness.

In the weeks that followed, I watched for signs that the period in quarantine had affected them in any way – and I realised Boss had stopped 'talking'. In fact, he never 'talked' again. However, that aside, they both seemed to have taken everything in their stride and they settled happily in England.

We moved to our current home, the new Clayton House in Buckinghamshire, early in 1999 and again took the precaution of fencing a large area where the dogs would be safe to roam. Boss and Bugsy seemed perfectly happy, and Helen and I treated them and loved them as our children. Day after day, they were a constant source of comfort and happiness for us both.

Bugsy had come to us fully trained by Bill Meldrum, a Field Dog Trials world champion in his own right. Even though I thought my Lab might have forgotten his gun dog skills after six years living in Switzerland, I decided to take him out shooting. It wasn't a complete success. He had no problem with sitting patiently at my side, but, when I sent him out to retrieve a pheasant at the end of a drive, when a Labrador would normally be expected to sprint, Bugsy strutted out with considerable style, found the bird and even stopped for a pee on the way back – a performance of which Bill would not have been enormously proud.

He had become accustomed to his home comforts. Like so many Labradors, he had a mild and gentle nature, and more than anything a soft mouth. He was wonderfully patient and, when Paul and Mark brought their families over for lunch, our grandchildren would climb all over him, pulling and tugging, and he would just lie there and take it and almost seem to enjoy it.

One day in 2004, after feeding them, I took the dogs out for a walk, and, as he often did, Bugsy went for a dip in the pond on our way back to the house. Emerging from the water, he suddenly seemed to stagger and fell over on his side. There was blood coming out of his mouth, and I thought something had bitten him. He was clearly not in a good way, and I genuinely thought I was going to lose him there and then. I didn't know what to do. I felt lost. I had no phone with me to call for help and I wouldn't leave him. He needed comforting so I lay with him and cuddled close. I thought he would be cold, but he wasn't. Boss was looking at us anxiously and I started thinking I would have to carry Bugsy back. However, after fifteen minutes, gaining some strength from somewhere, he managed to stand up. Looking a tad unsteady, he walked slowly back to the house, gradually gaining confidence. I wondered if he had had a stroke, but that would not account for the bleeding from his mouth.

Having dried him off, I called Martin Watson and explained what had happened.

'You had better bring him down here,' he said.

So Bugsy was taken straight down to Ascot, and, when Martin called me, he said it was not good news.

'He's got a tumour in his mouth,' he said.

'So what now?'

'Jackie, we could try and remove it, but, to be honest, I think the operation would be too cruel for a fourteen-year-old dog.'

'So we have to make a decision?' I asked.

'Yes, I'm afraid so.'

I cancelled whatever I had planned for the rest of the day, and Helen and I drove to the surgery, taking Boss with us. We arrived and realised there was really no option. Once Boss had been taken to Martin's office, Helen and I knelt down beside Bugsy on the floor of this small room and stroked our old Labrador friend as Martin gave him his last injection. He just lay there and died, as Helen and I wept.

'Maybe you should bring Boss back,' Martin said, when it was all over. 'I think it would be for the best.'

So Boss came back in and, very oddly, he walked right around the body of his departed companion, almost without looking at him, staying close to the wall. I picked him up and put him down, and he did precisely the same thing all over again. He seemed to be distancing himself from the death. Dogs won't immediately mourn a loss – but they will do so four or five days later, when they start missing their companions.

Bugsy was cremated, and his ashes were buried beneath a white headstone in the garden at Clayton House.

Unsurprisingly, Boss seemed to cling to us even more in the weeks that followed and he travelled almost everywhere with Helen and me. Into the spring of 2005, this wee man, who had always been so energetic, clearly began to slow down and he reached a stage where he seldom ran and only walked when necessary. I took him to see Martin, and a series of tests indicated there was some problem with a valve in his heart. Within a week, he had become very poorly, and Martin told me there was nothing more he could do. I said I certainly didn't want Boss to suffer, and Martin kindly offered to come up to Clayton House.

That last morning, Helen and I took Boss for one final, gentle walk. I remember the bluebell forest was looking wonderful, and we took some photographs together. It's almost impossible for anybody who has not experienced such moments to appreciate the depths of emotion, but, for what was the fourth time in my life, there was no alternative but to do what was best for Boss, however hard it was for us. Sitting at my desk in my study at home, I held wee Boss in my arms as Martin gave him a sedative. Boss drifted off to sleep, and we walked through to the TV room, where he had so often sat with me. Around five minutes passed, then Martin gave him the final injection, and, literally lying in my arms, his head against my chest, Boss peacefully passed away. It's difficult to explain, but, as I have said at the start of this chapter, in that precise moment, I felt as if part of my soul went with him. Martin took him away to be cremated, and we later buried his ashes beneath a black headstone, beside Bugsy.

I was profoundly and deeply affected by losing Boss. There were other things happening which made it a difficult period in my life, and my frustrations with the situation at Jaguar Racing and the struggle to save the British Grand Prix at Silverstone did not help, but I simply didn't feel right for six months or more. Helen, Paul and Mark were starting to be seriously worried. Come on, I would urge myself, get your act together. I was meant to be a three-time F1 world champion, a racing driver who had supposedly shown great courage and mental strength in being able to carry on competing when so many of his friends were being killed, but it was starting to look as if I had been deflated and defeated by the death of a small dog.

Maybe it was just a natural symptom of age: it had occurred to me that people do become more emotional and more easily moved to tears as they get older. Maybe it was just a question of time: when I was a racing driver, my life was so full and consuming that there had almost been no time to stop and mourn. That sounds harsh, but that was the reality – I was always rushing to the next thing. Whatever the reason, I found it exceptionally hard to recover. The grandchildren would come to visit, and they would take flowers to put on the graves of Bugsy and Boss, and I would have to make an excuse not to go with them because I knew that, in all probability, I would simply burst into tears.

I regularly telephoned Bill Meldrum during these difficult days. He understood exactly how I felt and indeed had lived through the same experience many times before. One day, he asked me if he could send me a poem. It duly arrived in the post, and it was so touching and, sadly, so real, reflecting the emotions every loving dog owner must face at some stage – not an easy read.

With Bill's permission, and with thanks to the author whose name I have unfortunately been unable to find, I include the poem in full here. It is called 'A Dog's Prayer':

> If it should be that I grow weak
> And pain should keep me from my sleep
> Then you must do what must be done
> For this last battle cannot be won
>
> You will be sad, I understand
> Don't let your grief then stay your hand
> For this day more than all the rest
> Your love for me must stand the test
>
> We've had so many happy years
> What is to come can hold no fears
> You'd not want me to suffer so
> The time has come, please let me go
>
> Take me where my need they'll tend
> And please stay with me till the end

Hold me firm and speak to me
Until my eyes no longer see

I know in time that you will see
The kindness that you did for me
Although my tail its last has waved
From pain and suffering, I've been saved

Please do not grieve, it must be you
Who has this painful thing to do.
We've been so close, we two, these years,
Don't let your heart hold back its tears

Boss could have written exactly these words for me.

Time moved on, and Helen felt getting a new dog would help, but I wasn't keen because I felt nothing could ever replace what we had lost and that trying would be pointless and unfair.

'Come on,' she said. 'We have to move on.' Her persistence paid off just over a year later when I agreed to visit the breeder of Norfolk terriers who had bred Boss. There was apparently a new litter, so we drove up to Rugby to have a look. We arrived to find four little balls of fluff huddled together in a cardboard box, all boys. Our 'look' quickly became two hours of amusement at how these little fellows reacted to us being there. Helen and I had such fun that we decided to buy not one puppy, but two because they seemed to get along so well.

'I don't think that's wise,' said the breeder. 'If you take two boys, the likelihood is that, as they grow up, they will fight a lot. I have a bitch who's going to have a litter soon. Why don't you come back in a couple of months for the second puppy?'

The discussion continued and, in the end, the breeder succumbed. Helen and I made it clear we would like to have both the wee boys together. A month later, when they were ten weeks old, we brought them home and decided to call the larger dog of the pair Whisky and the smaller one Pimms.

They have both become a central part of our lives, and we both miss them terribly when we are away. Watching them play together is so enjoyable. They truly love each other and, when they run, it's almost as if they are tied together, side by side; and even now, as he gets older, Pimms still jumps around like a bunny rabbit when he wants Whisky to play with him. Pimms is the one who seems full of life and always looking for trouble. He runs everywhere, with no time to walk. Whisky is more docile, never wanting to stray far from me when I'm home. Both get jealous if one or the other gets a little bit more attention and they'll starting pushing in and jumping up to get ahead. They are also great lovers of watching television, sometimes getting quite aggressive when other animals appear, first trying to snap at the screen and then, when the animals disappear from view, excitedly rushing round behind the television to find out where they have gone. It's a great cabaret.

Norfolk terriers are renowned for their characters, even among terriers, and our boys are no exception. They are so affectionate and upbeat. It's as if they wake up every morning, and suddenly it's a new day: they are so alert and full of excitement and expectation, wondering what adventures lie in store for them. The world would certainly be a happier place if more humans were to awake with such joy.

CHAPTER 21

Securing the Future

THE FACT THAT EVERY NEW F1 motor racing season brings new cars, new technology, new drivers and new regulations means it is impossible to compare one era with another. As a result, I find myself having to give slightly unsatisfactory answers to the two questions I am most often asked.

Was being a F1 racing driver more difficult in your era than it is today?

It was more dangerous, but it was neither any more difficult nor any easier. The job remains the same, because the core challenge of driving a high-performance car at the absolute limit has not changed. In temperament and ability, modern F1 drivers are still the same animal as drivers in the past.

Who is the greatest F1 racing driver of all time?

All anyone can be is the best in their time. Juan Manuel Fangio was my hero when I was young and he was undoubtedly the best of his era, and Jim Clark was the best driver I ever raced against. However, the sport has changed so much over the years that it is impossible to compare these two alongside multiple world champions such as Jack Brabham, Niki Lauda, Nelson

Piquet, Alain Prost, Ayrton Senna, Mika Häkkinen, Michael Schumacher and Fernando Alonso.

Many of these changes have been for the better, and, by general consent, F1 motor racing appears to be thriving. The sport is safer than ever, the competition among countries to host a Grand Prix is more intense than ever, the annual race calendar continues to expand, and the global television audience is growing at a healthy rate, particularly in China, India and other fast-developing countries. What was once, many years ago, a gentleman's sport has become a highly efficient and effective business, although I daresay many will mourn the passing of the private entrants motivated more by a real passion for motor sport than by the opportunity to add a few more noughts to their bank balance. Today it is a serious business of considerable size.

Ken Tyrrell was one such gentleman. He continued to run his F1 team during the 1990s but became increasingly disenchanted and at one stage raged against the introduction to F1 racing of the Turbo engine. 'It's unnecessarily expensive,' he declared, 'and beyond the reach of ordinary individuals, so it's turning the sport into the exclusive domain of the major car manufacturers . . .' and he would yearn for the relatively recent past when almost every F1 car used the 3 litre normally aspirated Ford Cosworth engine, which was affordable so private entrants could compete on a level playing field; the result was probably the most exciting and competitive era in the history of F1 racing.

People were starting to say Ken was 'too honest' for the sport, and eventually, in 1999, with dignity and integrity intact, he decided to sell his Tyrrell team to British American Racing. Visit the site of the old Tyrrell headquarters in Ockham, Surrey today, and you'll find a modern factory. Look across the car park and you'll see the famous old wood hut with the blue door still standing. Considering the remarkable success of the racing cars that were built inside, that building should be a national monument.

Ken was sad to leave the stage. I remember we went to watch the following year's Canadian Grand Prix in Montreal and were sitting together in a hospitality area; he suddenly turned to me and, jabbing his finger towards the pit lane, said, 'This is just not the same, Jackie. I want to be down there.' By then, he had been diagnosed with cancer of the pancreas. The outlook was not encouraging, but he went to the Mayo Clinic, and underwent an operation that probably gave him an extra couple of years with his beloved wife, Norah, and he never stopped fighting against the disease. On one occasion, he insisted on getting up at five in the morning to drive four and half hours so we could go shooting together in the depths of Derbyshire.

I saw Ken regularly towards the end of his life and we spent precious hours, recalling all the stories from the days we spent together and reliving the amazing times we shared.

One day, he suddenly sat up in bed and said, 'Jackie, there are two things I want you to do for me.'

'OK,' I replied.

'First, I want you to get the BRDC to give me a memorial service and I want you to organise it.' He was still president of the British Racing Drivers' Club, the owners of Silverstone, so I told him that I didn't think there would be any problem with that.

'Second, I want you to succeed me as president. You know all about the problems at Silverstone and you're the one man who can sort everything out. Will you do that, Jackie?'

'Really?'

'Yes.'

'What did I do to deserve that?'

He smiled.

It was a BRDC tradition that the outgoing president identified his successor, and invariably this candidate was then elected by the members, so he had decided to pass the torch to me.

'All right,' I said. 'I'll do it.'

Ken Tyrrell, giant of British motor sport, passed away on 25 August 2001, at the age of seventy-seven, and I was left to keep the two promises I had made on his deathbed. The memorial service was held at Guildford Cathedral, and 1,100 people came to pay their respects. Four Tyrrell racing cars were parked outside the main door, and the music was provided by the band of the Royal Air Force, the Guildford Cathedral choir and Dame Kiri Te Kanawa accompanied by a sixteen-piece orchestra. At the end, the congregation filed away to the rousing strains of 'When the Saints Go Marching In', played by Chris Barber's jazz band, and I felt Ken had been given the kind of send-off he would have enjoyed.

For my part, I would rather go to a good memorial service than a good wedding. That might sound odd, but the best memorial services are genuine celebrations, one-off reunions of family and friends, many of whom have known each other for a number of years, who want to reflect kindly on the good times and the achievements they have shared with the deceased. A wedding is also a celebration, but it marks a union that everybody trusts and hopes will be successful, as opposed to something that has already been achieved; and, with half the guests having been invited by the groom and half by the bride, you often seem to be surrounded by people you don't know.

Keeping my second promise proved substantially more challenging. As actors often advise each other to avoid working with children and animals, so businessmen warn against getting involved with private members' clubs.

The BRDC is the ultimate private members' club, because full membership is restricted to approximately 500 former and current racing drivers of varying standards from across the UK and the Commonwealth; in addition, a group of around 300 people – constructors, mechanics, journalists, photographers and others, all of whom have been deeply involved in the sport – are associate members with no voting rights. Its main business is to run the famous old racing circuit at Silverstone and, by extension, to stage the British F1 Grand Prix. In 2000, following Ken's wishes, I was elected as president.

'You're mad,' warned many of my friends. Perhaps I was, but I had no choice.

What followed was a difficult period of my life, when I worked hard to safeguard the future of the circuit and the British Grand Prix but felt increasingly isolated among the demanding F1 authorities, apathetic politicians and a club in which there was a vocal body resistant to change. There were many times when I felt like walking away from all the hassle, from the internal politics and different agendas, but I stuck it out because I had made my promise to Ken and also because I felt an obligation to 'do my bit' for British motor sport. It may sound trite, but the reality was that I felt that the sport had been good to me and I wanted to give something back.

A complete account of my six years as president of the BRDC would require another book on its own, and probably keep the lawyers busy, so a summary must suffice.

- When I took over as president, the BRDC was in negotiations with IPG, a large American company listed on the New York Stock Exchange that had bought four of Britain's racing circuits, not including Silverstone, as well as the rights to stage the British F1 Grand Prix. They initially wanted to stage the race at Brands Hatch, which was one of the four, but, unfortunately for them, Brands did not come close to meeting the standards required to host a modern F1 Grand Prix. So, if they were going to use their rights, they had to start talking to Silverstone, the only circuit in the UK that offered adequate facilities.

- A deal was agreed whereby IPG would lease Silverstone from the BRDC for £8 million per year, with the club retaining control of the clubhouse and the rights of its members being preserved – this was an amazingly good financial arrangement for the BRDC, perhaps too good, and it seemed to secure the future of the race.
- A complaint was lodged at the Competitions Commission because, allegedly, our deal with IPG gave them control of more than 20 per cent of the racing circuits in the UK. The issue dragged on for many months, making huge time demands on Martin Brundle, the hard-working BRDC chairman at the time, and on me, and also leaving us with substantial, but unavoidable, legal costs.
- When torrential rain disrupted the 2001 British Grand Prix, prompting a senior F1 official to declare famously that 'you can't hold a Grand Prix at the end of a farm road', the need to improve access to the circuit became urgent, and we spent £17.1 million on building a new access road and creating new parking areas and new spectator facilities.
- The IPG deal was finally approved, but, when they began losing considerable sums of money, not only on the Grand Prix but also in their other motor sport activities and at Silverstone, they changed their minds and said they wanted to buy their way out of their contract to stage the race and also their contract to lease the circuit from us. This process took more time, fed more lawyers and caused more disruption, but the BRDC reluctantly regained control of the race and Silverstone. We set about rebuilding the business, which had been damaged by uncertainty, and worked out how to make ends meet on the existing Grand Prix contract.
- This was the board's task, but we found it difficult to get on with the job we had been elected to do. In every private club, there will almost always be a group of members who are unhappy about something. Some of them just make their

voices heard, but a few try to disrupt things. The group within the BRDC was of the latter variety and they contributed to the creation of a mood of discontent.

- In an attempt to address this problem, I had for some months been trying to persuade the board to create a new structure that would separate the business of the BRDC and Silverstone from club membership matters. In the end, this proposal was supported by both the board and a clear majority of the membership.

- A motion of no confidence in the president and the board was tabled at an Extraordinary General Meeting in 2006 and defeated. However, after six intense and demanding years, I felt I had done as much as I could for the club, the circuit and the British F1 Grand Prix and, at the following Annual General Meeting a month or so later, I announced my intention to step down.

Aside from all the politics and the nonsense, what was the issue? It was – and, in fact, it remains – the future of British motor sport. If we don't find the funding to improve facilities at Silverstone, we will lose the British F1 Grand Prix; and if we lose the race, we will start to lose the British motor sport industry. In my view, that was something worth fighting for.

It was worth fighting to protect the future of Silverstone.

The former World War II airfield may be flat and sometimes bleak with little vegetation or few mature trees, and it may be some distance from a major city, yet it remains a place of history and tradition that hosted its first F1 race in 1948 and then staged the first-ever world championship Grande Epreuve in 1950. It has become universally acknowledged as one of the fastest and safest motor racing circuits in the world. It is a place with a distinguished past, and I am confident it can have a distinguished future. Any move to build a purpose-built circuit elsewhere in the UK would make no sense. Of course,

Silverstone needs investment, but, even now, its facilities are far from the worst on the F1 rota.

It was worth fighting to protect the future of the British F1 Grand Prix.

It's more than a great day out, although it has always been that for the many hundreds of thousands of British motor sport enthusiasts who have camped in the fields and packed the stands at what has been, for fifty years and more, one of the great events on the British sporting calendar. It's more than a great occasion, although it has always been that for so many people, and for me ever since 1953 when, as an excited fourteen-year-old, I first arrived at Silverstone to watch my older brother drive in the race. The British Grand Prix is the spark that ignites enthusiasm and passion for the sport across the country. Television is a wonderful medium, but it simply does not do justice to the spectacle of motor racing. Sitting at home and watching a long shot of a F1 car approaching Copse Corner is, to say the least, underwhelming compared to the thrill of attending the race and having all your senses bombarded by the experience. Year after year, young people make their way to Silverstone and hear the roar of the engines and smell the cars and see the speed. On that very day, they can catch the motor sport bug, and it is precisely these people who grow up to be F1 drivers, or engineers, or designers, or even constructors.

For so many of us who have contributed to motor sport over the years, it all started at the British Grand Prix. For Patrick Head, who became one of the great technical geniuses of the sport, for Adrian Newey, who became the highest-paid designer of racing cars in the world, for Ross Brawn, who masterminded Ferrari's domination in the Michael Schumacher era, for all of us, and many more, everything began at Silverstone, where we first saw the sport at close quarters and became intoxicated. For all those young Britons who will contribute in the future, for the next Lewis Hamilton and many more, we must safeguard the future of the race. Kill the spark, and we will kill the fire.

It was worth fighting to protect the future of the British motor sport industry.

The connection between the race, the sport and the industry is unique. The FA Premier League is hailed as the finest domestic league in football, yet the supporting industries that manufacture replica strips and boots are based in other countries. In contrast, British motor sport is inextricably linked to an entire industry of UK manufacturers, UK constructors and various UK suppliers.

Britain has been recognised as the capital of motor sport technology ever since the late 1960s, and F1 teams such as McLaren, Williams, Renault, Red Bull and Honda are all based in this country. The industry now includes around 3,000 associated companies, employing as many as 50,000 people, generating in excess of £5 billion in sales per year and exporting approximately 60 per cent of its total output. In my view, there is no doubt that if we lose the British Grand Prix, job by job, team by team, we will start to lose the industry to Germany, France, Italy and, in due course, to China.

It was worth fighting to sustain the heritage of British motor sport.

Too many people have worked too hard to create this heritage for it to be casually tossed away. Too many fine drivers in the early years – like Stirling Moss, whom I so revered as the epitome of an exciting modern racing driver, a man who walked and talked in the way I thought a racing driver should; and Mike Hawthorn, who raced wearing a bow tie beneath his overalls; and John Surtees, the only man who started in motorcycling, moved to cars and became F1 world champion. Too many fine drivers in my era – like Graham Hill and Jim Clark. Too many fine drivers in the following generation – like the charismatic James Hunt, who attracted a new audience; like

Nigel Mansell, the fast and furious world champion who mortgaged his house to get a drive and thrilled the crowds by almost grabbing his car by the scruff of the neck and man-handling it around the circuit; like Damon Hill who overcame many obstacles and showed his quality by becoming F1 world champion.

In addition, too many British team owners, principals, designers, engineers, mechanics and truckies had given too much to our heritage. It would be impossible to name everybody, but six individuals stand out.

John Cooper, together with his father Charles, was the originator of the rear-engined racing car in the UK and built the car that Jack Brabham drove to victory over Ferrari in 1959 and 1960; this success created demand for what became the most advanced small-batch engineering industry in the world.

Colin Chapman arrived and, through his achievements with Lotus, became probably the most brilliant and innovative design engineer and constructor in the history of the sport.

Eric Broadley, the wonderful creator of Lola Cars, which became the largest producer of racing cars in the world at one time. Ken Tyrrell worked his way to the highest level and, through the strength of his personality and the team that he gathered around him, became a major influence.

Sir Frank Williams has operated at the highest level of the sport for more than thirty years. We first met in 1964, when he spotted me walking along a road near Silverstone because my car had run out of petrol. He stopped and gave me a lift to the nearest garage, and we have been friends ever since.

Frank started as a driver in club racing, alongside people like Charlie Crichton-Stuart, Jonathan Williams, Piers Courage and Charles Lucas; in 1966, he started buying and selling racing cars until he had enough money to buy his own F3 car and trailer and become an entrant on the European tour. The Williams legend was born, and, today, he remains established as a grandee of the sport, wonderfully supported by his wife Jenny and as committed and hungry for success as he has ever been. Inspired by the partnership between Frank and Patrick Head, Williams have won no fewer than nine F1 constructors' world championships and seven F1 drivers' world championships.

We have shared so much over all these years, and we have laughed. I remember how, in the early days of Stewart Grand Prix, Frank took great delight in mocking our tartan trousers.

'You know, it would considerably improve your image if you wore a pair,' I told him.

A proud Englishman, he scoffed at the idea. 'I tell you what,' he replied, laughing, 'if your team ever wins a Grand Prix, I will wear a pair.'

He wasn't laughing when we won the Grand Prix of Europe at the Nurburgring in 1999 – and, just before the last race of that season in Malaysia, Paul and I took great delight in personally delivering to Frank a new pair of Racing Stewart tartan trousers, perfectly made in his size by Doug Hayward, the tailor in London who we had shared for so many years. As good as his word, he put them on and was duly photographed in the paddock. There is now an outstanding bet that, when Williams wins another F1 Grand Prix, Frank will wear the Royal Bank of Scotland tartan trousers.

Ron Dennis built the McLaren team into an immense power. He started as a mechanic with Cooper and Brabham and ran an operation that employs more than 1,200 people and operates from a futuristic headquarters in Surrey. This remarkable facility was designed by Sir Norman Foster, with two-thirds of the building underground. Ron has always been driven by a quest for excellence, and, over the thirty-eight years we have known each other, I have greatly admired his attention to detail in building the McLaren culture into what it is today. The team has won eight drivers' F1 world championships and eleven constructors' F1 world championships. Many great F1 racing teams have owed their success to the inspiring leadership of one highly respected and highly motivated individual. There is no better example than the role Ron Dennis has played in the development of McLaren; and, in 2007, I was pleased to see Ron receiving the accolades he deserves for developing the skills of Lewis Hamilton, certainly the best-prepared young driver ever to enter F1 motor racing.

These are the men who have helped build British motor sport into what it is today – without the British Grand Prix in the past, they may never have even entered the sport; without the British Grand Prix in the future, their legacy will be threatened.

'OK, but Jackie,' people ask, 'do you really think we could lose the race?'

'There's no doubt,' I reply. 'The British Grand Prix has been confirmed on the F1 calendar until the end of 2009. Beyond that, there are no guarantees at all.'

'Why?'

'Because the UK does not have a motor racing circuit that offers the level of facilities that people have come to expect at a major sporting event. People go to places like the new Wembley Stadium, the Millennium Stadium in Cardiff and the Emirates Stadium at Arsenal, and their expectations are raised to a level that a place like Silverstone simply cannot match.'

'Why not?'

'Because the circuit is owned by the BRDC, a private members' club that must first meet the costs associated with the Grand Prix contract and cannot provide the money to make the improvements that are required.'

'So what is required?'

'Public funding,' I reply.

This was a conversation I pursued hundreds of times during my six years as president of the BRDC, as I lobbied politicians of all parties to support and retain the British Grand Prix beyond 2009. I pointed out how governments worldwide invest huge sums to host a F1 Grand Prix because they recognise 1) the value of projecting their country as a high-tech, modern destination to a vast television audience in more than 200 countries, and 2) the race's impact on the local and regional economy. I told them that countries like Australia, Malaysia, Bahrain, Turkey and China had committed many millions of dollars to secure a F1 race, and that the likes of Korea, Singapore, Abu Dhabi, India and Russia would follow.

I explained that only two races on the F1 calendar receive no government support: the British Grand Prix and the US Grand Prix. 'But,' I added, 'the State of Indiana provides all traffic management services for free whereas at Silverstone the BRDC gets a bill for half a million pounds.' I said this situation was not sustainable.

'Yes, but,' the politicians replied, 'we can't spend public money on a F1 Grand Prix. This is a democracy, and we believe health and education need the money more than an elite sport.'

'We're not asking for a charitable donation,' I said. 'We are requesting investment in a race and an industry that contributes £5 billion to the UK economy and is under serious threat.'

'OK,' they said, 'but why can't the British Grand Prix just carry on as before?'

'The competition to host a F1 race is increasing, which means the fee has risen from around $5 million to more than three times that amount, and the costs of meeting all the requirements have escalated. The BRDC is not in a position to meet these costs.'

'So how much do you need?'

'Well,' I replied, 'around £100 million would transform Silverstone into a fully serviced modern circuit. People always talk about the importance of improving the pit and paddock complex, the administration buildings and the media centre – and these are all important, but none of these projects generate revenue or have any impact on the ordinary spectator. The Silverstone of the future must offer the paying public comfortable grandstands, good food and convenient parking; they must be kept warm on cold days and cool on hot days; they should be made to feel welcome and safe, and they should leave the venue with an enthusiasm and energy to return. In addition, it must provide facilities that meet the requirements of the increasingly demanding corporate hospitality sector. All of this could cost £100 million, but government might need to provide as little as 25 per cent of that because there is real potential for a public–private partnership – and that really is a small amount of money when compared to the sums allocated by the British government to other sports and projects.'

I can't say I particularly enjoyed my regular trips to Westminster – I had never previously met so many people who seemed so keen to find reasons not to make things happen – but I did put our case in one-on-one meetings with more than eighty MPs, including a series of Cabinet ministers.

Prime Minister Tony Blair was sympathetic and helpful, particularly when he personally supported a grant of £8 million to ensure the Silverstone bypass was largely completed in time for the race in 2003. Construction of the road had been delayed by the foot and mouth epidemic, and he acted to avoid the negative worldwide publicity that would have followed if one of Britain's largest sporting events had taken place in the middle of a construction site.

The British Grand Prix has been held at Silverstone ever since but, in the summer of 2008, it was announced that, with effect from the 2010 season, the race would be moved to Donington Park. This news obviously came as a great disappointment to those of us who hold Silverstone close to our hearts, but it was hardly a surprise. In simple terms, in the midst of an economic downturn, the BRDC had sadly reached the conclusion that, in the absence of direct government support, the club was unable to pay the extremely high fee being demanded by the governing body of the sport and the F1 commercial rights holder and also to fund the considerable improvements to the circuit being required by these same authorities. The combined burden of the fee and the improvements would have bankrupted the club.

Meanwhile a consortium of investors was developing a vision at Donington, and they felt able to agree terms which may have been even more onerous. Their task will grow as the recession deepens, and many believe the future of the British Grand Prix remains profoundly uncertain. Maybe the Donington plan will go ahead or perhaps a deal will be done and the race will remain at Silverstone after all . . . or maybe the race will simply disappear altogether from the F1 calendar, just as the French Grand Prix has gone.

Some people say this just won't happen. I think they're wrong. Complacency could easily prove to be our downfall. Whatever people like me say, and however many times we say it, a significant number of people in important places still believe deep down some kind of agreement will be reached and, somehow, the British Grand Prix will continue. I'm not sure. In the current F1 environment, unless some form of public funding is agreed, British motor sport and the industry may well be mortally damaged.

Some progress has been made. When we first asked for government support, the F1 authorities publicly declared we should not be seeking public money. It was encouraging to see them revise their view, and say the UK Government should contribute. All said and done, the British Grand Prix needs to find a safe and secure place within the current F1 landscape, as it has been developed by the authorities, most notably Bernie Ecclestone.

I have known Bernard since 1964, and he has been tremendously successful in transforming F1 motor racing into a multi-billion-dollar business. He is the most intensely focused person I have ever met. Mark McCormack was very bright, astute and successful, but Bernie is enormously clever and he has shown amazing foresight. Our approach to concluding a deal is different: I have always subscribed to the saying 'good business is profit on both sides' because that creates a feel-good factor and often leads to a long-term association, whereas Bernie has sometimes tended to take a more aggressive line and leave very little on the table. Having said that, his record speaks for itself, and there is no doubt he has played the leading role in the extraordinary success of F1 motor racing. For that, many of us who have derived substantial benefit from this growth certainly do have cause to be grateful. Bernie is a very tough man, but he does have an extremely generous side to his nature and when he's nice, he's very nice.

Maybe the deal the authorities have been seeking with the cities and venues that host the traditional Grands Prix in Europe has been too tough – the French Grand Prix has gone, the British Grand Prix is under threat and we have even lost the US and Canadian events. Other races such as Malaysia, Bahrain, China, Singapore, Australia, Turkey and Abu Dhabi are only sustained by local, regional or federal government funding. In a similar vein, the two races located in Spain – at Valencia and Barcelona – have also been greatly assisted.

The commercial rights holders will reply they don't need to reduce their fees or ease their terms because they still have a long list of cities and countries wishing to stage a race on the F1 calendar. That may have been true, but these proposed races are almost exclusively funded by governments prepared to invest many millions of dollars into hosting a race and projecting the profile of their city or country. We have seen this model work in places like Singapore, where the inaugural night race in the 2008 season was a wonderfully exciting event, and in Abu Dhabi which will host its first Grand Prix in November 2009, but clearly it does not work in most of Europe or the USA, where governments may not be prepared to financially support a Grand Prix. And it may not even work in India now and also China in the future.

In my view, tradition and history remain important and the challenge for the authorities is to develop a model that provides a balance, allowing the traditional Grands Prix to continue and the new races to be developed.

It is interesting that an imbalance appears to have been suggested, with the governing body and the commercial rights holders apparently indicating that some of the major vehicle manufacturers have accelerated the costs in F1, thereby leaving behind those teams not blessed with partners exhibiting such deep pockets. There seems to be a desire to return to a more level playing field. A similar argument could also be mooted in terms of the hosting of the races. Those supported with public sector spending can afford to do so; those without, struggle. If the governing body is pushing for technology cost reductions, would it not also be worthy to consider reducing the fees charged to the circuits to put on a Grand Prix, so that countries such as Britain, France, the US and Canada could enjoy long-term stability in hosting such events?

Maybe the recession will force a change of tack. I believe the governance of the sport will have to change. Maybe, as the structures change, more of the money generated by F1 will find its way back into motor sport and be distributed among the shareholders in a manner I believe would be more equitable. Nothing ever stays the same forever, not even the governance of F1 motor racing. Even the Roman Empire fell in the end.

Perhaps, if all that happens, somebody will address the ludicrous anomaly whereby many of the officials at F1 races are still eager, unpaid amateurs, who change from race to race and whose sole qualification may be that they have been an observer at one previous Grand Prix. These people are playing an increasingly important role in the sport, and their decisions affect the results of races and entire championships. It is surely sensible for this responsibility to be placed in the hands of experienced professionals.

The sport does remain a uniquely attractive proposition for commercial partners, continuing to offer outstanding global exposure all year round, but nobody should be complacent. There's that dangerous word cropping up again. Everyone in F1 should be aware of it.

Today, I remain close to the sport through my commercial relationship with RBS and my involvement with two associated charities. More than twenty years ago, most of the F1 teams could not afford to provide insurance cover and pension funds to look after their current and former mechanics in times of hardship. This situation prompted me to create the Grand Prix Mechanics Charitable Trust. With Ken Tyrrell as our first trustee, we started staging events and raising funds, which have been distributed to F1 mechanics and their families in times of hardship. The F1 teams are better organised and financed today, and appropriate policies and funds are in place. Some prominent people have questioned whether the Trust is still required. The answer is a resounding 'yes' because, while the current mechanics may be all right, it still needs to support those former mechanics who are now approaching or past the age of retirement. So we continue raising money and making grants to people in need.

Our annual lunch has become a wonderful reunion of more than 120 mechanics, past and present, the oldest of whom still recall the days when they prepared cars for the likes of Fangio, Gonzales and Moss. 'You are the only true professionals in the business,' I always tell them, year after year.

The continuing status of the Trust is neatly reflected in the quality of people who have agreed to serve on our board of trustees; in 2007, this included Martin Brundle (former F1 driver), Brian Clark (solicitor to F1 teams), Norbert Haug (vice-president of Mercedes-Benz responsible for F1 projects), Patrick Head (technical director, Williams F1), Peter Hetherington (charitable trust expert at Rawlinson & Hunter), Michael Jakeman (former F1 mechanic), Dave Ryan (McLaren team manager), Michael Tee (GP photographer), Professor Sid Watkins (F1 surgeon), Jo Ramirez (former F1 mechanic and team manager), John Hogan (former vice-president of Philip Morris), James Allen (F1 commentator) and me, as chairman.

I also continue to serve as president of the Springfield Club in the borough of Hackney, in the East End of London, a wonderful sports and social youth club that has been supported by generations of F1 motor racing drivers. I first visited the club in 1965, in the company of Graham Hill, who was president, and Jim Clark, a vice-president. On that visit I too was made a vice-president and since then I have been privileged to assist in the development of a club that has provided motivation and opportunities for boys and girls.

An exuberant annual awards evening is staged every November, and, by tradition, we arrange for a racing driver or well-known person to attend and address the members. David Coulthard was the principal guest in 2004, Zara Phillips came along in 2005, and Lewis Hamilton attended the event in November 2006.

I have been more formally involved with the club since 1976, when I succeeded Graham as president, and the family connection has continued, with Paul now serving as chairman. However, the key to Springfield's success is the day-to-day commitment of many remarkable people, notably Rita Berry, John Brumwell, Peter Jopp, Michael Keogh, Vibert Murdoch, Stephen Herbert and others, and many, many willing parents.

The passing years have in no way dimmed my enthusiasm for the sport, and I still attend seven or eight F1 Grands Prix each year, still getting excited, still enjoying the spectacle and still feeling comfortable walking down the paddock and seeing so many friends who I have known for so many years.

Nothing ever stands still, and, in 2007, we saw a changing of the guard to follow the era when Michael Schumacher and Ferrari swept all before them. Michael's defining genius was his ability to recognise F1 motor racing is a sport where a vast team of people must work together, and the driver gets most of the credit. He never believed he could win all on his own and he worked tirelessly to gather the very best people around him.

Prior to his arrival, Ferrari had not won a world championship in twenty-one years, but the Italian manufacturer was prepared to do whatever was required to recruit the people that Michael identified, and the result was the best team, the best car and a sustained period of F1 domination and success. Michael won an unprecedented six F1 world championships with Ferrari and he would not have done so without the direction provided by brilliant men like Jean Todt and Ross Brawn, but they would be the first to accept that Michael did much more than drive the car – he galvanised the entire team.

Many people assumed his retirement at the end of 2006 would usher in a period of domination by Fernando Alonso, who had shown incredible maturity beyond his years in winning back-to-back F1 world championships in 2005 and 2006. The young Spaniard is a beautifully smooth driver, who often seems so unflustered as he coaxes the car around the circuit in a way that not only generates speed but also ensures reliability. However, there is much more to being a world champion than just driving the car. As Fernando becomes a little more outgoing, and learns to assist the media and effectively project his team and its commercial partners, he has the potential to become one of the great world champions.

The same is undoubtedly true of Lewis Hamilton. In 2007, the talented young British driver announced his arrival in F1 motor racing in the most extraordinary fashion, claiming a podium finish in each of his first five starts and then winning both the Canadian Grand Prix in Montreal and the US Grand Prix at Indianapolis within the space of eight days. He came within a whisker of winning the world championship in his debut season, eventually being pipped at the post by Kimi Raikkonen at a dramatic Brazilian Grand Prix.

In 2008, a wonderfully exciting championship also reached its conclusion in São Paulo and, on this occasion, Lewis managed to get the job done, edging out Felipe Massa and securing his first world championship, the first of what I hope and believe will be many world titles.

Lewis is spectacularly talented, and he is brilliantly fulfilling the potential that first appeared when he competed in his first organised race at the age of eight. He joined the McLaren driver development programme at the age of thirteen, finished fifth in the senior British Formula Renault Winter Series at the age of fifteen and rose through the formative classes of the sport, winning the F3 Euroseries in 2005 and the GP2 series in 2006.

It is a fact that, when he arrived in F1 at the age of twenty-two, Lewis had negotiated more starts and more first corners than I did during my entire motor racing career. He also had available to him the world's most sophisticated F1 simulator – an incredible advantage for a young driver. This meticulous education, this almost unprecedented scale of preparation gave him the opportunity to master the techniques of driving, combining an ability to spot a gap and get past people and also to drive with consistency – and he has seized that opportunity.

Many people have pointed out that, in the entire history of our sport, no young driver has ever arrived in F1 and immediately been hired to drive for one of the two strongest teams. In this respect, Lewis has certainly benefited from the vast expertise within the McLaren team.

The great Ayrton Senna started with Toleman, a small team with minimal resources and no real potential to win a Grand

Prix. Fernando Alonso got his big break in F1 when he was employed by Minardi, but again his team did not have the capacity to challenge at the front of the grid. In fact, among F1 drivers in the past forty years, I may be the closest example of a rookie being drafted straight into a genuinely competitive team – BRM were not the strongest team in 1965, but they were certainly far from the worst.

Lewis owed his unique opportunity to Ron Dennis, the McLaren boss who was famously impressed at an awards ceremony when the twelve-year-old Hamilton walked up and declared he would like be his driver one day. Ron recognised the potential, and his faith has been vindicated.

Success has brought a tidal wave of commercial opportunities and, to date, this side of Lewis's life has been handled by his father, Anthony. Most people who operate at this rarefied level of international sport consider it wise to appoint a professional company to maximise commercial revenue and manage all the issues that come with a truly global profile. It will be interesting to see whether Lewis and Anthony eventually reach the same conclusion. So far, it must be said, they are doing an excellent job.

In my experience, Lewis is an outstanding ambassador not only for the sport but also for young people. He has twice visited the Springfield Club, and it was remarkable to witness the profound impact he made on the youngsters present.

His future is unbelievably bright, so long as he keeps his support system in place and does not get carried away by the celebrity cult. Make no mistake, this can happen in an intoxicating world where competitive media like nothing more than to build up a hero, and knock them down.

As he continues his rocket-ship ride – where life must surely become a blur, as he jets from race to race, from appearance to appearance, and from country to country – he will certainly have cause to be grateful for the backing of a strong and loyal family unit. Lewis is constantly supported by his father Anthony and his brother Nicholas, a fantastic young man, as well as by his mother and his step-mother.

Amid the media frenzy that developed around Lewis, another highly talented British racing driver suddenly seemed to have been pushed into the shadows. While his young compatriot was thriving at the front of the grid, Jenson Button was struggling in a less competitive car. Yet Jenson remains extremely gifted, and, if any of the leading drivers slipped on a banana skin, there is no doubt in my mind that, given the chance, he could step into the cockpit of a McLaren or a Ferrari and be instantly competitive, claiming pole positions and winning races. I hope his chance will come.

We will see.

I have often said there are hundreds of millions of people on this planet who drive cars.

Of these, only a few million have a competition licence.

Of these, a few thousand make a living from driving.

Of these, a few hundred make quite a lot of money.

Of these, at any one time, there are just twenty-two individuals who are given the opportunity to take their place on the starting grid of a F1 world championship Grand Prix.

Of those twenty-two, only six are truly outstanding.

Of those six, perhaps three are extraordinary.

History suggests that, at any one time, of those three, there is probably only one genius.

The continuing quest for that genius has sparked the enthusiasm of many millions of F1 followers all around the world, and I'm sure it will continue to do so for many years to come.

CHAPTER 22

What Is Enough?

T HE TITLE OF THIS BOOK – 'Winning Is Not Enough' – has real integrity for me. Those four words represent the central theme of my life, and they fully reflect the search for excellence, the partial satisfaction of achieving, the frustration of losing and the ever-present hunger to prove myself.

I have been fortunate to have enjoyed my fair share of winning but, as my life has progressed, it has become abundantly clear to me that simply winning is not enough.

As I pursued my goals in shooting, in motor racing, in television and business, and in the social structure that came my way, I found myself in the company of so many people who had achieved so much more than me, and I realised the ultimate goal is not winning . . . it is achieving long-term success not just in sport or just in business but across every aspect of life.

It is my sincere hope that this underlying theme has emerged from all the various episodes I have recalled in this book – the euphoric and the tragic, the gratifying and the frustrating.

When I started this project, almost fifteen months ago, I set out to portray as accurately and graphically as possible all the significant events of my life; however, as the book passed the halfway mark, it became clear that I would have to be content with recalling only the *most* significant events.

There was not enough space to incorporate everything I would have liked to include, and the process of deciding what to leave out proved frustrating for somebody like me, who has always attached so much importance to paying attention to detail and covering all the bases. Nonetheless, I hope the book provides a correct and vivid representation of what has made the past sixty-eight years so totally satisfying for me.

The central pillar of my life has always been the closeness of my family unit, from the care and support of my parents and my brother, the influence of my grandparents, my happy and fulfilling marriage to Helen and the immense love, pride and pleasure we have shared in watching Paul and Mark grow and develop, their marriages to Victoria and Anne, and on to the joy we take in watching the progress of our eight grandchildren.

I am conscious that Paul has featured heavily in these pages, by virtue of the fact that for so much of his life we were actually working together, in his own racing career, in the creation and development of Paul Stewart Racing and then Stewart Grand Prix, and also on account of his traumatic struggle with cancer.

Mark has been equally successful in the world of producing films and programmes for television, and I am so proud of his creative ability and the manner in which he has built his business, Mark Stewart Productions (MSP), surrounding himself with a group of wonderfully gifted and talented people.

I didn't identify and recruit these people – Mark did. I did not develop the concepts or make the programmes that have been nominated for awards – Mark did. He has written his own success story.

MSP has earned a strong reputation for documentaries and

corporate communications on subjects ranging from motor sport to Egyptian archaeology and its programmes are broadcast in Britain and worldwide, notably on the Discovery Channel, National Geographic and Smithsonian networks.

In 2001, Mark and his colleagues produced a two-hour documentary film on my life, which combined archive footage of my racing career with various interviews. This was an outstanding piece of work, broadcast on Channel 4 in the UK and on other major channels as far afield as Australia and New Zealand, and it was nominated in the Best Sports Documentary category at the Royal Television Society's award dinner in London.

MSP's documentary on Ken Tyrrell was a masterpiece, and the MSP film on the life of Graham Hill, released in late 2007, captured the essence of the man and his era, and received rave reviews.

None of this success has surprised me. I clearly remember the day in 1980 when Akai delivered one of their brand new video cameras to our home in Switzerland. It was a present for me, but I have never been an expert on technology – I still don't use a computer – and it was my excited twelve-year-old son who was soon working out what to do with the cables and power packs. Before long, Mark was running around the house, shooting short films and spoof commercials, keeping us all entertained.

As he grew up, he overcame the effects of serious dyslexia, every bit as potent as mine, and completed his education in the United States. He returned home, became a member of the Perth Repertory Theatre in Scotland, and subsequently worked for Trans World International, the television division of IMG, covering major sports events around the world; at one stage, he spent a year living and working in Australia.

This experience and knowledge gave him the confidence to create MSP in 1994, and, in the early years, he played an important role in Paul Stewart Racing and Stewart Grand Prix by filming many of our races and test sessions, and producing quality films that we used to enhance our media launches and commercial presentations.

Mark's company has never been backward in being innovative, not least in producing the upbeat video montage of my life, set to 'Supreme' by Robbie Williams, which I use as an introduction before a speech.

MSP has also been responsible for producing the Visual Book Enhancement (ViBE) that accompanied the hardback edition of this book. This concept of supplying a DVD to complement the book, bringing into vision and sound many of the people and the events described in the text, breaks new ground in publishing for biographies and autobiographies, and I believe provides an extra dimension, enhancing the reader's understanding and enjoyment.

It may also represent another example of a dyslexic person being able to think out of the box and come up with an entirely fresh way of doing things.

As I mentioned in the Introduction, I don't want this book to seem preached from any kind of pulpit, with a finger wagging. I certainly don't have all the answers, and I don't feel in any way qualified to tell anybody what to do. All I have tried to achieve is to relate my experiences in sport and in business, and indeed on a personal level; if the reader has gained something along the way, that would be pleasing.

It is a fact that lessons seldom come cheaply and, in my experience, achievement and success has usually only come after several errors of judgement and wrong turns. My life has often felt like a frenetic, emotional and disruptive rollercoaster. On the one hand, the ride has left scars, inside and out, but on the other hand it has given me so many opportunities to gain experience and make a positive contribution in various fields.

I consider myself extremely fortunate to have reached my late sixties and, genuinely, to have so few regrets and to reflect on so many wonderful experiences and long-term friendships.

It is impossible to exaggerate the importance of such long-term friendships, both in a business context and on a personal level, and the lubricant that maintains such relationships is effective communication.

When I was working with Ford, I often used to talk about the 'vital organs' of a car. Well, there is no doubt in my mind that smooth communication is one of the vital organs of life and, just by observing people along the way, I have picked up a couple of tips that have been useful to me.

The first is the importance of being prepared. When people speak on the spur of the moment, usually in an overly emotional state, things can go wrong and often be misunderstood. I find it is much better to take a little bit of time to work out exactly what I want to say and, without appearing too clinical, to deliver it calmly and clearly. Not being prepared creates anxiety and apprehension, and such disruption can distort the message.

Being prepared, and consequently being calm and clear, is an important element in every form of successful communication, in a personal or business context, or even in the way a racing driver is able to 'communicate' with his car.

Less than an hour before the start of the 2007 British Grand Prix at Silverstone, I was conducting a question and answer session at the circuit; somebody in the RBS audience asked me to explain exactly how the young British driver would be feeling at that precise moment as he prepared to start his first-ever British Grand Prix from pole position – a nerve-racking prospect.

In reply, I said I could not speak for Lewis but, if it were me in that situation, I would have tried to remove all the emotion from the experience. I wouldn't have wanted anyone to make me happy, and I certainly wouldn't have wanted anyone upsetting me. I would have wanted to create a neutral mental state.

'A racing car does not live and breathe like an animal,' I continued, 'but it still behaves like a highly strung, sophisticated thoroughbred, which will react either positively or negatively to how the driver communicates and functions. If a driver can be so prepared and clear-minded that he communicates smoothly with the car, the overall performance will be enhanced.

'Imagine you are bouncing a rubber ball along the pavement or sidewalk: if the ball is over-inflated, it can land on a pebble or a crack in the surface and violently bounce away; on the other hand, if you progressively deflate that same ball, it will behave in a more lethargic fashion and be easier to control. Whenever I was preparing for a Grand Prix, I tried to remove the emotion and so ensure that, by the time I stepped into the cockpit, the "rubber ball" of my mentality was completely deflated.

'In the same way, if Zara Phillips jumps on the back of her wonderful horse, Toytown, in an agitated mental state, her mood would be communicated to the horse and the overall performance would be negatively affected.'

I concluded by saying that, whether it is Lewis in his car or Zara on her horse, being fully prepared and removing any kind of volatile emotion will usually lead to smooth communication and optimum performance. Some athletes say they need an adrenalin rush to perform at their best but, for me, it was the removal of that hyper condition that enabled me to be successful.

The second tip was to ensure the start of any message hits precisely the right note. Whether it is the first words of a discussion, the opening line of a letter or the first statement of a presentation, the first impression is critical. It may be a racing driver coaxing his car into the first corner, or a husband starting a conversation with his wife at the end of a long and tiring day, or an executive alerting his staff to a complex problem –

the manner in which an action or subject is introduced very often determines how it is received.

Effective communication is often regarded as a God-given talent, something you either have or don't have. Some great communicators may well be born, but this is also a skill that can be learned.

In my mind, there are four stages of learning: first, a person has to gain experience, seeing what works and what doesn't; second, if he or she has consumed that experience in the fullest sense, they can gain knowledge; third, the combination of experience and knowledge can over a period of time produce wisdom; fourth, with more than a little bit of luck, drawing on a tower of wisdom, he or she can achieve maturity.

It is at that stage that the mature racing driver is able to lead his car through the many complexities of the corner smoothly and efficiently. It is at that stage that a mature husband comes home in the evening and is able to talk to his wife without starting an argument. It is at that stage that a mature executive is able to outline a problem to his staff without creating disruption, grievances and distress.

In my experience, effective communication solves problems, and poor communication creates problems.

The racing driver who hurls his car into a corner will upset the car, waste time and maybe even create an accident; the man who takes out his frustration on his wife will create unnecessary aggravation; and executives who shout at and ridicule their staff will usually create a bigger problem. Each of these negative outcomes can be repaired, and any sense of antagonism may well be forgiven. However, it is seldom forgotten.

All these consequences can be avoided by taking a little care. Anybody can do it. In fact, we all do it almost every day of our lives, almost without thinking. Before we jump into the bath or shower, each of us instinctively takes a moment to test the temperature with our finger and make sure the water is neither too hot nor too cold. If everybody applied the same principle to the way they communicate, the world would be a more peaceful place.

It also helps to be calm. I have seen many executives walk into a meeting and antagonise everybody in the room by their arrogant body language, and that's before they have even opened their mouth. They seem to think a tough approach will frighten people into agreeing with them, but this confront-ational attitude rarely succeeds in the long term.

Conversely, the behaviour of an overly relaxed individual, who is trying so hard to conceal his nerves that he just looks cocky, can also create a negative reaction.

It also helps to be concise. Waffling or over-complicating the message will result in people losing track of what you are saying, and then losing interest in what you are trying to say. This urge to explain issues fully is a dyslexic trend and, personally, I have to take care not to over-explain my point.

It also helps to be approachable. Direct eye-contact, a dis-arming smile or a simple nod of recognition invariably softens the first impression. I remember when Roger Penske, the widely respected American businessman, first met Paul and Mark; the boys were only small at the time but he made a point of teaching them always to look the other person in the eye when you shake hands with them. It was a small thing, but it was a useful piece of advice and both my young sons took it on board.

It also helps to be even-handed – the most effective com-municators address switchboard operators, junior secretaries and personal assistants with the same personal touch and respect as they address the chairman or chief executive.

Why does it matter? It matters because the way you communicate, combined with the way you dress and the way you conduct yourself, influences the way other people perceive you and to what extent they are prepared to help you. If they feel you are more courteous than most of the people they speak to, they will invariably go out of their way to assist.

Perception is nine-tenths of the law. You may be the most considerate, intelligent and talented person, but if you don't take care to sound or look considerate, intelligent and talented, your qualities may well be overlooked.

Roger Penske is a world-class communicator. He controls some of the most successful motor dealerships in the world, he communicates with all his staff and customers in an exemplary manner, appearing to have time for everyone. These skills have helped him achieve extraordinary success.

I first met Roger in 1964, and we have been friends ever since. He has led many successful businesses, including the Penske Racing team, Penske Truck Rental and Detroit Diesel (which he bought and sold), and he has been a director of many highly respected corporations. Once a member of the board of Philip Morris, he now sits on the board of General Electric.

At a much earlier stage of life, Peter Phillips is also an excellent communicator with people in all stations. He came to work for Stewart Grand Prix during his school holidays, and mixed easily throughout the entire team. It is not always easy being one of the Queen's grandsons, but these skills have helped him greatly as he developed his career with Jaguar Racing, Williams Grand Prix Engineering and now as a sports sponsorship manager at the Royal Bank of Scotland Group.

There are other elements, which can be considered within an overall communications strategy.

Appearances are important, but they are not everything. Sometimes you do meet somebody who looks and sounds impressive, but who simply doesn't deliver; as the saying goes, they are 'all gong and no dinner'. Equally, a person who dresses badly and often says the wrong thing should not be instantly discounted because, beyond that poor first impression, they could yet be an outstanding performer in their field.

Dealing with extreme rudeness can be awkward. Being rude and difficult back to them is rarely a solution because if you fight with the pigs, you just get dirty. If somebody needs to be pacified, maybe the best option is to follow the advice once given to me by Lord King. 'All you can do,' he said, 'is drown them in cream and sugar.'

In my little world, the first point of contact for anyone wanting to reach me is my front office and, over the years, I have committed considerable time and effort to ensuring my office is as effective and efficiently run as possible. The key ingredient is the people, and I have tended to set a premium on energy, enthusiasm and an ability to be pro-active. The human factor is more of a priority to me than the exams an applicant may or may not have passed when he or she was completing their education.

The first function of any office is to provide access and, while it may be surprising, my experience is that the most important people are often the easiest to reach because their offices are set up in such a way that they are almost always able to find a moment when the boss can take or return a call, even if it is in the car on the way to a meeting or in a departure lounge before boarding a flight. There's never ever 'no time'.

On the other hand, it is often the people with an inflated opinion of their own importance who are the hardest to reach, usually because their front office is overprotective. In such cases, an aggressive PA gives the impression of believing their boss is the busiest and most sought-after person in the whole damn world, when invariably they are not. This behaviour can provoke a negative perception of the entire operation; and, once again, perception is nine-tenths of the law.

I have been extremely fortunate to have worked with a series of exceptional secretaries and assistants. The first was Anne Rennie at Dumbuck; she proved tremendously efficient and supportive not only in organising my part of our business at the garage but also in helping to arrange my life as my early motor racing commitments became more demanding.

Ruth Kinnear worked with me in Switzerland for no fewer than thirty-two years, and became an extremely important person for me. We were introduced to each other by a friend of Helen's from Helensburgh and, soon after we arrived in Geneva in 1968, Ruth phoned us just to say hello. A fellow Scot, she was working for the GATT (General Agreement on Tariffs and Trade) organisation at the time, and was certainly not looking for a job.

Helen and I met her socially and, eventually, I managed to persuade her to help me out on a part-time basis. We used to meet during her lunch hour at a restaurant not far from her office, and she would take down some letters and we would run through my schedule. She proved tremendously well organised, and she had a wonderful way with people, which reflected well on her, and on me as well. I was delighted when, not long afterwards, she agreed to work for me on a full-time basis.

Ruth made everything seem so easy. She used to work incredibly long hours, and her amazing attention to detail washed through from my motor racing to my business life and my family life, to an extent that long-standing friends like Edsel Ford grew to know Ruth almost as well as they knew me. She eventually retired when I began spending more time in the UK, when Stewart Grand Prix was being established, but she still lives near Geneva and remains close to the entire family.

Jacqueline Rochat is another who has long since qualified for a long service award. She started working in my office in Switzerland in February 1972 and, more than thirty-five years later, she is still with us, dealing with matters that arise concerning our home in Genolier, our correspondence, the vehicles or anything else.

Jean Albrecht became my secretary during the Stewart Grand Prix years, and was based at the team headquarters in Milton Keynes. She coped exceptionally well with the heavy workload, the long hours and the pressure, and today works for Paul in his office, when he is in the UK.

My office is run by two outstanding secretaries, who both maintain high standards of efficiency. Karen Moss worked for Adrian Reynard's company that manufactured racing cars, and now takes responsibility for all my correspondence that comes into the UK. Sue Pilat looks after my diary, travel and accommodation arrangements – which accounts for a large part of my life – in a very competent and experienced manner. Both Sue and Karen have extremely strong communication skills; whether it is by telephone, email or face to face, they have the precious ability of being able to make people feel welcome.

Day by day, week by week, we keep everything ticking over, and I find myself implementing a series of little habits that, just by keeping my eyes open, I have managed to pick up along the way. I have always watched the way other people behave, and looked for ways I can improve myself and my systems:

I write instructions to my office on incoming letters. Many years ago, I happened to notice that the late Sir Ian Stewart, the respected Scottish industrialist, dealt with his mail in this manner; so I decided to follow his lead, scribbling the action required and adding my initials for authority – 'R' is to say I have read it, 'F' is for file, 'tape' means I have dictated a reply.

I write hard copy letters on an embossed letterhead, with a motif of my old racing helmet decorated by the Royal Stewart tartan. Email is ideal for speed and efficiency, but I still believe there is nothing quite like receiving a properly constructed letter on high-quality headed paper in the post. Whenever I return from a trip, I take care to write to almost everybody I have met during my time away. This may not always seem necessary but, in my experience, it is taking the trouble to 'go the extra yard' in such matters that can create opportunities, benefits, privileges and access over the long term.

I do whatever is necessary to be punctual. Based on the

premise that I usually attend meetings with people who are more important than me, I always try to make sure that I arrive ahead of them and am fully prepared when the meeting starts. Among the really successful people I have met, very few are ever late for a meeting.

Whenever in doubt, I seek counsel. Whether it was Jim Clark, Ken Tyrrell or Walter Hayes in my racing days, or whether it was His Majesty King Hussein or Lord King through the 1990s, or whether it is Sir Fred Goodwin, the former CEO of the Royal Bank of Scotland Group, today, I have never hesitated to seek the advice of a wise and trusted friend. It has always amazed me that so many people seem so reluctant to ask for a bit of guidance.

The attention to detail that we attach to every phone call, letter, email, and indeed every issue, is always time-consuming, and yet everything combines to project a particular image of our office, and I very much hope it is an image of efficiency, integrity and warmth. The entire operation is quite expensive in monetary terms, yet I could not afford to do without it.

In addition to my permanent offices, ever since 1996, I have employed a personal assistant who travels with me to meetings and engagements both in Europe and abroad. In fact, I took the idea from Sir Rocco Forte, who explained to me the advantages of having this kind of person constantly at your side, ensuring both that every aspect of your business is noted and that your life runs smoothly and efficiently, and follow-up is policed and executed on business meetings and activities while on the road.

As it has turned out, all my PAs have been relatively young men with an Army background. I decided to employ a man to avoid the inevitable nudges and winks if I was seen to be travelling with a young lady, and I recognised that people with a military training bring many qualities: typically, they have the discipline and energy to work with accuracy and speed at all hours of the day if necessary, they present themselves neatly and they are able to mix comfortably in all walks of life. Over the past eleven years, I have worked with three former captains and two former majors.

Each appointment has been relatively short term, simply because I realise these men have the capacity to assume greater responsibility and earn more money elsewhere. I have always been happy to give them experience on various levels and perhaps to position them for a successful career.

William Parry was my first PA, and he went on to become Head of Sponsorship at HSBC. Andy Foster came next, and he has started a successful head-hunting and problem-solving business. David Webb followed, and he is now Head of Sponsorship at the Royal Bank of Scotland Group. Will Griffiths worked with me for the longest period, from 2001 until 2006, and is now Special Assistant to His Highness Crown Prince of Bahrain. Will became a very good example of how a PA can be exposed to high-powered people, who recognise his ability and eventually offer him a position that advances his career and enriches his life.

I first met Shaikh Salman bin Hamad Al Khalifa, now Crown Prince of Bahrain, when we happened to be travelling together on Concorde. He was a keen motor sports enthusiast, and he invited me to visit his country and explore ways of developing the sport in the Middle East. We became friends, and I was happy to offer advice to the Crown Prince as he developed an initiative that eventually secured the rights to stage a F1 Grand Prix in Bahrain, the first in the region. Within sixteen months, an area of barren desert was transformed into a fully equipped racing circuit, including hospitality facilities that surpassed anything anywhere else in the world.

The official opening of the circuit was due to be held just before the inaugural Grand Prix, and I was told His Majesty wished to confer upon me the Order of the Kingdom of

Bahrain. However, it seemed I would not be able to attend because I was in Australia at the time.

'What are your plans?' the Crown Prince's office asked.

I explained that Helen and I, along with my PA, Will Griffiths, needed to be in Australia and then go to Malaysia, and I said we had checked the flight schedules, and there was just no way we could get to Bahrain in the appropriate window of time.

'Maybe we could send our Gulfstream to collect you in Kuala Lumpur, and then fly you back?'

'Well, that would get around the travel problem,' I said, 'and that would be extremely kind.'

In the event, we all flew commercially from Australia to Malaysia, and Helen decided to stay in Kuala Lumpur while Will and I boarded the Gulfstream G4 corporate jet, complete with beds and every creature comfort. We flew overnight to Bahrain, and arrived the next morning in Manama, the capital. After a quick shower and change at the Ritz Carlton hotel, we were taken to the circuit.

The opening ceremony was conducted by His Majesty The King, Shaikh Hamad bin Isa Al Khalifa, and this event was immediately followed by an elegant and well-organised investiture, attended by a significant number of people, where I was presented with the decoration. It was a great honour, and a wonderful occasion.

After a short meeting with the Crown Prince and his two main advisers, Shaikh Mohammad and Shaikh Abdullah, we were driven back to the airport, where the G4 was waiting for us. We arrived back in Kuala Lumpur in time for dinner with Helen – a full day!

My current PA is Oliver Anderson, known as Oli, a former captain in the Queen's Royal Hussars, who previously served in Kosovo and Iraq. He is effective and efficient and, like his predecessors, he spends enormous amounts of time with me, travelling around the world and he no doubt will gain the same broad experience.

Another important element of any effective communications strategy is working with the print and electronic media, something I have done regularly for more than forty years. Throughout this period, I have always appreciated the central role these professionals play within our sport and business lives.

In fact, it disappoints me when people dismiss the media as some kind of necessary evil. I recently heard a top F1 racing driver say thirty minutes spent with the press is more of an ordeal than driving a race, and I just didn't understand what he meant. Of course there are a handful of exceptions but, in my experience, the overwhelming majority of people working in the press room are committed, dedicated and professional.

As I have often said, if you're straight with them, they will be straight with you. I have always responded to telephone calls from journalists, particularly at times when I have been embroiled in controversies such as the safety campaign when I was still driving and more recently the issues at Silverstone. Some people tend to run from the media when the pressure is on, but it is at these moments that it is critical to take time to clarify the issues and communicate in a calm and coherent way.

I have met many exceptional motor racing journalists, most notably in the UK the quartet of Alan Henry, Maurice Hamilton, David Tremayne and Nigel Roebuck, each of whom I have known for a good many years and continue to see regularly.

During my early driving career, I remember dealing with outstanding correspondents such as Basil Cardew, of the *Daily Express*, and his successor David Benson. In Scotland, there was Malcolm McDougall, a real character from the *Daily Record*, and I have never forgotten Alistair Cameron who wrote an article in 1963 that started with the words 'I predict . . .' and went on to forecast a successful racing career ahead of me.

Motor sport has traditionally been well served by magazines worldwide, and I particularly respected Mike Doodson at *Motoring News* and the late Denis Jenkinson of *Motor Sport*, the revered doyen of the industry. In France, I always enjoyed dealing with the late Jabby Crombac, a wonderful man from *Sport Auto* who was friends with Colin Chapman as well as Jim Clark, and even called his dog 'Lotus'. Johnny Rives was a fine writer at *L'Equipe* and Bernard Cahier wrote for various publications, took wonderful photographs and always knew the right folks both in the sport and the industry.

In Austria, Heinz Prueller and Helmut Zwickl have both been in F1 as long as me, and are rightly recognised as authorities – Heinz still sends me *Sachertorte* on special occasions. And, whenever I was in the United States, I always used to look forward to meeting Henry Manney from *Road and Track* magazine, until he died in the late 1980s, and I still see Brock Yates, a fine writer who created the famous Cannonball event in the US and still writes for *Car and Driver* today. I have known and respected David E. Davis since the mid-1960s, and he is now editor of *Automobile Magazine*, a high-quality motoring publication in the US.

Not long ago, an experienced journalist paid me a compliment when he told me that I was one of the few people in the 'business' who phoned him from time to time just for a chat, not because I was in trouble or wanted coverage of any particular story. Some people may regard such regular contact as unnecessary, but I have always enjoyed chatting to specialists, especially those with knowledge and experience gathered from covering the sport or the business world at the highest level over an extended period of time. In many respects, they have been my colleagues – indeed, I was a card-carrying member of Equity for more than twenty years.

Effective communication, both to and from my office and with the media, lies at the heart of my ongoing responsibility as a global ambassador for the Royal Bank of Scotland. I must confess to having been surprised when Sir Fred Goodwin, CEO of RBS, contacted me in 2003 and asked if we could meet for a chat. We had met socially on a couple of occasions, but I was intrigued to discover what he wanted to discuss. Over dinner at the Savoy Grill in London, Sir Fred outlined his ambition for the bank, building on the foundations of its inherent Scottishness and more than 280 years of service since 1727, and developing a global profile. He felt there was clear synergy, and said he believed I could make a valuable contribution to the business.

It was an interesting proposal, but I immediately realised that, for me, any association with RBS might, in some people's eyes, have created a conflict of interests because I was still sitting on the board of Jaguar Racing, and still servicing HSBC as one of the team's major sponsors.

In such situations, the best policy is always to be completely open and to clear every issue up front. So I arranged to meet Sir John Bond, Chairman of HSBC, and told him about the approach that had been made. He was completely understanding and courteous, and agreed that, since I had no personal contract with HSBC, I was free to continue my discussions with RBS.

The next meeting with Sir Fred was held at his London office in Bishopsgate. 'I think we should call you a global ambassador,' he said, 'but I'm sure your role will evolve. Let's discuss it more fully as we go along.'

The only other person contracted to RBS in a similar capacity was Jack Nicklaus, which made sense because of the bank's role as a patron of The Open Championship and a sponsor of golf on television. However, when I signed a five-year contract, RBS had no plans whatever to get involved in F1 motor racing.

Timing is everything and, as I became acquainted with RBS and its core strategy, I kept hearing how the bank was eager to increase global awareness of its brand image and logo. 'There is no better vehicle to secure a global profile than F1 motor racing,' I told Sir Fred, explaining the sport attracted an immense and growing television audience across five continents.

Sir Fred and Howard Moody, the Director of Communications, recognised the business sense in developing an association with a F1 team, so I identified sponsorship opportunities with McLaren, Williams and BAR and arranged for them both to visit each of the three teams in the course of one single day, travelling by helicopter from one team headquarters to the next. It eventually came down to a straight choice between McLaren and Williams.

The criterion for the Group's decision was not simply which team we believed would be the most successful because our specific goal was to secure maximum recognition of the RBS logo, so we had to consider precisely how the white on royal blue RBS emblem would be displayed on the respective liveries.

The McLaren Mercedes team were understandably eager to preserve the integrity of their silver colour scheme, and they said the RBS logo would have to be black on a silver background. In contrast, quite literally, the match with the existing Williams colours was ideal, and they confirmed it would be possible for the RBS logo to be displayed on their car in its proper corporate colours, white on blue.

A series of advanced definition tests was conducted and, when they realised the logo was less visible on the McLaren, the bank decided to enter into a sponsorship agreement with Williams. The results have been outstanding, with research reporting a substantial increase in global awareness of the RBS brand.

The association is underpinned by the profound human relationship that has developed between Sir Fred and Sir Frank Williams with enormous respect on both sides, and I have been able to enhance the RBS investment in F1 motor racing by wearing their branding on my clothes and assisting in hosting their guests at Grand Prix events around the world.

RBS endured a traumatic period as an economic crisis gripped global banking during the latter months of 2008 and into 2009, with their share price slipping to an all-time low. On a personal level, Sir Fred Goodwin endured some tough times, both before and since he resigned from RBS. However, he remains one of the brightest minds and most decent men that I know.

My ongoing relationship with RBS extends beyond motor racing into the business community on a global basis, involving not only multinational corporations but also governments, and I have enjoyed facilitating meetings between various influential people and the bank.

For whatever reason, the media, most specifically in the United Kingdom it seems, have been guided towards the belief that the banking community is responsible for the economic downturn that has reached global dimensions. Other industries are greatly affected by the economic climate which is not all down to the banking sector. Government must take some responsibility for what has happened, as must the regulatory authorities. Other business sectors are having difficult times whether it's airlines, shipping, consumer products, and tourism, to name a few. Across the globe, car manufacturing plants are closing down and production is grinding to a halt, with acres and acres of unsold cars sitting in mothballs. This has a devastating effect on the wider communities around these facilities, and on the supporting industries. As the production and sales drop off, so does the money available for R&D which in itself will impact heavily on the development of increasingly environmentally friendly vehicles and other important innovations.

The pace of life remains fast and consuming. Yet, as time goes on, Helen and I have tried to take the wrinkles out of it, by surrounding ourselves with high-quality people at our homes in Switzerland and Buckinghamshire, as well as those that surround me within my business activities.

Gerry Webb has been working with me since 1974; that was when I joined the board of Britex, a seat-belt company. Since we were living in Switzerland, the company said they would provide me with one of their chauffeurs whenever I was in the UK, and that turned out to be Gerry. He eventually came to work for us and, over the years, has driven not only us but also an array of well-known people, including such motor racing legends as Ayrton Senna, Alain Prost and Michael Schumacher.

Gerry is now eighty-one, but he still drives well and he's a great mimic, especially of me. He has become a real friend of our entire family, and I trust him absolutely and completely.

Stuart Dean has been my chauffeur for the past nine years. A retired sergeant-major, he is rigorously punctual and well organised, and he keeps the cars in excellent condition. His wife Kay is our loyal cook/housekeeper. Eric Bennett is the very model of a professional modern butler and house manager. He can turn his hand towards almost anything, having spent many years working on large private yachts.

Even allowing for my hectic schedule, Helen and I still make time for ourselves, maybe taking a week at Gleneagles, playing some golf and walking the dogs, or spending a few days in transit being pampered at what I consider to be probably the best city hotel in the world, the Mandarin Oriental in Bangkok.

One of our favourite events of the year is watching tennis at the All England Club in Wimbledon, where we have been invited as guests of the Duke and Duchess of Kent each year since 1968. It is a remarkable event with a unique atmosphere, and we both enjoy and very much appreciate the privilege.

The Duke of Kent has always been a keen motorist, and we have known each other since we first met at a motor racing event at the Charterhall circuit, in the Scottish borders, in 1963.

I still remember him arriving at the wheel of a 3.8 litre Jaguar with wire wheels. More than four decades later, we still see a fair amount of each other through motor sport, as His Royal Highness is President-in-Chief of the British Racing Drivers' Club.

We also take delight in spending time with Mark and Paul and their respective families, whether we are away together or whether the entire gang descends on us for Sunday lunch.

Paul and Victoria have four children: Dylan, Lucas, Zac and Ashton; Mark and Anne also have four: Leona, Marcus, Andreas and Johann. Helen and I enjoy being doting grandparents, and feel extraordinarily lucky to have been blessed with such a robust, loving family unit.

Helen often gets tired of all the travelling, and I understand her frustration. I am the first to concede that I find it difficult to slow down – it's difficult, but not impossible. There are times when we will decide to go somewhere warm, and I will be perfectly happy doing nothing at all, just reading, relaxing and maybe going for a leisurely walk now and then. Maybe such breaks are too rare, maybe I should take on fewer projects, but the fact is I am stimulated by everything that I do.

My head runs, and I find myself constantly wanting to do something else. It's not a question of needing to achieve, or needing to earn more money. If something is there to be done – whether it's a business opportunity or a weed that needs to be uprooted in the garden, or a piece of rubbish that needs to be picked up – my restless nature seems to drive me to do it there and then. That's just how I am.

However, living at such a relentless pace means we often have little distilling time to enjoy each experience to the full. Everything always seems such a rush, and I often find myself getting home late at night and having to go somewhere else early the next day. There is invariably somebody to call, someone to see, something to do and somewhere to go; and I often feel as if I don't have two minutes to myself.

In recent years, an enormous amount of my time has been spent putting out fires. As you grow older and become more experienced, people start to see you as somebody who can solve problems. They sense you are able to judge the direction of the wind and effectively extinguish the fire that threatens them, whether it is a business issue, a career matter or a medical problem that needs to be referred to the Mayo Clinic.

I am naturally flattered to be asked, and eager to help, not least because I am acutely aware how often in my life I have been assisted by somebody else's help.

The task of writing this book has forced me to slow down for a moment and reflect on much of what I have seen and done over the years. Inevitably I will have omitted people and events that should have been included – not too many, I hope.

Ian Wooldridge, the great sportswriter and broadcaster, was kind enough to read the first three chapters of the manuscript before he died in April 2007, and he said he was impressed, but he doubted it would be possible to maintain the quality to the last chapter. Well, wherever he is reading this, I hope he has been pleasantly surprised.

I am also aware that human nature recalls the good times more clearly than the bad times. So I am eager this account should not be perceived as one long litany of success. For every success in my life, there has been a failure; if there is one reason why I have achieved anything, it is that I refused to be defeated by disappointment, and carried on . . . and on and on.

I know some sports people say they pay little attention to awards. That was never the case with me. It meant a great deal to me when I was named Sportsman of the Year by the American magazine *Sports Illustrated*, and when I became BBC Sports Personality of the Year in 1973, and when I was presented with the 1973 World Sportsman of the Year award by Muhammad Ali, and all the others. It meant a great deal to me precisely because these accolades represented indisputable evidence that, against whatever odds, I was managing to be successful.

The same was true on that day in 1971, when I was deeply honoured to be awarded the Order of the British Empire.

Eighteen years later, I was woken at five o'clock in the morning in Detroit and told the Honours Office had telephoned my office and asked whether I cared.

'About what?' I asked.

It transpired a letter had been sent to an old address, and not been forwarded. The letter was to enquire whether I would be willing to accept a knighthood. A copy of the correspondence was eventually faxed to me in Detroit; I was told to sign, and immediately return it by fax to my office.

The public announcement that I was to become Sir Jackie Stewart was made on the Queen's official birthday in June 2000, and Helen and I celebrated by having lunch with Ken and Norah Tyrrell, who seemed every bit as thrilled as we were. Ken was such an ardent royalist that I always used to tell people how I saw him, in my imagination, each night at bedtime, standing to attention at the bottom of his bed, wearing his Union Jack pyjamas and saluting as he played a 78 rpm record of 'God Save the Queen'. The four of us enjoyed a memorable celebration together.

Needless to say, it was an enormous thrill and a privilege for me to be recognised in this fashion. I was duly knighted at an investiture conducted by HRH The Prince of Wales at Buckingham Palace, and we celebrated at what I thought was going to be a family lunch at Harry's Bar, but which Paul and Mark had turned into a surprise party. They had taken over the whole place, and invited many of our friends. What a day!

'Titles mean different things to different people' – that was the opening line of this book, and I have no hesitation in confirming my particular title means a great deal to me.

All of which brings us back once again to the actual title of the book, and the still unanswered question – if 'winning is not enough', what is enough?

In my view, 'enough' is winning over an extended period of time in a variety of different fields and, as the recurring theme of this book may suggest, the key to achieving long-term success lies in nurturing meaningful long-term relationships.

This has been my experience. In whatever field I have worked – as a clay pigeon shooter, a racing driver, a corporate spokesman, a colour commentator, a television presenter, a vehicle assessor, a F1 team owner, a club president, a member of the board, a public speaker, a campaigner or a global brand ambassador – I have always tried to develop meaningful long-term relationships with the highest quality people and companies and, in all these fields, it has been the people around me who have made the difference.

It may have been my father who introduced me to fishing on the River Spey, or Duncan Macbeth, who took me stalking in the hills and imbued me with a deep love of the countryside, or Bob MacIntyre and Glynne Jones who first made me believe I could succeed. It may have been John Lindsay and Allan Jones who have blessed me with lifelong friendship.

It may have been Jim Clark or Graham Hill who taught me so much about motor racing, or Ken Tyrrell who created the team and guided and inspired me to win three F1 world championships. It may have been Roone Arledge who gave me an opportunity in television, or Walter Hayes, Edsel Ford, Don Petersen, Red Poling and Jac Nasser who helped me contribute to the Ford Motor Company over a forty-year period.

It may have been His Majesty King Hussein, Lord King or George Harrison, each of whom gave me so much wise counsel and support over the years, or HRH The Princess Royal who has been such a good friend, or Sir Fred Goodwin who has opened up a new dimension to my life.

It is certainly these extraordinary people, and others, who

have enabled the small boy who was made to feel so stupid at school to grow up and make something of himself.

The greatest long-term relationship in my life has been my marriage. Helen and I are very different in many ways, in temperament and approach to life; that may explain why we have been so happy together for so many years. However, thinking back over all this time, through all the dramas, excitement and indeed grief, through all the travelling and the demands on my time, I am truly humbled by the depth of her support. She has stood by me. She has turned houses into homes. She has raised two fine sons, Paul and Mark. She has enjoyed the good times and survived the bad times. She has put up with so much, and brought such love and stability to my restless life. More than forty-five years on, she is still standing beside me and, God willing, we will have many more years together.

I have no burning desire to realise any specific goal. I never have had. Even as a boy, I never harboured any particular ambition to become a racing driver. My focus has always been to work hard and make the most of every day and the most of every opportunity, and to see where that takes me. Life continues, relationships endure and, I'm sure, many fulfilling adventures lie ahead.

When I was young, my father told me: 'If you fly with the crows, you are liable to be shot at.'

I have tried to follow his advice and now, looking back over all these years, I realise I have been privileged to soar with the eagles, and, far beyond winning, that has been more than enough.

Career Record

WORLD CHAMPIONSHIP GRANDS PRIX

1965
South African GP, East London   BRM P261   6th
Steady run to claim point on championship debut.
Monaco GP, Monte Carlo   BRM P261   3rd
Challenged boldly for the lead but spun after clipping kerb.
Belgian GP, Spa-Francorchamps   BRM P261   2nd
Well-paced second place to Jim Clark's dominant Lotus.
French GP, Clermont-Ferrand   BRM P261   2nd
Second again to Clark on this particularly demanding circuit.
British GP, Silverstone   BRM P261   5th
Struggled slightly with handling balance and never quite with the leaders.
Dutch GP, Zandvoort   BRM P261   2nd
Back on form again, following Clark home for their third 1–2 of the season.
German GP, Nurburgring   BRM P261   Rtd
Qualified on the front row, but damaged suspension on opening lap.
Italian GP, Monza   BRM P261   1st
Great first GP win after outfumbling team-mate Graham Hill in closing stages.

US GP, Watkins Glen   BRM P261   Rtd
Disappointing retirement at popular upstate New York circuit with suspension trouble.
Mexican GP, Mexico City   BRM P261   Rtd
Failed to finish again in final race under 1.5-litre F1 regulations, this time with clutch failure.

1966
Monaco GP, Monte Carlo   BRM P261   1st
Took a commanding win after John Surtees' leading Ferrari hit trouble.
Belgian GP, Spa-Francorchamps   BRM P261   Rtd
Broke collarbone after first lap accident in torrential cloud burst.
British GP, Brands Hatch   BRM P261   Rtd
Sidelined by engine problems on first race back after injury.
Dutch GP, Zandvoort   BRM P261   4th
Steady run to claim points at the popular Dutch seaside circuit.
German GP, Nurburgring   BRM P261   5th
First helping of points at track which was central to his safety crusade.
Italian GP, Monza   BRM P83   Rtd
Fast but fragile H-16 succumbed to a fuel leak.
US GP, Watkins Glen   BRM P83   Rtd
More disappointment as he retires at the Glen with engine failure.
Mexican GP, Mexico City   BRM P83   Rtd
No luck at the high altitude Mexico City track thanks to oil leak.

1967
South African GP, Kyalami   BRM P83   Rtd
Engine problems sidelined him in the opening race of the new year.
Monaco GP, Monte Carlo   BRM P261   Rtd
On the pace again with the 2-litre V8 but stopped with gearbox breakage.
Dutch GP, Zandvoort   BRM P83   Rtd
Brake failure for the H-16 on this occasion.
Belgian GP, Spa-Francorchamps   BRM P83   2nd
Great drive on this daunting track, holding the car in gear at 170mph.
French GP, Le Mans   BRM P261   3rd
Back in the 'baby' BRM V8 again for some long overdue points.
British GP, Silverstone   BRM P83   Rtd
Transmission problems sidelined JYS yet again.

German GP, Nurburgring   BRM P115 Rtd
You've guessed it; transmission problems again.
Canadian GP, Mosport Park   BRM P115 Rtd
Spun off in pouring rain when sand jammed the throttle slides.
Italian GP, Monza   BRM P115 Rtd
Engine failure again at this high speed venue.
US GP, Watkins Glen   BRM P115 Rtd
A broken belt to the fuel metering unit brought the car to a silent halt.
Mexican GP, Mexico City   BRM P115 Rtd
Engine vibration rounded off his final outing for BRM on a dismal note.

1968
South African GP, Kyalami   Matra MS9 Rtd
Retired with engine failure while running 2nd to Jim Clark's Lotus.
Belgian GP, Spa-Francorchamps Matra MS10 4th
Finished fourth after losing the lead with a late pit stop for fuel.
Dutch GP, Zandvoort   Matra MS10 1st
Dominant run to score first win for F1 Matra-Ford partnership.
French GP, Rouen-les-Essarts   Matra MS10 3rd
Lost a lap changing to fresh tyres in the torrential rain.
British GP, Brands Hatch   Matra MS10 6th
Struggled with pain from wrist brace to finish two laps down.
German GP, Nurburgring   Matra MS10 1st
Masterly victory in appalling conditions of mist and rain.
Italian GP, Monza   Matra MS10 Rtd
Ran in the leading bunch until engine failure caused his retirement.
Canadian GP, Mont Tremblant, St Jovite Matra MS10 6th
Lost time with pit stop to investigate possible suspension problem.
US GP, Watkins Glen   Matra MS10 1st
Confident run to victory backed up convincing fastest lap.
Mexican GP, Mexico City   Matra MS10 7th
Slowed and eventually dropped from the points with fuel feed trouble.

1969
South African GP, Kyalami   Matra MS10 1st
Dominant run to kick off first championship campaign.
Spanish GP, Montjuic Park   Matra MS80 1st
Debut win in Spain for Matra's new MS80 contender.
Monaco GP, Monte Carlo   Matra MS80 Rtd
Driveshaft failure sidelined him while running at the front.

Dutch GP, Zandvoort	Matra MS80	1st

Great battle with Lotus 49s of Jochen Rindt and Graham Hill.

French GP, Clermont-Ferrand	Matra MS80	1st

Heads Matra 1–2 ahead of team-mate Jean-Pierre Beltoise.

British GP, Silverstone	Matra MS80	1st

Home victory after surviving big shunt at Woodcote in practice.

German GP, Nurburgring	Matra MS80	2nd

Gearbox problems drop him to second behind Jacky Ickx's Brabham.

Italian GP, Monza	Matra MS80	1st

Split-second victory over Rindt's Lotus clinches first world championship.

Canadian GP, Mosport Park	Matra MS80	Rtd

Spun off the track by Ickx during their battle for the lead.

US GP, Watkins Glen	Matra MS80	Rtd

Engine failure sidelines the new champion.

Mexican GP, Mexico City	Matra MS80	4th

Off the pace in the final race of the season.

1970

South African GP, Kyalami	March 701	3rd

Cautiously optimistic debut for the successor to the Matra.

Spanish GP, Jarama	March 701	1st

Unexpected win with a little bit of luck.

Monaco GP, Monte Carlo	March 701	Rtd

Pole position start spoiled by eventual engine failure.

Belgian GP, Spa-Francorchamps	March 701	Rtd

Engine failure sidelines him again.

Dutch GP, Zandvoort	March 701	2nd

Second to Rindt's Lotus 72 on the dreadful day Piers Courage died.

French GP, Clermont-Ferrand	March 701	9th

A distant ninth after a long pit stop to check ignition problems.

British GP, Brands Hatch	March 701	Rtd

Car not competitive, retired with split fuel line fire.

German GP, Hockenheim	March 701	Rtd

Gearbox problems on a day he was not a contender.

Austrian GP, Osterreichring	March 701	Rtd

Another split fuel line, but this time without the fire.

Italian GP, Monza	March 701	2nd

Runner-up on another bitter weekend, this time the death of Jochen Rindt.

Canadian GP, Mont Tremblant, St Jovite	Tyrrell 001	Rtd

Broken stub axle sidelines impressive new Tyrrell on debut.

US GP, Watkins Glen	Tyrrell 001	Rtd

Engine oil leak thwarts pole winning effort.

Mexican GP, Mexico City	Tyrrell 001	Rtd

Damaged steering after hitting dog on circuit.

1971

South African GP, Kyalami	Tyrrell 001	2nd

Good run to finish behind Mario Andretti's Ferrari.

Spanish GP, Montjuic Park	Tyrrell 003	1st

Commanding victory over Jacky Ickx's Ferrari.

Monaco GP, Monte Carlo	Tyrrell 003	1st

Start to finish victory despite broken brake balance bar.

Dutch GP, Zandvoort	Tyrrell 003	11th

Outclassed as Goodyear rain tyres could not match Firestone opposition.

French GP, Paul Ricard	Tyrrell 003	1st

Another tour de force from pole position.

British GP, Silverstone	Tyrrell 003	1st

Untouchable again on the Tyrrell team's home turf.

German GP, Nurburgring	Tyrrell 003	1st

A second win at this legendary venue, but this time in the dry.

Austrian GP, Osterreichring	Tyrrell 003	Rtd

Lost a wheel in the race, but clinched his second world championship.

Italian GP, Monza	Tyrrell 003	Rtd

Engine failure intervened to cause his retirement.

Canadian GP, Mosport Park	Tyrrell 003	1st

Great run in the rain to beat Ronnie Peterson's March in close fight.

US GP, Watkins Glen	Tyrrell 003	5th

Slowed by chunking tyres on the day that team-mate François Cevert won.

1972

Argentine GP, Buenos Aires	Tyrrell 003	1st

Won impressively from second on grid behind Reutemann's Brabham.

South African GP, Kyalami	Tyrrell 003	Rtd

Retired with gearbox trouble.

Spanish GP, Jarama	Tyrrell 003	Rtd

Retired after spinning off and holing water radiator.

Monaco GP, Monte Carlo	Tyrrell 004	4th

Battled torrential rain and had two spins during lurid race.

French GP, Clermont-Ferrand	Tyrrell 003	1st

Disciplined run to win on stone-strewn track.

British GP, Brands Hatch	Tyrrell 003	2nd

Could not quite get the better of Emerson Fittipaldi's winning Lotus.

German GP, Nurburgring	Tyrrell 003	Rtd

Retired after collision with Clay Regazzoni's Ferrari.

Austrian GP, Osterreichring	Tyrrell 005	7th

Handling problems dropped him out of points-scoring placings.

Italian GP, Monza	Tyrrell 005	Rtd

Broken transmission left him stranded on starting grid.

Canadian GP, Mosport Park	Tyrrell 005	1st

Commanding win and fastest race lap.

US GP, Watkins Glen	Tyrrell 005	1st

Commanding win and fastest race lap again.

1973

Argentine GP, Buenos Aires	Tyrrell 005	3rd

Opening race of year handicapped by slow puncture.

Brazilian GP, Interlagos	Tyrrell 005	2nd

Short-wheelbase Tyrrell struggled over the bumpy surface.

South African GP, Kyalami	Tyrrell 006	1st

Won after practice crash due to brake failure.

Spanish GP, Montjuic Park	Tyrrell 006	Rtd

Retired with broken brake disc mounting.

Belgian GP, Zolder	Tyrrell 006	1st

Shrewd drive on precariously resurfaced track.

Monaco GP, Monte Carlo	Tyrrell 006	1st

Great win, then collided with Fittipaldi's Lotus on slowing down lap.

Swedish GP, Anderstorp	Tyrrell 006	5th

Brake problems kept him at the back of the leading bunch.

French GP, Paul Ricard	Tyrrell 006	4th

Running with the leaders, but Lotus 72s had the edge.

British GP, Silverstone	Tyrrell 006	10th

Spun off into cornfield due to gear selection problems.

Dutch GP, Zandvoort	Tyrrell 006	1st

Headed Cevert in 1–2 on the day Roger Williamson was killed.

German GP, Nurburgring	Tyrrell 006	1st

The last 1–2 finish for Tyrrell twins Stewart and Cevert.

Austrian GP, Osterreichring   Tyrrell 006   2nd
Good run to finish runner-up behind Peterson's Lotus.
Italian GP, Monza   Tyrrell 006   4th
Great recovery from early tyre stop clinches third world championship title.
Canadian GP, Mosport Park   Tyrrell 006   5th
Distant finish at the end of chaotic wet/dry race.
US GP, Watkins Glen   Tyrrell 006   DNS
Withdrew from race after team-mate Cevert was killed in practice.

NON-CHAMPIONSHIP F1 RACES

Year	Race	Car	Result
1964	Rand GP, Kyalami	Lotus 33	winner one heat
1965	Race of Champions, Brands Hatch	BRM P261	2nd
1965	Sunday Mirror Trophy, Goodwood	BRM P261	Rtd
1965	Daily Express International Trophy, Silverstone	BRM P261	1st
1966	Gold Cup, Oulton Park	BRM H-16	Rtd
1967	Spring Cup, Oulton Park	BRM H-16	Rtd
1967	Daily Express International Trophy, Silverstone	BRM H-16	Rtd
1967	Gold Cup, Oulton Park	F2 Matra MS7	2nd
1967	Spanish GP, Jarama	F2 Matra MS7	Rtd
1968	Race of Champions, Brands Hatch	Matra MS10	6th
1968	Gold Cup, Oulton Park	Matra MS10	1st
1969	Race of Champions, Brands Hatch	Matra MS80	1st
1969	Daily Express International Trophy, Silverstone	Matra MS10	3rd
1969	Gold Cup, Oulton Park	Matra MS80	Rtd
1970	Race of Champions, Brands Hatch	March 701	1st
1970	Daily Express International Trophy, Silverstone	March 701	2nd
1970	Gold Cup, Oulton Park	Tyrrell 001	Rtd
1971	Race of Champions, Brands Hatch	Tyrrell 001	2nd
1971	Questor GP, Ontario Motor Speedway	Tyrrell 001	2nd
1971	Rothmans Trophy, Oulton Park	Tyrrell 001	3rd
1971	Daily Express International Trophy, Silverstone	Tyrrell 003	Rtd

| 1971 | World Champion Victory Race, Brands Hatch | Tyrrell 003 | 3rd |
| 1973 | Daily Express International Trophy, Silverstone | Tyrrell 006/2 | 1st |

FORMULA 3

1964

Snetterton, UK	Cooper T72	1st
Goodwood, UK	Cooper T72	1st
Oulton Park, UK	Cooper T72	1st
Aintree, UK	Cooper T72	1st
Silverstone, UK	Cooper T72	1st
Monaco F3, Monte Carlo	Cooper T72	1st
Mallory Park, UK	Cooper T72	1st
Rouen-les-Essarts	Cooper T72	1st
Reims	Cooper T72	1st
Brands Hatch, UK	Cooper T72	6th
Zandvoort	Cooper T72	1st
Oulton Park, UK	Cooper T72	1st

FORMULA 2

1964

Trophée d'Auvergne, Clermont-Ferrand	Lotus 32	2nd
Kanonloppet, Karlskoga	Cooper T72	Rtd
Gold Cup, Oulton Park	Lotus 32	3rd
GP Ile de France, Montlhery	Lotus 32	2nd
Vanwall Trophy, Snetterton	Lotus 32	1st
GP de Albi	Lotus 32	Rtd
GP Limburg, Zolder	Lotus 32	Rtd

1965

Spring Trophy, Oulton Park	Cooper T75	2nd
Autocar Trophy, Snetterton	Cooper T75	Rtd
GP de Pau	Cooper T75	5th
London Trophy, Crystal Palace	Cooper T75	Rtd
GP de Reims	Cooper T75	5th
GP de Rouen-les-Essarts	Cooper T75	Rtd
Kanonloppet, Karlskoga	Cooper T75	Rtd
Gold Cup, Oulton Park	Cooper T75	Rtd

1966

Sunday Mirror Trophy, Goodwood	Matra MS5	6th
GP de Pau	Matra MS5	4th
Juan Jover Trophy, Barcelona	Matra MS5	2nd
GP Ile de France, Montlhery	Matra MS5	4th
Trophée Craven A, Le Mans Bugatti	Matra MS5	4th
GP de Albi	Matra MS5	Rtd

1967

Guards 100 race, Snetterton	Matra MS5	10th
Wills Trophy, Silverstone	Matra MS5	5th
GP de Pau	Matra MS5	Rtd
Juan Jover Trophy, Barcelona	Matra MS5	Rtd
London Trophy, Crystal Palace	Matra MS5	4th
GP de Reims	Matra MS5	Rtd
GP de Madrid	Matra MS7	2nd
Kanonloppet, Karlskoga	Matra MS7	1st
Mediterranean GP, Enna Pergusa	Matra MS7	1st
Guards Trophy, Brands Hatch	Matra MS7	2nd
GP de Albi	Matra MS7	1st

1968

Juan Jover Trophy, Barcelona	Matra MS7	1st
GP de Pau	Matra MS7	1st
GP de Madrid	Matra MS7	DNS
GP de Reims	Matra MS7	1st
GP de Albi	Matra MS7	Rtd

1969

Wills Trophy, Thruxton	Matra MS7	2nd
GP de Pau	Matra MS7	Rtd
Eifelrennen, Nurburgring	Matra MS7	1st
GP de Madrid	Matra MS7	1st
GP de Limburg, Zolder	Matra MS7	12th
GP de Rouen	Matra MS7	4th
Tulln Langenlebarn, Austria	Matra MS7	2nd
GP de Albi	Matra MS7	Rtd

1970
Wills Trophy, Thruxton	Brabham BT30 2nd
London Trophy, Crystal Palace	Brabham BT30 1st
Trophée de France, Paul Ricard	Brabham BT30 Rtd

CANAM

1970	Watkins Glen CanAm	Chaparral 2J	Rtd
1971	Labatts Blue race, Mosport Park	Lola T260	Rtd
1971	Labatts CanAm, Mont Tremblant, St Jovite	Lola T260	1st
1971	CanAm challenge, Road Atlanta	Lola T260	Rtd
1971	CanAm challenge, Watkins Glen	Lola T260	Rtd
1971	Valvoline CanAm race, Mid-Ohio	Lola T260	1st
1971	CanAm Challenge Cup, Road Atlanta	Lola T260	Rtd
1971	Minneapolis Tribune race, Donnybrooke	Lola T260	6th
1971	Molson Cup race, Edmonton	Lola T260	2nd
1971	Monterey-Castrol GP, Laguna Seca	Lola T260	2nd
1971	Los Angeles Times GP, Riverside	Lola T260	Rtd

SPORTS CAR RACES

1965	24 Hour of Le Mans	Rover BRM Turbine	10th
1965	Surfers' Paradise	Ferrari 250LM	1st
1967	BOAC Brands Hatch six-hour	Ferrari 330P4	2nd

INDYCAR RACES
1966	Indianapolis 500	Lola-Ford	Rtd (6th)
1966	Fuji, Japan	Lola-Ford	1st
1967	Indianapolis 500	Lola-Ford	Rtd

TASMAN SERIES RACES

1966
New Zealand GP	BRM P261	2nd
Levin, NZ	BRM P261	Rtd
Lady Wigram Trophy, NZ	BRM P261	1st
Teretonga, NZ	BRM P261	1st

Warwick Farm, Aus	BRM P261	4th
Australian GP, Lakeside	BRM P261	Rtd
Sandown Park, Aus	BRM P261	1st
Longford, Tasmania	BRM P261	1st

1967

New Zealand GP	BRM P261	1st
Levin, NZ	BRM P261	2nd
Lady Wigram Trophy, NZ	BRM P261	Rtd
Lakeside, Aus	BRM P261	Rtd
Australian GP, Warwick Farm	BRM P261	1st
Sandown Park, Aus	BRM P261	Rtd

Picture Credits

Credits are listed according to the order the pictures appear on each page, left to right, top to bottom.

'JYS' denotes photographs that are courtesy of Jackie Stewart.

Section 1
Page 1: JYS, JYS, JYS, JYS, JYS; page 2: JYS, JYS, JYS, JYS; page 3: Sutton Images, JYS, Ronald Dumont/Daily Express; page 4: JYS, Geoffrey Goddard, Keystone Press Agency, The Rover Car Company; page 5: Indianapolis Motor Speedway Official Photos, JYS, Sutton Image, Sutton Images; page 6: Sutton Images; page 7: JYS, JYS, JYS; page 8: RSK, George Outram & Co., JYS, Autocar, JYS.

Section 2
Page 1: JYS, Sutton Images, JYS; page 2: Daily Express, Scottish Sunday Express, JYS; page 3: Sutton Images, Sutton Images, Sutton Images, Bernard Cahier; page 4: JYS, Sutton Images, Sutton Images, Rainer Schlegermilch, Sutton Images; page 5: JYS, Sutton Images; page 6: JYS, JYS, JYS, DPPI, Gianni Vescovi, JYS; page 7: The Drivers Collection/Serge Pozzoli,

Manfred Gygli; page 8: The Associated Press, JYS, Michael R. Hewett, Sutton Images.

Section 3
Page 1: JYS, Sutton Images, Sutton Images; page 2: Sutton Images, Daily Express/Hilaria McCarthy, JYS, JYS; page 3: JYS, JYS, Adrian Meredith, JYS, JYS; page 4: Ford of Britain, Jeff Bloxham, DALDA, JYS; page 5: Gary Talbot, JYS, JYS, Pip Calvert; page 6: Sutton Images, Sutton Images, Sutton Images, Sutton Images; page 7: Sutton Images, Sutton Images, Sutton Images, Sutton Images; page 8: BCA Film, JYS, William Thorton, JYS, JYS.

Index

Note: JS = Jackie Stewart

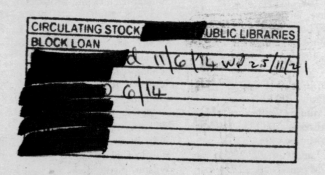